Official Publications of Western Europe

VOLUME 2

Austria, Belgium, Federal Republic of Germany, Greece, Norway, Portugal, Sweden, Switzerland and United Kingdom

EDITED BY
Eve Johansson

Mansell Publishing Limited

London and New York

First published 1988 by
Mansell Publishing Limited
6 All Saints Street, London N1 9RL, England

© Mansell Publishing Limited 1988

All rights reserved. No part of this publication may be reproduced or transmitted in any form or by any means, electronic or mechanical, including photocopy, recording or any information storage or retrieval system, without permission in writing from the publishers or their appointed agents.

British Library Cataloguing in Publication Data

Official publications of Western Europe.
  Vol. 2: Austria, Belgium, Federal Republic
of Germany, Greece, Norway, Portugal,
Sweden, Switzerland and United Kingdom.
  1. Europe—Government publications
  I. Johansson, Eve
070.5′95′094   Z2000

ISBN 0-7201-1662-7

Library of Congress Cataloging in Publication Data
(Revised for vol. 2)

Official publications of Western Europe.

  Includes bibliographies and indexes.
  Contents: v. 1. Denmark, Finland, France, Ireland, Italy, Luxembourg, Netherlands, Spain and Turkey—v. 2. Austria, Belgium, Federal Republic of Germany, Greece, Norway, Portugal, Sweden, Switzerland, and United Kingdom.
  1. Europe—Government publications. 2. Europe—Government publications—Bibliography—Methodology. 3. Libraries—Special collections—Government publications. 4. Acquisition of European publications. 5. Europe—Government publications—Library resources. I. Johansson, Eve.
Z291.038 1984   011′.53   83-22246
ISBN 0-7201-1623-6 (v. 1)
ISBN 0-7201-1662-7 (v. 2)

This book has been printed and bound in Great Britain: typeset in Compugraphic Plantin by Colset (Private) Ltd., Singapore, printed by Redwood Burn Ltd. on Redwood Book Wove, and bound by Western Book Company.

Contents

The contributors ix

Preface x

AUSTRIA (Ilse Dosoudil; translated by Stephen Hanger) 1

1. Introduction 1
2. Principal publications of the federal government 4
   - 2.1 The *Bundesgesetzblatt* 4
   - 2.2 Legislative proceedings 5
   - 2.3 Publications of government departments and executive agencies 6
   - 2.4 The judiciary 9
   - 2.5 Non-official publications of public bodies 11
3. Official publishing 11
   - 3.1 The Österreichische Staatsdruckerei 11
   - 3.2 Other official publishing 13
4. Bibliographic control 13
5. Publications of the Provinces and Municipalities 14
   - 5.1 The Provinces 14
   - 5.2 The Municipalities 15
6. Library collections and availability 16
7. Bibliography 18

CONTENTS

BELGIUM (Gloria Westfall) — 19

1. Introduction — 19
2. Principal publications of central government — 28
   - 2.1 Legislation — 28
   - 2.2 Parliamentary publications — 29
   - 2.3 Publications of the courts — 31
   - 2.4 Publications of the executive — 32
3. Official publishing — 46
4. Bibliographic control — 46
5. Publications of regional, provincial and municipal governments — 46
   - 5.1 Regional — 48
   - 5.2 Provincial — 50
   - 5.3 Municipal — 50
6. Library collections and availability — 51
7. Bibliography — 52

FEDERAL REPUBLIC OF GERMANY
(Siegfried Detemple; translated by Stephen Hanger) — 55

1. Introduction — 55
2. Principal publications of the federal government — 57
   - 2.1 Statutes and decrees — 57
   - 2.2 Parliamentary publications — 60
   - 2.3 Publications of the federal government, ministries and authorities — 65
   - 2.4 Other official agencies of the federal government — 93
3. Manner of publication — 94
4. Bibliographic control — 95
   - 4.1 Bibliographies of official publications — 95
   - 4.2 The national bibliography — 96
   - 4.3 Catalogues and lists of publications — 97
   - 4.4 Data-bases — 98

5.	Library collections and availability	99
	5.1 The national library and legal deposit of official publications	99
	5.2 Availability	100
6.	Publications of the Länder, districts and municipalities	101
7.	Bibliography	102

Appendix 104

GREECE (Panay.otis Ph. Christopoulos) 107

1.	Introduction	107
2.	Principal publications of central government	108
	2.1 Legislation	108
	2.2 Legislative proceedings, debates and documents	109
	2.3 Publications of the executive agencies of government	110
3.	Manner of publication	117
4.	Bibliographic control	117
5.	Library collections and availability	118
6.	Bibliography	118

NORWAY (Olaf Chr. Torp, Gerd B. Krag, Hilde Rødland and Kjell Frank) 121

1.	Introduction	121
2.	Principal publications of central government	124
	2.1 Legislative proceedings	124
	2.2 Legislation and secondary legislation	130
	2.3 The executive agencies of government	131
3.	Manner of publication	137
4.	Bibliographic control	138
	4.1 Government publishers' catalogues	139
	4.2 National bibliography of official publications	139
	4.3 Publications lists of the executive agencies	140

5. Publications of regional and local government	143
5.1 Regional government	143
5.2 Local government	144
6. Library collections and availability	144
7. Bibliography	147

PORTUGAL (Robert Howes) — 149

1. Introduction	149
2. Principal publications of central government	152
2.1 Legislation	152
2.2 The official gazette	154
2.3 Legislative proceedings	155
2.4 Publications of the executive	157
3. Manner of publication	166
3.1 Imprensa Nacional-Casa da Moeda	166
3.2 Departmental publications	167
4. Bibliographic control	168
5. Publications of regional and local government	168
6. Bibliography	170

SWEDEN (Lennart Grönberg, Lucia Mitlid and Rolf Nygren) — 171

1. Introduction	171
2. Legislation and legislative proceedings	175
2.1 Legislative proceedings	175
2.2 Legislation and secondary legislation	184
2.3 Local government statutory codes	185
2.4 Church Assembly measures	186
2.5 Principal publications of the executive agencies of government	186
3. Manner of publication	194
4. Bibliographic control	195

5. Library collections and availability	196
6. Bibliography	197

SWITZERLAND (Ingunn Rüfenacht; translated by Stephen Hanger) — 199

1. Introduction	199
2. Principal publications of the federal government	201
2.1 Legislation and subordinate legislation	201
2.2 Legislative proceedings, debates and documents	201
2.3 Publications of the executive agencies of government	202
2.4 Publications of the judiciary	204
3. Manner of publication	205
4. Bibliographic control	205
4.1 Government publishers' catalogues	206
4.2 National bibliography of official publications	206
4.3 Other lists	206
5. Library collections and availability	206
5.1 National library	206
5.2 Other principal collections	206
5.3 Collections abroad and acquisitions problems	207
6. Publications of state, regional and local governments	207
7. Bibliography	207

UNITED KINGDOM (Eve Johansson) — 209

1. Introduction	209
2. Principal publications of central government	212
2.1 Laws and legislation	212
2.2 Secondary legislation	213
2.3 Parliamentary publications	213
2.4 Non-parliamentary official publications	216
2.5 The *London Gazette*	229

	2.6 Publications of the judiciary	229
	2.7 Northern Ireland	229
	2.8 Channel Islands	230
3.	Manner of publication	230
4.	Bibliographic control	231
	4.1 The national bibliography	231
	4.2 The HMSO catalogues	231
	4.3 Non-HMSO publications	233
	4.4 Other sources	233
5.	Local government publications	234
6.	Library collections and availability	234
7.	Bibliography	235
Appendix 1		240
Appendix 2		241

Indexes   247

   Organizations and Titles Index   249

   Subject Index   269

The contributors

Panayotis Ph. Christòpoulos, Deputy Director, Parliament Library, Athens

Siegfried Detemple, Abteilung Amtsdruckschriften und Tausch, Staatsbibliothek Preussischer Kulturbesitz, Berlin

Ilse Dosoudil, responsible for law, social sciences and economics in the Information Service of the University Library, Vienna

Kjell Frank, Deputy Librarian, Stortingsbiblioteket, Oslo

Lennart Grönberg, former Chief Librarian, Riksdagsbiblioteket, Stockholm

Stephen Hanger, St Pancras Planning Office, British Library, London

Robert Howes, Central Administration, British Library, London (formerly Research Assistant in the Official Publications Library of the British Library, London)

Eve Johansson, Head of the British Library Newspaper Library, formerly of the Official Publications Library of the British Library, London

Gerd B. Krag, former Head Librarian, Utenriksdepartementet, Oslo

Lucia Mitlid, Library Assistant, Riksdagsbiblioteket, Stockholm

Rolf Nygren, Professor of Law, Uppsala University, former Chief Archivist of the Riksdag, Stockholm

Hilde Rødland, Head Librarian, Statistisk Sentralbyrå, Oslo

Ingunn Rüfenacht, Schweizerische Landesbibliothek, Berne

Olaf Chr. Torp, Parliamentary Librarian, Stortingsbiblioteket, Oslo

Gloria Westfall, Government Documents Department, Indiana University Library, Bloomington, Indiana, USA

Preface

This volume was planned at the same time as Volume 1, which was published in 1984. Its objectives are the same: to present a state-of-the-art record of government publishing in the late twentieth century, and to provide a practical reference work of lasting value.

There have been surprisingly few changes since planning of the chapters began. On-line access to bibliographic records and to statistical data is more extensive, but by no means general. There is some private-sector exploitation of information produced in the public sector, and some concern that information in the public domain will be less accessible to the citizen than previously. Overall bibliographic control and availability of official publications are no more satisfactory than before.

The chapters in this volume have been prepared over a period of nine years, and completed at different times, but every effort has been made to bring them up to date.

The editor is particularly grateful to all the authors for carrying out their brief and responding to the aims behind the book so successfully: the editor's task has been a thoroughly rewarding one. I would like in addition to acknowledge the efforts of the contributors who stepped in rather late to help with the chapters on Greece and Portugal; to Natália Nunes Rocha of the Procuradoria Geral da República in Lisbon, who helped in commenting on the Portuguese chapter, and Monsieur Brock of the Bibliothèque Royale in Brussels for his help with the Belgian chapter; to Chris Penn of Her Majesty's Stationery Office and Valerie J. Nurcombe, who offered comments on the United Kingdom chapter; to the translators and the language experts in the British Library who helped with the checking of publications from their countries. Willi Steiner, retired librarian of the Institute of Advanced Legal Studies in the University of London, gave invaluable help in the translation of the chapter on Austria; and the editors at Mansell Publishing Limited have given support and commitment without which the completion of this very complex project would not have been possible.

Austria

ILSE DOSOUDIL

Translated by Stephen Hanger

1. INTRODUCTION

Constitution and structure of the Republic of Austria

Following the end of World War I and the fixing of the frontiers of the state of Austria by the Treaty of St. Germain, a constitution for the Republic of Austria was formulated, principally by Hans Kelsen. It was accepted by parliament on 1 October 1920, and was published in the *Staatsgesetzblatt* [State law gazette] as statute no. 1920/450. This constitution of the first Austrian Republic, subsequently amended in 1925 and 1929, was re-enacted in its 1929 version on 1 May 1945, after the end of World War II and the restoration of the state of Austria. Together with the *Verfassungsüberleitungsgesetz* [Transitional constitution law], the *Rechtsüberleitungsgesetz* [Transitional justice law], the *Staatsvertrag* [State Treaty] of 15 May 1955, and the declaration of Austrian neutrality of 26 October 1955, this constitution forms the legal basis of the second Austrian Republic.

The guiding precepts of the Austrian constitution are the principles of the rule of law, of the separation of powers, of indirect, parliamentary and democratic republicanism, and of federalism. From the federal principle, there results the sharing of legislative and executive powers between the federal and provincial governments. Those matters which the federal government regulates centrally for the Republic as a whole are laid down in Art. 10–14 of the federal constitution.

Austria is a federal state comprising nine separate provinces: Burgenland, Carinthia (Kärnten), Lower Austria (Niederösterreich), Salzburg, Styria (Steiermark), Tyrol (Tirol), Upper Austria (Oberösterreich), Vienna (Wien) and Vorarlberg. Each federal province is relatively autonomous in matters of provincial legislation and administration, but also participates, through its rights of veto and assent in the Bundesrat [Federal Council], in federal legislation and within the framework of delegated administration in the activities of the federal executive. The agencies for, and procedures of, provincial legislation, and the organization of provincial administration, are laid down in the constitution of the individual Provinces. The legislative body of each Province is the democratically elected provincial Diet (Landtag), which in its turn elects the provincial government (Landesregierung) as the highest collegiate body of the provincial administration. The government is led by the provincial governor (Landeshauptmann), who is also the central agent for the indirect federal administration of the Province.

Legislative and administrative powers are basically allocated by the federal authority. The administration of justice is exclusively a federal matter. Principal responsibility for federal legislation rests with the Nationalrat [National Council], which is composed of 183 democratically elected deputies. In collaboration with this works the Bundesrat [Federal Council], the body representing the Provinces, which has the right to initiate legislation. The highest executive agencies are the democratically elected President (Bundespräsident) and the federal government (Bundesregierung). The leader of the government is the federal Chancellor (Bundeskanzler), who is assisted in the conduct of the government by 14 ministers (Bundesminister). Each minister is responsible for enforcing those statutes which fall within the scope of his ministry.

Ministries have been established for the following areas:

Bundeskanzleramt [Federal Chancellor's Office]
Bundesministerium für Auswärtige Angelegenheiten [Federal Ministry for External Affairs]
Bundesministerium für Bauten und Technik [Federal Ministry for Building and Engineering]
Bundesministerium für Familie, Jugend und Konsumentschutz [Federal Ministry for the Family, Youth and Consumer Affairs]
Bundesministerium für Finanzen [Federal Ministry for Finance]
Bundesministerium für Gesundheit und Umweltschutz [Federal Ministry for Health and Environmental Protection]
Bundesministerium für Handel, Gewerbe und Industrie [Federal Ministry for Trade, Business and Industry]
Bundesministerium für Inneres [Federal Ministry for Home Affairs]
Bundesministerium für Justiz [Federal Ministry for Justice]
Bundesministerium für Landesverteidigung [Federal Ministry for National Defence]
Bundesministerium für Soziale Verwaltung [Federal Ministry for Welfare]
Bundesministerium für Unterricht, Kunst und Sport [Federal Ministry for Education and the Arts]
Bundesministerium für Verkehr [Federal Ministry for Transport]
Bundesministerium für Wissenschaft und Forschung [Federal Ministry for Science and Research].

The Bundesversammlung [Federal Assembly], which is composed of the Nationalrat [National Council] and the Bundesrat [Federal Council], convenes for the swearing-in of the President. Its competence is limited to this swearing-in, to the decision on a declaration of war, to the arrangement of a referendum on the removal from office of a President, and to the impeachment of the President for violation of the constitution.

The ordinary administration of justice is a federal matter. It is separated from the administrative arm at all judicial levels. In accordance with Art. 6 of the Convention on Human Rights, all civil and criminal cases must be decided by the courts, with the exception of those governed by the laws of administrative procedure. The judges are in their official capacity free, independent and permanent agents, having obligation only to the law. In certain criminal cases, the public assists in the administration of justice through jury service in particular courts (Schöffengerichte, Geschworenengerichte).

The Municipalities of Austria and the bodies representing the interests of various professional groups (e.g. Chambers of Commerce, Workers' Chambers, etc.) are established as autonomous administrative bodies (Selbstverwaltungskörper). In their own spheres of activity, they conduct the administration without outside interference, and there is no appeal to another administrative authority, which at most performs only a supervisory rôle. Their officials are elected by the members on the basis of legally compulsory membership.

The Verwaltungsgerichtshof [Court of Administration] is appointed to ensure the legality of every aspect of public administration. The Verfassungsgerichtshof [Constitutional Court] is the supreme judicial body empowered to act to maintain rights guaranteed by the constitution, against unconstitutional statutes, in claims against the federal, provincial or municipal governments for the recovery of property, and in conflicts of jurisdiction.

The Rechnungshof [Audit Office] is a special government body set up to control the accounting and management of the federal and provincial governments and of Municipalities and corporate bodies governed by public law. As an agency which supervises the executive, it is independent of the latter, and is directly subordinate to the Nationalrat [National Council]. Its scrutiny extends to numerical accuracy, legality, economy, efficiency and suitability of management, with the right of recommendation to the Nationalrat.

The administration as a whole is conducted by government bodies which are termed authorities (Behörden) not only because of their position within the governmental organization, but also because executive powers are conferred upon them by law. They have the power to enact unilaterally-binding rules or decrees and to issue orders with the sanction of police powers. These individual acts of government are regulated by special procedural law. In contrast to the judicial bodies, the administrative ones are fundamentally subject to direction by executive agencies superior to them.

Manuals of government organization

A very useful practical reference work is the *Österreichischer Amtskalender* [Austrian official yearbook], compiled from official sources and published in Vienna by the Österreichische Staatsdruckerei [Austrian State Printing Office] since 1922. It lists all Austrian federal and provincial authorities with their departments and areas of responsibility of those departments, their officials and addresses of the individual offices. Ecclesiastical authorities, bodies representing sectional interests, and commercial bodies such as banks, insurance firms, the mass media, the tourist industry and so on are also included, and there is a list of Austrian place-names arranged alphabetically and by district and Municipality, an historical survey section on the federal and provincial governments, a list of the heads of state since 1918, and a calendar.

Definition of official publications

Official publications are defined in the *Mediengesetz* [Media Law] (BGBl. 324/1981). Non-print media are included. A 'media work' (Medienwerk) is an item intended for wide dissemination among a large number of people, carrying information or presenting something with an intellectual content. It may be produced in any medium by some process of mass production. A 'printed publication' (Druckwerk) is a class of media work through which information is presented exclusively in type or non-moving pictures.

'Official media works' are those issued by a specified range of official bodies in the direct exercise of their administrative or juridical functions, or issued as an indirect aid in the exercise of those functions, or forming part of a non-official work (for example, when an official gazette is issued as a supplement to a daily newspaper). In so far as an official body produces a publication acting under private law in the exercise of its functions, the publication is regarded as non-official. Hence works published through a contract with a publisher or intended for sale on the open market such as school textbooks are regarded as non-official. The content and the legal form are thus critical in defining an official publication (Amtsdruckschrift) in Austria.

The official bodies concerned are defined as consisting of the Nationalrat [National Council], Bundesrat [Federal Council] Bundesversammlung [Federal Assembly], provincial Diets (Landtag) or public authorities (Behörde in funktionellem Sinn) as defined in the federal constitution—administrative bodies which through legislation have at their disposal the legal forms of regulations and decrees and the power of direct order and compulsion.

Publications of banks, nationalized industries, corporations under public law, and political parties are not considered as 'official media works' within the terms of the *Mediengesetz*.

'Official media works' are exempted from the provisions of the *Mediengesetz*.

Austrian law expresses the concept of the official publication somewhat narrowly. According to it, official media works are law gazettes, official gazettes, decrees, collections of judicial decisions, reports of legislative proceedings, etc.

2. PRINCIPAL PUBLICATIONS OF THE FEDERAL GOVERNMENT

2.1. The Bundesgesetzblatt

The most important publication of the state of Austria is the *Bundesgesetzblatt für die Republik Österreich* [Federal law gazette of the Republic of Austria], which is issued by the Bundeskanzleramt [Federal Chancellor's Office] in accordance with a special federal law. All statutes passed by the Nationalrat, all international treaties, as well as those statutes which must be re-promulgated in accordance with the *Wiederverlautbarungsgesetz* [Re-promulgation law] (*Bundesgesetzblatt* no. 114/1947), must be published in the *Bundesgesetzblatt*, and attain the full force of law on the day of publication, unless the Nationalrat has determined on a different date.

Since 1850, this gazette has appeared under the following titles:

Allgemeines Reichsgesetz- und Regierungsblatt für das Kaiserthum Österreich [General imperial law and government gazette for the Austrian Empire] Vienna, 1850–1917

Staatsgesetzblatt für den Staat Deutschösterreich [State law gazette for the state of German Austria] Vienna, 1918

Staatsgesetzblatt für die Republik Österreich [State law gazette for the Republic of Austria] Vienna, 1919

Bundesgesetzblatt für die Republik Österreich [Federal law gazette of the Republic of Austria] Vienna, 1920–1934, pt. 1

Bundesgesetzblatt für den Bundesstaat Österreich [Federal law gazette for the Federal State of Austria] Vienna, 1934, pt. 2–1938, pt. 26

Gesetzblatt für das Land Österreich [Law gazette for the Province of Austria] Vienna, 1938, pt. 1–1940, pt. 25

Staatsgesetzblatt für die Republik Österreich [State law gazette for the Republic of Austria] Vienna, 1945, pt. 1–61

Bundesgesetzblatt für die Republik Österreich [Federal law gazette of the Republic of Austria] Vienna, 1945–.

The *Bundesgesetzblatt* appears in annual volumes comprising separate parts (Stücke). Each part contains several statutes. It may be obtained by subscription or in individual parts from the Österreichische Staatsdruckerei [Austrian State Printing Office] in Vienna. Citations refer to the number of the statute and the year, for example BGBl. 324/1981.

A valuable aid in using the law gazette is the *Index zum Österreichischen Reichs-, Staats- und Bundesgesetzblatt* [Index to the Austrian imperial, state and federal law gazette], published in Vienna in a loose-leaf edition with annual supplements. It is arranged in sections as follows:

Schlagwortindex [Keyword index]
A: *Verzeichnis der zur Gänze aufgehobenen österreichischen Vorschriften* [Index of wholly-repealed Austrian regulations]
B: *Verzeichnis der zur Gänze aufgehobenen deutschen Vorschriften* [Index of wholly-repealed German regulations]
C: *Verzeichnis der abgeänderten österreichischen Vorschriften* [Index of amended Austrian regulations]
D: *Verzeichnis der abgeänderten deutschen Vorschriften* [Index of amended German regulations].

As a supplement to the *Bundesgesetzblatt*, the Österreichische Staatsdruckerei issues the *Amtliche Sammlung wiederverlautbarter österreichischer Rechtsvorschriften* [Official collection of re-promulgated Austrian legal regulations]. This has been published since 1945.

2.2. Legislative proceedings

The activities of the legislative bodies are recorded in the *Protokolle* [Official record] of the sessions of the Nationalrat and the Bundesrat. These comprise the deliberations and resolutions of the two Councils, together with the motions, debates, questions, reports and so on. The official records have been published by the Österreichische Staatsdruckerei since 1862, under the following titles:

Stenographische Protokolle des Hauses der Abgeordneten des Reichsrates

[Stenographic reports of the House of Representatives of the Imperial Council] 1862–1918

Stenographische Protokolle des Herrenhauses des Reichsrates [Stenographic reports of the House of Peers of the Imperial Council] 1862–1918

Stenographische Protokolle über die Sitzungen der Provisorischen Nationalversammlung für Deutschösterreich [Stenographic reports on the sessions of the Provisional National Assembly for German Austria] 1918–1919

Stenographische Protokolle über die Sitzungen der Konstituierenden Nationalversammlung der Republik Österreich [Stenographic reports on the sessions of the National Constituent Assembly for the Republic of Austria] 1919–1920

Stenographische Protokolle über die Sitzungen des Nationalrates der Republik Österreich [Stenographic reports on the sessions of the National Council of the Republic of Austria] 1920–1934, 1945–

Stenographische Protokolle über die Sitzungen des Bundesrates der Republik Österreich [Stenographic reports on the sessions of the Federal Council of the Republic of Austria] 1920–1934, 1945–.

Both current series of these official records are numbered according to legislative period and session. The corresponding supplementary volumes contain government bills and reports of parliamentary committees. For each legislative period, a separate *Index für die Protokolle des Nationalrates/des Bundesrates* [Index to the records of the National/Federal Council] is published. These indexes are arranged in personal name, subject and keyword sequences.

The annual listing of members of parliament and parliamentary offices, committees and clubs, published in Vienna under the title *Nationalrat und Bundesrat* [National Council and Federal Council], is a ready source of information. A *Biographisches Handbuch des Nationalrates und des Bundesrates der Republik Österreich* [Biographical handbook of the National Council and the Federal Council of the Republic of Austria] has been published by the Österreichische Staatsdruckerei since 1978 in a continuously updated loose-leaf edition.

Parliamentary correspondence—communications and pronouncements of the parties in parliament concerning parliamentary matters and drafts of bills, addressed to the parliamentary parties and to the press—is produced by the parliament's own copying service and distributed by its press office. This material is not generally available, and is controlled by the Dokumentationsstelle der parlamentarischen Materialien der Parlamentsdirektion [Department of Parliamentary Documentation of the Parliament Directorate] and by the Dokumentation an der Bibliothek des Verwaltungsgerichtshofes [Documentation Department of the Library of the Court of Administration].

The Rechnungshof [Audit Office] produces each year a report of its activities and the *Bundesrechnungsabschluss der Republik Österreich* [Balance of federal accounts of the Republic of Austria].

2.3. Publications of government departments and executive agencies

The federal ministries and the more important administrative authorities issue official journals covering their spheres of responsibility, in which all regulations, decrees and announcements are published. A few of these may serve as examples here:

PRINCIPAL PUBLICATIONS OF THE FEDERAL GOVERNMENT

Verordnungsblatt für die Dienstbereiche der Bundesministerien für Unterricht, Kunst und Sport und für Wissenschaft und Forschung [Official gazette for the Federal Ministries for Education, the Arts and Sport and for Science and Research] Vienna, 1970–

Amtsblatt der österreichischen Justizverwaltung [Official gazette of the Austrian judicature] Vienna, 1945–

Amtsblatt der österreichischen Finanzverwaltung [Official gazette of the Austrian exchequer] Vienna, 1947/48–

Amtliche Nachrichten des Bundesministerium für Soziale Verwaltung und des Bundesministerium für Gesundheit und Umweltschutz [Official reports of the Federal Ministry for Welfare and the Federal Ministry for Health and Environmental Protection] Vienna, 1945–

Amtliche Veterinärnachrichten des Bundesministerium für Gesundheit und Umweltschutz, Veterinärverwaltung [Official veterinary reports of the Veterinary Administration of the Federal Ministry for Health and Environmental Protection] Vienna, 1974–

Mitteilungen des österreichischen Sanitätsverwaltung [Communications of the Austrian Health Administration] Bundesministerium für Gesundheit und Umweltschutz [Federal Ministry for Health and Environmental Protection] Vienna, 1950–

Anzeigeblatt für Verkehr [Transport reports gazette] Bundesministerium für Verkehr [Federal Ministry for Transport] Vienna, 1945–

Post- und Telegraphenverordnungsblatt [Official postal and telegraph gazette] Vienna, 1945–. (The managements of the postal and telegraph services in Linz, Klagenfurt, Graz, Innsbruck and Vienna each issue their own official gazettes.)

Amtliche Verlautbarungen für die österreichische Bundesgendarmerie [Official announcements for the Austrian Federal Gendarmerie] Vienna, 1946–

Öffentliche Sicherheit [Public safety] Bundesministerium für Inneres [Federal Ministry for Home Affairs] Vienna, 1954–

Österreichisches Patentblatt [Austrian patents gazette] Vienna, 1947–

Legislation laying down the basic principles of education in Austria is a federal matter. Its implementation as it affects the universities, secondary schools, the curricula for schools at which attendance is compulsory, and so on, is also a federal matter. The competence of the Provinces in education is set out in art. 14 of the federal constitution. The schools are administered by collegiate school authorities and provincial and district school councils (Landesschulräte, Bezirksschulräte). The universities and art academies do not fall within their domain. These are institutions established by law, with their own partial legal corporate identity and autonomous spheres of activity. In the national sphere, they are directly subordinate to the Bundesministerium für Wissenschaft und Forschung [Federal Ministry for Science and Research].

The provincial schools councils each publish a *Verordnungsblatt des Landesschulrates* [Official gazette of the Provincial Schools Council for the different Provinces]. In Vienna, this periodical is entitled *Verordnungsblatt des Stadtschulrates in Wien* [Official gazette of the City Schools Council in Vienna]. These gazettes are produced by local printers.

Austrian universities are obliged by law to issue information gazettes in which all their regulations, advertisements for posts and announcements to students are to be published. These are displayed on official notice boards or distributed at university establishments. They are produced by the universities' own printers.

The publications described so far contain almost exclusively legal regulations binding on the general public and particularly on the administrative bodies themselves. Besides these, however, the federal authorities issue reports of activities, statistical publications, guides and handbooks. For example, the Österreichisches Statistisches Zentralamt [Austrian Central Statistical Office], a body subordinate to the Bundeskanzleramt [Federal Chancellor's Office], issues a wide range of statistical material. The series *Beiträge zur österreichischen Statistik* [Contributions to Austrian statistics] has been published since 1946, and comprises to date about 670 volumes. A considerable part of this series consists of statistical yearbooks such as the *Demographisches Jahrbuch Österreichs* [Austrian demographic yearbook], *Mikrozensus-Jahresergebnisse* [Annual results of the micro-census], *Österreichische Hochschulstatistik* [Austrian higher education statistics], and so on. The Statistisches Zentralamt collaborates with the parliament to produce the annual *Statistisches Handbuch für die Republik Österreich* [Statistical handbook for the Republic of Austria].

The Bundespressedienst des österreichischen Bundeskanzleramtes [Federal Press Service of the Austrian Chancellor's Office] is responsible for producing the *Österreichisches Jahrbuch* [Austrian yearbook], and the *Österreich-Bericht* [Austria report] and for publishing information bulletins and press notices such as *Informationen aus Österreich* [Information from Austria], *Österreich-Nachrichten für die arabische Welt* [Austrian news for the Arab world], and so on.

The Bundespolizeidirektion [Federal Police Directorate] in Vienna issues leaflets and brochures which in the main recommend effective measures for the prevention of crime. This series, with titles beginning *Tips für . . .* [Tips for . . .], is produced by the Amtsdruckerei der Bundespolizeidirektion [Official Printing Office of the Federal Police Directorate] in Vienna, and is distributed free of charge to interested parties at police stations, at public events, and so on.

The Bundesministerium für Gesundheit und Umweltschutz [Federal Ministry for Health and Environmental Protection] produces and distributes brochures and leaflets giving the public information for the early recognition of serious illnesses, warning against the dangers of alcohol and nicotine abuse, calling on the public to participate in vaccination campaigns, as well as pamphlets on family planning, parenthood, etc.

The Bundesministerium für Soziale Verwaltung [Federal Ministry for Welfare] publishes a central bulletin listing situations vacant and wanted, which covers the whole of Austria, entitled *Der Arbeitsmarkt* [The labour market]. It appears fortnightly and is available free of charge.

The Bundesministerium für Verkehr [Federal Ministry for Transport] which is responsible for postal and telegraph services as well as for the country's rail system publishes amongst other things the *Postlexikon der Republik Österreich* [Postal lexicon for the Republic of Austria], leaflets concerning telephone and data transmission services, postal tariffs, special issues of postage stamps, etc. The rail and bus timetable *Das Österreichische Kursbuch* [The Austrian timetable], postal tariffs, and telephone directories and tariffs for every Province are obtainable (some without charge) from all Austrian post offices.

The Bundesministerium für Finanzen [Federal Ministry for Finance] issues the periodical *Finanz intern* [Inside finance], an information journal for revenue officers, the *Steuerfibel* [Tax primer], etc.

A further group of publications is the 'Official Aids' (Dienstbehelfe). These are procedural regulations, chancellery orders, instructional materials, etc., which serve as supporting documents for the administrative bodies in the performance of their functions. The larger federal departments produce daily press digests and information bulletins produced by in-house copying services, which are intended for internal use only. Many authorities also issue periodicals containing information on activities and on planned or completed reforms within their administrative domains, such as *Postrundschau* [Postal review], *Eich- und Vermessungsmagazin* [Weights and measures magazine], *Die Energieversorgung Österreichs* [Austria's energy supply], *ÖBB-Journal* [Austrian Federal Railways Journal], *Österreichischer Markenanzeiger* [Austrian trade marks advertiser], and so on.

2.4. The judiciary

The administration of justice in Austria consists in the execution of the laws by judicial bodies independent of the administration. It comprises the ordinary administration of justice (ordentliche Gerichtsbarkeit) and the administration of justice by the courts of public law (die Gerichtsbarkeit des öffentlichen Rechtes). The latter is the province of the Verwaltungsgerichtshof [Court of Administration] and the Verfassungsgerichtshof [Constitutional Court]. Its organization and powers are regulated by federal law, since according to the constitution it is a federal matter. The highest authority in private jurisdiction is the Oberste Gerichtshof [Supreme Court of Justice]. Its rulings are published annually by the Österreichische Staatsdruckerei as follows:

Entscheidungen des Österreichischen Obersten Gerichtshofes in Strafsachen und Disziplinarangelegenheiten [Rulings of the Austrian Supreme Court of Justice in criminal cases and disciplinary matters] Bd. 1–. Vienna, 1920–. A general index to Bd. 1–30 (1919–1959), entitled *Generalindex zu den Entscheidungen des österreichischen Obersten Gerichtshofes in Strafsachen* [General index to the rulings of the Austrian Supreme Court of Justice in Criminal cases], was published in Vienna in 1959.

Entscheidungen des Österreichischen Obersten Gerichtshofes in Zivilsachen [Rulings of the Austrian Supreme Court of Justice in civil cases] Bd. 1–. Vienna, 1919–. General indexes to Bd. 1–30 (1919–1957) and Bd. 31–40 (1958–1967), entitled *Generalindex zu den Entscheidungen des österreichischen Obersten Gerichtshofes in Zivil- und Justizverwaltungssachen* [General index to the rulings of the Austrian Supreme Court of Justice in civil and jurisdictional cases], were published in Vienna in 1957 and 1967 respectively.

The rulings of the Verwaltungsgerichtshof [Court of Administration] have been collected and published since as long ago as 1867, as this supreme court was created in imperial times. They have been published under the following titles:

Erkenntnisse des k.k. Verwaltungsgerichtshofes [Judgements of the Imperial and Royal Court of Administration] 1–24 (1867/77–1900). Vienna, 1878–1901. (From Jahrg. 22 (1898), this was divided into an Administrativrechtlicher Teil [Administrative law section] and a Finanzrechtlicher Teil [Fiscal law section]

Budwinskis Sammlung der Erkenntnisse des k.k. Verwaltungsgerichtshofes [Budwinski's collection of the judgements of the Imperial and Royal Court of

Administration] 25–42 (1901–1918). Vienna, 1902–1919

Sammlung der Erkenntnisse des Verwaltungsgerichtshofes [Collection of the judgements of the Court of Administration] 43–58 (1919–1934). Vienna, 1920–1935. (From 1935 to 1940/41 this was combined with the *Sammlung der Erkenntnisse und wichtigsten Beschlüsse des Verfassungsgerichtshofes* [Collection of the judgements and most important orders of the Constitutional Court] to form the *Sammlung der Erkenntnisse, Beschlüsse und Rechtssätze des Bundesgerichtshofes* [Collection of the judgements, orders and provisions of the Federal Court of Justice])

Erkenntnisse und Beschlüsse des Verwaltungsgerichtshofes [Judgements and orders of the Court of Administration] Neue Folge, 1–, (1946–). Vienna, 1948–.

In the series *Handausgabe österreichischer Gesetze und Verordnungen, Gruppe 3* [Pocket edition of Austrian laws and regulations, group 3] published by the Österreichische Staatsdruckerei, the following volumes containing collections of the most important case law established by the Verwaltungsgerichtshof have appeared:

Bd.22 *Die Rechtsprechung des Verwaltungsgerichtshofes 1946–1959* [The decisions of the Court of Administration 1946–1959] Vienna, 1963

Bd. 22a *Die Rechtsprechung des Verwaltungsgerichtshofes 1960–1964* Vienna, 1968

Bd. 22b *Die Rechtsprechung des Verwaltungsgerichtshofes 1965–1970* Vienna, 1972

Bd. 22c *Die Rechtsprechung des Verwaltungsgerichtshofes 1971–1974* Vienna, 1976

Bd. 22d *Die Rechtsprechung des Verwaltungsgerichtshofes 1975–1977* Vienna, 1978

Bd. 22e *Die Rechtsprechung des Verwaltungsgerichtshofes 1978–1980* Vienna, 1982

Bd. 24 *Generalregister zur Rechtsprechung des Verwaltungsgerichtshofes. Administrativrechtlicher Teil 1946–1974* [General index to the decisions of the Court of Administration. Administrative law section 1946–1974] Vienna, 1977.

Collections of decisions of the Verfassungsgerichtshof [Constitutional Court] have appeared under the following titles:

Sammlung der Erkenntnisse des durch das Gesetz vom 25 Jänner 1919, STGBl. Nr. 48 geschaffenen österreichischen Verfassungsgerichtshofes [Collection of the judgements of the Austrian Constitutional Court created by the law of 25 January 1919, State law gazette no. 48] 1–2. Vienna, 1919–1920

Sammlung der Erkenntnisse des Verfassungsgerichtshofes [Collection of the judgements of the Constitutional Court] Neue Folge, 1–6. Vienna, 1921–1926

Sammlung der Erkenntnisse und wichtigsten Beschlüsse des Verfassungsgerichtshofes [Collection of the judgements and most important orders of the Constitutional Court] Neue Folge, 7–32. Vienna, 1927–1933, 1946–1967. (Between 1934 and 1940/41, this was combined with the *Sammlung der Erkenntnisse des Verwaltungsgerichtshofes* [Collection of the judgements of the Court of Administration] to form the *Sammlung der Erkenntnisse, Beschlüsse und Rechtssätze des Bundesgerichtshofes* [Collection of the judgements, orders and provisions of the Federal Court of Justice].)

Erkenntnisse und Beschlüsse des Verfassungsgerichtshofes [Judgements and orders of the Constitutional Court] Neue Folge, 33– (1968–). Vienna, 1969–. (From Bd. 38 (1973), this collection has been published twice yearly.)

In addition, the Verfassungsgerichtshof issues a cumulative selection of its most important judgements, entitled *Die Judikatur des Verfassungsgerichtshofes* [The case law established by the Constitutional Court]. To date, three of these have been published, covering the years 1919–1964 (2 vols., 1966), 1965–1969 (1971), 1970–1974 (1975) and 1975–1979 (1984).

2.5. Non-official publications of public bodies

The publications described so far all conform in the broadest sense to the concept of the 'official media work' or 'media aid' as defined in the Mediengesetz [Media law]. However, Austrian authorities issue a large number of publications which, despite being published by an official body, are not by virtue of their content a part of the exercise of its official powers by that body as required by law. These publications are not published by the Österreichische Staatsdruckerei or other official printers, but by publishers and printers in the private sector, and are obtainable through the book trade.

In addition, in the category of autonomous bodies, there is the group of statutory bodies representing the professions which has been accorded by law the right to advise in the legislative process and to participate in the executive process. As legal entities governed by public law (juristische Personen des öffentlichen Rechts), accorded the compulsory membership of all those in the professions they represent, they are subject to the supervision of the appropriate ministry, but are not governmental authorities. The most important of these bodies are the chamber of commerce (Kammer der gewerblichen Wirtschaft), the workers' and employees' chamber (Kammer für Arbeiter und Angestellte), and the agricultural chamber (Landwirtschaftskammer). Each Province has its own provincial chamber (Landeskammer), and for the country as a whole there are the Bundeskammer der gewerblichen Wirtschaft [Federal Chamber of Commerce], the Österreichischer Arbeiterkammertag [Austrian Diet of Workers' Chamber], and the Präsidentenkonferenz der Landwirtschaftskammern Österreichs [Presidential Conference of Austrian Agricultural Chambers]. In addition, there are a number of chambers for various professions, established according to different systems, for lawyers, doctors, dentists and so on. Each of these issues a bulletin to its members free of charge, usually weekly or monthly. Annual reports of activities, statistics and occasional publications giving information on themes of current interest may also be issued.

The publications of Austria's nationalized industries, and of other commercial undertakings largely or wholly in the ownership of the Republic, also cannot be considered to be official publications in the broadest sense. These bodies publish mainly periodicals and information brochures which are primarily intended for distribution to their employees. These publications are listed in the *Bibliographie der verstaatlichten Industrie* [Bibliography of nationalized industry], Vienna, 1981.

3. OFFICIAL PUBLISHING

3.1. The Österreichische Staatsdruckerei

Austria's own Hof- und Staatsdruckerei [Court and State Printing Office] was created by the imperial charter of 18 September 1804, and came under state control in 1814 by imperial decree. From the invention of printing until the founding of this printing office, imperial decrees, charters and legal regulations were published by court printers who had been granted the imperial privilege. One of the most important of these was the Trattner works in Vienna. They produced, amongst other things, Maria Theresa's criminal law code, the *Constitutio Criminalis Theresiana* of 1768, as well as the first part of the *Allgemeines Bürgerliches Gesetzbuch* [General code of civil law] of 1786 and the legal code of the Emperor Joseph II.

From its creation until 1 January 1982, the State Printing Office was a government-run concern which was incorporated into the imperial, later the federal, administration. Most recently, it has come under the Bundeskanzleramt [Federal Chancellor's Office], as its most important duty is to issue the *Bundesgesetzblatt*. Under the 1982 revision, the Österreichische Staatsdruckerei attained the legal status of a corporate body with independent legal personality, and became a trader within the terms of the *Handelsgesetzbuch* [Code of commercial law]. It no longer has to conduct its business under the provisions of public law, but under those of the *Handelsgesetzbuch* and of the *Allgemeines Bürgerliches Gesetzbuch* [General code of civil law]. The rights and duties of the Österreichische Staatsdruckerei are regulated by the *Staatsdruckereigesetz* [Law on the State Printing Office], published in the *Bundesgesetzblatt* as no. 340/1981.

The Österreichische Staatsdruckerei has to produce all printed items defined under the terms of the *Mediengesetz* [Media law] as official media works of the federal government. It is the exclusive producer of the *Bundesgesetzblatt*, the stenographic reports of the proceedings of the Nationalrat and the Bundesrat, the reports of the Volksanwaltschaft [Ombudsman], the official gazettes of the federal ministries, and the collections of laws and administrative decisions on behalf of the federal government. It also produces and publishes the *Wiener Zeitung* [Viennese gazette]. It has the statutory responsibility for the printing, for the federal administration, of items whose production involves security regulations or secrecy. These include, for example, the *Bundesrechnungsabschluss* [Federal accounts], reports of the activities of the Rechnungshof [Audit Office], lists of wanted persons, banknotes, etc. In addition it has to produce forms and other printed material for the federal government departments and state concerns in so far as it has the resources and can produce them more cheaply or efficiently than the departments themselves. It prints passports, driving licences, identity papers and bonds. With regard to the printing of postage stamps, it is worth noting that the Österreichische Staatsdruckerei has for some time produced the stamps of 44 countries in Europe and elsewhere on account of its high quality of production.

It may undertake to print other kinds of material, and to publish and distribute books, newspapers, periodicals and so on, either on its own behalf or on behalf of others. As an independent commercial body it produces pictures of the Austrian President, of the arms of Austria and so on. About three quarters of its production is undertaken for other bodies. Among its chief customers are the Österreichische Postverwaltung [Austrian Postal Administration], the Postsparkassenamt [Postal Savings Bank Office], the Finanzlandesdirektion Wien [Financial Directorate of the Province of Vienna], and the Österreichisches Statistisches Zentralamt [Austrian Central Statistical Office].

The Österreichische Staatsdruckerei produces an annual report, which however is not published and is only for internal use or for submission to its controlling bodies. Since it became an autonomous body in 1982, it has been obliged to produce, at the end of every financial year, a balance sheet and a profit-and-loss account, and to publish them in the official supplement to the *Wiener Zeitung* [Viennese gazette]. From these statements of account, the basic principles of the marketing and pricing policy of the Österreichische Staatsdruckerei may be deduced.

For its 175th anniversary in 1979, the Österreichischer Staatsdruckerei issued a list of its publications. All items entered are obtainable either directly from the Verlag der Österreichischen Staatsdruckerei, 1037 Wien, Rennweg 12a and 16, Austria, or else from their own bookshop or through the Austrian book trade.

3.2. Other official publishing

The official publications of the Provinces and Municipalities are printed and published by the official printers of the provincial governments or commissioned from private printing houses.

4. BIBLIOGRAPHIC CONTROL

No special bibliography of official publications is published in Austria. As a consequence of the legal deposit obligation applying to all Austrian printers and publishers laid down in the *Mediengesetz*, the Österreichische Nationalbibliothek [Austrian National Library] in Vienna receives four copies of every periodical printed or published in Austria, and two copies of other kinds of printed publication. These form the basis for the production of the *Österreichische Nationalbibliographie* [Austrian national bibliography], which is compiled by the Österreichische Nationalbibliothek and published by the Hauptverband des Österreichischen Buchhandels in Vienna. It is published fortnightly. Its contents are divided into 24 subject areas and equipped with an author and subject index. Corporate bodies acting as authors or publishers are included in the index. Items not available through the book trade are listed separately within each subject area.

The *Österreichische Nationalbibliographie* aims to list all official and non-official publications of the federal and provincial authorities, but it should be mentioned that this cannot be guaranteed, as the Österreichische Nationalbibliothek is not in a position to check on the fulfilment of the legal deposit obligation. It notes whether non-official publications are commercially available. Items published through the book trade can be checked and claimed with the aid of the publishers' catalogues and the *Anzeiger des österreichischen Buchhandels* [Austrian book trade advertiser].

Officially-published periodicals are also to be found in the printed *Zeitschriftenliste 1978* [Periodicals list 1978], issued by the Planungsstelle für wissenschaftliches Bibliothekswesen [Planning Office for Library Science] at the Österreichische Nationalbibliothek (Vienna, 1979) and in the *Periodika-Zentralkatalog der Universitätsbibliothek Wien* [Central periodicals catalogue of Vienna University Library], published in four volumes (Vienna, 1986), with a supplement (1986).

The Planungsstelle has for some time been working on a periodicals data base for the whole of Austria, which is to include records and locations of all Austrian officially-published periodicals.

The federal authorities do not issue catalogues of their publications. The libraries of the federal ministries produce monthly to yearly lists of new accessions, which include the publications of their respective ministries.

5. PUBLICATIONS OF THE PROVINCES AND MUNICIPALITIES

5.1. The Provinces

The constitution provides for the Provinces to establish an autonomous legislative and administrative authority for those matters assigned to them by the federal authority (*see* section 1.1). The laws and regulations issued by the Provinces, in accordance with the various provincial constitutions, are published in the respective provincial law gazettes. The titles of these are as follows:

Landesgesetzblatt für das Burgenland [Provincial law gazette for the Burgenland] Eisenstadt, 1922–1938, 1945–

Landesgesetzblatt für das Land Niederösterreich [Provincial law gazette for the Province of Lower Austria] Vienna, 1922–1938, 1945–. (Formerly *Landesgesetzblatt für das Land Niederösterreich Land* [Provincial law gazette for the Province of Lower Austria] 1920–1921)

Landesgesetzblatt für Oberösterreich [Provincial law gazette for Upper Austria] Linz, 1929–1938, 1947–. (Formerly *Landesgesetz- und Verordnungsblatt für Oberösterreich* [Provincial law and regulation gazette for Upper Austria] 1919–1928)

Landesgesetzblatt für das Land Salzburg [Provincial law gazette for the Province of Salzburg] Salzburg, 1921–1938, 1945–. (Formerly *Landesgesetz- und Verordnungsblatt für das Land Salzburg* [Provincial law and regulation gazette for the Province of Salzburg] 1918–1920)

Landesgesetzblatt für Kärnten [Provincial law gazette for Carinthia] Klagenfurt, 1918–1938, 1950–

Landesgesetzblatt für das Land Steiermark [Provincial law gazette for the Province of Styria] Graz, 1921–1938, 1946–1976 no. 5. (Continued as *Landesgesetzblatt für die Steiermark* [Provincial law gazette for Styria] Graz, 1976 no. 6–. Previously *Landesgesetz- und Verordnungsblatt für das Land Steiermark* [Provincial law and regulation gazette for the Province of Styria] Graz, 1918–1920)

Landesgesetzblatt für Tirol [Provincial law gazette for Tyrol] Innsbruck, 1959–. (Formerly *Landes-Gesetz- und Verordnungsblatt für Tirol* [Provincial law and regulation gazette for Tyrol] 1919–1938, 1946–1958)

Vorarlberger Landesgesetzblatt [Vorarlberg provincial law gazette] Bregenz, 1918–1934, 1935–1938, 1946–

Landesgesetzblatt für Wien [Provincial law gazette for Vienna] Vienna, 1920–1934, 1946–.

The legislative body of each Province is the provincial diet (Landtag). Its sessions and resolutions are, like those of the Nationalrat and Bundesrat, published as *Protokolle* by the respective provincial diets.

The administration of each Province is conducted by the provincial government (Landesregierung), presided over by the provincial governor (Landeshauptmann). The executive body is the office of the provincial government (Amt der Landesregierung), which handles both the administration of the Land and the matters of federal administration entrusted to it. Each of these offices issues a weekly official gazette, as follows:

PUBLICATIONS OF THE PROVINCES AND MUNICIPALITIES

Landesamtsblatt für das Burgenland [Provincial official gazette for the Burgenland] Eisenstadt, 1949–
Amtliche Nachrichten der niederösterreichischen Landesregierung [Official reports of the provincial government of Lower Austria] 1945–
Amtliche Linzer Zeitung [Official Linz gazette] Linz 1945–
Kärntner Landes-Zeitung [Carinthian provincial gazette] Klagenfurt, 1951–
Salzburger Landeszeitung [Salzburg provincial gazette] Salzburg, 1945–
Bote für Tirol [Courier for Tyrol] Innsbruck, 1946–
Grazer Zeitung [Graz gazette] Graz, 1959–. (Formerly *Verordnungs- und Amtsblatt für das Land Steiermark* [Regulatory and official gazette for the Province of Styria] 1944–1958)
Amtsblatt für das Land Vorarlberg [Official gazette for the Province of Vorarlberg] Bregenz, 1946–
Amtsblatt der Stadt Wien [Official gazette of the city of Vienna] Vienna, 1948–.

Each provincial government publishes an annual *Rechnungsabschluss* [Balance sheet], most of which consist of three or four volumes.

The office of the provincial government in each Province has its own press service, which is responsible for the provincial press notices and for the issuing of periodical information bulletins and other occasional publications. These are printed either by an official printer attached to the office itself, or by publishers or printers commissioned for the purpose. The range and number of these publications varies from Province to Province. Their content extends from the programmes of provincial organizations, current developments in the provincial administration, statistical material and reports of activities, to the publication of important individual provincial statutes. The publications may in some cases be obtained without charge on demand or through distribution lists, or are distributed to all households.

District administrative officers (Bezirkshauptmannschaften) handle all matters of federal and provincial administration which have not been specifically assigned to any other authority, although some towns and cities are exempt from District administration and come under the Provinces directly.

Each District head office issues a twice-monthly *Amtsblatt der Bezirkshauptmannschaft* [Official gazette of the District Head Office] which contains all official orders and announcements relating to its administrative domains. These gazettes are produced by appointed printers located in the seats of the respective offices. They may be obtained separately or by annual subscription.

Many provincial authorities issue informational publications, for example the provincial employment offices (Landesarbeitsämter) and the employment offices (Arbeitsämter). These publish, monthly to half-yearly, employment information bulletins with situations vacant and wanted, which are distributed without charge to interested parties.

5.2. The Municipalities

The Municipalities of Austria are, under the provisions of the federal constitution, area authorities (Gebietskörperschaften) with legal personality and administrative autonomy. They are also the local administrative bodies which handle tasks delegated to them by the federal or provincial governments.

Municipal law is regulated by the Provinces in municipal orders (Gemeindeordnungen) and published in the provincial law gazette. All legal regulations pertaining to the autonomous sphere of operation of the Municipalities are published in gazettes or by posting them on the official notice boards of the municipal authority. These gazettes appear under a great variety of titles, such as *Gemeindeblatt der Gemeinde* . . . [Municipal gazette of . . . Municipality], *Gemeindepost* [Municipal post], *Gemeindenachrichten* [Municipal news], *Der Gemeindekurier* [The municipal courier], and so on. Often a number of small municipalities combine to issue a joint gazette. In addition to the resolutions and orders of the Municipal Council (Gemeinderat), these periodicals keep the inhabitants of the Municipalities informed of all important and interesting aspects of community life—events, agricultural information, medical care, births and marriages and so on. These municipal gazettes appear fortnightly to quarterly, and are obtainable free or for a minimal charge.

The provincial capitals and other towns and cities of Austria likewise issue gazettes with various titles which contain, besides official communications, articles and cultural and other information. The titles take the form of *Amtsblatt der Stadt* . . . [Official gazette of the town of . . .], *Nachrichten der Stadtgemeinde* . . . [Municipality of . . . news], *Stadt* . . . [The town of . . .], *Mitteilungen der Stadt* . . . [Communications from the town of . . .], and so on. These official gazettes appear fortnightly to quarterly and are mostly available free of charge.

6. LIBRARY COLLECTIONS AND AVAILABILITY

The following Austrian libraries acquire official publications as a consequence of the legal deposit obligation:

For the country as a whole:
Österreichische Nationalbibliothek [Austrian National Library], Vienna, Heldenplatz
Administrative Bibliothek und Österreichische Rechtsdokumentation im Bundeskanzleramt [Administrative Library and Department of Austrian Legal Documentation in the Federal Chancellor's Office], Vienna, Herrengasse 23
Parlamentsbibliothek [Parliament Library], Vienna, Dr. Karl Renner-Ring 3

For the Burgenland:
Universitätsbibliothek Wien [Vienna University Library], Vienna, Dr. Karl Lueger-Ring 1
Burgenländische Landesbibliothek [Library of the Province of Burgenland], Eisenstadt, Landhaus

For Carinthia:
Universitätsbibliothek der Universität für Bildungswissenschaften [Library of the University for Pedagogics], Klagenfurt, Universitätsstrasse 67
Landesmuseum für Kärnten, Bibliothek [Library of the Museum for the Province of Carinthia], Klagenfurt, Museumgasse 2

For Lower Austria:
Universitätsbibliothek Wien [Vienna University Library], Vienna, Dr. Karl Lueger-Ring 1
Niederösterreichische Landesbibliothek [Library of the Province of Lower Austria], Vienna, Teinfaltstrasse 8

For Salzburg:
Universitätsbibliothek Salzburg [Salzburg University Library], Salzburg, Mirabellplatz 1
Salzburger Landesarchiv, Bibliothek [Library of the Salzburg Provincial Record Office], Salzburg, Michael Pacher Strasse 40

For Styria:
Steiermärkische Landesbibliothek [Library of the Province of Styria], Graz, Kalchberggasse 2
Universitätsbibliothek Graz [Graz University Library], Graz, Universitätsplatz 3

For Tyrol:
Tiroler Landesarchiv [Tyrol Provincial Record Office], Innsbruck, Herrengasse 1
Universitätsbibliothek Innsbruck [Innsbruck University Library], Innsbruck, Innrain 50

For Upper Austria:
Bundesstaatliche Studienbibliothek [Federal Studies Library], Linz, Schillerplatz 2
Universitätsbibliothek Linz [Linz University Library], Linz-Auhof

For Vienna:
Wiener Stadt- und Landesbibliothek [Library of the City and Province of Vienna], Vienna, Rathaus
Universitätsbibliothek Wien [Vienna University Library], Vienna, Dr. Karl Lueger-Ring 1

For Vorarlberg:
Vorarlberger Landesbibliothek [Library of the Province of Vorarlberg], Bregenz, Kirchstrasse 28
Universitätsbibliothek Innsbruck [Innsbruck University Library], Innsbruck, Innrain 50.

Official libraries have been established in every federal ministry, at the Sicherheitsdirektion [Security Directorate] in Vienna, at the Generaldirektion der österreichischen Bundesbahnen [General Directorate of the Austrian Federal Railways], at the Generaldirektion für die Post- und Telegraphenverwaltung [General Directorate for the Administration of Posts and Telegraphs], and so on. These libraries look after the official publications of their respective departments.

In April 1983, the Bundesministerium für Wissenschaft und Forschung [Federal Ministry for Science and Research] issued an *Informationsführer: Bibliotheken und Dokumentationsstellen Österreichs* [Guide to libraries and documentation centres in Austria] published by the Verlag der Österreichischen Staatsdruckerei in Vienna. This lists all Austrian libraries and documentation centres, their areas of acquisition and the procedures for their use. An index by subjects and names aids consultation.

Austrian official publications are acquired by exchange under different treaties by libraries in other countries, such as the Library of Congress and the British Library from whom some are available on inter-library loan. These exchanges are operated by the Österreichische Nationalbibliothek.

The principal series, the *Bundesgesetzblatt*, the *Stenographische Protokolle* of the

Bundesrat and of the Nationalrat and their supplements, and the official gazettes of the federal government, may be obtained by annual subscription or in separate parts from the Österreichische Staatsdruckerei or through the Austrian book trade. The *Österreichischer Amtskalender*, the *Postlexicon der Republik Österreich*, the publications of the Österreichisches Statistisches Zentralamt, the *Österreichisches Jahrbuch* and other titles may be purchased from any bookshop or from the Österreichische Staatsdruckerei.

Non-official publications put out by the federal authorities (handbooks, guides, informational publications, periodicals, etc.) are produced and distributed by various Austrian printers and publishers on the authorities' behalf, or distributed without charge to interested parties by the authorities concerned. Most of these may be obtained through the book trade or from the issuing body.

7. BIBLIOGRAPHY

Adamovich, Ludwig K. and Funk, Bernd-Christian. *Österreichisches Verfassungsrecht*. Vienna, 1982. pp. 239–255.

——. *Allgemeines Verwaltungsrecht*. Vienna, 1980, pp. 155–168, 268–280.

Berchtold, Klaus. *Gemeindeaufsicht*. Vienna, 1972. pp. 7–8.

Ermacora, Felix. *Österreichische Verfassungslehre*. 2 vols. Vienna, Stuttgart, 1970, 1980. (Studienreihe zum öffentlichen Recht und zu den politischen wissenschaften, Bd. 1, 5.) 427, 176 p.

——. *Österreichischer Föderalismus*. Vom patrimonialen zum kooperativen Bundesstaat. Vienna, 1976. (Schriftenreihe des Institutes für Föderalismusforschung, Bd. 3.) 364 p.

Neuhofer, Hans. *Handbuch des Gemeinderechts*. Vienna, 1972, pp. 17, 27–28, 223–225.

Ringhofer, Kurt. *Die österreichischen Verwaltungsverfahrengesetze*. 9th ed. Vienna, 1983. 26 p.

Schambeck, Herbert (ed.) *Das österreichische Bundesverfassungsgesetz und seine Entwicklung*. Berlin, 1980. 35, 800 p.

Stamprech, Franz. *175 Jahre Österreichische Staatsdruckerei*. Vienna, 1979. 241 p.

Walter, Robert. *Österreichisches Bundesverfassungsrecht*. Vienna, 1972. pp. 799–811.

——. *Verfassung und Gerichtsbarkeit*. Vienna, 1960. 209 p.

Walter, Robert and Mayer, Heinz. *Grundriss des besonderen Verwaltungsrechts*. Vienna, 1981. 163 p.

——. *Grundriss des österreichischen Bundesverfassungsrechts*. Vienna, 1980. 32, 415 p.

——. *Grundriss des österreichischen Verwaltungsverfahrensrechts*. 2nd ed. Vienna, 1980. pp. 25–34.

Welan, Manfred, et al. *Theorie und Praxis des Bundesstaates*. Salzburg, Munich, 1974. (Föderative Ordnung, Bd. 3.) 219 p.

Belgium

GLORIA WESTFALL

1. INTRODUCTION

The Belgian state as we know it today came into existence on 21 July 1831 when Leopold I, the first king of modern Belgium, swore allegiance to the constitution promulgated the previous February by the Constituent Assembly. The summoning of the Assembly, one of the first acts of the revolutionary government which had seized power the previous autumn, occurred on the same day that the provisional government declared the independence of Belgium from the Netherlands, 4 October 1830. As early as the fourteenth and fifteenth centuries, the territories comprising modern Belgium had achieved a high level of economic development and administrative sophistication under the Dukes of Burgundy, only to fall under the dominion of four major European powers—Spain, Austria, France and the Netherlands—for almost three centuries.

Although the constitution of 1831 proved to be remarkably stable (it was amended only twice in the period from 1831 to 1967), conflicts between the various cultural and linguistic groups composing the Belgian population have led to profound changes in the last fifteen years.

Official languages

To the north, in the region of Flanders, the majority of the people speak Dutch, while to the south in Wallonia French is the language of the majority. In 1979, these two regions held 56.77% and 32.11% of the population respectively, while a German-speaking region concentrated in the area bordering West Germany accounted for another 0.6% of the population. The remaining population is in the Brussels metropolitan area, an officially-bilingual district with a French-speaking majority situated in the midst of the Flemish region. Official language policy has varied over the years. French was the only official language until 1898, when Dutch was also declared official. In 1932, this policy of bilingualism was replaced by one of regional unilingualism. The use of both languages for the conduct of official business was permitted only in municipalities in which a sizeable majority spoke a second language. The number of such municipalities was reviewed each time a national census was taken and a second language made official if 30% or more of the municipality's population customarily spoke it. In 1963, regional unilingualism was made official by the coordinated laws on the use of languages in administrative matters (laws of 18 July 1966), which provided that all government employees must use the language of the region in which they serve in the conduct of official business. The areas of the linguistic regions were to be those laid down in the law of 8 November 1962 defining the French- and Dutch-speaking regions and that of 23 December 1970 outlining the boundaries of the Brussels region. Every inch of Belgian territory was attached to one of these regions, and the decennial census reviews of municipalities entitled to bilingual status were discontinued. The boundaries of these linguistic regions, plus one for the German-speaking area, were incorporated into the constitution as art. 3–B in 1970.

In this chapter, the names of government organizations and bilingual titles are given in both French and Dutch, accompanied by an English translation the first time they appear in the text. Since reversing the order of the languages each time they are used (the only truly correct way to handle the order of priority where two official languages are involved) would confuse readers, I have taken the liberty of placing French, the language I assume to be best known to the international audience for whom this volume is primarily intended, first. Where the name of an organization is repeated after its initial appearance, only the English translation is used. Bilingual titles are separated by a slash when the texts in both languages appear in the same work. When the French and Dutch versions appear in separate editions, the word 'and' is inserted between the two titles in place of a slash. Subsequent references to a bilingual title are given in French only.

Unless otherwise specified, the government responsible for the publications cited is the central government of Belgium and the place of publication Brussels.

I would like to add at this point that it would have been impossible for me to write this contribution without the generous aid of the following librarians, who did their best to make the intricacies of the world of Belgian official publications clear to an outsider: Léon Danse, Joseph Brock, Nicole Tassoul and Anne-Marie Vastesaeger, all of the Royal Library, and Huguette de Clerck of the Parliamentary Library.

Structure of the government

It is difficult to offer a definitive description of the organization of the Belgian government since it is still in the process of undergoing changes which are transforming it from a unitary state to one in which representation of the different linguistic regions plays an increasingly important rôle. The basic form of government established by the constitution of 1831, that of a constitutional monarchy with the traditional separation of powers among executive, legislative and judicial branches, has changed only slightly at the national level during the recent reforms. An executive, composed of the King and government (Prime Minister and Cabinet), and a legislature, consisting of two houses, a Chambre des Représentants/Kamer van Volksvertegenwoordigers [Chamber of Representatives]a and a Sénat/Senaat [Senate]a and the King, function in much the same way as do their British counterparts, but there are the following important differences. Belgium has a written constitution. Its sovereign must be male. The two houses of Parliament have equal powers. There are no hereditary seats (with one exception: royal princes are guaranteed the right to sit in the Senate from the age of 18 by the constitution). There are several political parties, rather than two major ones.

The 212 members of the Chamber of Representatives are elected by a system of proportional representation based on universal compulsory suffrage, while the 182 Senators are currently chosen by a complicated formula providing for three methods of selection: direct election, indirect election by Provincial Councils, and co-option by the elected members. A provision for changing to a system of direct election of Senators through the revision of arts. 53 and 54 of the constitution was included in the recent reorganization legislation and is expected to be enacted in the near future. The question of retaining bicameralism is also expected to be reviewed in the near future. Parliament shares legislative power with the King who has the power to approve and promulgate laws. Although he could, in theory, exercise a veto by withholding his signature from a law, in practice he has never done so.

The executive

Executive power is vested in the King and his ministers, but it is the ministers alone who are responsible for all decisions. The King's inviolability, which is assured by art. 63 of the constitution, makes it impossible for him to be held responsible, while the provision of art. 64 stating that no act of his is valid unless countersigned by a minister removes any possibility of his acting on his own. The powers of the king, as spelled out in art. 65–76 of the constitution, include the following: appointment and recall of ministers; appointment of other civil and military officials; declaration of war; granting of pardons; conferring of titles of nobility; and the making of treaties and regulations necessary to carry out the law. The King also serves as commander-in-chief of the armed forces. He closes regular sessions of Parliament and may call special sessions or prorogue or dissolve it upon the advice of the Prime Minister. The recent creation of regional governments has taken away some powers formerly exercised by the King and his ministers, particularly those concerned with the supervision of provincial and local governments. A new category of minister, called a Secretary of State or a Minister-Secretary of State, has been added to the government in recent years. Each of these officials is attached to a regular ministry. They may not sit in Cabinet meetings and may countersign legislation only in those cases where the King has determined that they shall have that power. They are appointed and recalled by the King.

The legislature

In addition to the usual parliamentary parties, the elected members of each house of the Belgian Parliament are aligned by linguistic groups whenever a question involving linguistic interests is under consideration. Membership in linguistic groups is determined in the following way. Deputies and Senators elected in French- and German-speaking regions belong to the French-language group. Those elected in the Dutch-speaking region belong to the Dutch-language group. Those elected from the constituency of Brussels, plus Senators chosen by the Brabant Provincial Council and co-opted Senators, belong to the French group if they take their oath of office in French or German, and to the Dutch if they take the oath in that language. Members who take the oath in several languages are considered to belong to the language group in which they first take the oath. The term 'elected members' is used in determining the membership in Senate linguistic groups in order to exclude the royal princes.

The judiciary

The judicial system remains basically the same as outlined in the constitution of 1831. For an overall view of the system, see Figure I. At the national level, there is a Supreme

BELGIUM

LEVEL		
National	Cour de Cassation/Hof van Cassatie [Supreme Court]	
Regional	Cour d'Appel/Hof van Beroep [Court of Appeal]	Cour du Travail/Arbeidshof [Labour Court]
District	Tribunal de Première Instance/Rechtbank van Eerste Aanleg [Court of Primary Jurisdiction] • Tribunal de Commerce/Rechtbank van Koophandel [Commercial Court] • Chambre Civile/Burgerlijke Rechtbank [Civil Court] • Tribunal Correctionnel/Correctionele Rechtbank [Criminal Court] • Tribunal de la Jeunesse/Jeugdrechtbank [Juvenile Court] Cour d'Assises/Hof van Assise [Court of Assize]	Tribunal du Travail/Arbeidsrechtbank [Labour Tribunal]
Canton	Justice de Paix/Vredegericht [Justice of the Peace]	Tribunal de Police/Politierechtbank [Police Court]

Kindly provided by Anne-Marie Vastesaeger, Bibliothèque Royale, Brussels

Figure I. The Belgian judicial system

Court in Brussels, the Cour de Cassation/Hof van Cassatie. This court decides whether the decisions of lower courts brought before it are in strict compliance with the law; it does not consider the content of cases, except in cases concerning ministers. When it quashes a decision, the case in question is referred back to a lower court for the settlement of the litigation between the parties concerned. This court also resolves conflicts of jurisdiction between governmental bodies.

At the regional and provincial level there are two types of court, appeals courts, the Cours d'Appel/Hoven van Beroep, and assize courts, the Cours d' Assises/Assisenhoven. The latter courts are the only courts which have juries. Cases involving crimes liable to the death penalty, hard labour, imprisonment or internment, and those concerning political or press misdemeanours, are tried in the assize courts. As might be expected, it is at the regional level that changes have taken place in the court system in recent years. A constitutional amendment, which went into effect in 1974, added two new appeals courts, one at Antwerp and one at Mons, to the existing three at Ghent, Brussels and Liège, and redefined the boundaries of the areas served by each court so that four out of the five are contained within a single linguistic region. These changes have halved the number of bilingual appeals courts: only the court at Brussels remains bilingual. Another change was made in 1980, when a constitutional amendment provided for the establishment of an Arbitration Court to resolve disputes between the regional governments or between them and the national government. The competence, structure and functions of this court were laid down in the law of 28 June 1983.

Lower courts fall into two categories. Those at the district level include a number of courts of primary jurisdiction, 'tribunaux de première instance/rechtbanken van eerste aanleg', while those at the municipal level consist of justices of the peace, 'justices de paix/vredegerechten' and police courts, 'tribunaux de police/politierechtbanken'. There are also a number of special courts for questions involving labour and commercial disputes, as well as separate courts for cases involving members of the armed forces or the government. Judges, including justices of the peace, are appointed by the Crown for life and can only be removed by a specific judgement. Public prosecutors are also appointed by the King; he may also remove them.

Relations between the three branches

Parliament can force the resignation of a government through a vote of no confidence at any time in the legislative proceedings. The monarch remains free to accept or refuse the resignation of the government. In actual practice, he has sometimes refused to accept its resignation, as happened six times in 1944, when the Prince Regent judged that the loss of support of a Parliamentary majority did not constitute a true loss of Parliamentary confidence. The executive can dissolve Parliament and call for new elections. Ministers can speak on the floor of Parliament if they wish, and Parliament can require their presence. Ministers cannot however participate in the deliberations of a chamber unless they are members of it.

The King has several judicial powers. In addition to appointing judges and prosecutors, he may grant pardons. He himself is above the law and cannot be tried in any of the courts. Ministers may not be tried for acts committed during the exercise of their office. They may however be tried for acts committed outside the exercise of their office, in which case action must be initiated by the Chamber of Representatives. If indicted by the Chamber, they are tried by the two chambers of the Supreme Court sitting together. Members of Parliament enjoy Parliamentary immunity and can only be arrested or held during a session of Parliament if caught *in flagrante delicto*.

Regional institutions

The new institutions designed to give greater representation to the various linguistic groups in Belgium are still in the process of development. Those described here are those existing on 9 November 1981. There will be further changes in the next few years until the structures already mandated by law reach the final stages and until definitive arrangements are worked out for the Brussels Region and the German-speaking area.

There are two types of regional organization, one based on the Community and the other on the Region. Communities, the first governing institutions at a level other than the national to be recognized, acquired legal existence by a constitutional amendment, art. 3–C, in 1970. (Provinces and Municipalities had of course existed prior to this time, but had been considered extensions of the national government.) No boundaries for the three Communities, French, Flemish and German, were laid out in the amendment. They followed the boundaries for the linguistic regions mentioned earlier, except in the case of Brussels. Institutions in the Brussels bilingual region which conduct their activities exclusively in French were considered to be part of the French Community, with those using exclusively Dutch considered part of the Flemish Community. Each Community was endowed with a cultural council empowered to act in a specific number of matters concerning education and the use of languages. The powers and structures of the Communities have evolved since their establishment. The Communities now have very large responsibilities in the areas of health and social security, as well as culture, education and language usage. They are sovereign in the areas in which they have jurisdiction. They have the power to make decrees in these areas which have the force of law within the Community concerned. They may also establish their own budgets.

The French Community is headed by an assembly of 138 members, the Conseil de la Communauté Française. It is composed of members of the Chamber of Representatives and those directly-elected Senators who belong to the French linguistic groups of their respective houses. After revision of the method of electing Senators expected to occur in the near future, it is anticipated that the total number of members will fall to 91. The executive is made up of three members and at least one of the three must be from the bilingual region of Brussels. The members of the executive are elected by the assembly by a system of proportional representation which will change to one based on a simple majority in 1985. The executive may pose a question of confidence and any member of the assembly may introduce a motion of no confidence. The executive must resign in the case of a vote of no confidence against it.

The organization of the Flemish Community, the Vlaamse Gemeenschap, is similar to that of the French Community, except that the assembly, the Vlaamse Raad [Council], and the executive also handle matters concerning the Flemish Region, which is described below, as well as the Flemish Community. The Vlaamse Raad now consists of 180 members and the executive of nine members, of whom one at least must be from the Brussels linguistic region. The size of the assembly will fall to 121 after the revision of the method of electing Senators.

The German Community has possessed a cultural council, the Rat der Deutschen Kulturgemeinschaft, since the law of 10 July 1973, but this council has had the power to issue decrees having the force of law only since December 1983.

INTRODUCTION

The second type of regional structure is the Region. When appearing with a capital letter in this chapter, the word Region refers to one of the three sub-national political units set up to handle economic and political questions at regional level. When used with lower case it refers to the linguistic regions described above.

The three Regions, Walloon, Flemish and Brussels, were created by constitutional amendment during the reforms of the period 1968–1971. Their boundaries are yet to be fixed and may or may not follow the same lines as those of the linguistic regions described earlier. In the case of the Flemish regions, the economic and linguistic boundaries are the same and the same legislative and executive organs conduct Community affairs (cultural and social matters) as well as Regional (economic policy) affairs (with one exception: members of the Flemish Council from Brussels may not vote when matters coming within the purview of the Flemish Region, as distinct from the Community, are under consideration).

The Walloon Region differs from the French Community territorially, in that it includes the German linguistic regions within it. At present the Walloon Region has its own legislature and executive, completely separate from those of the French Community, called the Conseil Régional Wallon and the Exécutif de la Région Wallonne. These organs are chosen in much the same way as their Community counterparts, except that the law has been written in such a way as to eliminate any representation from Brussels in the Regional Council. The Council now consists of 106 members (this will fall to 70 after the revision of the Senate electoral laws) and the executive of six members. The eventual merger of the Walloon Regional Council and the French Community Council is provided for in existing legislation, but this has not yet been implemented.

Regional governments have power in the following areas: economic development; territorial and urban planning; housing; employment; rural renovation; environmental matters and conservation of natural resources; energy; public works; intergovernmental relations; and research in these areas. As in the case of the Communities, Regions enact their own budgets and pay their operating and capital expenditures. The national budget allocates funds for cultural and social security affairs directly to the French and Flemish Communities. Some funds budgeted by the national government to the two national Ministries of Education (one for education in French and the other for education in Dutch) may also be expended by the Communities for cultural matters. The national budget also provides funds to the Walloon and Flemish Regional governments for Regional economic affairs. Expenses incurred beyond the funds provided by the national government must be covered by Regional governments through one of four ways: non-tax revenue, such as receipts from the sale of hunting and fishing licences; refunds on certain fees collected by the national government, among them proceeds from radio and television licences; additional levies on existing taxes in the preceding category; and borrowing. In short, the Regional and Community governments do not have power to institute new taxes. The Regional governments must assume all responsibility for paying interest charges and principal on loans they contract; the national government will not guarantee their loans.

The definitive structure of the Brussels Region, which includes the 19 Municipalities comprising the administrative district of Brussels-Capital, has yet to be worked out. Until a law on the structure of self-government for the area acceptable to all parties is passed, Brussels is still governed under the law of 20 July 1979 and the regulations implementing it. This legislation provides for the following divisions of power.

Responsibility for national matters and the supervision of local authorities belongs to the two houses of Parliament and the national Cabinet. Matters lying within the scope of the Communities are handled by the appropriate Community Council and Executive where unilingual institutions are involved and by Parliament and the Cabinet where bilingual institutions are concerned. The executive organ responsible for bilingual institutions differs depending on whether cultural or social security matters are involved. The national government as a whole acts in the former case, and the two secretaries of state for the Brussels Region in the latter. Economic affairs lying within the competence of Regional governments are handled by the two houses of Parliament and the Executive of the Brussels Region. This Executive, a three-member committee called the Comité Ministériel de la Région Bruxelloise/Ministerieel Comite van het Brusselse Gewest, is a Cabinet committee and consists of the Ministre de la Région Bruxelloise et des Classes Moyennes/Minister van het Brusselse Gewest en van Middenstand[1] [Minister for the Brussels Region and the Middle Classes], plus the two secretaries of state for the Brussels Region. At least one of the secretaries of state must be from a different linguistic group from the chairman of the committee.

Local taxes in the Region are levied by the national government, leaving the Region with no revenue sources of its own. Parliament votes appropriations for Regional (economic) matters and receipts from local taxes are apportioned to the two Communities by royal decree.

It will be remembered that provision for the representation of Brussels on the executives of the Communities is guaranteed by the stipulation that at least one member of the Executive of each Community must be from Brussels. On the other hand, representation on the Walloon Regional Council is denied to residents of Brussels, and they must refrain from voting in the Flemish Council when Regional (economic) affairs are under discussion.

Provincial government

Art. 1 of the constitution provides that Belgium can be divided into nine Provinces: Antwerp, Brabant, East Flanders, West Flanders, Hainaut, Liège, Limburg, Luxemburg and Namur. The boundaries of the Provinces and the 'arrondissements', the districts into which they are subdivided, were last fixed by the law of 1 October 1979. Provincial governments consist of a governor, appointed and dismissed by the King, a Provincial Council, the Conseil Provincial/Provincieraad of members elected for four-year terms, and an executive committee known as the Députation Permanente/Bestendige Deputatie, which is composed of six members of the Provincial Council and conducts the affairs of the Province when the Council is not in session.

Provincial governments have power to issue provincial regulations in the form of resolutions. Such resolutions must of course be in accord with national and regional legislation. The Council considers all matters of provincial interest, except financial questions. It is chiefly involved with education, welfare, public works and services involving associations of several municipalities. It also elects Senators representing the Provinces and nominates candidates for some judicial posts.

The chief changes in Provincial administration in the recent restructuring of the Belgian government have been the removal of the power of the Provinces to tax and a change in the chain of command which makes them now responsible to the Regional governments rather than as formerly to the national government (Brabant is an exception). To compensate them for the loss of revenue formerly received from the taxes they levied, the Provinces are to receive funds equal to the sum of the taxes they levied in 1981, adjusted annually for inflation in line with the consumer price index.

Local government

Municipal government structure is uniform throughout Belgium. Each Municipality possesses a council of members elected for six-year terms, called the Conseil Communal/Gemeenteraad, a mayor named by the King on the recommendation of the Council, who is known as the Bourgmestre/Burgemeester, and aldermen elected by the Council, called Echevins/Schepenen. The mayor, council and aldermen together have the power to make local regulations, usually called délibérations/beraadslagingen or arrêtés/besluiten. These must be countersigned by Regional authorities in most cases. Municipal officials must see that laws and regulations issued at all the levels of government above them, as well as their own, are carried out. They receive subsidies from their Regional government for their operating and capital expenses.

In the interests of reducing the large number of Municipalities in existence in Belgium, there has been legislation to encourage the merger of Municipalities. Between the passage of the law of 26 July 1971 and 1 January 1977, the total number of municipal governments has been reduced from over 2,000 to 596. Municipal governments have also been encouraged to band together for the provision of a number of services. These organizations, known as 'associations de communes/verenigingen van gemeenten', also possess governing institutions.

Relations between the levels of government

The restructuring of the Belgian government, which is still in progress, has changed it from a unitary state in which power flowed from the capital in Brussels down through the various subdivisions of the national government to a state in which there are two centres of political power, which may under certain circumstances be at variance with each other. It will be noted that the national government is the source of sovereignty. All powers not expressly delegated to the Regions and Communities reside in the national government. Governments at the regional and national levels are linked together by the fact that some officials serve in both: the members of the Regional and Community councils and the executives they elect are members of the national Parliament. Members of Regional governments and the national government do differ in linguistic group membership, however. Each Regional government, except for the Brussels Region, represents the interests of only a single linguistic group, whereas the national government and the government of the Brussels Region represent the interests of the nation as a whole or of all the people in the Brussels area regardless of language affiliation.

Guides to government organization

The two best tools for keeping abreast of changes in government organization are the two annual directories, both non-official, the *Annuaire administratif et judiciaire de Belgique/Administratief en gerechtelijk jaarboek voor Belgie* [Administrative and judicial yearbook of Belgium], published since 1869, and the *Guide des Ministères: revue de l'administration belge/Gids der Ministeries: tijdschrift van de Belgische administratie* [Guide to ministries: review of Belgian administration], published since 1951. Both are distributed by Bruylant. Both list members of the Royal Household, names and addresses of all official and semi-official bodies at national, Regional, Provincial and local level, and names of their top officials. The former also includes universities and secondary schools, churches, scientific, professional and literary organizations, and libraries, museums and archives. The latter gives the political affiliations of members of Parliament and mayors, and information on political parties. It is an excellent source for the history of changes in ministerial organization. The table entitled 'Composition successive des Ministères depuis 1830/Samenstelling der verschillende ministeries sedert 1830', which appears in every edition, shows all name changes in ministries from 1830, along with the dates on which they occurred. In addition, the table lists the names of all ministers and the dates they held office. Both directories have alphabetical lists of all Municipalities in Belgium and subject indexes. More detailed descriptions of the structure and functions of individual agencies will be found in the loose-leaf *Dictionnaire des services publics relevant de l'État* [Dictionary of state public services] of the Centre de Droit de la Gestion et de l'Économie Publiques of the Université Catholique de Louvain, published by Oyez in 1978. The third part of this volume, issued under the direction of Jean le Brun, gives name, address, mission, organization, activities, and financing for each agency. Also included are a description of the personnel system, a list of the laws and regulations covering the agency, and the names of the bodies responsible for overseeing its operations. Updates are provided at regular intervals, the most recent in 1982.

A convenient tool for finding the latest changes in Cabinet membership is *Chiefs of state and cabinet members of foreign governments*, published monthly by the Central Intelligence Agency of the US government. All names of government departments appear in English translation only, and no addresses are given.

The best source of historical information on government organization and personnel is the *Almanach royal officiel* [Official royal almanac], published annually by Guyot for the Ministère de l'Intérieur/Ministerie van Binnenlandse Zaken [Ministry of the Interior] from 1840 to 1939. It covers all levels of government for both Belgium and her colonies and includes a list of treaties in force.

2. PRINCIPAL PUBLICATIONS OF CENTRAL GOVERNMENT

2.1. Legislation

Article 129 of the Belgian constitution provides that no law, decree or administrative regulation is binding upon the governed until it has been published in the manner laid down by law. Since 1845, all national legislation has appeared in the *Moniteur belge/Belgisch Staatsblad* [Official gazette], which is published five times a week and is rigorously bilingual, the French and Dutch versions appearing in columns side by side on the same page. The order of the columns is reversed each year. It contains the full texts of constitutional amendments, international agreements, laws and subsidiary legislation, usually within ten days to two weeks of signature. Also included are appointments, resignations and promotions of government officials and employees, notices of positions vacant, summaries of parliamentary proceedings and selected court decisions. Citations to all texts comprising the legislative history of an item are given. The *Moniteur belge* has a number of annexes, which contain legislation concerning private companies, non-profit organizations, mutual societies and professional organizations. A bulletin announcing government contracts for tender or awarded is also published as an annexe under the title *Bulletin des adjudications/Bulletin der aanbestedingen* [Bulletin of the award of contracts].

Annual alphabetical subject and personal name indexes are provided as part of a year's subscription to the *Moniteur belge*. Monthly alphabetical subject indexes and chronological lists are provided by a private publisher, Larcier, as *Tables legislatives mensuelles indiquant la date et la page du Moniteur belge* [Monthly legislative indexes to date and page in the *Moniteur belge*]. Subscribers to the monthly indexes also receive an annual cumulated index.

Information as to how to obtain subscriptions to the *Moniteur belge* is given in section 3, below, on official publishing. It is also available in microfilm: the New York Public Library has filmed 1944-1952 and 1970 to date. The intervening years are available from Kraus Microforms.

In addition to the *Moniteur*, which is the primary source of Belgian laws and decrees, there are a number of official and non-official compilations of laws which may be more convenient to use. The Office of the *Moniteur belge* offers an unannotated selective compilation, entitled *Recueil des lois, décrets et arrêtés/Verzameling der wetten, decreten en besluiten* [Collection of laws, decrees and orders], which has been published since 1830. There are alphabetical and chronological indexes, with cumulated indexes for 1830-1860, 1860-1870 and 1871-1880. The most widely used compilation in French is the semi-official *Pasinomie: Collection complète des lois, décrets, arrêtés et règlements généraux* [*Pasinomie*: complete collection of the laws, decrees and general orders], which first appeared in 1780 and is published monthly by Bruylant. It does not include the Dutch texts of legislation.

Annotated editions of the laws in force have been issued by a number of non-official publishers, among them Bruylant and Larcier, who have produced *Les codes belges* [Belgian codes of law] and *Les codes Larcier* [Larcier codes of law] respectively. Legislation for the territory comprising Belgium before the foundation of the Belgian state may be found in the *Recueil des actes des princes belges* [Collection of acts of the Belgian princes], published by the Commission Royale d'Histoire of the Académie Royale des Sciences, des Lettres et des Beaux-Arts [Royal Historical Commission of the Royal Academy of Science, Literature and the Arts] between 1936 and 1938, and the *Recueil des ordonnances des anciens Pays-Bas* [Collection of ordinances of the former Low Countries] and the *Recueil des anciennes coutumes de la Belgique* [Collection of the ancient customs of Belgium], both of which were published by Gomaere for the Commission Royale pour la Publication des Anciennes Lois et Ordonnances de la Belgique [Royal Commission for the Publication of the Ancient Laws and Ordinances of Begium], between 1847 and 1912 and 1867 and 1911 respectively. The latter title records the customary law of the various counties, duchies and cities.

2.2. Parliamentary publications

A brief summary of the activities of the Chamber of Representatives may be found in the weekly bulletin published by the Legislative Service of the Chamber every Friday during session, *Informations parlementaires* [Parliamentary information]. In addition to mentioning all subjects treated in committee or on the floor during the week, and listing events scheduled for the following week, it contains information on such topics as elections and characteristics of members.

The debates of each house are issued in two forms by the Office of the *Moniteur belge*. The official version containing the full text for the Chamber of Representatives appears in the *Annales parlementaires/Parlementaire handelingen: Chambre/Kamer* [Annals of Parliament: Chamber of Representatives], published since 1845/46, in the language of the original speaker. A similarly-titled series for the Senate was begun in 1848. Before that its debates were published in the series for the Chamber of Representatives. From 1831 to 1844 the debates were published in the *Moniteur belge*. Members may correct the speeches in these versions, but must return them within four days for the Chamber of Representatives and two days for the Senate. A summary of the proceedings appears the day after the session in both French and Dutch as *Compte rendu analytique/Beknopt verslag* [Summary proceedings]. The Dutch series began in 1912/1913 and the French for the Chamber of Representatives in 1878/79 and for the Senate in 1886/87. Divisions and answers to oral questions to ministers from members of parliament appear in both series.

Written questions and answers appear in a separate series, *Bulletin des questions de Messieurs les senateurs et représentants et réponses de Messieurs les ministres/Bulletin van Vragen der volksvertegenwoordigers en Antwoorden der Ministers* [Bulletin of questions of senators and representatives and answers from ministers], from 1908/09 for the two houses and from 1954 for each house separately. Before these dates, they were included in annexes to the summarized version of the debates.

Subject and personal name indexes to the debates are published annually in both French and Dutch. There is also an annual index of laws arranged alphabetically by subject. Entries include the date of introduction of the bill, dates of passage by each house, and dates of approval, promulgation and publication. Written questions are indexed in the debates indexes for the Senate, while separate indexes by subject, name of questioner and name of ministry to which the official answering the question is attached are published for the Chamber of Representatives.

Bills, amendments, committee reports and other documents prepared by or for Parliament for the conduct of its business appear in both languages in a series edited by each house and printed for it by a commercial publisher. These series are entitled *Recueil des pièces imprimées par ordre de la Chambre des Représentants (Senat)/Parlementaire bescheiden, Kamer (Senaat)* [Collection of papers printed by order of the Chamber of Representatives (Senate)], published since 1831/32 and 1832/33 respectively. They are also referred to as *Documents parlementaires/Parlementaire stukken* [Parliamentary documents]. The individual documents are numbered consecutively throughout the life of a legislature (four years, unless Parliament is dissolved and new elections called earlier). All items related to a bill have the same basic number, followed by the dates of the session and a dash. Numbers after the dash distinguish the various documents related to the bill from one another. For example, bill no. 521 of session 1980/81 concerned the entry, stay, settlement and departure of foreigners. This bill was numbered 521 (1980/81)—no. 1. The report of the Justice Committee on this bill received the number 521 (1980/81)—no. 2. If there had been amendments they would have been nos. 3, 4, 5 and so on.

This system is a little more complicated for the first six basic numbers used each year: these are used for lists of members of the two houses, member of committees and other organizational matters and for the national budget, and the numbers remain the same every session. Thus each year the budget is document no. 5. The huge number of documents generated in the consideration of a budget requires more symbols to differentiate them from each other. Accordingly, a Roman numeral indicating the agency whose budget is the subject of the document is inserted between the base number and the number showing the type of document. A Senate bill on appropriations for the Foreign Ministry during the special session of 1979 might be numbered 5 (1979)—VIII—no. 1. A report on appropriations for external trade might be no. 2. No. 3 might concern appropriations for foreign relations, and no. 4 appropriations for overseas development, with no. 5 an amendment to the bill whose text was given in no. 1.

Before 1862 the parliamentary documents were printed with the *Annales parlementaires*. Prior to 1845, both the debates and documents appeared in the *Moniteur belge*.

There are currently three indexes to the documents of the Chamber of Representatives. Alphabetical author and subject indexes and a numerical list of documents are all issued annually and for the entire legislative period. There are also decennial cumulated indexes for the period 1831-1911, and one covering the documents of both houses for the period 1911-1931. Senate documents are included in the annual indexes to its debates. Cumulated indexes for the Senate were issued for 1831/32-1851/52 and 1851/52-1871/72. A useful non-official tool for tracing laws, bills and other parliamentary documents is the last issue each year of the *Annales* [Annals] of the Faculté de Droit, d'Économie et des Sciences Sociales de Liège [Liège Faculty of Law, Economics and Social Sciences], which contains an index entitled 'Documentation juridique belge' [Belgian law documentation].

In addition to the lists found in the personal name indexes to the debates and in the parliamentary documents at the beginning of each session, names and addresses of members will be found in the government manuals mentioned earlier. Biographical directories with photographs are also issued after each election as *Notices biographiques/Levensberichten* [Biographical notices]. A cumulative biographical directory by Paul van Molle, entitled *Le Parlement belge/Het Belgisch Parlement* [The Belgian Parliament], offers biographical sketches of senators, deputies and ministers who were not members of Parliament, for the period from 1894 to 1972. This work, which was published in Antwerp in 1972 by Standaard, includes photographs of some members.

The results of parliamentary elections are published by the Ministère de l'Intérieur/Ministerie van Binnenlandse Zaken[2] [Ministry of the Interior]. Records of committee meetings are not published, but are usually reported in the daily press. Recommendations of committees and summaries of their deliberations are contained in their reports issued in the parliamentary documents series discussed above. The rules and procedures of each house are published in their *Règlement/Reglement* [Rules of procedure].

2.3. Publications of the courts

Most court decisions are published by non-official publishers. The most widely-used compilation of court reports is the *Pasicrisie: recueil général de la jurisprudence* [*Pasicrisie*: general collection of jurisprudence], published by Bruylant. An official edition of the decisions of the Cour de Cassation/Hof van Cassatie [Supreme Court] is published monthly: the French edition, *Bulletin des arrêts de la Cour de Cassation* [Bulletin of decisions of the Supreme Court], is published by Bruylant, while the Dutch edition, *Arresten van het Hof van Cassatie*, is issued by the Ministère de la Justice et des Réformes Institutionnelles/Ministerie van Justitie en Institutionele Hervormingen[3] [Ministry of Justice and Institutional Reform].

2.4. Publications of the executive

General information

The Institut Belge d'Information et de Documentation/Belgisch Instituut voor Voorlichting en Documentatie (INBEL) [Central Information Office] has published numerous editions of a popular handbook on Belgium, available in some twelve languages, *Belgium at the heart of Europe* (latest edition, 1980). It is also responsible for several series describing various aspects of Belgian life and culture. *Vu par les Belges/More about Belgium* (formerly *Belgian news*) appears bimonthly. *Quid* answers questions most frequently received by INBEL and Belgian Embassies and appears weekly in French, Dutch, and English. Government departments and public institutions are the subject of each number in the monographic series *Ce qu'il faut savoir de . . .* and *Wat men moet weten over . . .* [What you need to know about . . .], available in French and Dutch. INBEL has also issued two directories of information services in Belgium: *Répertoire de l'information 1981* and *Repertorium van de voorlichting 1981* [Information guide 1981], a guide to mass media and both official and nonofficial information agencies. A round-up of official information and public relations agencies is found in *Les services d'information et de relations publiques* and *De openbare voorlichtings- en public relations diensten* [Official information and public relations services] (latest edition 1977). In addition to names and addresses, it includes a brief description of the mission and accomplishments of each body.

A number of serious studies of Belgian institutions appear in a series prepared by the Ministère des Relations Extérieures/Ministerie van Buitenlandse Zaken[4] [Ministry of External Relations] for its personnel abroad. This series, which is published at irregular intervals in six languages, is entitled *Textes et documents* and *Teksten en documenten* [Texts and documents]. The English version is entitled *Memo from Belgium*. Numbers which are unparalleled for an understanding of the Belgian system of government are no. 166, *The Belgian constitution: commentary*, 1974, and nos. 179, 182 and 189, *The reform of the Belgian state*, 1978–1980, all by Robert Senelle. Other issues have discussed such topics as music, cartoons, social communications and unemployment policy in Belgium.

Political affairs and foreign policy

There is no official series devoted exclusively to texts and statements on foreign relations or to treaties. Summaries of Belgian foreign policy may be found from time to time in the two series discussed above, *Memo from Belgium* and *More about Belgium*. Texts of treaties usually appear in the *Moniteur belge* as an annex to the law approving them, but they may be published in a completely different issue of the *Moniteur* from the law. There is no general legislation making the publication of treaties mandatory, although a provision requiring publication may of course be written into an individual treaty. Texts of treaties which have appeared in the *Moniteur belge* may also be found in the *Pasinomie* and the *Recueil des lois et arrêtés*. Acts of ratification, adhesion, accession and extension of treaties are never published in full, but a summary notice of such action appears in the *Moniteur*.

The fact that not all treaties are published has led to some interesting legal ramifications. In cases where a citizen contravenes a provision of a treaty which has not been published, the courts have decided that the citizen cannot be held responsible.

Until 1939, a list of all treaties in force was published annually in the *Almanach royal officiel*, mentioned earlier. Citations to the texts of treaties published in the *Moniteur belge* or other sources were included. Bilateral treaties were arranged alphabetically by country, while multilateral treaties were in chronological sequence, with a subject index at the end.

French texts of treaties for the period 1831–1913 are published in the *Recueil des traités et conventions concernant le royaume de Belgique* [Collection of treaties and conventions affecting the Kingdom of Belgium], edited by Desiré de Garcia de la Vega and continued by Alphonse de Busschère, 1850–1914, in 21 volumes.

One of the subjects on which the Ministry of External Relations has published a good deal is third world aid. The sub-agency responsible for development aid, the Administration Générale de la Coöpération au Développement (AGCD)/Algemeen Bestuur van de Ontwikkelingssamenwerking (ABOS) [General Administration for Development Cooperation], publishes a bimonthly record of policy and programmes, *Dimension 3* and *Dimensie 3* [Third dimension]. It has also issued a number of brochures offering general economic information about individual countries aided and a summary of development projects carried out in two series, *Les Belges au . . .* and *Belgen in . . .* [The Belgians in . . .], and *Projets de coöpération entre la Belgique et . . .* and *Ontwikkelingsprojecten tussen België en . . .* [Cooperation projects between Belgium and . . .]. It also issues manuals for participants in aid programmes and studies of development aid. An annual report of its activities, *Rapport annuel* and *Jaarverslag*, is also available.

Responsibility for external cultural relations is shared with the two ministries for education and culture, the Ministère de l'Éducation Nationale et de la Culture Française[5] and the Ministerie van Nationale Opvoeding en Nederlandse Cultuur,[6] and also the Counseil National de la Politique Scientifique/Nationale Raad voor Wetenschapsbeleid [National Council for Science Policy]. The latter does not produce many publications in this area, but it does issue one series of great importance, the annual list of doctoral theses completed in Belgium, the *Répertoire des thèses de doctorat/Repertorium van doctorale proefschriften*, which began in 1971/72.

The Ministry of External Relations maintains its own archives, rather than depositing them in the national archives, the Archives Générales du Royaume/Algemeen Rijksarchief. A description of the archives, their history, organization and classification, and inventories and guides to them, will be found in the chapter on Belgium by Daniel M. Thomas in *The new guide to the diplomatic archives of Western Europe*, edited by Daniel M. Thomas and Lynn M. Case, Philadelphia, University of Pennsylvania Press, 1975, pp. 20–42.

The Ministère de l'Intérieur/Ministerie van Binnenlandse Zaken[7] [Ministry of the Interior] has ceased publication of two well-known series which it began publishing in the first half of the nineteenth century—its official bulletin, *Bulletin du Ministère de l'Intérieur* and *Bulletin van het Ministerie van Binnenlandse Zaken*, and the *Almanach royal officiel* mentioned earlier. It is still the publisher of Parliamentary election results, *Elections législatives: résultats des élections du . . . /Parlementsverkiezingen: uitslagen der verkiezingen van. . . .*

In addition to bearing the responsibility for publication of the official gazette, the parliamentary debates, and other publications of the official gazette office, the Ministère de la Justice et des Réformes Institutionnelles/Ministerie van Justitie en Institutionele Hervormingen[8] [Ministry of Justice and Institutional Reform] publishes series concerned with prison administration and juvenile delinquency. The quarterly bulletin *Bulletin de l'administration pénitentiaire/Bulletin van het bestuur strafinrichtingen* [Bulletin of prison administration] contains statistics of the prison population and reports of prison activities and personnel actions, as well as texts of prison regulations and articles on prison administration. Studies, news, bibliographies and other material on the protection of youth appear in the *Bulletin de liaison de l'Office de la Protection de la Jeunesse/Contactblad van de Dienst voor Jeugdbescherming* [Contact bulletin of the Office for the Protection of Youth]. Judicial statistics will be discussed below in the section on statistics.

The Ministère de la Défense Nationale/Ministerie van Landsverdediging [Ministry of National Defence] issues very little material for public distribution, other than its magazine for servicemen, *Vox: hebdomadaire militaire* and *Vox: militair weekblad* [Vox: forces weekly].

Economic affairs

The ministry most active in publishing economic information is the Ministère des Affaires Économiques/Ministerie van Economische Zaken [Ministry of Economic Affairs]. Its chief publishers are the Direction Générale des Études et de la Documentation/Algemene Directie voor Studiën en Documentatie [General Directorate for Surveys and Documentation], and the Institut National de Statistique/Nationaal Instituut voor de Statistiek [National Statistical Institute].

Some of the most important series produced by the former are:

L'économie belge en . . . and *De Belgische economie in* . . . [The Belgian economy in . . .], an annual account of the macroeconomic aspects of the Belgian economy, with detailed analyses, accompanied by statistical tables and graphs for each sector of economic activity

Aperçu de l'évolution économique/Overzicht van de economische ontwikkeling [Review of economic development], a monthly review of the economic situation in Belgium and a number of other countries, with regular supplements, *Bilans énergetiques/Energiebalansen* [Energy accounts], and *Principales mesures de politique économique, financière et sociale/Belangrijkste economische, financiële en sociale beleidsmaatregelen* [Principal indicators of economic, financial and social policy]

Budget économique de . . . and *Economisch budget* . . . [Economic budget for . . .], a description of the economic situation and outlook based on the national accounts, which appears in three versions each year, preliminary, final and revised.

All of these contain a wealth of statistical material on the economy. The General Directorate for Surveys and Documentation also produces a handbook for businessmen outlining procedures which must be carried out in order to establish a business in Belgium, entitled *Entreprises industrielles et commerciales en Belgique* and *Handels- en nijverheidsondernemingen in België* [Industrial enterprises in Belgium].

The publications of the Institut National de Statistique are described in the section on statistics below.

Other sub-agencies of the Ministry of Economic Affairs with active publishing programmes are the Administrations de l'Industrie, du Commerce, des Mines and the Administration de l'Énergie/Administraties van de Nijverheid, de Handel, het

Mijnwezen and Energie [Administrations for Industry, Commerce, Mines and Energy].

The Administration for Industry is responsible for an annual series on foreign investment in Belgium, *Investissements étrangers en Belgique, année* . . . and *Buitenlandse investeringen in België, jaar* . . . [Foreign investment in Belgium in . . .], which contains data on activities related to the first phase of the investment programmes of firms established in Belgium between 1959 and the year covered. Statistics are broken down by economic sector, product group and country of origin as well as by region. Investments aided by economic expansion legislation in the period from 1959 are shown, as are the number of new establishments, the number of jobs and the amount invested by a number of countries in each Province of Belgium. The names and addresses of all foreign companies that have invested in Belgium during the year are included.

The Administration for Commerce publishes a number of bulletins containing regulations, information on weights and measures, and so on. It is also the publisher of the official patent journal, *Recueil des brevets d'invention/Verzameling der Uitvindingsoctrooien* [Collection of patents], which appears monthly.

The Administration for Mines publishes weekly, monthly and annual statistics on the mineral industries, which are available free. It also publishes the monthly *Annales des mines de Belgique/Annalen der mijnen van België* [Annals of Belgian mines]. The Service Géologique/Geologische Dienst [Geological Service] prepares a series of detailed maps, the *Carte géologique détaillée de la Belgique/Gedetailleerde geologische kaart van België* [Detailed geological map of Belgium], scale 1:25,000.

The chief series published by the Administration for Energy are the *Bilans énergétiques* and *Energiebalansen* [Energy accounts], issued quarterly, *Statistiques électriques* and *Elektriciteitsstatistieken* [Electricity statistics], issued annually, *Production et consommation d'énergie électrique/Produktie en verbruik van electrische energie* [Production and consumption of electricity], which is monthly, and *Organisation du secteur de l'énergie électrique/Organisatie van de sector electrische energie* [Organization of the electricity industry], which are annual or biennial. There are similar series for gas and petroleum.

Two of the most important of the many independent institutions reporting to the Ministry of Economic Affairs are the Conseil Central de l'Économie/Centrale Raad voor het Bedrijfsleven [Central Economic Council] and the Bureau du Plan/Planbureau [Planning Bureau]. The former is a consultative group set up to bring together representatives of varied economic interest groups, such as trade unions, management, consumers and small businessmen, to participate in drawing up economic policy. A description of the Council, its work and its publications, is found in a brochure published by it at regular intervals, entitled simply *Le conseil central* and *De Centrale Raad*. The latest edition was that for 1980. It also publishes an annual report of its activities, *Rapport du Secrétaire sur l'activité du Conseil/Verslag van de Secretaris over de werkzaamheden van de Raad* [Report of the Secretary on the work of the Council]. There is a monthly economic survey, *Note mensuelle sur la situation économique* and *Maandnota betreffende de economische toestand* [Monthly note on the economic situation], and an annual or semi-annual assessment of the economic situation, *Avis sur la situation économique* and *Advies betreffende de economische toestand* [Information on the economic situation].

Four- or five-year development plans have been drawn up by the government since

1961. The Planning Bureau prepares the plans in collaboration with the Regional Councils and sees that the plans are implemented. The plans themselves are published in the parliamentary documents, usually, but not always, accompanying the bills approving the plan. They may be entitled *Programme d'expansion économique/Economisch Expansieprogramma* [Plan for economic expansion] or quite simply *Le plan/Het Plan* [The plan]. The texts of the plans are also issued in separate editions by the Planning Bureau. The first three, covering the period 1961–1975, are available on microfiche from InterDocumentation Co. This company also offers the investment programmes which preceded the plans in the period 1948–1960 on fiche.

Other ministries and autonomous organizations which publish in the area of economic affairs are the Ministère des Finances et du Commerce Extérieur/Ministerie van Financiën en Buitenlandse Handel[9] [Ministry of Finance and External Trade], the Ministère du Budget, de la Politique Scientifique et du Plan/Ministerie van Begroting, Wetenschapsbeleid en het Plan [Ministry of the Budget, Science Policy and Planning], the Banque Nationale/Nationale Bank [Central Bank], the Ministère de la Région Bruxelloise et des Classes Moyennes/Ministerie van het Brusselse Gewest en van Middenstand[10] [Ministry of the Brussels Region and the Middle Classes] and the Secrétariat d'État aux Affaires Européennes et à l'Agriculture/Staatssecretaris voor Europese Zaken en Landbouw [Secretary of State for European Affairs and Agriculture].

The first two of these, the Ministry of Finance and External Trade and the Ministry of the Budget, Science Policy and Planning, handle budgetary and fiscal matters. It is difficult to keep up with the current organization of these ministries and the division of responsibilities between them, since they have undergone many changes in recent years. Their chief publication is the budget, which actually appears in the parliamentary documents series of the Chamber of Representatives, usually in September or October of the year preceding that covered by the budget. A popularized edition of the budget, *Les finances de l'État en . . . /Die Staatsfinanciën in . . .* [The state finances in . . .] is available free from the Service d'Études et de Documentation/Studie- en Documentatiedienst [Reports and documents service], 14 rue de la Loi, 1000 Brussels, at irregular intervals, as is a series of reports and studies on the budget designed for the layman, *Études et documents budgétaires/Studiën en begrotingsbescheiden* [Budget studies and documents]. Information on taxes, including court decisions, parliamentary questions and answers and statistics, is contained in the monthly *Bulletin des contributions* and *Bulletin der Belastingen* [Tax bulletin] of the Ministry of Finance and External Trade. It also issues a loose-leaf compilation of legislation pertaining to pensions, *Recueil des dispositions légales et réglementaires en matière de pensions civiles/Verzameling van de wettelijke en reglementaire bepalingen inzake burgerlijke pensioenen . . .* [Collection of laws and regulations concerning civil pensions]. Its information bulletin for staff, which is unfortunately not for public distribution, the *Bulletin de documentation/Documentatieblad*, is a treasury of up-to-date economic and financial statistics, with citations to sources of information.

Finance

The determination of monetary policy is of course the function of the Central Bank. Each issue of the Bank's monthly *Bulletin*, published since 1926 (formerly with the titles *Bulletin hebdomadaire d'information et de documentation* and *Tijdschrift voor documentatie en voorlichting* [Weekly bulletin of information and documentation], includes a round-up of economic legislation for the month, a bibliography of economic and financial books and articles, and a graph showing the overall trend of economic indicators during the preceding month based on the Bank's monthly economic survey. In addition, it contains statistics on population, national accounts, employment, industry, agriculture, services, price indexes, wages, foreign trade, the balance of payments, exchange markets, public finance, credit operations, the balance sheets and discount rates of the principal Belgian banks and other monetary institutions, money stock, the money market, savings, stocks and bonds, discount and interest rates, public and private assets and the activities of foreign banks. The legislative section gives citations to the original texts in the *Moniteur belge* and the *Journal officiel* of the European Communities and reprints the texts of major laws and regulations. Issues may also include articles and studies on topics such as the European Monetary System or the balance of payments of the Benelux countries.

Another useful publication of the Bank is its annual report, *Rapport*, published since 1851 and appearing in English as well as French and Dutch. Each report contains a thorough review of the year's economic and financial developments. Weekly figures showing assets and liabilities of the Bank are published in the *Moniteur belge* and reprinted in an annex to the annual report. Of special value to English-speaking readers is the glossary of French and English organization names appearing in the report.

Foreign trade

The Office Belge du Commerce Extérieur/Belgische Dienst voor de Buitenlandse Handel [Office of External Trade] prepares publications for businessmen interested in international trade. Its quarterly bulletin describing new industrial organizations, products and techniques developed in Belgium and Luxembourg and sales of Benelux products abroad is entitled *Belgique: économie et technique* and *België: economie en techniek* [Belgium: economy and technology]. It is also printed in Spanish and English: the English title is *Belgium: economic and technical information*. This office is also responsible for the publication of detailed annual foreign trade figures, *Le commerce extérieur de l'Union Belgo-Luxembourgeoise* and *De Buitenlandse Handel van de Belgisch–Luxemburgse Economische Unie* [External trade of the Belgium–Luxembourg Union]. These figures were previously published in the following series:

> *Statistique annuelle du commerce extérieur de l'Union Économique Belgo-Luxembourgeoise/Jaarstatistiek over de buitenlandse handel van de Belgisch–Luxemburgse Economische Unie* [Annual statistics of external trade of the Belgium–Luxembourg Economic Union], published from 1932 by the Institut National de Statistique
>
> *Tableau général (annuel) du commerce extérieur de la Belgique avec les pays étrangers* [General annual table of the external trade of Belgium with other countries], published by the Ministère des Finances [Ministry of Finance] from 1914 to 1931 and by the Ministère de l'Intérieur [Ministry of the Interior] from 1831 to 1913.

Volumes for each major geographical region of the world show the value and quantity of imports and exports cross-classified by product and country of origin or destination.

This office also publishes a variety of promotional material designed to increase Belgian exports and aid both importers and exporters in doing business. Most of this information appears in supplements to *ICE* (*Informations du commerce extérieur*) and

BBH (*Berichten over de Buitenlandse Handel*) [Information on external trade] which appears bi-weekly.

Other agencies concerned with economic affairs which have active publishing programmes are those concerned with agriculture and small businesses. Agriculture is currently handled by a Secretary of State attached to the Ministry of External Affairs, the Secrétaire d'État aux Affaires Européennes et à l'Agriculture/Staatssecretaris voor Europese Zaken en Landbouw [Secretary of State for European Affairs and Agriculture]. Some of the best-known series in this area began under former ministries of agriculture, such as the monthly *Agricontact: le courrier du Ministère de l'Agriculture/Agricontact: Koerier van het Ministerie van Landbouw* [Agricontact: newsletter of the Ministry of Agriculture] and the quarterly *Revue de l'agriculture/Landbouwtijdschrift* [Review of agriculture]. The semi-autonomous Institut Économique Agricole [Economic Institute for Agriculture] publishes a number of periodicals and monographic series for farmers, including *Cahiers de l'IEA/LEI schriften* [IEA notebooks], which are irregular, the *Courrier de l'IEA/LEI Koerier* [IEA newsletter], which is issued monthly, and *Notes de l'IEA/LEI Nota's* [IEA notes], issued irregularly.

Small business, which was formerly the province of a separate ministry, the Ministère des Classes Moyennes/Ministerie van Middenstand [Ministry of the Middle Classes], is now combined with responsibility for the administration of the Brussels Region in the hands of the Ministre de la Région Bruxelloise et des Classes Moyennes/Ministerie van het Brusselse Gewest en van Middenstand [Minister for the Brussels Region and the Middle Classes].[11] The most active publisher in the field is an independent establishment, the Institut Économique et Social des Classes Moyennes/Economisch en Sociaal Instituut voor de Middenstand [Social and Economic Institute for the Middle Classes], which produces news and articles of interest to small businessmen in its monthly *Informations/Informatieblad* [Information] and a digest of Belgian and foreign newspaper and magazine articles concerning small business in its monthly *Revue de la presse/Persoverzicht* [Review of the press]. It also prepares a number of brochures offering information on aid available to business.

Statistics

An excellent guide to official statistics is found in an article by R. Dereymaeker, 'Statistiques au service des entreprises: description et méthodologie', *Bulletin de statistique*, 12/1979 and 1/1980, and *Études statistiques*, 58/1980. Both were published by the Institut National de Statistique/Nationaal Instituut voor de Statistiek [National Statistical Institute] and are described below. In addition to an explanation of business statistics, there is a brief description of the organization and history of the National Statistical Institute.

Publications of the Institute are listed in its annual catalogue and monthly updates.

Statistical publications from the nineteenth and early twentieth centuries are listed in the statistical yearbook published by the Institute, the *Annuaire statistique/Statistisch jaarboek*, which is also described below, vol. 2, 1911, pp. cxiii–cxxiii.

The most widely-used publications of the Institute are the yearbook, which has been published annually since 1870, and the censuses of population. The former was known as the *Annuaire statistique de la Belgique et du Congo Belge* prior to 1960 and is available on microfiche from Chadwyck-Healey Ltd. for the period 1870–1962 (a few years are available only in full size). It includes statistics on climate, territory, population, health, housing, elections, education, culture, science policy, justice, agriculture, forestry, fishing, industry, domestic and foreign trade, transport, tourism, the postal system and telephones, the press, radio, television, cinema, public finance, banking and credit, income and wealth, employment, prices, salaries and wages, consumption, social security and the national accounts. Tables are accompanied by notes identifying the agency but not the specific title from which the data were obtained. There is also a condensed version of the yearbook, the *Annuaire statistique de poche* and *Zakjaarboek* [Statistical pocket yearbook], which has been published since 1965. The yearbooks are updated by the monthly *Bulletin de statistique/Statistisch bulletin* [Statistical bulletin], which began in 1909 (it was quarterly until 1955), and the weekly *Communiqué hebdomadaire/Weekbericht*, provided free on demand with a subscription to the *Bulletin*.

Statistics for the nineteenth century are available in two compilations, *Documents statistiques sur le Royaume . . . 1832 à 1841; 1857 à 1869* [Statistical documents on the kingdom . . . 1832 to 1841; 1857 to 1869], in 13 volumes, and *Exposé de la situation du Royaume, 1841-1850; 1851-1860; 1861-1875; 1876-1900* [Statement on the situation of the Kingdom, 1841-1850; 1851-1860; 1861-1875; 1876-1900] in four volumes. Both were published by the Commission Centrale de Statistique [Central Commission on Statistics]. The latter title, which includes census results, vital statistics and state budgets, is available on microfiche from Chadwyck-Healey Ltd.

Population censuses were taken every ten years from 1846 to 1876 and again from 1880 to the present, though with some exceptions. The only census between 1930 and 1961 was taken in 1947, and two have been taken a year later than the normal schedule, one in 1961 and one in 1981. The results were published as *Recensement* and *Volkstelling* from 1846 to 1930 and as *Recensement général de la population* and *Algemene volkstelling* from 1961. The 1947 census was entitled *Recensement général de la population, de l'industrie et du commerce* and *Algemene Volks- nijverheids- en handelstelling* [General census of population, industry and trade]. Censuses from 1846 to 1970 are available on microfilm from Research Publications, Inc., and those from 1846 to 1920 from InterDocumentation Co. on microfiche.

Census results showing population by Province, Arrondissement and town broken down by sex are published by the *Moniteur belge* about two years after the taking of a census. They appear in a separate edition available from the Office of the *Moniteur belge* entitled *Recensement général . . . : relevé du nombre des habitants par province, par arrondissement administratif, et par commune/Algemene volkstelling . . . :opgave van het bevolkingscijfer per provincie, per administratief arrondissement en per gemeente* [General census . . . : extract of the number of inhabitants by Province, District and Commune]. Population estimates also appear annually in the *Moniteur belge* and in a separate edition also put out by the Office of the *Moniteur belge* entitled *Chiffres officiels de la population à la date du . . . /Officiële bevolkingscijfers . . .* [Official figures for the population at . . .]. Population projections are published from time to time in the National Statistical Insitute's *Bulletin de statistique* and in *Études statistiques* and *Statistische Studiën*.

Housing data are included in the population censuses from 1890 to 1970. There was a separate census of buildings, *Recensement des bâtiments* and *Gebouwentelling* [Census of buildings] in 1968.

Socio-economic information is found in most of the population censuses, except that for 1876. Included are occupations (1846-1970), literacy and/or educational attainment (1846-1947, except 1930), number of clergy (1846-1947), and languages spoken (1846-1947, except 1856). In the years 1910 and 1920, both the languages people could speak and the ones they most often used were reported. The 1930 census included a full volume devoted to languages.

A number of specialized censuses are also taken. Full agricultural censuses were taken in 1846, 1866, 1880, 1895, 1910, 1929, 1950, 1959 and 1970. A briefer enumeration of crops, livestock, agricultural machinery and labour has also been taken annually or semi-annually since 1941 as *Recensement agricole et horticole au* . . . and *Landbouw- en tuinbouwtelling op* . . . [Census of agriculture and horticulture in . . .]. A census of industry and commerce was first taken in 1910 and repeated in 1930, 1937, 1961 and 1970. In 1947 it formed part of the population census. Prior to 1910, there were three censuses of industry—1846, 1880 and 1896.

The National Statistical Institute also publishes a number of series of specialized statistics on a monthly, quarterly or annual basis. The most important of these are:

Statistiques agricoles and *Landbouwstatistieken* [Agricultural statistics], issued monthly (annual before 1975). Previously entitled *La statistique agricole* and *De landbouwstatistieken* from 1946 to 1966 and *Statistiques agricoles* and *Landbouwstatistieken* from 1900 to 1945

Statistiques de la construction et du logement and *Statistieken over bouwnijverheid en huisvesting* [Statistics of building and housing], published irregularly. Preceded by *Bâtiments et logements* and *Gebouwen en woningen* [Building and housing], 1957–1967, and *Autorisations de bâtir* and *Bouwvergunningen*, 1953–1956 [Building authorizations]

Statistiques démographiques and *Demografische statistieken* [Demographic statistics], normally issued quarterly. Preceded by *Statistique du mouvement de la population et de l'état civil [Statistics on the movement of population]*, 1890, 1900, 1901–1910 and 1911–1920

Causes de décès and *Doodsoorzaaken [Causes of death]*, published annually

Bulletin mensuel du commerce extérieur de l'Union Économique Belgo-Luxembourgeoise and *Maandelijks bulletin over de buitenlandse handel van de Belgisch–Luxemburgse Economische Unie*, published monthly, with annual figures in the December issue (annual foreign trade statistics have been mentioned above)

Statistiques du commerce and *Handelsstatistieken* [Trade statistics], issued annually. Entitled *Statistiques du commerce et des transports* and *Statistieken van handel en vervoer* [Statistics of trade and transport] before 1972

Statistiques des transports and *Vervoerstatistieken* [Transport statistics], appearing annually. There are also quarterly statistics of air and sea transport and annual statistics of motor vehicles and accidents

Statistiques industrielles and *Industriële statistieken* [Statistics of industry], monthly. Entitled *Statistique annuelle de la production* and *Jaarlijkse produktiestatistieken* [Annual statistics of production] before 1972

Statistiques financières and *Financiële statistieken* [Financial statistics], published irregularly. Previously entitled *Statistique fiscale des revenus soumis a l'impôt des personnes physiques* and *Fiscale statistiek van de inkomens onderworpen aan de personenbelasting* [Statistics of taxable personal income]

Population scolaire and *Schoolbevolking* [The school population], issued annually

Annuaire statistique de l' enseignement and *Statistisch Jaarboek van het Onderwijs* [Annual education statistics] was published jointly with the Ministry of Education from 1956 to 1971

Statistiques judiciaires and *Gerechtelijke statistieken* [Judicial statistics], published irregularly. Preceded by *Statistique judiciaire* and *Gerechtelijke statistiek* [Judicial statistics] from 1931 to 1943 and *Statistique criminelle de la Belgique* and *Criminele statistiek van België* [Criminal statistics of Belgium] from 1944 to 1967, both issued annually. (Statistics on the years 1841 to 1897 appear in the *Exposé de la situation du Royaume* already mentioned from 1873 to 1898, and are available in microform from Chadwyck-Healey Ltd.)

Statistiques sociales and *Sociale statistieken* [Social statistics], published irregularly. Wages, wholesale and retail prices, strikes and workplace accidents are included. A compilation covering the years 1900–1964 was issued in 1965 as *Statistiques des prix—statistiques du travail—autres statistiques sociales* and *Prijzen-, arbeids- en sociale statistieken* [Statistics on prices and labour and other social statistics].

The National Statistical Institute also publishes statistical and econometric studies. Many of these appear in the *Bulletin de statistique* or *Études statistiques* already mentioned. In addition to the national accounts, topics such as household budgets, input–output tables, life tables, revisions of price indexes, and statistics on immigration and migrant labour have been discussed in them.

Other surveys and studies are published separately. Examples of recent titles have been the *Enquête socio-économique* and *Sociaal-economisch onderzoek* [Social and economic survey] issued in three volumes in 1977–78 and *Perspectives de population, 1976-2000* and *Bevolkingsvooruitzichten, 1976-2000* [Population prospects], published in 1979.

The Institute also provides codes and nomenclatures by geographic region, product and economic activity.

Health and social security

The ministry responsible for these areas at present is the Ministère des Affaires Sociales et des Réformes Institutionnelles/Ministerie van Sociale Zaken en Institutionele Hervormingen [Ministry of Social Affairs and Institutional Reform], formed in 1981. Until the formation of this ministry, the main official publisher in health affairs was the Ministère de la Santé et de la Famille/Ministerie van Volksgezondheid en van het Gezin [Ministry of Public Health and the Family]. Its publications fell into three main categories: legislation, statistics and research studies. In the first group, the chief series were the quarterly bulletin of laws and regulations on health, the *Bulletin du Ministère/Bulletin van het Ministerie*, and compilations of legislation concerning food products, the *Recueil de la législation belge en matière de denrées alimentaires* and *Verzameling der Belgische Wetgeving betreffende voedingsmiddelen*. Its main statistical publications were the *Annuaire statistique de la santé publique/Statistisch Jaarboek van Volksgezondheid* [Yearbook of public health statistics], which contained figures on demography, vital statistics, public and environmental health, the capacity and utilization of the medical infrastructure, medical assistance, personnel, medical education, health research and health costs. Many health statistics are also issued by the National Statistical Institute whose publications were discussed earlier. Research results are presented in *Archives belges de médecine sociale, hygiène, médecine du travail et médecine legale/Belgisch archief van sociale geneeskunde, hygiëne, arbeidsgeneeskunde en gerechtelijke geneeskunde* [Belgian archives of social medicine, hygiene, industrial medicine and medical law]. An independent research institute, the Centre d'Étude de la Population et de la Famille/Centrum voor Bevolking en Gezin [Centre for the Study of Population and the Family] is responsible for collecting information and coordinating demographic policy. Its periodical, *Population et famille/Bevolking en Gezin* [Population and the family], which appears three times a year and includes English abstracts, contains studies of demographic and family matters. It has also published a number of monographs on such demographic topics as natality.

Until the establishment of the present ministry, social security affairs were the responsibility of the Ministère de la Prévoyance Sociale/Ministerie van Sociale Voorzorg [Ministry of Social Security]. In addition to a guide to social security benefits and legislation published at irregular intervals, the *Aperçu de la sécurité sociale en Belgique* and *Beknopt overzicht van de sociale zekerheid en België* [Summary of social security in Belgium], it produced an annual compilation of statistics on social security funding and expenditures, the *Annuaire statistique de la sécurité sociale* and *Statistisch jaarboek van de sociale zekerheid* [Statistical yearbook of social security]. Its monthly review, *Revue belge de sécurité sociale* and *Belgisch Tijdschrift voor sociale zekerheid* [Belgian review of social security], contained articles on the theory and practice of social security, a round-up of the latest legislation on sickness and workplace accidents, court decisions in social security cases and book reviews of works on social security. Detailed statistics on revenue collected, benefits paid and numbers of people covered by the system appear in the annual report of the Office National de la Sécurité Sociale/Rijksdienst voor Sociale Zekerheid [National Office of Social Security], an autonomous organization reporting to the minister responsible for social security.

Family allowances are handled by a semi-independent agency, the Office National d'Allocations Familiales pour Travailleurs Salariés/Rijksdienst voor Kinderbijslag voor Werknemers [National Office for Family Allowances for Employed Persons], which publishes an annual report that often contains statistics and special surveys of family allowances in its annexes.

Employment

The principal official publication in this area since 1896 has been the *Revue du travail* and *Arbeidsblad* [Employment review], issued monthly, currently by the Ministère de l'Emploi et du Travail/Ministerie van Tewerkstelling en Arbeid [Ministry for Employment and Labour]. In addition to statistics on employment, wages, strikes, prices and work permits granted to foreigners, its issues regularly include articles and book reviews on labour questions, news of trade unions, and a list of acquisitions of the Ministry's library. Reports of activities of subsidiary agencies of the Ministry also appear from time to time.

A major report on labour conditions in Belgium in the nineteenth century has been made available by Hachette in its microfiche series, *La condition ouvrière en France au 19e siècle* [The condition of the French working classes in the nineteenth century in France]. The report, which is entitled *Enquête sur la condition des classes ouvrières et sur le travail des enfants* [Study of the condition of the working classes and of the employment of children], was published by Lesigne for the Ministère de l'Intérieur [Ministry of the Interior] in 1846–48 in three volumes. It presents the results of a survey of manufacturers, mining engineers, chambers of commerce, medical societies and provincial health agencies, conducted by a commission set up to prepare a bill on child labour and the regulation of workshops.

Education

The discussion of official publications in the field of education is complicated by the fact that since 1968 there have been two ministries for education, one for the Dutch-speaking community, the Ministerie van Nationale Opvoeding en Nederlandse Cultuur,[12] and one for the French-speaking community, the Ministère de l'Éducation Nationale et de la Culture Française.[13] Education is further complicated by the existence of two systems of schools, both receiving state support—provincial and municipal schools, 'écoles officielles/officiële scholen' on the one hand, and church schools, 'écoles libres/vrije scholen', on the other. Higher education is split along the same lines as the lower schools. There are six full universities in Belgium today, three French and three Flemish. Two are state controlled, the French one at Liège and the Flemish one at Ghent. Two are Roman Catholic, one for each language, at Louvain and Louvain-la-Neuve, and two, both situated in Brussels, are autonomous.

The main publications of the two ministries fall into four categories: legislation concerning education; reports and statistics on education and culture in Belgium; teaching aids; and research results. The most important series in the first category are the monthly bulletins of each ministry, called simply *Bulletin* in each case. These contain laws, regulations, circulars and instructions, as well as all personnel changes.

The Ministerie van Nationale Opvoeding en Nederlandse Cultuur publishes three monthly reviews of Flemish educational and cultural activities, the *Informatieblad* [Information sheet], *Open deur* [Open door], and *Informatiebulletin* [Information bulletin]. The Ministère de l'Éducation Nationale et de la Culture Française publishes an account of trends in education, *Le mouvement éducatif en Belgique: principales tendances* [Educational developments in Belgium: main trends] biennially. New developments in education are presented in its series *Faire le point sur . . .* [The point about . . .]. As was mentioned earlier, statistics on the school population are now found in the National Statistical Institute's *Statistiques démographiques* [Demographic statistics] in the issues entitled 'Population scolaire'. There is usually a lag of three or four years between the year covered and the year of publication. A series published by the French ministry, entitled *Collection études et documents statistiques de l'enseignement* [Statistical studies and documents collection on education], also offers educational statistics, usually within a year of the academic year covered.

The numerous teaching aids produced by both ministries of education will be found in their catalogues. Important official sources for research in education are *Recherche en éducation* [Research in education] and *Pédagogie et recherche* [Teaching and research], both published by the French ministry.

The two ministries also lend their support to the publication of a prominent Belgian journal of political science, *Res publica: revue de science politique/tijdschrift voor politologie* [*Res publica*: review of political science]. As was mentioned earlier, a publication frequently produced by ministries of education in other countries, the annual list of theses submitted at doctoral level, is published by the Ministère des Relations Extérieures/Ministerie van Buitenlandse Zaken [Ministry of External Relations] rather than by the ministries of education.

Scientific and cultural affairs

Although the language question makes the administration of cultural policy much more complicated in Belgium than in other countries, the government has pursued a vigorous policy of encouraging scientific research and cultural activity. Policy and action in these areas is spearheaded by the Conseil National de la Politique Scientifique/Nationale Raad voor Wetenschapsbeleid [National Council for Scientific Policy] and the Commission Royale Belge de Folklore/Koninklijke Belgische Commissie voor Volkskunde [Belgian Royal Folklore Commission].

The former, which is composed of scientific and academic experts and representatives of business and finance, was established in 1960 to coordinate science policy. Acting in conjunction with the universities, it promotes and finances scientific research through several independent agencies—the Fonds National de la Recherche Scientifique/Nationaal Fonds voor Wetenschappelijk Onderzoek (FNRS) [National Fund for Scientific Research], the Institut pour l'Encouragement de la Recherche Scientifique dans l'Industrie et l'Agriculture/Instituut tot Aanmoediging van het Wetenschappelijk Onderzoek in Nijverheid en Landbouw (IRSIA/IWONL) [Institute for the Encouragement of Scientific Research in Industry and Agriculture], the Institut Interuniversitaire des Sciences Nucléaires/Interuniversitair Instituut voor Kernwetenschappen [Interuniversity Institute of Nuclear Science], the Fonds de la Recherche Fondamentale Collective/Fonds voor Kollektief Fundamenteel Onderzoek [Collective Fund for Fundamental Research], and the Fonds de la Recherche Scientifique Médicale/Fonds voor Geneeskundig Wetenschappelijk Onderzoek [Medical Research Fund].

The Council has been primarily concerned with analysing the optimum conditions under which scientific research should take place. It inventories scientific potential in Belgium every two years and prepares studies, plans and guidelines for research, which are published under the imprint of the Council itself or that of the Services de Programmation de la Politique Scientifique du Premier Ministre/Diensten voor Programmatie van het Wetenschapsbeleid (SPPS) [Planning Service for Science Policy of the Prime Minister]. Among the best-known of these publications is *Recherche et croissance économique* and *Wetenschappelijk onderzoek en economische groei* [Research and economic growth], issued since 1964, a series of reports on the role of research in promoting economic growth in various sectors of Belgian industry. The annual report of IRSIA lists recipients of all subsidies given during the year and their topics of research. It also lists publications resulting from the research it has funded. Reports of results of individual research projects it has supported appear in the series *Comptes rendus de recherches/Verslagen over navorsingen* [Accounts of research].

The Belgian Royal Folklore Commission which was instituted in 1937 is composed of a Flemish and a Walloon section, the Vlaamse Afdeling and the Section Wallonne. Since 1939 it has published a yearbook, the *Annuaire* and *Jaarboek*, which contains reports on the membership and activities of the Commission and unannotated bibliographies on folklore prepared by members of the Commission. The Walloon Section also publishes a series devoted to folklore studies entitled *Collection Contributions au Renouveau de Folklore en Wallonie* [Collection of contributions to the revival of folklore in Wallonia]. It has also encouraged the publication of a number of folktales and folksongs. All these publications will be found listed in *La Commission Royale Belge de Folklore, ses statuts, ses membres, ses publications (bibliographie complète)* [The Belgian Royal Folklore Commission, its statutes, membership and publications, a complete bibliography], published in 1975 by the then Ministère de la Culture Française.

Linguistic research is supported by the Commission Royale de Toponymie et Dialectologie/Koninklijke Commissie voor Toponymie en Dialectologie [Royal Commission for the Study of Place Names and Dialects]. The Flemish and Walloon sections of this Commission publish a bulletin, the *Bulletin/Handelingen*, at irregular intervals, and a series of historical and linguistic studies, *Mémoires/Werken*.

Another area in which there has been vigorous effort to preserve the cultural heritage is that of the preservation of historical monuments. The agencies directing this programme are the two sections of the Commission Royale des Monuments et des Sites/Koninklijke Commissie voor Monumenten en Landschappen [Royal Commission on Historical Monuments and Sites]. Each publishes an illustrated bulletin containing architectural, archaeological and technical information on the restoration of buildings.

Libraries

The foremost library in the country is of course the Bibliothèque Royale Albert I [Royal Library of Albert I]. The present library, which became the national library by royal decree on 25 July 1837, traces its origins to an order of Philip II in 1559, creating a royal library composed of the collections of the Dukes of Burgundy, commonly referred to as the Burgundian Library, and those of later rulers of Belgium. As both the national library and the central research library of Belgium, the Royal Library is charged with acquiring and preserving all books produced in Belgium and a selection of the major books and serials in the sciences, social sciences, humanities and arts produced elsewhere. The library has been entitled to one copy of all works published in Belgium and all works published abroad by Belgian authors residing in Belgium since the legal deposit law of 8 April 1965 went into effect in January 1966. Descriptions of the library and its collections are found in *The National Library in Belgium* by Robert Senelle (Memo from Belgium no. 93, 1967). The most important publication of the library is the national bibliography, the *Bibliographie de Belgique*, mentioned below on the section on bibliographic control (section 4). It also prepares catalogues of its exhibitions.

Public libraries are the concern of the Conseil Supérieur des Bibliothèques and the Hoge Raad voor de Openbare Bibliotheken [Higher Councils for Public Libraries], which serve each of the education ministries. The Councils have established a number of aids for public libraries, including a list of basic reference works, *Ouvrages de référence* and *Referentiewerken*, 1968. Supplements to both were published in 1971.

Archives

Most records of agencies of the central government no longer needed by the offices generating them are housed in the Archives Générales du Royaume/Algemeen Rijksarchief [National Archives]. Two exceptions are the Ministry of National Defence and the Ministry of External Relations, which have their own archives.

The National Archives have published two guides to Belgian archives for materials in specific geographical areas, one for Africa and one for Latin America. These guides, which are entitled *Guide des sources de l'histoire d'Afrique du Nord, d'Asie et d'Océanie conservées en Belgique* [Guide to the sources for the history of North Africa, Asia and Oceania in Belgium], edited by Émile Vandewoude and André Vanrie, 1972, and *Guide des sources de l'histoire de l'Amérique latine conservées en Belgique* [Guide to the sources for the history of Latin America in Belgium], edited by Léone Liagre and Jean Baerten, 1967, form part of the International Council on Archives series, *Guide to the sources of the history of the nations*, and include the holdings of local public archives and private collections, as well as the National Archives. A list of the many inventories and guides to the holdings of the National Archives will be found in *Archives et bibliothèques de Belgique: revue trimestrielle de l'Association des Archivistes et Bibliothécaires/Archief en bibliotheekwezen en België: driemaandelijks tijdschrift van de Vereniging van Archivarissen en Bibliothecarissen* [Archives and libraries in Belgium: four-monthly review of the Association of Archivists and Librarians], numéro special 2, 1970, in an article edited by Jacques Nicodème entitled 'Répertoire des inventaires des archives conserveés en Belgique parus avant le 1er janvier 1969'. This list is updated by articles in the same journal. The National Archives also frequently publish catalogues of the exhibitions they have mounted.

3. OFFICIAL PUBLISHING

There is no central government printer or distributor of publications. The most active official publishers are the Office of the *Moniteur belge*, the Institut National de Statistique/Nationaal Instituut voor de Statistiek [National Statistical Institute] and formerly the Institut Belge d'Information et de Documentation/Belgisch Instituut voor Voorlichting en Dokumentatie (INBEL) [Central Information Office].

The first of these, the Direction du Moniteur Belge/Bestuur van het Belgische Staatsblad, is the only official publisher. It is attached to the Ministry of Justice. It receives government subsidies and sells its publications at less than cost. All domestic subscriptions to serials published by this office are sold through Belgian post offices. Foreign subscriptions, however, are sold by the Direction du Moniteur Belge, 40–42 rue Louvain, 1000, Brussels.

The central information office, the Institut Belge du'Information et de Documentation/Belgisch Instituut voor Voorlichting en Documentatie (INBEL), an autonomous public establishment (établissement d'utilité public) founded in 1962 to carry out an ambitious programme in the area of public relations and official publishing, publishes for other government agencies and maintains a bookshop at 3 avenue des Arts in Brussels, which sells the publications it distributes and its own publications. At the same address are two libraries open to the public which contain a collection of photographs and slides on all aspects of Belgium.

As in most countries, the national statistical institute, the Institut National de Statistique/Nationaal Instituut voor de Statistiek, is among the most active of official publishers.

Apart from the Office of the *Moniteur belge*, the Central Information Office and the National Statistical Institute, all materials are published by the individual agencies. There is little provision for control over or advice on design and marketing. Except for the legal and parliamentary publications of the Office of the *Moniteur belge*, for which subscriptions can be placed at post offices, official publications are extremely difficult to acquire. Most appear to be issued free.

4. BIBLIOGRAPHIC CONTROL

There is no easy bibliographic access to Belgian official publications. Those that reach the Royal Library are recorded in the *Bibliographie de Belgique/Belgische Bibliografie* [Belgian national bibliography], which has been issued since 1875 and is currently published monthly by the Royal Library. Although the coverage of publications has improved immensely since the national deposit law of 8 April 1965, which includes government publications among those required to be deposited, only a selection of the total output appears in it. Official publications are not distinguished from others in any way. Entry is by title, with the name of the agency responsible appearing just after the title: in earlier issues, the agency appeared in the imprint. Entries are arranged in subject categories. There are monthly author, title and subject indexes, with cumulated annual indexes. Beginning with 1982, there is a separate index of corporate authors which includes government agencies. Annual indexes also include a directory of government publishers whose work is represented in the bibliography.

There are several excellent retrospective bibliographies covering earlier periods. Denise de Weerdt's monumental *Bibliographie rétrospective des publications officielles de la Belgique, 1794-1914* [Retrospective bibliography of Belgian official publications, 1794-1914] (Centre Interuniversitaire d'Histoire Contemporaine, Cahiers no. 30/Interuniversitair Centrum voor Hedendaagse Geschiedenis Bijdragen no. 30), Paris, 1963, is based on a landmark list of Belgian official publications published in 1912, to which she has added publications found in the catalogues of the Royal Library, the National Archives, and other sources. The work is divided into three sections, one for the French period, one for the Dutch period and one for the period since independence. Arrangement is alphabetical by title or personal author, with a subject index which includes the names of agencies. Provincial and local government publications are included and call numbers given for holdings of the Royal Library and the National Archives.

Official and semi-official serials that were being published in 1954 are listed in *Les publications périodiques éditées par les services centraux des Ministères* [Periodicals published by the central services of government ministries], compiled by Marie Keppenne and published in 1957 by the Commission Belge de Bibliographie/Belgische Commissie voor Bibliografie [Belgian Commission on Bibliography] as no. 22 in its series *Bibliographia Belgica*. Arrangement is by issuing agency, with an alphabetical title index.

Although not devoted exclusively to official periodicals, Julien van Hove's general list of periodicals published in Belgium, *Répertoire des périodiques paraissant en Belgique/Repertorium van de in Belgë verschijnende tijdschriften*, 1951, with its four supplements published in 1955, 1960, 1964 and 1972, is another possible place to find official serials. Arrangement is alphabetical by title, with indexes by geographical name, subject and publishing organization, including government agencies.

A selective list of publications of national scientific and cultural institutions, compiled for an exhibition at the Royal Library in Brussels in January 1966, was published by the Library in 1966 as *Publications scientifiques de l'État* and *Wetenschappelijke publicaties van het Rijk*. In addition to a description of the mission and in some cases a brief history of each official body it includes a summary of the publishing programme of each.

Two listings of official publications of a number of governments may be useful for tracing official publications from earlier periods. *Official publications of European governments*, compiled by José Meyer and published by the American Library in Paris in 1929, lists Belgian publications by ministry on pp. 60-108. English translations of titles are included. Winifred Gregory's *Serial publications of foreign governments* remains one of the best resources for official serials published up to 1931.

The three most important government publishers who are described above each produce a catalogue of their publications (usually entitled simply *Catalogue* or *Cata-*

logus or *Liste des publications/Lijst der uitgaven*) which may be obtained by writing to them at the following address:

> INBEL, 3 avenue des Arts, 1040 Brussels
> Institut National de Statistique, 44 rue de Louvain, 1000 Brussels
> Direction du Moniteur Belge, 40–42 rue de Louvain, 1000 Brussels.

The last lists individual laws, decrees and compilations of legislation on specific topics which have been issued as separate numbers in a series of brochures issued by the Office of the *Moniteur belge*. It does not however include information on the parliamentary and legislative serials published by the Office. Subscription prices, methods of payment and brief descriptions of the contents of these last publications are found in a supplement to the *Moniteur belge*, which may also be obtained by writing to the address above.

Other agencies which produce catalogues of their publications include:

> Ministère de l'Éducation Nationale et de la Culture Française, 26–28 Bd. de Berlaimont, 1000 Brussels
> Ministère des Finances/Ministerie van Financiën, 12 rue de la Loi, 1000 Brussels
> Ministère des Affaires Économiques/Ministerie van Economische Zaken, 23 square de Meeûs, 1040 Brussels.

The latter ministry includes a list of all its serial publications in its frequently-updated organization manual, *Organisation administrative du Département* . . . and *Administratieve Inrichting*. . . . The Institut Géographique National/Nationaal Geographisch Instituut [National Geographic Institute], 13 Abbaye de la Cambre, 1050 Brussels, offers the best listing for maps, and the Archives Générales du Royaume/Algemeen Rijksarchief [National Archives], 4–6 rue de Ruysbroeck, 1000 Brussels, publish a listing of published inventories to archives and catalogues of exhibitions.

Until 1960, the Ministère des Colonies/Ministerie van Koloniën [Ministry for the Colonies] produced an excellent list of its own publications and those of the Office de l'Information et des Relations Publiques pour le Congo Belge et le Ruanda-Urundi/Dienst voor de Voorlichting en de Publieke Relaties van Belgisch-Congo en Ruanda-Urundi [Information and Public Relations Office for the Belgian Congo and Ruanda-Urundi] and other official and semi-official institutions concerned with the colonies.

5. PUBLICATIONS OF REGIONAL, PROVINCIAL AND MUNICIPAL GOVERNMENTS

5.1. Regional

Legislative branch

The new regional institutions described in the section on government organization (section 1 above) have developed their own publishing programmes, which include parliamentary series similar to those of the two houses of the national Parliament. Verbatim debates are issued by the assemblies of the Communities and Regions as *Compte rendu intégral* and *Handelingen* [Complete proceedings]. Summaries of the debates appear in series entitled *Compte rendu analytique* or *Beknopt verslag*, while bills, reports and other working documents appear in a series entitled simply *Documents* or *Gedrukte stukken* [Documents or printed papers]. Questions and answers are found in the *Bulletin des questions et réponses* or *Bulletin van vragen en antwoorden* [Bulletin of questions and answers]. Most of these series have annual personal name and subject indexes: some have indexes covering the whole legislative period. The various series may be difficult to trace because of the changes in agency names that have occurred. A list of names and dates for the various regional assemblies is given below:

French Community
Conseil de la Communauté Française, 1980–, 6 rue de la Loi, 1000 Brussels. Prior to November, 1980, the Council of the Community was known as the Conseil Culturel de la Communauté Culturelle Française

Flemish Community
Vlaamse Raad, 1980–, Paleis der Natie, 2 Natieplain, 1000 Brussels. From 1971 to 21 October 1980 the Council of the Flemish Community was called the Cultuurraad voor de Nederlandse Cultuurgemeenschap

German Community
Rat der Deutschen Kulturgemeinschaft, 1974–, 8 Kaperberg, 4700 Eupen. The titles of its series are: *Ausführliche Berichte* [Verbatim debates], *Kurzberichte* [Summary debates], *Dokumenten* [Documents], *Fragen und Antworten* [Questions and answers], and *Mitteilungen* [Communications]

Walloon Region
Conseil Régional Wallon, 1974–1977 and 1980–, 24 rue Saint-Nicolas, 5000 Namur. This Council was dissolved by the law of 19 July 1977 and recreated by the laws of 8 and 9 August 1980

Flemish Region
Vlaamse Raad, 1980–. In the period from 1974 to 1977, the Council of this Region was called the Vlaamse Gewestraad

Brussels Region
At present there is no assembly. Prior to 1980, some legislative documents were issued by the Conseil Régional Bruxellois/Brusselse Gewestraad, from 1974 to 1979, and by the Assemblée de Parlementaires Bruxellois/Vergadering van de Brusselse Parlementsleden from 14 May 1979 to 15 December 1980. The latter published only summary debates.

Legislation passed by the Regional assemblies must be published in the *Moniteur belge*.

Executive branch

The Regional executives have only very recently attained independent existence outside the national government. During the period when they were still within the national Cabinet, it was the ministries charged with administering the Communities, the Ministère de la Communauté Française, the Ministère de la Région Wallonne and the Minister van de Nederlandse Gemeenschap en van het Vlaamse Gewest, which were responsible for non-legislative publications concerning the Communities and

Regions. This is still the case for the Brussels Region, which is administered by a minister in the national Cabinet, rather than by an independent executive. Among the publications of the new Regional executives are *Wallonie: une Région, un Parlement, un Gouvernement* [Wallonia: a Region, a parliament, a government] and *Région wallonne: premier bilan* [The Walloon Region: the first balance sheet], both published by the Exécutif Régional Wallon in 1981, and *Een regering voor de Vlamingen* [A government for the Flemish], published by the Vlaamse Executieve in 1982.

To secure publications of the Communities and Regions, one must write to them directly. Addresses for the assemblies are included in the listing given above. Addresses for the Regional executives are:

Exécutif Régional Wallon, 11 bd. de l'Empereur, 1000 Brussels
Vlaamse Executieve, 30 Jozef II-straat, 1040 Brussels
Exécutif de la Région Bruxelloise/Executieve van het Brusselse Gewest, 21–23 bd. du Régent, 1000 Brussels.

5.2. Provincial

The main publications of the Provinces are compilations of legislation concerning the Provinces. These appear in the *Mémorial administratif de la province de . . .* or *Verslag over het Bestuur van de provincie . . .* [Report on the administration of the Province of . . .] published annually or semi-annually by each Province. Included are resolutions and other acts of Provincial Councils, circulars concerning provincial administration from the national ministries (these will be replaced by directives from the Regional level) and municipal regulations. Reports and statistics on the Provinces also appear in these series. Provincial officials are listed in the *Annuaire administratif et judiciaire* mentioned in section 1.

Annual reports to the Provincial Councils by the executives of the Provinces have been required since 1836. Many of those made before 1914 will be found listed in De Weerdt's bibliography (mentioned in the previous section) where they usually appear under the title *Exposé de la situation administrative de la province de . . . fait au conseil provincial par la députation permanente* [Account of the administration of . . . Province presented to the Provincial Council by the executive committee]. These are a very rich source of detailed information and statistics on many aspects of the Provinces, including population, government, charities, public health, religion, justice, the militia, taxes, public works, agriculture, industry and commerce. Directories and budgets for individual Provinces were also published from time to time, and appear in De Weerdt's bibliography under the titles *Almanach* or *Annuaire de la province de . . .* and *Budget de la province de . . .*

5.3. Municipal

In the absence of any adequate bibliographic control of local government publications, it would seem that the only way to learn what is being published by local governments, aside from their regulations which are published in the *Mémoriaux* of the Provincial governments, is to apply directly to the government of the local area concerned. Fortunately, the names and addresses of all municipal officials are listed in the *Guide des Ministères* mentioned in section 1 above.

Some local governments have embarked upon publishing programmes in an attempt to improve relations between the local administration and the public. An example of such an effort is the publication of a directory designed to aid new immigrants undertaken by the commune of Woluwe-Saint-Lambert in the Brussels area.

6. LIBRARY COLLECTIONS AND AVAILABILITY

The most complete collection of Belgian official publications in Belgium is that of the Royal Library. Belgian official publications received before 1 January 1966 are found in the main catalogue, while those received after that date are found in the catalogue of the legal deposit section, the Section du Dépôt Légal/Afdeling van het Wettelijk Depot. They are difficult to trace because they are usually entered under title or personal author and are not distinguished from other publications by any symbols. A few kinds of material are entered under the names of ministries, but the agency name is not preceded by the name of the country. Publications of Provinces or towns, on the other hand, are usually entered under the name of the jurisdiction. De Weerdt's bibliography of official publications issued before 1914 provides call numbers for a great many of the library's earlier holdings.

The publications themselves may be shelved in any one of four places. Most of them received before 1966 are in the main reading room or main stacks. A few of the most heavily-used are shelved in the Section des Documents Officiels/Afdeling der Officiële Documenten [Official Publications Section]. Catalogue cards for materials shelved here include the symbols OFF at the end of the call number. Although the section was set up primarily to handle documents of international organizations, it acts as a clearing house for information on all types of official publications and is the first place anyone wanting to use Belgian official publications should visit. Its small but efficient staff will help the user to locate official publications shelved anywhere in the library. It has several catalogues of materials shelved in the section, which duplicate entries in the main catalogues. The most recent issues of selected serials, including the *Moniteur belge* and many of the series published by the Institut National de Statistique, are in the Salle des Périodiques/Tijdschriftenzaal [Periodicals reading room].

Publications received since January 1966 are shelved in the Legal Deposit Section, which has its own catalogues and reading room and is approached from a separate entrance from that of the main reading room. It should be noted that the Official Publications and Legal Deposit sections keep slightly different hours from those of the main and periodicals reading rooms.

Other libraries which are good for materials in specialized areas include:

> Bibliothèque du Parlement/Bibliotheek van het Parlement [Library of Parliament], 2 place de la Nation, 1000 Brussels, the prime source for parliamentary documents
>
> Bibliothèque Centrale 'Fonds Quetelet' du Ministère des Affaires Économiques/Centrale Bibliotheek 'Queteletfonds' [Central Library of the Ministry of Economic Affairs], 6 rue l'Industrie, 1040 Brussels, excellent for economic and financial materials
>
> Bibliothèque Africaine/Afrika Bibliotheek [African Library of the Ministry of External Relations], 7 place Royale, 1000 Brussels, for materials on former Belgian colonies.

The most important collections of Belgian official publications in the USA are found at the Library of Congress, the New York Public Library, the Hoover Institution and

Stanford University, and the University of California at Berkeley. Printed catalogues which will be helpful in tracing the holdings of these libraries include the *Catalogue of government publications* of the Research Libraries of New York Public Library, 1972, and its annual supplements, *Bibliographic guide to government publications: foreign*, which include entries from the Library of Congress MARC tapes, and the *Catalogue of the Western language collections of the Hoover Institution*, 1969, and its supplements. All are published by G. K. Hall, Boston.

The National Library of Canada has actively collected Belgian official publications since 1970. Its holdings and those of the Legislative library of Quebec are listed in the National Library publication *Research collections in Canadian libraries*, II: special studies, 5: Collections of official publications in Canada. Ottawa, 1976, p. 552.

The Service Belge des Échanges Internationaux of the Royal Library exchanges the official journal and parliamentary annals and documents with 58 libraries, exchange centres and institutes in 36 countries, mainly in Europe, Latin America and North America, and sends other official and semi-official publications more widely still.

NOTES

This chapter was prepared in 1981, and revised in 1986. At that time no further changes had occured in the process of constitutional reform: the arrangements for the regions referred to in section 1 were unaltered and the provisional arrangements for the Brussels Region were still in force. For simplicity, the names of government ministries in the main body of the text have been left as they were in 1981 but any changes are recorded in the notes below.

1. In 1985, Ministère de la Région Bruxelloise/Ministerie van het Brusselse Gewest.
2. In 1985, Ministère de l'Intérieur et de la Fonction Publique/Ministerie van Binnenlandse Zaken en Openbaar Ambt.
3. In 1985, Ministère de la Justice/Ministerie van Justitie.
4. In 1985, Ministère des Affaires Étrangères, du Commerce Extérieur et de la Coöpération au Développement/Ministerie van Buitenlandse Zaken, Buitenlandse Handel en Ontwikkelingssamenwerking.
5. In 1985, Ministère de l'Éducation Nationale.
6. In 1985, Ministerie van Onderwijs.
7. In 1985, as in note 2.
8. In 1985, as in note 3.
9. In 1985, Ministère des Finances/Ministerie van Financiën.
10. In 1985, as in note 1.
11. In 1985, the Ministère des Classes Moyennes/Ministerie van Middenstand is again a separate ministry.
12. In 1985, as in note 6.
13. In 1985, as in note 5.

7. BIBLIOGRAPHY

Guides to Belgian official publications

There is no book-length guide to Belgian official publications. The most recent discussion of official publishing in Belgium is the brief account in J.J. Cherns' *Official publishing: an overview*. An international survey of the role, organization and principles of official publishing (Guides to official publications, vol. 3), Oxford, Pergamon Press, 1979, pp. 64–66. Attention is focussed on the activities of INBEL and the Office of the *Moniteur belge*, with little treatment of bibliographic access. Two earlier articles, one in French and the other in Dutch, review the general situation of government documents in Belgium, with special attention to efforts at bibliographic control. The first, National official publications of Belgium, by Frans Vanwijngaerden, appeared in English in *Aslib proceedings* 26, July–Aug. 1974, pp. 267–273, while the latter, Status quaestionus van de officiële en semi-officiële uitgaven in België, by A. van Iseghem, appeared in the *Bulletin* of the Commission Belge de Bibliographie, 16, 1972, pp. 111–128. An older account which is now of historical interest is H. Kessels' contribution on Belgium in the proceedings of a conference on official publications held by the Carnegie Endowment for International Peace's European Centre in 1951, edited by Michel Roussier and published as *Les publications officielles et la documentation internationale* [Official publications and international documents], Paris, 1952, 81 p.

A detailed description of the nature and characteristics of the publications produced by the various agencies of the Belgian government published in 1965 has not become widely-known, possibly because it is contained within a larger work devoted to an analysis of government communication techniques. Although it is now out of date, J. Lhoest's *Information et propagande officielles en Belgique: organisation et aspects budgétaires* [Government information and propaganda in Belgium: organization and financial aspects] (Techniques de diffusion collective: études et recherches, nos. 11–12), Centre National d'Étude des Techniques de Diffusion Collective, 1965, provides valuable material on such topics as legislation requiring the government to divulge information, the history of the *Moniteur belge* and INBEL, and funding for information and public relations services by the government from 1954 to 1965. The organization and activities of government information services in operation at that time are described and their major publications are listed.

Guides to the government of Belgium

Although the restructuring of the Belgian government in progress at the present time makes it impossible to find any single book which describes the current government completely and accurately, one can get a good idea of the basic system by consulting some older works, such as Robert Senelle's *The Belgian constitution: commentary* (Memo from Belgium, no. 166), 1974, 493 p., and André Molitor's *L'Administration de la Belgique: essai*, Institut Belge de Science Politique and Centre de Recherche et d'Informations Socio-politiques (CRISP), 1974, together with two studies of the recent reforms by Jacques Brassine, *Les institutions de la Flandre, de la Communauté Française et de la Région Wallonne* [The institutions of Flanders, the French Community and the Walloon Region] (Dossiers du CRISP, no. 14), 1981, and L'après 8 novembre 1981: la mise en oeuvre de la deuxième phase de la réforme des institutions [After 8 November 1981: the implementation of the second phase of institutional reform], *Courrier hebdomadaire du CRISP* [CRISP weekly bulletin], no. 940, 1981.

The constitutional revisions of 1968–1971 have been the subject of a number of studies, among them the following:

Lagasse, Charles-Etienne and Remiche, Bernard. *Une constitution inachevée.* La Renaissance du Livre (Collection droit actualité), 1973.

Senelle, Robert. *The reform of the Belgian state.* (Memo from Belgium, nos. 179, 182, 189.) 1978, 1979, 1980. 378, 498, 299 p.

——. *La réforme de l'Etat Belge.* Tome IV. (Textes et documents. Collection Idées et Études, no. 333). Brussels, Ministère des Affaires Étrangères, du Commerce Extérieur et de la Cooperation au Développement, 1985.

Stexhe, Paul de. *La révision de la constitution Belge, 1968–1971.* (Travaux de la Faculté de Droit de Namur, no. 8.) Larcier, 1972.

Wigny, Pierre. *Comprendre la Belgique après la révision constitutionnelle.* Verviers, André Gérard, 2nd ed. 1974. 255 p.

Pre-reform studies which are important for an understanding of later changes are:

Impe, Herman van. *Le régime parlementaire en Belgique.* (Centre Interuniversitaire de droit public. Thèses et mémoires, no. 3). Brussels, Bruylant, 1968. 11, 270 p.

International Institute of Administrative Sciences. *Les structures politiques et administratives de la Belgique.* 1968.

A useful English source is *The constitution of Belgium and the Belgian civil code (as amended to Sept. 1 1982 in the Moniteur Belge).* Translated and introduced by John H. Crabb. Littleton, Rothman, 1982. 428 p.

Federal Republic of Germany

SIEGFRIED DETEMPLE

Translated by Stephen Hanger

1. INTRODUCTION

After the collapse of the German Reich in 1945 and the administration of the territory by the victorious Allied Powers, on 23 May 1949 the population of the three Western occupied zones, represented by a Parlamentarischer Rat [Parliamentary Council], accorded itself a provisional constitution, the *Grundgesetz*, and thus founded the Federal Republic of Germany. The new state remained for a time thereafter under the political control of the Allied High Commission, and attained full sovereignty in all internal and external matters only on 5 May 1955 by repealing the Occupation Statute of 1949. The first official publications of the Federal Republic are therefore the records of the preparatory sessions of the Parlamentarischer Rat; the sessional records of the Deutscher Bundestag [Federal Assembly] and of the Bundesrat [Federal Council], which convened first on 7 September 1949; and the first issue of the *Bundesgesetzblatt* [Federal law gazette], which contained the text of the constitution.

In accordance with article 20 of the constitution, the Federal Republic of Germany is a democratic and social federal state, in which the separation of powers prevails. It comprises the Länder of Baden-Württemberg, Bavaria, Bremen, Hamburg, Hesse, Lower Saxony, North Rhine-Westphalia, Rhineland-Palatinate, Saarland and Schleswig-Holstein. The constitution and that of Berlin designate Berlin a Land also. In the Four Power Agreement of 1971, however, the three Western Powers ruled that, while the close ties between the western sectors of Berlin and the Federal Republic should be maintained and developed, the sectors were not an integral part of the Federal Republic and should not be governed by it. The terms of the federal constitution, and those of the constitution operative in the western sectors, remain in this respect without force. As the Abgeordnetenhaus [Chamber of Deputiesa] of Berlin (West) in all cases decides, with the consent of the three western allies, to adopt federal statutes for Berlin (West), and as the Federal Republic and Berlin (West) continue to assert that west Berlin is part of the Federal Republic, the official publications of Berlin (West) will be dealt with in this chapter. Thus what will be described here—to express it exactly and in the official form—is the official publications of the Federal Republic of Germany and Berlin (West).

According to the constitution, the federal authorities are:

(a) the Bundestag [Federal Assembly], whose deputies are directly elected by the people every four years, by proportional representation
(b) the Bundesrat [Federal Council], through which the Länder collaborate in legislation and in the administration of the Federal Republic, and whose members are delegated by the Länder governments
(c) the Bundespräsident [Federal President], the head of state, elected for five-year terms by
(d) the Bundesversammlung [Federal Convention], which consists of all members of the Bundestag and an equal number of delegates of the Länder parliaments
(e) the Bundesregierung [federal government], consisting of
(f) the Bundeskanzler [Federal Chancellor], proposed by the Federal President and elected by the Bundestag, and of
(g) the Bundesminister [federal ministers], appointed and dismissed by the Federal President on the recommendation of the Chancellor
(h) the Bundesverfassungsgericht [Federal Constitutional Court], the highest federal court, half of whose members are elected by the Bundestag and half by the Bundesrat. For particular spheres of the law, the following specialized courts of justice have been established: the Bundesgerichtshof [Federal Court of Justice], the Bundesverwaltungsgericht [Federal Administrative Court], the Bundesfinanzhof [Federal Fiscal Court], the Bundesarbeitsgericht [Federal Labour Court] and the Bundessozialgericht [Federal Social Court].

The Bundestag, the Bundesrat, the President and the government have their seats in Bonn, the Bundesverfassungsgericht in Karlsruhe.

In consequence of article 28 of the constitution, which prescribes the establishment in each Land of a constitutional order conforming to the basic principles of the republican, democratic and social government as defined in the constitution, the 11 Länder have all accorded themselves constitutions of their own. In each Land and in all further constitutional subdivisions—the Kreise [Districts] and Gemeinden [Municipalities]—there are representative bodies elected by general, direct, free, equal and secret suffrage. Each Land has its own capital as the seat of its parliament, government and central authorities.

Of particular influence on the system of official publications in the Federal Republic is the regulation in article 70 of the constitution, according to which not only the federal government but also the Länder have the right to legislate. On the one hand, the federal government has exclusive legislative competence in areas such as foreign affairs, tariffs and trade, the federal railways and air transport, posts and telecommunications, federal statistics, and so on. On the other hand, there exists in certain areas concurrent legislation on the part of the Länder. The details are laid down in articles 70–75 of the constitution. Thus there may be cases in which anyone wishing to obtain information in the Federal Republic must consult not only federal legal publications, but also the publications of the Länder.

Government organization manuals

The best survey of the Federal Republic's official bodies and their structure is provided by the *Bundesrepublik Deutschland: Staatshandbuch* [Federal Republic of Germany: official handbook], which appears in 14 parts, frequently updated. It is commercially published by Carl Heymanns Verlag but is produced from information supplied by the ministries in response to questionnaires.

Definition of official publications

There is no official definition of official publications in the Federal Republic. The Staatsbibliothek Preussischer Kulturbesitz [State Library of the Prussian Cultural Foundation] takes the view that all publications deposited in accordance with the federal and Länder governments' decrees are official.

2. PRINCIPAL PUBLICATIONS OF THE FEDERAL GOVERNMENT

2.1. Statutes and decrees

In the Federal Republic of Germany, the legislative and the executive organs work more closely together in the legislative process than is the case in other countries with parliamentary systems of government. Bills originate generally with the Bundesregierung [federal government], seldom with the Bundestag and still more rarely with the Bundesrat. In their 'first passage', they are initially examined by the Bundesrat, then introduced into the Bundestag, which after a first reading forwards them to one of its 20 subject-oriented committees for intensive discussion. After a second and a third reading in the Bundestag, a bill agreed by majority decision goes back to the Bundesrat for the 'second passage'. The Bundesrat then either gives consent to the statute or appeals to a Vermittlungsausschuss [Committee for joint consideration of bills] composed of members of both houses. If a bill has passed these last hurdles it is signed by the Federal President and attains the force of law through publication in the *Bundesgesetzblatt* [Federal law gazette].

A statute may include the proviso that, for it to be implemented, decrees (Rechtsverordnungen) having the force of law must be promulgated by the federal government, by particular federal ministries or by Länder governments. These are published either in the *Bundesgesetzblatt* or in the *Bundesanzeiger* [Federal gazette], with the exception of rail and transport tariffs, which appear in the official gazette of the Bundesministerium für Verkehr [Federal Ministry of Transport] (*see* section 2.3. below).

The *Bundesgesetzblatt* is not issued by parliament, as it is in many other countries, but by the Bundesminister der Justiz [Federal Minister of Justice]. However, it is published by a non-official publishing house, the Bundesanzeiger Verlagsgesellschaft m.b.H. in Bonn.

Part 1 of the *Bundesgesetzblatt* contains statutes, decrees, orders and related notices, as well as references to announcements in Part 2 of the *Bundesgesetzblatt* and in the *Bundesanzeiger*, and to European Communities' regulations which have attained direct legal force in the Federal Republic. Individual issues (Hefte) appear as required, in general weekly, and are identified by running numbers within each annual series (Jahrgang). Occasional supplements (Beilagen) are also published, containing either more comprehensive information on individual decrees or surveys on particular themes. These supplements are sent to subscribers to the *Bundesgesetzblatt* on demand only. At the end of each year, the publishers produce a *Zeitliche Übersicht* [Chronological survey] of Parts 1 and 2, in which all statutes and decrees are arranged according to the date of their enactment. This should be placed at the front of each annual series. The series is divided by title pages into several volumes, and at the end of the last volume contains a subject index to Parts 1 and 2. The supplements do not form part of these volumes, and should be catalogued by their individual titles.

Part 2 contains firstly international conventions, bilateral treaties with foreign states, Intra-German treaties and related decrees and notices; and secondly the regulations for customs duties. Issues are published irregularly. As for Part 1, the publishers provide title pages to divide the annual series into volumes, a chronological survey and another subject index to close the last volume. Part 2 also has its supplements, for example the *Deutscher Zolltarif* [German customs duties] which appeared from 1959 to 1968 (currently issued in a different form by the Bundesministerium der Finanzen [Federal Ministry of Finance]). These supplements too are supplied by the publishers on demand only.

Part 3 of the *Bundesgesetzblatt* contains the *Sammlung des Bundesrechts* [Federal law digest]. This will be dealt with at the end of this section, as part of a survey of the Federal Republic's official law digests and their indexes.

The application of many statutes and decrees occasionally necessitates the publication of deadlines, schedules, etc. Notices emanating from federal and Länder authorities and agencies and from the courts, in so far as they apply to the country as a whole, are published in the *Bundesanzeiger* [Federal gazette]. This also is issued by the Bundesminister der Justiz and published by the Bundesanzeiger Verlagsgesellschaft m.b.H. It appears in newspaper format, daily from Tuesday to Saturday. The issues (Hefte) have running numeration within each annual series (Jahrgang), and are 60–70 pages long. The *Amtlicher Teil* [Official section] contains announcements by federal and Länder authorities, notices, and references to the contents of other federal legal publications. The *Nicht-amtlicher Teil* [Non-official section] contains other notices and, at irregular intervals, the Übersicht über den Stand der Bundesgesetzgebung [Survey of current federal legislation]. There is also a third section, *Gerichtliche und sonstige Bekanntmachungen* [Judicial and other announcements].

A regular (separately paginated) supplement to the *Bundesanzeiger* is the *Zentralhandelsregister-Beilage* [Central trade register supplement], which publishes entries to the trade register, property law register, register of associations, and bankruptcy and composition proceedings. Fuller announcements, listings, and surveys on particular themes appear in the series of running supplements (Beilagen): until 1984 these were numbered within each annual series, but were also designated 'a'-numbers of the corresponding issues of the *Bundesanzeiger*. Thus for example the supplement entitled *Wärmeschutzverordnungen und Stoffwerte*, by Otto Schaible, has the running number 29/82, but is also issue 110a of Jahrg. 34 of the *Bundesanzeiger*, published on 22 July 1982. Since 1985, these supplements have been given 'a'-numbers only.

The varied contents of the *Bundesanzeiger* are listed in a subject index (Sachregister) to the official and non-official sections and the supplements, which is published quarterly.

Since 1981, the Bundesanzeiger Verlagsgesellschaft has published (with the permission of the Bundesminister der Justiz, but as a commercial undertaking) a microfiche edition of the *Bundesanzeiger* (reduction ratio 1:36). This reproduces in full the daily issues and the quarterly subject index. A keyword index (Stichwortverzeichnis), cumulating monthly, covers the whole of the current annual series of the *Bundesanzeiger*, with the exception of sections 1–4d of the *Gerichtliche und sonstige Bekanntmachungen*. The publishers plan to film issues of the *Bundesanzeiger* for 1948–1980.

In contrast to the digests of Länder legislation, there is no complete and continuously updated official digest of federal statutes in force. The *Gesetz über die Sammlung des Bundesrechts* [Law on the Digest of federal law] of 10 July 1958 instructed the Bundesminister der Justiz [Federal Minister of Justice] to prepare such a digest: para. 1(1) reads: 'Federal law is to be established and published in a separate section (part 3) of the *Bundesgesetzblatt*, arranged according to subject'. But on 28 December 1968 another law announced the termination of this digest with effect from 31 December 1963. From 1960 to 1963, the *Sammlung des Bundesrechts* [Digest of federal law] appeared as Part 3 of the *Bundesgesetzblatt*, but it contains only the statutes and decrees in force in 1963, systematically arranged in the following subject groups: (a) Constitutional law; (b) Public administration; (c) Administration of justice; (d) Civil and criminal law; (e) Defence; (f) Finance; (g) Commercial law; (h) Labour law, social security law, assistance to war victims; (i) Posts and telecommunications, traffic, federal waterways. These subject areas are further subdivided. The digest of course includes those statutes of the German Reich which were still in force at that time. It now serves as an initial point of reference: subsequent updating has taken the form, not of revisions of the digest, but only of lists of statutes and decrees in force and references to those which have been repealed.

This purpose was served by the *Fundstellennachweis über die Bundesgesetzgebung* [Federal legislation finding list], which appeared from 1951 to 1958 as a supplement to Part 1 of the *Bundesgesetzblatt*. This took the form of a subject listing with a keyword index. From 1959 to 1967, this list was treated as an update of the *Sammlung des Bundesrechts*, and appeared under the following titles:

1959: *Fundstellen der Bundesgesetzgebung, Fortschreibung und Sammlung des Bundesrechts (Bundesgesetzblatt Teil III) und Nachweis der Bundesgesetzgebung (Bundesgesetzblatt Teil I und II, Bundesanzeiger) 1949–1958 nach dem Stand vom 1. Januar 1959* [Guide to Federal legislation: update and digest of Federal law (Federal law gazette, Part 3) and list of Federal legislation (Federal law gazette, Parts 1 and 2, Federal gazette) 1949–1958 as of 1 January 1959]

1960–1965: *Fundstellen der Bundesgesetzgebung und Fortschreibung der Sammlung des Bundesrechts—Bundesgesetzblatt Teil III nach dem Stand vom* . . . [Guide to Federal legislation and update of the Digest of Federal law—Federal law gazette, Part 3, as of . . .]

1966–1967: *Fundstellennachweis der Sammlung des Bundesrechts—Bundesgesetzblatt Teil III und der Bundesgesetzgebung, Bundesgesetzblatt Teil I und II ab 1. Januar 1964. Stand* . . . [Finding list of the Digest of Federal law—Federal law gazette, Part 3—and of Federal legislation, Federal law gazette, Parts 1 and 2, from 1 January 1964. As of . . .]

From 1968 on, the practice has been to publish an annual supplement to Part 1 of the

Bundesgesetzblatt, entitled *Fundstellennachweis A* [Finding list A], subtitled: 'Federal law excluding international conventions and treaties with the German Democratic Republic, as of 31 December 19--'. The division of this list into subject areas, and the numeration of these, are based on the *Sammlung des Bundesrechts*. Statutes repealed in the course of the year are printed in italics, and are deleted the following year. Section 9 is followed by a keyword index, then by an index of abbreviations of statutes listed.

An annual supplement to Part 2 of the *Bundesgesetzblatt* is also published, entitled *Fundstellennachweis B* [Finding list B], subtitled: 'International treaties and treaties with the German Democratic Republic, as of 31 December 19--'. This lists all international conventions concluded by the Federal Republic which have been made public and which are still in force, or might have some other practical significance. Bilateral treaties with states and communities or organizations are listed first, followed by multilateral treaties, and finally treaties with the German Democratic Republic and declarations of the Federal Republic. After these, there is a chronological survey of multilateral treaties, a listing of treaties by subject, and a keyword index (covering the multilateral treaties only).

2.2. Parliamentary publications

The restoration of German political autonomy after World War II began, in the Western zones, with the establishment of Länder by the military administrations in the British and American zones in autumn 1945. In the Frankfurt Documents of July 1948, the military governors of the American, British and French zones authorized the prime ministers of the Länder to convene a constituent assembly, which would draft a constitution and, after its ratification, be dissolved. The individual Länder then drafted a statute setting up a Parlamentarischer Rat [Parliamentary Council], which was inaugurated on 1 September 1948 with 65 delegates from the Länder and five non-voting representatives from Berlin. To debate the text of the constitution, the Council formed a Central Committee (Hauptausschuss). The records of both these bodies are contained in:

> *Parlamentarischer Rat. Stenographische Berichte* [Stenographic records of the Parliamentary Council] Nr. 1–12, 1948–1949. 273 p.
> *Parlamentarischer Rat. Verhandlungen des Hauptausschusses* [Proceedings of the Central Committee of the Parliamentary Council] 1–59. Session 1948—1949. 791 p.

Both publications are indexed by a 200-page *Sach- und Sprechregister zu den Verhandlungen des Parlamentarischen Rates und seines Hauptausschusses 1948* [Subject and speaker index to the proceedings of the Parliamentary Council and its Central Committee 1948]. All three of these publications were printed and distributed by the Bonner Universitäts-Buchdruckerei Gebr. Scheuer, Bonn.

Deutscher Bundestag [Federal Assembly]

In accordance with an injunction from the Allied military authorities of the Western zones, the constitution formulated by the Parlamentarischer Rat provides for a federal system of government in West Germany. Two parliamentary chambers were instituted: the Deutscher Bundestag, the body which provides political representation for all citizens of the Federal Republic; and the Bundesrat, representing the governmental interests of the Länder. Both chambers convened for the first time on 7 September 1949.

The deputies (Abgeordnete) to the Bundestag are elected every four years, on the basis of proportional representation, by universal, free and secret suffrage. All publications of the Bundestag are numbered according to these electoral periods (Wahlperioden). The sessional records are entitled *Verhandlungen des Deutschen Bundestages*. 1–. Wahlperiode 1949–. *Stenographische Berichte* [Proceedings of the Lower House of Parliament ... Stenographic reports]. The reports are arranged according to the date of the session (Sitzung), the sessions of each electoral period being numbered in sequences beginning with no. 1. From the eighth electoral period (1976–1980) onwards, the sessional reports have been designated plenary reports (Plenarprotokolle). These reports are combined to form volumes, which have been numbered consecutively from Bd. 1, 1949, onwards. The pagination begins afresh with each electoral period.

Documents laid before the Bundestag were formerly designated 'appendices to the Stenographic reports', and are nowadays subsumed under the term 'Drucksachen' (literally, printed matter or documents). The full title reads: *Verhandlungen des Deutschen Bundestages ... Anlagen zu den Stenographischen Berichten* [Proceedings of the Federal Assembly ... Appendices to the Stenographic reports]. These documents are numbered in sequence from the beginning of each electoral period, and (as before) collected in volumes numbered consecutively from 1949 onwards.

For each electoral period, a *Register zu den Verhandlungen des Deutschen Bundestages und zu den Anlagen* [Index to the Proceedings of the Federal Assembly and to the Appendices] is published, in two parts: 1, a keyword subject index; and 2, a speaker index. From the eighth electoral period onwards, it also contains the index to the proceedings of the Bundesrat, and is entitled: *Register zu den Verhandlungen des Deutschen Bundestages und des Bundesrates* [Index to the proceedings of the Federal Assembly and the Federal Council]. It is compiled with the aid of a computer; the thesaurus of headings also is handled by a data-base system. The index is issued by the Abteilung Wissenschaftliche Dokumentation [Specialized Documentation Department] of the Bundestag and the documentation and data-processing service of the Bundesrat. It cumulates annually within each electoral period, at the end of which the annual volumes are replaced by an overall index.

All the above publications are obtainable from the Verlag Dr. Hans Heger, Bonn.

As the *Register zu den Verhandlungen* is not published before the end of the first year of an electoral period, it was necessary to produce indexes covering shorter time-spans in order to provide an up-to-date survey of parliamentary deliberations. From September 1957, therefore, the Interparlamentarische Arbeitsgemeinschaft [Interparliamentary Study Group] issued a *Parlamentsspiegel* [Parliament news], a subject index covering not only the current legislative debates in the Bundestag, but also the proceedings and documents of the Länder parliaments and of the European Parliament in Strasbourg. The weekly issues are subsequently replaced by annual cumulations. For its first six years, the *Parlamentsspiegel* was published by the Verlag Max Gehlen, Bonn. After splitting with this firm, the Interparlamentarische Arbeitsgemeinschaft were in 1964 able only to issue a keyword index. At this time, the archive of the parliament (Landtag) of North Rhine-Westphalia began to assemble a subject card file. The cards were copied and sent each month to the archives of the federal and Länder parliaments. At the end of a parliamentary year, before the mid-July recess, the subject file was printed as an annual index and published under the imprint of the parliament of North Rhine-Westphalia itself. The volume numeration began with Jahrg. 8. The title now became: *Parlamentsspiegel (Jahresregister): Dokumentation über die Arbeit des Europäischen Parlaments, der Bundes- und Länderparlamente der Bundesrepublik Deutschland (einschliesslich Berlin) und über die Gesetz- und Verordnungsblätter der Europäischen Gemeinschaften, der Bundesrepublik Deutschland und der Länder* [Parliament news (Annual index): documentation on the work of the European Parliament, the federal and Länder parliaments of the German Federal Republic (including Berlin), and on the legal and other official gazettes of the European Communities, the German Federal Republic and its Länder]. Since Jahrg. 12 (1968/69), the title has been: *Dokumentation Parlamentsspiegel. Jahresregister* [Parliament news documentation: annual index]. From the mid-1970s, only documents of supra-regional significance have been covered: the primary criterion for inclusion is 'inter-parliamentary relevance'. Since 1980, the printed version of the index has been complemented by an updating microfiche which cumulates fortnightly. The printed annual index is produced from the same data-base. Both editions are obtainable from the parliament of North Rhine-Westphalia (Zentraldokumentation Parlamentsspiegel), Düsseldorf.

The deliberations of the 20 committees, whose areas of competence run parallel to those of the ministries, are for the most part not public; the relevant reports are thus not published, apart from occasional reports of public sessions and hearings.

Statutes and standing orders relating to the Bundestag, details of its composition and brief biographies of its deputies are collected in the *Amtliches Handbuch des Deutschen Bundestages* [Official handbook of the Federal Assembly], issued by the Bundestag and edited by the Bundestagverwaltung [Administration of the Bundestag]. A new edition of this handbook is issued each electoral period. It is loose-leaf, with supplements. The publisher is the Verlag Neue Darmstädter Verlagsanstalt.

The Bundestag's Presse- und Informationszentrum [Press and Information Centre] reports on the work of the Bundestag in a periodical entitled *Woche im Bundestag: Parlamentskorrespondenz* [This week in the Bundestag: parliamentary correspondence]. This first appeared in 1971, and is published weekly when Parliament is in session (as a rule, two weeks of sessions are followed by two free weeks, with recesses at Christmas, Easter, and in July and August). Each issue starts with a *Gesetzesdokumentation* [Documentation of statutes], a survey of the draft statutes under discussion in the current week and their subsequent fate, and then proceeds to survey systematically individual subjects by means of brief reports. At the end of each annual series, a keyword index is published.

The older-established weekly *Das Parlament: die Woche im Bundeshaus* [Parliament: this week in the two Houses] is intended to disseminate information on proceedings in Parliament to a wider audience. First published in 1951, it is issued by the Bundeszentrale für politische Bildung [Federal Centre for Political Education], a body subordinate to the Bundesministerium des Innern [Federal Ministry of the Interior], and distributed by the Paulinus-Druckerei, Trier. It may be bought at any news-stand in the Federal Republic. Its principal contents are programmatic extracts from speeches delivered in the Bundestag and the Bundesrat. It also has a supplement, *Aus Politik und Zeitgeschichte* [Politics and current affairs], of some scholarly interest, containing articles on controversial political problems of the moment. At the end of each year, the publishers issue a bound version of these supplements which replaces the separate issues.

For the first six electoral periods, the Presse- und Informationszentrum of the Bundestag compiled a six-volume survey with the title *Chronik: Debatten, Gesetze, Kommentare* [Chronicle: debates, statutes, commentaries], published in 1974. This summarizes the most important themes of each sessional day in chronological sequence, occasionally with press comments added. Each volume closes with an index of personal names, which also serves as an index of speakers; an index of the newspapers quoted; and a keyword title index of statutes passed.

Since the seventh electoral period, the Gruppe Datenverarbeitung [Data Processing Group] of the Bundestag and the Arbeitsbereich Archivierung und Dokumentation [Archive and Documentation Section] of the Bundesrat have been operating a computer-based information system on the current state of legislation (GESTA). The data-base contains all draft legislation laid before the Bundestag and the Bundesrat, with details of its passage through the Houses. For each electoral period, a loose-leaf publication is compiled, which is replaced by a bound volume at the end of the period. During the seventh electoral period (1972–1976), the loose-leaf version was available only for internal distribution within the Bundestag and the Bundesrat. The cumulative volume, and the entire publication from the eighth electoral period on, have been published by Nomos Verlagsgesellschaft, Baden-Baden. The title of the work is *Stand der Gesetzgebung des Bundes; verkündete Gesetze und anderweitig erledigte Gesetzentwürfe* [Current state of Federal legislation: promulgated statutes and otherwise settled bills]. Its main section consists of the statutes, systematically arranged and described by means of the following headings: subject class number, date of promulgation, abbreviated title, full title, initiation, endorsement clause, subjects, brief summary of content and brief summary of passage. There is in addition a subject index, which is placed at the beginning of the loose-leaf edition, but which is found at the end of the bound volumes. The latter also contain, at the front, contents lists and statistics on the legislative activity of the current electoral period. The loose-leaf edition is updated approximately monthly.

Another monthly survey, with the title *Übersicht über den Stand der Gesetzgebung* [Survey of current legislation], appears in the non-official section of the *Bundesanzeiger* [Federal gazette]. This too is produced by the GESTA data-base. There is daily information on the passage of statutes in another part of the non-official section, headed *Deutscher Bundestag. Berichte des Parlamentsdienstes des Bundesanzeigers. Ergebnis der . . . ten Sitzung* [Federal Assembly. Reports of the Parliament Service of the Federal gazette. Account of the . . . th session]. The *Bundesanzeiger* also publishes additional items, *Nachrichten des Parlamentdienstes* [News from the Parliament Service], which surveys the agendas for the parliamentary sessions.

Since 1970, the Bundestag's Presse- und Informationsdienst has published studies on particular themes of current parliamentary and public interest in the series *Zur Sache: Themen parlamentarischer Beratung* [To the point: themes of parliamentary debate]. By 1985, 50 volumes had appeared.

The Wissenschaftliche Abteilung [Research Department] of the Bundestag, created to provide information on all matters relating to legislation, has from 1965 published two series: *Materialien* [Data] and *Bibliographien* [Bibliographies]. *Materialien* contains collections of material on different themes: for example, Bd. 69 (1981), *Die Ausschüsse des Deutschen Bundestages, 1. bis 9. Wahlperiode* [The Committees of the Federal

Assembly, 1st–9th electoral periods]. *Bibliographien*, which began in 1964, contains bibliographies on themes of national interest, such as futurology, terrorism, nuclear energy, public health, etc.

Bundesrat [Federal Council]

Article 50 of the constitution ordains that the Länder should participate in federal legislation and administration through a second legislative body, the Bundesrat. According to article 51, this consists of members appointed and recalled by the Länder governments, their number in each case varying according to the population of the Land. At present the Bundesrat has 41 members with full voting rights, and four members with advisory rights from Berlin (West). Each year the Bundesrat elects a member from a different Land as its President (there is a prescribed sequence of Länder for this purpose). Thus, in contrast to the Bundestag, each period of business lasts only one year. The sessional reports of the Bundesrat appear under the title: *Verhandlungen des Bundesrates, Stenographische Berichte* [Proceedings of the Federal Council, Stenographic reports]. From 1949 to 1958, the individual issues bore the title *Deutscher Bundesrat. Sitzungsbericht* [Federal Council. Sessional report]; this was subsequently changed to *Bundesrat. Bericht über die . . . te Sitzung* [Federal Council. Report of the . . . th session]. The sessions are numbered in sequence from the first session, which was held on 7 September 1949. Each year's sessions are collected in annual volumes. Each sessional report is preceded by an agenda and a list of members present.

Documents submitted to the Bundesrat are published under the title *Bundesrat: Drucksachen* [Federal Council: documents]. Their numeration begins afresh each year. The documents are collected to form volumes, which are issued in annual series (Jahrg. 1980 consists of 16 volumes, for example). Each volume has a contents list.

Until 1975, the Sekretariat [Secretariat] of the Bundesrat compiled and issued an index to the proceedings and the documents, entitled: *Sach- und Sprechregister zu den Verhandlungen des Bundesrates und zu den Anlagen* [Subject and speaker index to the proceedings of the Federal Council and to the appendices]. A single volume covers the years 1949–1952, with annual volumes thereafter. Since 1976, these indexes have been combined with those of the Bundestag in a single publication.

All the aforementioned works are published by the Verlag Dr. Hans Heger, Bonn.

Surveys of the agendas and results of individual sessions of the Bundesrat appear in the *Bundesanzeiger*. The Bundesrat itself publishes irregularly a review of the press, which documents press comments and opinions on the work of the Bundesrat and of the Länder. (There were nine issues in 1981, for example.) It is issued by the Pressestelle [Press Office] of the Bundesrat's Sekretariat.

The *Handbuch des Bundesrates* [Handbook of the Federal Council] contains a collection of statutes and agendas, statistics and other related material. Part 6 contains brief surveys of the constitutions and structures of the various Länder; part 7 has biographical data on the members of the Bundesrat. The handbook is issued by the Bundesrat and published by the Neue Darmstädter Verlagsanstalt, Rheinbreitbach. It was first published in 1958. Since 1977, it has been issued as a loose-leaf publication, with 11 updating supplements to date.

Bundesversammlung [Federal Convention]

In accordance with article 54 of the constitution, the term of office of the President of the Federal Republic (Bundespräsident) lasts five years. At least 30 days before the expiry of this term, the Bundesversammlung must convene and (without debate) elect a President. The Bundesversammlung is composed of members of the Bundestag and an equal number of members chosen by the Länder parliaments. Sessional records of the Bundesversammlung appear under the title *Bundesversammlung der Bundesrepublik Deutschland. Sitzung 1-* [Federal Convention of the German Federal Republic. Session 1-] (1949-). A summary of the first seven sessions has been published as *Die Bundesversammlungen 1949-1979: eine Dokumentation aus Anlass der Wahl des Bundespräsidenten am 23. Mai 1984* [Federal Conventions 1949-1979: documentation prepared on the occasion of the election of the President on 23 May 1984] (Bonn, Deutscher Bundestag, Presse- und Informationszentrum, 1984).

2.3. Publications of the federal government, ministries and authorities

The Federal Chancellor (Bundeskanzler) has no official function according to the constitution. He is simply the head of the federal government, and determines overall policy. His directives are, however, binding on the ministries. He has various bodies at his disposal to assist him in performing these tasks, among them the Bundeskanzleramt [Federal Chancellor's Office] and the Presse- und Informationsamt der Bundesregierung [Federal Government Press and Information Office].

The Presse- und Informationsamt in Bonn does not act as the government publisher. Its activities cover the following areas:

(a) it must keep the President and the government informed of news and developments in all fields
(b) it must sound public opinion at home and abroad to provide a basis for the political work of the government
(c) it acts as a central office for the government's dealings with the home and foreign press
(d) it must keep the German people informed of the political aims and achievements of the government.

It is in its performance of the last of these activities that the Presse- und Informationsamt issues periodicals and other publications.

Since 1951, the Presse- und Informationsamt has issued an almost daily *Bulletin* [Bulletin], containing speeches and extracts from government announcements. Its numeration begins afresh each year. Occasionally, more comprehensive special issues (Sonderausgaben) are published on topics of current interest. There is a quarterly name and subject index. The Bulletin is obtainable from the Deutsche Reportagefilm Produktions-, Verlags- und Vertriebs-GmbH, Bonn.

The Presse- und Informationsamt issues an annual report on the government's achievements entitled *Bonner Almanach* [Bonn diary] (until 1967, *Leistung und Erfolg* [Performance and achievement]). Since 1968, it has also published the *Jahresbericht der Bundesregierung* [Annual report of the federal government]; each issue is of about 600 pages. Previously, this appeared under the titles *Deutschland im Wiederaufbau* [Germany rebuilding] (1950-1959), and *Deutsche Politik* [German policy] (1960-1966).

Two series which began publication in 1978 are designed to raise public awareness of topics of current interest: *Berichte und Dokumentationen* [Reports and documentation] and *Bürgerservice* [Citizens' service]. 26 issues of the former and 28 of the latter were issued between 1978 and 1981, since which time the series have been unnumbered. In addition, many separate publications are produced, most of which are distributed free of charge. These include information brochures such as *Deutschland heute* [Germany today], which are constantly reissued in new editions and in many languages, but also editions of speeches and essays by Presidents, Chancellors and ministers, and special offprints of recent important legislation or government reports.

The federal government (Bundesregierung) includes at present 17 ministers, who also head their respective ministries. In most instances, the ministries are also federal authorities; in other cases, an authority is created expressly by statutory means. The drafting and passage of many statutes and orders, and the control or monitoring of regulations, often demands specialized knowledge and scientific or technical expertise. Many ministries therefore run special research institutes (Bundesforschungsanstalten) created for this purpose. Their publications will be dealt with below, under the appropriate ministries. Other state research institutions will be discussed in section 2.4. below.

Auswärtiges Amt [Foreign Office] (AA)

The Auswärtiges Amt is responsible for the conduct of the relations of the Federal Republic with other states; it is under the direction of the Bundesminister des Auswärtigen [Federal Minister for Foreign Affairs]. Abroad, he has under his control 123 embassies, 59 general consulates, 7 consulates and 8 delegations to international or supranational organizations, as well as the Deutsches Archäologisches Institut [German Archaeological Institute].

Treaties between the Federal Republic and foreign states are published regularly in Part 2 of the *Bundesgesetzblatt*. Implementation orders (Ausführungsvorschriften), which are directed at the administration and authorities, do not appear in an official gazette of the Auswärtiges Amt, but in the *Gemeinsames Ministerialblatt* [Joint ministerial gazette], which is issued by the Bundesminister des Innern [Federal Minister of the Interior].

Since 1955, the Auswärtiges Amt has issued a collection of the multilateral treaties to which the Federal Republic is a signatory, entitled *Verträge der Bundesrepublik Deutschland. Serie A, Multilaterale Verträge* [Treaties of the Federal Republic of Germany. Series A, Multilateral treaties]. The series, which is published by Carl Heymanns Verlag, currently comprises 62 volumes and contains 821 treaties, numbered consecutively in chronological sequence. A four-volume loose-leaf supplement, *Stand und Verzeichnis der Verträge* [Current state and listing of treaties], updates the collection. A 'Series B', intended to contain the bilateral treaties, has so far not been published.

From 1961 to 1970, another loose-leaf compilation, *Dokumente zur auswärtigen Politik* [Documents on foreign policy], was published. It contained a list of documents, with subject and name indexes, and was compiled for the Auswärtiges Amt by the Deutsche Gesellschaft für Auswärtige Politik [German Society for Foreign Policy], Bonn.

Information on German cultural policy abroad may be found in the *Berichte* [Reports] of the Abteilung für Auswärtige Kulturpolitik [Foreign Cultural Policy Department]. These have been published since 1964, first as the *Jahresbericht der Kulturabteilung des Auswärtigen Amtes* [Annual report of the Cultural Department of the Foreign Office], then as *Berichte*, which are occasionally issued as *Zweijahresberichte* [Biennial reports] or *Dreijahresberichte* [Triennial reports].

The Auswärtiges Amt sometimes issues separate publications on foreign policy themes. These publications also appear in the series *Berichte und Dokumentationen* [Reports and documentation] of the Presse- und Informationsamt. Other publications take the form of handbooks or collections of reference material. An important recent example is *EPZ—EPC—CPE, 1969-1978. Phraseologie der Europäischen Politischen Zusammenarbeit* [EPZ—EPC—CPE, 1969-1978. Phraseology of the European Political Co-operation] (in German, French and English), which the Auswärtiges Amt published in 1980.

Embassies of the Federal Republic abroad each issue their own information sheets, under various titles. These mainly take the form of extracts from the press, and are intended to clarify or comment on German foreign policy for the benefit of the citizens of the country concerned.

Bundesminister des Innern [Federal Minister of the Interior] (BMI)

The Bundesministerium des Innern is the centre of the entire federal adminstration and the public service. Its many and varied responsibilities include questions of constitutional law, administration, safeguarding of the constitution, internal security, security of the frontiers, the legal position of officials, employees and workers in the public service, cultural and sporting matters, civil defence, the organization of administration, statistics and matters relating to displaced persons, refugees and war victims. Because of this profusion of tasks, the Ministry is advised by a large number of agencies, institutes, advisory bodies, committees and commissions. In many of the abovementioned areas, however, the federal government has only limited responsibility, for example in matters of law relating to the public service and the police. In the early years of the Federal Republic, there was much argument over the boundary between the responsibilities of the federal government and those of the governments of the Länder. The line of demarcation has since been clarified by the Bundesverfassungsgericht [Federal Constitutional Court] in a whole series of judgements.

As the minister with central responsibility for the federal administration, the Bundesminister des Innern [Federal Minister of the Interior] has since 1950 issued the *Gemeinsames Ministerialblatt* [Joint ministerial gazette], in which the administrative directives (Verwaltungsanordnungen) of a number of ministries are collected. Its more precise title is: *Gemeinsames Ministerialblatt des Auswärtigen Amtes, des Bundesministers des Innern, des Bundesministers für Ernährung, Landwirtschaft und Forsten, des Bundesministers für Jugend, Familie, Frauen und Gesundheit, des Bundesministers für Raumordnung, Bauwesen und Städtebau, des Bundesministers für Innerdeutsche Beziehungen, des Bundesministers für Forschung und Technologie, des Bundesministers für Bildung und Wissenschaft, des Bundesministers für wirtschaftliche Zusammenarbeit und des Bundesministers für Umwelt, Naturschutz und Reaktorsicherheit* [Joint ministerial gazette of the Foreign Office, the Federal Minister of the Interior, the Federal Minister for Food, Agriculture and Forestry, the Federal Minister for Youth, the Family, Women and Health, the Federal Minister for Regional Planning, Building and Urban Development, the Federal Minister for Intra-German Relations, the Federal Minister for Research and Technology, the Federal Minister for Education and Science, the

Federal Minister for Economic Co-operation and the Federal Minister for the Environment, Nature Conservation and Nuclear Safety]. It generally appears fortnightly, and is collected in annual volumes with a chronological survey and subject and name indexes. It is distributed by Carl Heymanns Verlag, Berlin and Bonn.

In the course of the Federal Republic's history, the distribution of areas of responsibility among individual ministries has often altered: consequently the full title of the *Gemeinsames Ministerialblatt* has not always been the same. Formerly, various ministries issued their own official gazettes with generic titles such as *Ministerialblatt* or *Amtsblatt*; these have since ceased publication. The extant gazettes issued by individual ministries will be described below. Administrative directives relating to individual cases or persons, or which are valid only in specific regions, and executive orders relating to directives, appear mainly in so-called 'Dienstblätter'. These are often intended for internal circulation only, and are not regarded as publications.

Since 1979, the Referat Öffentlichkeitsarbeit [Publicity Department] of the Bundesministerium des Innern has issued a free periodical entitled *BMI-Mitteilungen: Informationen des Bundesministeriums des Innern* [BMI news: information from the Federal Ministry of the Interior]. It is published irregularly, with between three and six issues per year. The Referat Öffentlichkeitsarbeit also issues the *Schriftenreihe des Bundesministeriums des Innern* [Publications series of the Federal Ministry of the Interior], which deals with questions of constitutional law and ongoing legislative projects. It has been published since 1971, with 16 volumes to date. In addition, there are many separate publications, such as the loose-leaf *Gemeinsame Geschäftsordnung der Bundesministerien. Geschäftsordnung der Bundesregierung* [Joint standing orders of the federal ministries. Standing orders of the federal government], which is issued by the Bundesministerium des Innern and published by Kohlhammer Verlag, Stuttgart (1974–).

The following important official bodies are subordinate to the Bundesministerium des Innern:

STATISTISCHES BUNDESAMT [FEDERAL STATISTICAL OFFICE] (StBA)

In order to fulfil its obligation to compile the official statistics for the Federal Republic, the Bundesministerium des Innern has the Statistisches Bundesamt in Wiesbaden subordinate to it. In accordance with the federal nature of the West German state, this office is responsible only for statistics relating to the territory as a whole. Regional statistics are compiled and published by the statistical offices of the Länder and the Municipalities (Gemeinden).

The Statistisches Bundesamt distinguishes between 'comprehensive publications' (Zusammenfassende Veröffentlichungen), 'specialized series' (Fachserien) and 'foreign statistics' (Statistik des Auslands). The most important of the comprehensive publications are the *Statistisches Jahrbuch für die Bundesrepublik Deutschland* [Statistical yearbook for the Federal Republic of Germany] (Stuttgart, Kohlhammer, 1952–); the monthly *Wirtschaft und Statistik* [Economy and statistics] (1949–), containing essays and survey tables; and the *Statistischer Wochendienst* [Weekly statistical service] (1950–), containing the statistics for a particular week with comparative figures. In addition there are so-called 'thematic cross-section publications' such as *Ausgewählte Zahlen zur Energiewirtschaft* [Selected figures on the energy industry] or *Wirtschaft in Zahlen* [The economy in figures].

The specialized statistics are currently issued in 19 series, which are further divided into various thematic sub-series. The individual series are published differently. The *Index der Grundstoffpreise* [Index of raw material prices], for example, appears as Reihe 3 of Fachserie 17, *Preise* [Prices]. It is published monthly with an annual cumulation.

The foreign statistical reports have been published under several successive titles. From 1985, the arrangement has been as follows: the *Allgemeine Auslandsstatistik* [General foreign statistics] appears quarterly as *Vierteljahreshefte zur Auslandsstatistik* [Foreign statistics quarterly] (1984–) and as a collection of *Länderberichte* [Country reports]. The latter were formerly divided into *Länderberichte* and *Länderkurzberichte* [Short country reports]. Since 1985, they have been published in five series (Reihen): 1, Europe; 2, Africa; 3, America; 4, Asia; and 5, Australia, Oceania and other countries. Each series contains reports on individual countries, e.g. the Soviet Union (published 1984, as part of Reihe 1) or New Zealand (1983, in Reihe 5). New editions of a particular volume appear irregularly.

The Statistisches Bundesamt issues an annual *Veröffentlichungsverzeichnis* [List of publications] which serves as a useful guide to their publications, all of which (including the *Veröffentlichungsverzeichnis)* are available from Kohlhammer Verlag, Stuttgart.

BUNDESZENTRALE FÜR POLITISCHE BILDUNG [FEDERAL CENTRE FOR POLITICAL EDUCATION] (BpB)

Political education plays a significant part in the educational system of the Federal Republic. In 1952, a Bundeszentrale für Heimatdienst [Federal Centre for Service to the Nation] was created within the Bundesministerium des Innern; it was renamed the Bundeszentrale für politische Bildung in 1963. Its task was to encourage the growth of public political awareness on a non-party-political basis. In addition to the periodical *Das Parlament* and its supplement *Aus Politik und Zeitgeschichte* (see section 2.2. above), the Bundeszentrale issues the following periodicals: the *Politische Zeitung* [Political news] (1971–); *Zeitlupe: Analysen, Daten, Meinungen* [Slow motion: analyses, data, opinions] (1975–); *Informationen zur politischen Bildung* [Information on political education] (1982–). The *Schriftenreihe der Bundeszentrale für politische Bildung* [Publications series of the Federal Centre for Political Education], which began in 1957, consists (as of 1984) of 222 volumes.

BUNDESARCHIV [FEDERAL ARCHIVE] (BArch)

The Bundesarchiv was founded by the Federal Government in 1952 as the central archive for the government and for all federal authorities. It is located in Koblenz. It also collects and makes available archival material from the earlier German states, the papers of famous persons, and films and sound recordings of national historical interest.

As well as the records of the Parlamentarischer Rat [Parliamentary Council] of 1948–1949 (see section 2.2. above), the Bundesarchiv issues the following series:

Schriften des Bundesarchivs [Publications of the Federal Archive] (Koblenz, 1955–)
Findbücher zu Beständen des Bundesarchivs [Guides to holdings of the Federal Archive] (Koblenz, 1970–). Arranged according to provenance
Akten der Reichskanzlei. Weimarer Republik [Documents of the State Chancery of the Weimar Republic] (Boppard, Boldt, 1970–). An unnumbered series of volumes

containing the documents of particular cabinets, e.g. *Das Kabinett Scheidemann* [The Scheidemann cabinet] (1971) or *Die Regierung Hitler* [The Hitler government] (1983–)

Akten zur Vorgeschichte der Bundesrepublik [Documents on the prehistory of the Federal Republic] (Munich, Oldenburg, 1976–)

Die Kabinettsprotokolle der Bundesregierung [The cabinet records of the federal government] (Boppard, Boldt, 1982–). A chronological series covering the years from 1949 onwards.

Also subordinate to the Bundesministerium des Innern are two institutions of great significance for West German librarianship: the Staatsbibliothek Preussischer Kulturbesitz [State Library of the Prussian Cultural Foundation] in Berlin, and the Deutsche Bibliothek [German National Library] in Frankfurt am Main, whose publications will be discussed later in section 4.

Bundesminister der Justiz [Federal Minister of Justice] (BMJ)

The principal task of the Bundesministerium der Justiz is the preparation of legislation relating to the constitution, the legal system, administration, finance, industrial property and defence, to civil law, criminal law and the law relating to trade and industry. It examines the draft statutes and regulations of other ministries to ensure their correct legal form. As mentioned previously (section 2.1.), its duties include the issuing of the *Bundesgesetzblatt* and the *Bundesanzeiger*. The supreme courts subordinate to the Bundesministerium der Justiz are the Bundesgerichtshof [Federal Court of Justice] in Karlsruhe, which is the highest federal court in civil and criminal matters; the Bundesverwaltungsgericht [Federal Administrative Court] in West Berlin; the Bundesfinanzhof [Federal Fiscal Court], the Bundespatentgericht [Federal Patent Court], and the Oberste Rückerstattungsgericht [Supreme Court of Restitution], all in Munich. The last-named is an international court which acts as the final court of appeal in questions relating to the restitution of property lost in the wartime and occupation periods.

The judgements of these courts are published, not by the courts themselves, but by individual members and through commercial publishing houses. Selected judgements only are published. The titles are as follows:

Entscheidungen des Bundesgerichtshofs in Zivilsachen [Judgements of the Federal Court of Justice in civil cases] (Cologne, Heymanns, 1951–). Edited by members of the Bundesgerichtshof and of the legal profession

Entscheidungen des Bundesgerichtshofs in Strafsachen [Judgements of the Federal Court of Justice in criminal cases] (Cologne, Heymanns, 1951–). Edited by members of the Bundesgerichtshof and of the legal profession

Entscheidungen des Bundesverwaltungsgerichts [Judgements of the Federal Administrative Court] (Cologne, Heymanns, 1955–). Edited by members of the Court

Sammlung der Entscheidungen des Bundesfinanzhofs [Collected judgements of the Federal Fiscal Court] (Bonn, Stollfuss, 1959–). Edited by the members. (The numeration continues that of the *Sammlung der Entscheidungen und Gutachten des Reichsfinanzhofs des Deutschen Reiches* [Collected judgements and opinions of the German State Court of Finance], which commenced publication in 1920)

Entscheidungen des Bundespatentgerichts [Judgements of the Federal Patent Court]

(Cologne, Heymanns, 1962–). Edited by judges of the Bundespatentgericht
Urteile = Arrets. Obserstes Rückerstattungsgericht, 1. Senat [Verdicts. Supreme Court of Restitution, 1st Division]
Ausgewählte Entscheidungen des Obersten Rückerstattungsgerichts, 2. Senat [Selected judgements of the Supreme Court of Restitution, 2nd Division]
Entscheidungen: Oberstes Rückerstattungsgericht, 3. Senat [Decisions: Supreme Court of Restitution, 3rd Division].

DEUTSCHES PATENTAMT [GERMAN PATENT OFFICE] (DPA)

The Deutsches Patentamt was founded in Munich in 1949 as a subordinate body of the Bundesministerium der Justiz, to deal with legal matters relating to industrial property. The application documents (Offenlegungsschriften), inspection documents (Auslegeschriften) and patent specifications (Patentschriften) are obtainable separately from the Deutsches Patentamt, Dienststelle Berlin (West) [German Patent Office, West Berlin Branch]. The office also publishes the following serials:

Blatt für Patent-, Muster- und Zeichenwesen [Patent, design and trademark gazette] (Cologne, Heymanns, 52. 1950–). Continuation of a similar publication issued by the Kaiserliches Patentamt [Imperial Patent Office] from 1894

Patentblatt: Bekanntmachungen auf Grund des Patentgesetzes und des Gebrauchsmustergesetzes [Patent gazette: announcements pursuant to patent and registered design law] (Cologne, Heymanns, 73. 1953–). Continuation of the corresponding publication of the Kaiserliches Patentamt (from 1877)

Vierteljährliches Namenverzeichnis zum Patentblatt [Quarterly name index to the Patent gazette] (Cologne, Heymanns, 1953–)

Warenzeichenblatt [Trademark gazette] (Munich, Wila-Verlag, 1950–). Published in two parts: Teil 1, *Angemeldete Warenzeichen* [Trademark applications] and Teil 2, *Eingetragene Warenzeichen* [Registered trademarks]

Taschenbuch des gewerblichen Rechtsschutzes [Industrial property pocket book] (Cologne, Heymanns, 1968–). Loose-leaf.

Bundesminister der Finanzen [Federal Minister of Finance] (BMF)

The Bundesminister der Finanzen has two areas of responsibility. In accordance with articles 110 and 115 of the constitution, he is the minister in charge of the budget: that is, he prepares the federal financial plan and the draft of the federal budget, and is responsible for the accounts of income and expenditure and for the administration of state assets and debts. In addition, he is head of the federal financial authorities, which by article 108 of the constitution have the task of administering customs duties, financial monopolies, federal excise duties including the import sales tax, and duties connected with the European Communities.

In his capacity as minister in charge of the budget, the Bundesminister der Finanzen publishes the *Bundeshaushaltsplan für das Haushaltsjahr* [Federal budget for the fiscal year] (1949–) and the *Haushaltsrechnung und Vermögensrechnung des Bundes für das Haushaltsjahr* [Federal budgetary and financial accounts for the fiscal year] (1949–).

As head of the federal financial authorities, he publishes:

Bundeshaushaltsordnung [Federal budgetary order] (Bonn, Stollfuss [in Komm.], 1979–). Loose-leaf

Vorschriftensammlung Bundesfinanzverwaltung: Amtsblatt des Bundesministers der Finanzen [Code of regulations for the federal financial administration: official gazette of the Federal Minister of Finance] (Cologne, Bundesanzeiger, 1974–). Divided into numerous subject areas, for which loose-leaf publications are issued

Ministerialblatt des Bundesministers der Finanzen und des Bundesministers für Wirtschaft: mit Veröffentlichungen des Bundesministers für Raumordnung, Bauwesen und Städtebau [Ministerial gazette of the Federal Minister of Finance and the Federal Minister for the Economy: with publications of the Federal Minister for Regional Planning, Building and Town Planning] (Cologne, Bundesanzeiger, 1973–). From 1949 to 1972, entitled *Ministerialblatt des Bundesministers für Wirtschaft und Finanzen* [Ministerial gazette of the Federal Minister for the Economy and Finance]

Bundessteuerblatt [Federal tax gazette] (Bonn, Stollfuss, 1951–). Published in two parts: Teil 1, *Veröffentlichungen des Bundesfinanzministers und der obersten Finanzbehörden der Länder* [Publications of the Federal Minister of Finance and of the supreme financial authorities of the Länder]; Teil 2, *Entscheidungen des Bundesfinanzhofs* [Judgements of the Federal Court of Finance]

Deutscher Gebrauchszolltarif [German customs tariff] (1953–). An annual loose-leaf publication for the Federal customs administration

Erläuterungen zum Zolltarif [Notes on the customs tariff]. Loose-leaf publication, also for the Federal customs administration

Reden und Interviews [Speeches and interviews] (1973–). A series of publications under the names of individual ministers, secretaries of state, etc.

Schriftenreihe des Bundesministers der Finanzen [Publications series of the Federal Minister of Finance] (Bonn, Stollfuss [in Komm.], 1962–).

Bundesminister für Wirtschaft [Federal Minister for the Economy] (BMWI)

The Bundesminister für Wirtschaft is responsible for all matters of economic policy. Subordinate to him are a number of important federal authorities whose purpose is to supervise the observance of state regulations in economic activities. The Minister's administrative regulations are published in the *Bundesanzeiger* or the *Gemeinsames Ministerialblatt*. In addition, he publishes various serials and monographs on matters of economic policy and law:

BMWI-Tagesnachrichten [BMWI daily news] (1957–)

Die wirtschaftliche Lage in der Bundesrepublik Deutschland: Monatsbericht (1955–). English edition entitled *The economic situation in the Federal Republic of Germany: monthly review* (1966–)

Leistung in Zahlen [Performance figures] (1958–). Annual

BMWI-Dokumentation [BMWI documentation] (1983–). Formerly *BMWI-Texte* [BMWI texts] (1973–1982); contains speeches by the Bundesminister für Wirtschaft and by secretaries of state, and reports on economic topics

Studien-Reihe [Study series] (1973–). Contains mainly expert opinions and investigations.

PRINCIPAL PUBLICATIONS OF THE FEDERAL GOVERNMENT

The Bundesstelle für Aussenhandelsinformation [Federal Office for Export Information], subordinate to the Bundesminister für Wirtschaft, issues the annual *Zoll- und Handelsinformation* [Customs and trade information] (1983–; loose-leaf), previously *Deutsches Handelsarchiv* [German trade archive] (1949–1982).

The other major subordinate institutions are:

PHYSIKALISCH-TECHNISCHE BUNDESANSTALT [FEDERAL PHYSICO-TECHNICAL AGENCY] (PTB)

The principal task of the Physikalisch-Technische Bundesanstalt (Braunschweig and Berlin)—apart from research and development in all areas of physico-technical metrology—is to carry out the legally prescribed tests for the approval of measuring instruments for the calibration of instruments used in radiation protection, medicine and traffic surveillance. Its *Jahresbericht* [Annual report] was first published in 1971. Its most important publications are:

PTB-Mitteilungen: Forschen und Prüfen, Fachorgan für Wirtschaft und Wissenschaft, Amts- und Mitteilungsblatt der Physikalisch-technischen Bundesanstalt Braunschweig-Berlin [PTB information: research and testing, publication for specialists in industry and research, official gazette and information journal of the Federal Physico-Technical Agency, Braunschweig and Berlin] (Wiesbaden: Vieweg, 1964–). Formerly *Amtsblatt der Physikalisch-technischen Bundesanstalt* [Official gazette of the Federal Physico-Technical Agency] (1950–1963)

PTB-Bericht [PTB report] (Braunschweig, 1972–). The reports are published in many sub-series on themes such as acoustics, dosimetry, mechanics, medical measuring, etc. Of considerable bibliographical significance is *Reihe L, Literaturzusammenstellungen und Veröffentlichungsverzeichnisse* [Series L, Bibliographies and lists of publications] (1974–)

PTB-Prüfregeln [PTB testing rules] (1980–)

Eichordnung (EO): vom 15. Januar 1975 [Calibration regulation of 15 January 1975] (Braunschweig: Deutscher Eichverlag, 1975). To date, the section *Allgemeine Vorschriften* [General provisions] has been published, with 10 volumes of appendices.

In addition, the Physikalisch-Technische Bundesanstalt publishes individual technical guidelines and circulars as required.

BUNDESANSTALT FÜR MATERIALPRÜFUNG [FEDERAL AGENCY FOR MATERIALS TESTING] (BAM)

Also subordinate to the Bundesminister für Wirtschaft is the Bundesanstalt für Materialprüfung in West Berlin, which advises the Minister on matters of materials research and testing and of chemical safety, and supports the German economic effort in general. It issues a quarterly *Amts und Mitteilungsblatt* [Official gazette and information journal] (1970–) and a *Jahresbericht* [Annual report] (1957–), which from 1957–1968 was entitled *Tätigkeitsbericht* [Report of activities]. Important scientific papers and research reports appear in the series *Forschungsbericht* [Research report] (from 1970–1978 issued as *BAM-Berichte: Forschung und Entwicklung in der Bundesanstalt für Materialprüfung* [BAM reports: research and development in the

Federal Agency for Materials Research]) and as *Seminar preprints* (1978–). As a consequence of its legal obligation to collect and make publicly accessible both its own research results and those of others in its field, the Agency issues *BAM-Information, BAM-Dokumentation* [BAM information, BAM documentation] (1979–), an important bibliography.

Other important areas of the economy are covered by the following bodies subordinate to the Bundesministerium für Wirtschaft: the Bundesamt für gewerbliche Wirtschaft [Federal Office for Trade and Industry] in Eschborn; the Bundeskartellamt [Federal Cartel Office] in Berlin; the Bundesamt für Geowissenschaften und Rohstoffe [Federal Institute for Geosciences and Raw Materials] in Hanover; the Filmförderungsanstalt [Film Promotion Institute] in Berlin; and the Bundesstelle für Aussenhandelsinformation [Federal Office for Export Information] in Cologne. All these institutions issue series relating to their particular spheres of activity.

Bundesminister für Ernährung, Landwirtschaft und Forsten [Federal Minister for Food, Agriculture and Forestry] (BMELF)

The Bundesministerium für Ernährung, Landwirtschaft und Forsten has three major areas of responsibility. It is responsible for the economic elements of policy relating to food, agriculture and forestry, but also investigates, supervises and supports the entire field of food and agriculture, and therefore has to mediate between the interests of producers and consumers. It issues the following serials:

Agrarbericht der Bundesregierung [Agriculture report of the federal government] (1956–). The title has changed several times

Statistischer Monatsbericht des BMELF [Monthly statistical report of the BMELF] (1950–)

Statistisches Jahrbuch über Ernährung, Landwirtschaft und Forsten [Statistical yearbook on food, agriculture and forestry] (Münster-Hiltrup, Landwirtschaftsverlag, 1957–)

Berichte über Landwirtschaft: Zeitschrift für Agrarpolitik und Landwirtschaft [Reports on agriculture: journal for agriculture and agricultural policy] (Hamburg, Berlin, Parey, 1952–).

Reports of research are published in the following series:

BMELF-Informationen: Nachrichten, Berichte, Dokumentation [BMELF information: news, reports, documentation] From 1957 to 1966, entitled *Informationsdienst für Ernährung und Landwirtschaft* [Information service for food and agriculture]

Forschung im Geschäftsbereich des BMELF [Research in the BMELF's field] (Münster-Hiltrup, Landwirtschaftsverlag, 1962–). Issued in sub-series designated Teil A to S, which are devoted to particular subjects

Schriftenreihe des BMELF [Publications series of the BMELF] (Münster-Hiltrup, Landwirtschaftsverlag, 1955–). Divided into R.A: *Angewandte Wissenschaft* [Applied science]; R.B: *Flurbereinigung* [Consolidation of farmland]; and R.C: *Agrarpolitische Berichte der OECD* [Agricultural policy reports of the OECD]. The title has changed several times.

To support and advise the Ministry, it has 14 research institutes, each of which carries out research within its own allotted area: these are the Bundesanstalten [Federal Research Agencies] für Landwirtschaft [Agriculture] (Braunschweig-Völkenrode), Milchforschung [Milk Research] (Kiel), Fischerei [Fisheries] (Hamburg), Forst- und Holzwirtschaft [Forestry and Timber Industries] (Hamburg), Getreide- und Kartoffelverarbeitung [Cereals and Potato Production] (Detmold), Viruskrankheiten der Tiere [Virus Diseases of Animals] (Tübingen), Rebenzüchtung [Viticulture] (Siebeldingen), Fleischforschung [Meat Research] (Kulmbach), Ernährung [Food] (Karlsruhe), Gartenbauliche Pflanzenzüchtung [Horticultural Plant Cultivation] (Ahrensburg), Naturschutz und Landschaftsökologie [Nature Conservation and Land Ecology] (Bonn), Fettforschung [Fat Research] (Münster), and Landwirtschaftliche Marktordnung [Agricultural Market Regulation] (Frankfurt am Main).

The best known of these institutes, however, is the Biologische Bundesanstalt für Land- und Forstwirtschaft [Federal Biological Research Institute for Agriculture and Forestry] (Berlin and Braunschweig), successor to the Biologische Reichsanstalt für Land- und Forstwirtschaft [State Biological Institute for Agriculture and Forestry]. It is at present responsible for all aspects of plant protection and the protection of provisions, and issues the following publications:

Mitteilungen aus der Biologischen Bundesanstalt für Land- und Forstwirtschaft, Berlin-Dahlem [Communications from the Federal Biological Research Institute for Agriculture and Forestry, Berlin-Dahlem] (Berlin, 1954–). Continuation of the series *Mitteilungen der Biologischen Zentralanstalt Braunschweig* [Communications from the Braunschweig Central Biological Institute]

Nachrichtenblatt des Deutschen Pflanzenschutzdienstes [News from the German Plant Protection Service] (Stuttgart, Ulmer, 1950–). Edited by the Biologische Bundesanstalt with the collaboration of the Plant Protection Offices of the Länder. Monthly. Continuation of the corresponding periodical of the Biologische Zentralanstalt Braunschweig

Bibliographie der Pflanzenschutzliteratur [Bibliography of plant protection] (Berlin, Parey [in Komm.], 1970–). Quarterly. A new series, superseding the *Jahresbericht über das Gebiet der Pflanzenkrankheiten* [Annual report on plant diseases] (1914–1958)

Amtliche Pflanzenschutzbestimmungen [Official plant protection regulations] (Berlin, Dahlem, 1951–). Five issues per volume. Continuation of a publication which appeared under various titles from 1924

Merkblätter der Biologischen Bundesanstalt für Land- und Forstwirtschaft [Memoranda from the Federal Biological Institute for Agriculture and Forestry] (Braunschweig, 1949–). Consists of over 60 titles, new editions of which appear irregularly

Bundesminister für Arbeit und Sozialordnung [Federal Minister for Employment and Social Affairs] (BMA)

The sphere of responsibility of the Bundesminister für Arbeit und Sozialordnung includes all areas connected with the administration of employment in the Federal Republic. West Germany has a state employment service in addition to the private labour market (recruitment by means of advertisement), and compulsory insurance in the areas of health and social security. The Bundesminister für Arbeit und Sozialordnung is in overall control of health, accident and employment insurance, each of which is itself administered by other official bodies.

The Bundesminister publishes the following serials:

Bundesarbeitsblatt [Federal employment gazette] (Stuttgart, Kohlhammer, 1950–). A monthly periodical which is the official gazette of the Bundesministerium, including the supplement *Bundesversorgungsblatt* [Federal war victim support gazette], which was a separate publication until 1978

Arbeitsplatz Deutschland [Workplace Germany] (Bonn, 1973–). A quarterly information journal for foreign workers, published in various languages

Statistisches Taschenbuch: Arbeits- und Sozialstatistik [Statistical pocket book: employment and social statistics] (Bonn, Bundesministerium für Arbeit und Sozialordnung, Referat Presse- und Öffentlichkeitsarbeit, 1977–). An annual publication supplementing the corresponding statistics from the Statistisches Bundesamt [Federal Statistical Office].

In addition, the ministry produces yearly reports on its most important areas of responsibility:

Sozialbericht [Social report] (Bonn, BMA, Referat Presse- und Öffentlichkeitsarbeit, 1970–)

Die Einkommens- und Vermögensverteilung in der Bundesrepublik Deutschland [The distribution of income and property in the German Federal Republic] (Bonn, BMA, Referat Öffentlichkeitsarbeit, 1970–)

Die gesetzliche Krankenversicherung in der Bundesrepublik Deutschland [Statutory health insurance in the German Federal Republic] (Bonn, BMA, 1967–). From 1963 to 1966, published under the title *Die gesetzliche Krankenversicherung im Jahre . . .* [Statutory health insurance in the year . . .]

Die gesetzliche Unfallversicherung in der Bundesrepublik Deutschland: statistischer und finanzieller Bericht [Statutory accident insurance in the Federal Republic of Germany: statistical and financial report] (Bonn, BMA, 1949–)

Die Rentenversicherung der Arbeiter und der Angestellten in der Bundesrepublik Deutschland: statistischer und finanzieller Bericht [Employment insurance for blue- and white-collar workers in the German Federal Republic: statistical and financial report] (Bonn, BMA, 1957–). Title varies.

The following series are also published:

Schriftenreihe des Bundesministers für Arbeit und Sozialordnung [Publications series of the Federal Minister for Employment and Social Affairs] (Stuttgart, etc., Kohlhammer, 1960–)

Forschungsbericht [Research report] (Bonn, BMA, Referat Presse- und Information, 1978–)

Arbeit und Gesundheit: medizinische Schriftenreihe des Bundesministers für Arbeit und Sozialordnung [Employment and Health: medical series of the Federal Minister for Employment and Social Affairs] (Stuttgart, Thieme, 1951–). A new series, superseding the *Schriftenreihe Reichsarbeitsblatt* [National employment gazette] (1926–1944).

In the Federal Republic, the administration of employment is characterized by the coexistence of private and state employment services, and the link between the state employment service and unemployment insurance. Anyone who has lost their job and wishes to receive payments from the (compulsory) unemployment insurance scheme, is obliged to allow the state employment service to find them another post. The Bundesanstalt für Arbeit [Federal Employment Agency] in Nuremberg, which is subordinate to the Bundesministerium für Arbeit und Sozialordnung, was created to perform the numerous tasks which arise as a result of this arrangement. According to the *Arbeitsförderungsgesetz* [Employment promotion law] of 25 June 1969, its duties are to provide careers advice, to act as an employment agent, to promote career development, to grant payments for job maintenance and creation, to pay unemployment and sickness benefits, and to conduct research into careers and the employment market. Because it combines administrative, advisory and research functions, the Bundesanstalt für Arbeit produces a particularly comprehensive range of publications which are of special importance for professional life.

The Bundesanstalt für Arbeit (BA) issues several report series:

Amtliche Nachrichten der Bundesanstalt für Arbeit [Official information from the Federal Employment Agency] (Nuremberg, BA, 1953–). Monthly, with a large number of supplements, of which the most significant are *Arbeitsstatistik: Jahreszahlen* [Employment statistics: yearly figures] and *Berufsberatung: Ergebnisse der Berufsberatungsstatistik*.

Haushaltsplan der Bundesanstalt für Arbeit [Careers advice: results of the careers advice statistics] [Budget of the Federal Employment Institute] (Nuremberg, BA, 1952–)

Geschäftsbericht [Business report] (Nuremberg, Spandel, 1952–)

Presse-Informationen [Press releases] (Nuremberg, Spandel, 1969–). Issued as required; supplements.

To assist the allocation of employment, the Bundesanstalt issues the serial *Markt und Chance* [Market and opportunity] (1970–). Edited by the Zentralstelle für Arbeitsvermittlung [Central Employment Office] at Frankfurt am Main, it is published in two sections: *Ausgabe A, Bewerberanzeiger* [Edition A, Situations wanted] and *Ausgabe B, Zentraler Stellenanzeiger* [Edition B, Central list of situations vacant].

The Bundesanstalt für Arbeit issues a great deal of information material relating to careers advice:

Blätter zur Berufskunde [Careers information] (Bielefeld, Bertelsmann, 1952–). A loose-leaf work consisting of brochures, constantly updated, on the aims and training requirements of particular professions. This widely available publication has for several years been supplemented by a collection of more detailed information brochures

Gabi: Grundwerk ausbildungs- und berufskundlicher Informationen [Gabi: reference work for training and careers information] (Nuremberg, FW Verlag für Fortbildung und Wissen, 1981–). Loose-leaf.

The Bundesanstalt also issues an annual publication entitled *Beruf aktuell* [Professions today] (Wiesbaden, Universum Verlags-Anstalt, 1971–).

An official survey of recognized professions in the Federal Republic is available in the *Klassifizierung der Berufe: systematisches und alphabetisches Verzeichnis der Berufsbenennungen* [Classification of professions: systematic and alphabetic listing of titles of professions], new editions of which are published irregularly by the Bundesanstalt für Arbeit.

Bundesminister für Verkehr [Federal Minister of Transport] (BMV)

The Bundesminister für Verkehr is in charge of all aspects of transportation, i.e. the railways, road transport, inland navigation, sea transport, air transport, road construction, waterways and the meteorological service. His most important serial publications are:

Verkehrsblatt: Amtsblatt des Bundesministers für Verkehr der Bundesrepublik Deutschland [Transport gazette: official gazette of the Federal Minister of Transport] (Dortmund, Verkehrsblatt-Verlag, 1949–). Fortnightly; continuation of the *Verkehrsblatt des Vereinigten Wirtschaftsgebiets* [Transport gazette of the Combined Economic Area] (1947–1948)

Allgemeiner statistischer Dienst des Bundesverkehrsministeriums [General statistical service of the Federal Transport Ministry] (Bonn, 1958–). Annual

Verkehr in Zahlen [Transport in figures] (Bonn, BMV, 1972–). Annual; edited by the Deutsches Institut für Wirtschaftsforschung [German Institute for Economic Research], Berlin

Strassenverkehrszählungen [Road traffic censuses] (Cologne, Bundesanstalt für Strassenwesen, 1976–). Issued on behalf of the Bundesministerium für Verkehr. The series contains reports on traffic censuses, which are regularly carried out

Forschung Strassenbau und Strassenverkehrstechnik: Forschungsberichte aus den Forschungsprogrammen des BMV und der Forschungsgesellschaft für das Strassenwesen e.V. [Road construction and road traffic technology research: research reports from the research programmes of the Federal Ministry of Transport and the Road Research Society] (Bonn, BMV, 1959–).

The Bundesministerium für Verkehr controls various bodies which perform the practical testing and supervisory tasks connected with the field of transport. The most important of these, from the point of view of publishing output, are:

DEUTSCHES HYDROGRAPHISCHES INSTITUT [GERMAN HYDROGRAPHIC AGENCY] (DHI)

The Deutsches Hydrographisches Institut, at Hamburg, is a 'higher federal authority' (Bundesoberbehörde), responsible for the control and promotion of sea navigation, the related maritime research and the supervision of maritime traffic. It continues the work of its predecessor, the Deutsche Seewarte [German Marine Observatory], Hamburg, and publishes serials containing all data required for maritime traffic:

Nachrichten für Seefahrer: Amtsblatt des Deutschen Hydrographischen Instituts [News for seafarers: official gazette of the German Hydrographic Agency] (Hamburg, 1945–). The title has appeared weekly since 1870, with many supplements such as the *Leuchtfeuerverzeichnis* [List of lights], *Berichtigungen Deutscher Seekarten* [Corrections to German maritime charts], etc.

PRINCIPAL PUBLICATIONS OF THE FEDERAL GOVERNMENT

Deutsche hydrographische Zeitschrift [German hydrographic journal] (Hamburg, DHI, 1948–). Bi-monthly; from 1955, it has included the *Hydrographische Bibliographie* [Hydrographic bibliography] (published on microfiche since 1983)

Nautisches Jahrbuch: oder Ephemeriden und Tafeln zur Bestimmung der Zeit, Länge und Breite zur See nach astronomischen Beobachtungen [Nautical yearbook: or ephemerides and tables for determining time, longitude and latitude at sea from astronomical observations] (Hamburg, DHI, 1948–). The title has been published since 1852

Erdmagnetisches Jahrbuch: numerische Ergebnisse und Magnetogramme Wingst [Geomagnetic yearbook: numerical results and Wingst magnetograms] (Hamburg, DHI, 1949–). Data supplied by the DHI's Erdmagnetisches Observatorium Wingst [Wingst Geomagnetic Observatory], covering the years from 1943 onwards

Gezeitentafeln [Tide tables] (Hamburg, DHI, 1952–). Published in two parts: Teil 1, *Europäische Gewässer* [European waters], and Teil 2, *Atlantischer und Indischer Ozean, Westküste Südamerikas* [Atlantic and Indian Oceans, West coast of South America]; continuation of a title first published in 1880

Eisbericht: Amtsblatt des Deutschen Hydrographischen Instituts [Ice report: official gazette of the German Hydrographic Institute] (Hamburg, DHI, 1946–). The title has been published irregularly, as required, since 1928; supplement *Eisübersichtskarte* [Ice survey chart]

Nautischer Funkdienst [Nautical radio service] (Hamburg, DHI, 1961–). Published monthly in three parts: *Funkverkehr* [Radio traffic], *Funkortung* [Radio location] and *Wetterfunk* [Radio weather forecasts]

Jahresbericht [Annual report] (Hamburg, DHI, 1946–)

Verzeichnis der Leuchtfeuer und Signalstellen [List of lights and signal positions] (Hamburg, DHI, 1961–). Loose-leaf.

Sea navigation regulations are collected in *Seeschiffahrtsstrassen-Ordnung und andere Seeverkehrsvorschriften* [Sea lane order and other maritime traffic regulations], issued by the Deutsches Hydrographisches Institut with the Bundesminister für Verkehr, 25th ed. (Herford, Mittler, 1983). The Institute also publishes the official maritime charts, and documents all its publications in the annual *Verzeichnis der Nautischen Karten und Bücher und sonstigen Veröffentlichungen* [List of the nautical charts and books and other publications] (Hamburg, DHI, 1955–).

DEUTSCHER WETTERDIENST [GERMAN WEATHER SERVICE] (DWD)

The Deutscher Wetterdienst at Offenbach am Main is charged with the supervision of, and research into, meteorology as an aid to transport, agriculture, the construction industry, the health service, and air and sea travel. The most important data and results of meteorological analysis are published under the following titles:

Europäischer Wetterbericht: Amtsblatt des Deutschen Wetterdienstes/European meteorological bulletin/Bulletin météorologique européen/Boletin meteorológico europeo (Offenbach am Main, Deutscher Wetterdienst, Zentralamt, 1976–). Daily; continuation of an earlier title, *Täglicher Wetterbericht* [Daily weather report], first published in 1948. Part 1 contains the charts, Part 2 the ground and aerological weather forecasts

Die Grosswetterlagen Europas: Amtsblatt des Deutschen Wetterdienstes [The general European weather situation: official gazette of the German Weather Service] (Offenbach am Main, Deutscher Wetterdienst, Zentralamt, 1975–). Monthly; continuation of an earlier title, *Die Grosswetterlagen Mitteleuropas* [The general Central European weather situation], first published in 1948

Wetterkarte des Deutschen Wetterdienstes: Amtsblatt des Wetteramtes . . . [Weather chart of the German Weather Service: official gazette of the . . . Weather Office] (Offenbach am Main, Wetteramt Frankfurt, 1953–). A series which is sometimes subdivided among the regional weather offices

Die Witterung im Übersee: monatlich erscheinender Weltwetterbericht [The weather overseas: monthly world weather report] (Hamburg, Seewetteramt, 1953–)

Agrarmeteorologischer Wochenhinweis für das Gebiet der Bundesrepublik Deutschland [Weekly agricultural weather guide for the Federal Republic] (Offenbach am Main, DWD, Zentralamt, 1957–)

Monatlicher Witterungsbericht: Amtsblatt des Deutschen Wetterdienstes [Monthly weather report: official gazette of the German Weather Service] (Offenbach am Main, DWD, Zentralamt, 1953–

Jahresbericht des deutschen Wetterdienstes [Annual report of the German Weather Service] (Offenbach am Main, DWD, Zentralamt, 1953–)

Deutsches meteorologisches Jahrbuch: Bundesrepublik [German meteorological yearbook: Federal Republic] (Offenbach am Main, DWD, Zentralamt, 1953–)

Annalen der Meteorologie [Annals of meteorology] (Offenbach am Main, DWD, Zentralamt, 1963–). New series

Berichte des Deutschen Wetterdienstes [Reports of the German Weather Service] (Offenbach am Main, DWD, Zentralamt, 1953–)

Das Klima der Bundesrepublik Deutschland [The climate of the German Federal Republic] (Offenbach am Main, DWD, Zentralamt, 1979–). Issued in parts

Klimadaten von Europa [European climatic data] (Offenbach am Main, DWD, Zentralamt, 1980–1982). 3 vols

Bibliographien des Deutschen Wetterdienstes [Bibliographies of the German Weather Service] (Offenbach am Main, DWD, Zentralamt, 1955–). Covers the years from 1950

Agrarmeteorologische Bibliographie [Agricultural–meteorological bibliography] (Offenbach am Main, DWD, Zentralamt, 1950–). Annual.

A survey of the Service's publications is provided by *Die Veröffentlichungen des Deutschen Wetterdienstes* [The publications of the German Weather Service] (Offenbach am Main, DWD, Zentralamt). Irregular; last issued 1981.

DEUTSCHE BUNDESBAHN [GERMAN STATE RAILWAYS] (DB)

Rail traffic in the Federal Republic is almost entirely under state control. The managing body, subordinate to the Bundesminister für Verkehr, is the Deutsche Bundesbahn, a state-owned corporation controlling its own finances. Its administrative headquarters are the Hauptverwaltung der DB [Head Office of the DB] in Frankfurt am Main. Ten regional directorates regulate traffic and are responsible for vehicles and lines; each issues its own *Amtsblatt* [Official gazette]. The main publications of the Deutsche Bundesbahn are:

Die Bundesbahn: Zeitschrift für aktuelle Verkehrsfragen: amtliches Organ der Hauptverwaltung der DB [The state railways: journal for current transport questions: official organ of the Head Office of the DB] (Darmstadt, Hestra Verlag, 1949–). Monthly.

The official timetables of the Deutsche Bundesbahn are:

Kursbuch: Gesamtausgabe [Railway guide: complete edition] (Mainz, DB, Kursbuchstelle, 1971–). Published twice yearly since 1949 under the title *Amtliches Kursbuch* [Official railway guide]

Buskursbuch [Bus guide] (Mainz, DB, Kursbuchstelle, 1984–). Published twice yearly since 1949 under various titles, it also contains details of the bus services of the Deutsche Bundespost [German Postal Service], giving a complete picture of the entire bus network

Güterkursbuch der Deutschen Bundesbahn: Jahresfahrplan [Goods services guide: the year's timetable] (Mainz, DB, Kursbuchstelle, 1955–).

The Deutsche Bundesbahn's tariffs and charges are announced in the *Tarif-und Verkehrsanzeiger für den Personen-, Gepäck-, Expressgut-, Güter- und Tierverkehr der Eisenbahnen des öffentlichen Verkehrs im Gebiet der Bundesrepublik Deutschland* [Tariff and transport advertiser for passenger, luggage, express goods, goods and animals carried by the public railways of the Federal Republic of Germany (Frankfurt am Main, 1950–). This weekly publication is issued by the Zentralstelle Absatz [Central Marketing Office], Mainz.

Further public information about the Deutsche Bundesbahn is available in the following:

Blickpunkt: Zeitung der Deutschen Bundesbahn [Viewpoint: journal of German State Railways] (Frankfurt am Main, 1973–). Issued by the DB-Hauptverwaltung, Pressedienst [DB Head Office, Press Service], this has appeared monthly since 1958, previously under the title *Rad und Schiene* [Wheel and rail]

Die schöne Welt: das Ideenmagazin der DB [Beautiful world: concept magazine of German State Railways] (Frankfurt am Main, DB, 1958–)

DB: Deutsches Bundesbahn-Adressbuch [DB: German State Railways directory] (Darmstadt, Hestra Verlag, 1951–). Annual

Geschäftsbericht der Deutschen Bundesbahn [Business report of German State Railways] (Frankfurt am Main, DB, Vorstand, 1949–). Annual.

A by-product of the DB-Hauptverwaltung is a monthly bibliography of railway literature, *Information Eisenbahn: Dokumentation des Fachschrifttums* [Railway information: documentation of the specialist literature] (Darmstadt, Tetzlaff (in Komm.), 1978–). This is edited by the Dokumentationsdienst [Documentation Service] of Deutsche Bundesbahn, at Frankfurt. It continues *Kurzauszüge aus dem Schrifttum für das Eisenbahnwesen* [Excerpts from railway literature] (1953–1978).

Bundesminister für das Post- und Fernmeldewesen [Federal Minister for Posts and Telecommunications] (BPM)

Postal and telecommunications services in the Federal Republic are administered by the state; the federal government alone is empowered to legislate in these areas. The transmission of data is a state monopoly. The Deutsche Bundespost [German Postal Service] (DBP) is responsible for all postal and telecommunications traffic. Technical research and development is carried out by the Fernmeldetechnisches Zentralamt [Central Telecommunications Office] (FTZ) in Darmstadt. The Posttechnisches Zentralamt [Central Postal Technical Office] (PTZ), also in Darmstadt, is in charge of all matters relating to the postal service.

A complete survey of the available publications of the Bundesminister für das Post- und Fernmeldewesen, the Deutsche Bundespost and the two Zentralämter is provided by the *Druckwerkeverzeichnis. Deutsche Bundespost* [List of publications of the German Postal Service] (1957–), an annual publication issued by the Ministry and compiled by the Posttechnisches Zentralamt. It was previously entitled *Amtliche Druckwerke der Deutschen Bundespost* [Official publications of the German Postal Service].

The Ministry also issues the following titles:

Amtsblatt des Bundesministers für das Post- und Fernmeldewesen [Official gazette of the Minister for Posts and Telecommunications] (Bonn, BPM, 1950–). Published at least twice weekly, with various supplements

Archiv für das Post- und Fernmeldewesen [Archive for Posts and Telecommunications] (Bonn, BPM, 1949–). Irregular, roughly quarterly

Geschäftsbericht. Deutsche Bundespost [Report of the German Postal Service] (Bonn, BPM, 1956–). Covers the years from 1955

Jahresrechnung: Nachweisung über die Einnahmen und Ausgaben der Deutschen Bundespost [Annual accounts: record of the income and expenditure of the German Postal Service] (Bonn, BPM, 1951–)

Jahrbuch der Deutschen Bundespost [German Postal Service yearbook] (Bad Windsheim, Verlag für Wissenschaft und Leben, 1949–)

Weltposthandbuch: Verträge des Weltpostvereins [World postal handbook: conventions of the Universal Postal Union] (Frankfurt, BPM, 1952–). Loose-leaf since 1984.

Publications of importance for the management of postal traffic are:

Ortsverzeichnis Post: Verzeichnis der Orte im Bereich der deutschen Postverwaltungen [Postal directory: list of places covered by the German postal agencies] (Darmstadt, Posttechnisches Zentralamt, 1959–). Biennial; compiled by the PTZ

Postleitzahlenverzeichnis [List of postal codes] (Darmstadt, Posttechnisches Zentralamt). Annual; two editions, *Abc-folge* [Alphabetical sequence] and *Numerische Folge* [Numerical sequence]

Postgebührenheft. Deutsche Bundespost [Postal charges. German Postal Service] (Bonn, BPM, 1951–). Annual

Postkursbuch [Postal timetable] (Bonn, BPM, 1950–). Compiled by the Posttechnisches Zentralamt. Published twice yearly in two parts, 1. *Postbeförderung auf Eisenbahnen* [Carriage of post by rail] and 2. *Postbeförderung*

PRINCIPAL PUBLICATIONS OF THE FEDERAL GOVERNMENT

auf Strassen: Überlandverkehr [Carriage of post by road: long-distance traffic]

Postmagazin: Zeitschrift der Deutschen Bundespost [Postal magazine: journal of the German Postal Service] (Munich, Thiemig (in Komm.), 1980–). Quarterly; issued by the Referat für Presse und Public Relations [Press and Public Relations Section] of the Ministry

Telepost: Zeitschrift der Deutschen Bundespost [Telepost: journal of the German Postal Service] (Munich, Süddeutscher Verlag, 1972–). Monthly.

The following publications relate to telecommunications:

Amtliches Verzeichnis der Ortsnetzkennzahlen für den Selbstwählferndienst: AVON: national–international [Official list of telephone dialling codes: national–international] (Darmstadt, FTZ). Irregular, published roughly every two years

Amtliches Fernsprechbuch der Deutschen Bundespost: Telefonbuch [Official telephone book of the German Postal Service]. There are currently 100 different regional editions, issued by the appropriate local postal authorities; new editions are issued each year

Amtliches Telex- und Teletexverzeichnis [Official telex and teletex list] (Darmstadt, FTZ, 1951–). Published annually in three volumes; the title has changed a number of times

Amtliches Telefax- und Telebriefverzeichnis der Deutschen Bundespost [Official telefax and teleletter list of the German Postal Service] (Nuremberg, Oberpostdirektion, 1983–). Annual

BTX: Amtliches Verzeichnis der Bildschirmtextteilnehmer der Deutschen Bundespost [BTX: Official list of teletext subscribers of the German Postal Service] (Frankfurt am Main, Deutsche Postreklame, 1985–). Annual

DATEX: Amtliches Verzeichnis der DATEX-L- und DATEX-P-Teilnehmer der Deutschen Bundespost [DATEX: official list of DATEX-L and DATEX-P subscribers of the German Postal Service] (Frankfurt am Main, Deutsche Postreklame, 1985–). Annual

Amtliches Verzeichnis der Teilnehmer des öffentlichen Bildübertragungsnetzes [Official list of subscribers to the public picture transmission network] (Darmstadt, FTZ, 1973–). Annual

DATEL-Handbuch: Handbuch für die Entwickler, Planer und Anwender von Datenfernverarbeitungssystemen [DATEL handbook: handbook for the developers, planners and users of teledata systems] (Darmstadt, FTZ, 1981–). Loose-leaf since 1985

DATEX-P-Handbuch: Detailinformation zu Technik und Betrieb der Datenpaketvermittlung [DATEX-P handbook: detailed technical and operational information on data packet switching] (Darmstadt, FTZ, 1985–). Loose-leaf.

The results of the research carried out by the Fernmeldetechnisches Zentralamt are published under the title *Technischer Bericht: Deutsche Bundespost, Forschungsinstitut des FTZ* [Technical report: German Postal Service, Research Institute of the Central Telecommunications Office] (Darmstadt, FTZ, 1972–). 20–30 issues with report numeration are published annually.

Bundesminister der Verteidigung [Federal Minister for Defence] (BMVg)

In accordance with article 73, para. 1 of the constitution, the federal government has exclusive jurisdiction in matters of defence. The Bundesminister der Verteidigung thus controls the Bundeswehr [Federal Armed Forces], consisting of the Army (Heer), the Navy (Marine) and the Air Force (Luftwaffe). The ministry's publications on the one hand inform the public of developments concerning the armed forces, and on the other assist the training and information of service personnel. The most important of these publications are:

Ministerialblatt des Bundesministers der Verteidigung [Official gazette of the Federal Minister for Defence] (Cologne, Bundesanzeiger Verlags-GmbH, 1956–). Published usually twice a month

Weissbuch . . . zur Lage und Entwicklung der Bundeswehr [White Book . . . on the situation and development of the Federal Armed Forces] (Bonn, Presse- und Informationsamt der Bundesregierung, 1969–). Biennial; published by the Bundesminister für Verteidigung for the federal government. The title constantly varies slightly; the publication is also known as the *Verteidigungsweissbuch* [Defence White Book]

Jahresbericht der Rüstung [Annual armament report] (Bonn, the Ministry, 1972–). Compiled by the Ministry's Rüstungshauptabteilung [Main Armament Department]; traceable since 1969 under the title *Jahresbericht der Wehrtechnik* [Annual weapons technology report]

Information für die Truppe: Hefte für politische Bildung und innere Führung [Information for the services: pamphlets for political education and moral leadership] (Bonn, Bundesministerium der Verteidigung, Führungsstab der Streitkräfte, 1956–). Monthly

Heer: Truppenzeitschrift des Heeres [Army: magazine for soldiers] (Koblenz, Mönch, 1972–)

Marine: Truppenzeitschrift der Marine [Navy: magazine for sailors] (Koblenz, Mönch, 1974–)

Luftwaffe: Truppenzeitschrift der Luftwaffe [Air Force: magazine for airmen] (Koblenz, Mönch, 1971–)

Truppenpraxis: Zeitschrift für Technik und Ausbildung [Practical information for the services: journal for technology and training] (Darmstadt, Wehr und Wissen, 1957–). Issued in collaboration with the Ministry

Soldat und Technik: Zeitschrift für die technische Ausbildung, Fortbildung und Information in der Bunderwehr [Soldier and technology: journal for technical training, advanced training and information in the Federal Armed Forces] (Frankfurt am Main, Umschau Verlag, 1958–). Issued in collaboration with the Ministry

Schriftenreihe Innere Führung [Moral leadership series] (Bonn, Bundesministerium der Verteidigung, Führungsstab der Streitkräfte, 1967–). Until 1978, published with the sub-series *Ausbildung* [Training], *Politische Bildung* [Political education], *Ausbildungspädagogik* [Training techniques].

The results of military research are made available through the following publications:

Berichte. Sozialwissenschaftliches Institut der Bundeswehr [Reports of the Social Sciences Institute of the Federal Armed Forces] (Munich, 1975–). Issued on behalf of the Ministry

Wehrpsychologische Untersuchungen [Military psychology studies] (Bonn, the Ministry, 1966–). Annual

Forschungsbericht aus der Wehrtechnik [Weapons technology research report] (Bonn, Dokumentationszentrum der Bundeswehr, 1970–). Issued on behalf of the Ministry; the issues have report numeration

BwDOK-Informationen. Sonderheft [BwDOK information: special issue] (Bonn, Informationszentrum der Bundeswehr, 1972–). Issued on behalf of the Ministry; also entitled *BwDOK-Sonderheft* [BwDOK special issue]

Wehrmedizinische Monatsschrift; offizielles Organ des Sanitäts- und Gesundheitswesens der Bundeswehr [Military medical monthly: official organ of the medical and health service of the Federal Armed Forces] (Munich, Lehmann, 1957–). Issued in collaboration with the Ministry.

To undertake research into military history, the Bundesministerium der Verteidigung maintains a Militärgeschichtliches Forschungsamt [Military Historical Research Office] in Freiburg. It publishes the following series:

Beiträge zur Militär- und Kriegsgeschichte: Schriftenreihe des Militärgeschichtlichen Forschungsamtes [Contributions to military and war history: publications series of the Military Historical Research Office] (Stuttgart, Deutsche Verlags-Anstalt, 1960–)

Militärgeschichtliche Mitteilungen [Military historical communications] (Karlsruhe, Braun, 1967–). Biannual

Vorträge zur Militärgeschichte [Lectures on military history] (Herford, Mittler, 1981–)

Militärgeschichte seit 1945 [Military history since 1945] (Boppard am Rhein, Boldt, 1975–). In progress

Wehrwissenschaftliche Forschungen [Military science research] (Boppard am Rhein, Boldt, 1966–)

Einzelschriften zur Militärischen Geschichte des Zweiten Weltkrieges [Monographs on the military history of World War II] (Freiburg im Breisgau, Rombach, 1967–).

Bundesminister für Jugend, Familie, Frauen und Gesundheit [Federal Minister for Youth, the Family, Women and Health] (BMJFG)

According to article 6 of the constitution, married life, the family and children's education in the Federal Republic are 'under the special protection of the state'. Federal and Länder governments each have their own ministries covering these areas. The federal ministry has the additional task of carrying out the government's legal obligations with regard to public health (*see* article 74, para. 19 of the constitution). The ministry's regulations and notices appear in the *Bundesanzeiger* and the *Gemeinsames Ministerialblatt*. Other serial publications include:

Daten des Gesundheitswesens [Public health data] (Stuttgart, Kohlhammer, 1977–)
Schriftenreihe des Bundesministers für Jugend, Familie, Frauen und Gesundheit

[Publications series of the Federal Minister for Youth, the Family, Women and Health] (Stuttgart, Kohlhammer, 1972–)

Forschung und Modellvorhaben des BMJFG [Research and model projects of the BMJFG] (Stuttgart, Kohlhammer, 1969–). Covers the years from 1965; title varies

Dokumentation Gefährdung durch Alkohol, Rauchen, Drogen, Arzneimittel [Documentation on the dangers of alcohol, smoking, drugs and pharmaceuticals] (Bielefeld, Institut für Dokumentation und Information über Sozialmedizin und öffentliches Gesundheitswesen, 1972–). Compiled by the Deutsches Institut für Medizinische Dokumentation und Information [German Institute for Medical Documentation and Information] for the Bundesminister für Jugend, Familie, Frauen und Gesundheit and the Minister für Arbeit, Gesundheit und Soziales des Landes Nordrhein-Westfalen [Minister for Employment, Health and Social Affairs of North Rhine-Westphalia]. 4 issues per year

Ernährungsbericht [Nutrition report] (Frankfurt am Main, Deutsche Gesellschaft für Ernährung, 1969–). Issued by the Deutsche Gesellschaft für Ernährung [German Nutrition Society] on behalf of the Bundesminister für Jugend, Familie, Frauen und Gesundheit and the Bundesminister für Ernährung, Landwirtschaft und Forsten; this appears once in every legislative period of the Bundestag as a report to the Bundestag, and consequently is also an appendix (Anlage) to the *Verhandlungen des Deutschen Bundestages*

Familienbericht: Familie und Sozialisation [Family report: family and socialization] (Bonn, the Ministry, 1968–). Also issued as an appendix to the *Verhandlungen des Deutschen Bundestages*

Informationen des Bundesministeriums für Jugend, Familie, Frauen und Gesundheit [Information from the Federal Ministry for Youth, the Family, Women and Health] (Bonn, the Ministry, Pressereferat). Traceable since 1975; roughly 8 to 10 issues per year

Pressedienst des BMJFG [Press service of the BMJFG] (Bonn, the Ministry, Pressereferat). Traceable since 1980; irregular

Treffpunkt: eine Informationsschrift des BMJFG [Meeting place: an information journal of the BMJFG] (Bonn, the Ministry, 1976–).

The Bundesgesundheitsamt [Federal Health Office] (BGA) in West Berlin, which is subordinate to the Bundesministerium für Jugend, Familie, Frauen und Gesundheit, has the task of monitoring health-related legislation, of carrying out research and providing expert advice in the field of public health. It consists of a Zentralabteilung [Central Divison] and a number of specialized research institutes, each publishing their own reports. The following serials are issued:

Bundesgesundheitsblatt [Federal health gazette] (Cologne, Heymann, 1958–). Fortnightly. Issued by the Bundesgesundheitsamt; imprint varies

Tätigkeitsbericht. Bundesgesundheitsamt [Report of activities. Federal Health Office] (Berlin, the Office). Annual; published by Reimer, Berlin, from 1959 to 1982

BGA-Schriften: Schriftenreihe des Bundesgesundheitsamtes [BGA publications: publications series of the Federal Health Office] (Munich, MMV Medizin Verlag, 1984–). From 1978 to 1983, published by Reimer, Berlin

AMI-Heft [AMI publication] (Berlin, Institut für Arzneimittel, 1985–). Issued by the Institut für Arzneimittel [Pharmaceutical Institute]; continues *AMI-Bericht* [AMI report] (Berlin, Reimer, 1978–1983)

ISH-Heft [ISH publication] (Heuherberg, Institut für Strahlenhygiene, 1983–). Issued by the Institut für Strahlenhygiene [Institute for Radiological Hygiene]; continues *ISH-Bericht* [ISH report] (1981–1983)

MvP-Hefte [MvP publications] (Berlin, Max-von-Pettenkofer-Institut, 1984–). Issued by the Max-von-Pettenkofer-Institut; continues *MvP-Berichte* [MvP reports] (Berlin, Reimer, 1978–82). The Institute conducts research in the fields of toxicology, food chemistry, chemical evaluation and nutritional medicine

RKI-Berichte [RKI reports] (Berlin, Reimer, 1978–). Issued by the Robert-Koch-Institut, which conducts research in virology, bacteriology and immunology

SOZEP-Hefte [SOZEP publications] (Berlin, Institut für Sozialmedizin und Epidemiologie, 1984–). Issued by the Institut für Sozialmedizin und Epidemiologie [Institute for Social Medicine and Epidemiology]; continues *SOZEP-Berichte* [SOZEP reports] (Berlin, Reimer, 1978–1982)

VETMED-Hefte [VETMED publications] (Berlin, Institut für Veterinärmedizin, 1984–). Issued by the Institut für Veterinärmedizin [Institute for Veterinary Medicine]; continues *VETMED-Berichte* [VETMED reports] (Berlin, Reimer, 1978–1983)

WaBoLu-Hefte [WaBoLu publications] (Berlin, Institut für Wasser-, Boden-und Lufthygiene, 1984–). Issued by the Institut für Wasser-, Boden- und Lufthygiene [Institute for Water, Soil and Air Hygiene]; continues *WaBoLu-Berichte* [WaBoLu reports] (Berlin, Reimer, 1978–1983)

ZEBS-Hefte [ZEBS publications] (Berlin, Zentrale Erfassungs- und Bewertungsstelle für Umweltchemikalien, 1984–). Issued by the Zentrale Erfassungs- und Bewertungsstelle für Umweltchemikalien [Central Recording and Evaluation Office for Environmental Chemicals]; continues *ZEBS-Berichte* [ZEBS reports] (Berlin, Reimer, 1978–1983).

Bundesminister für wirtschaftliche Zusammenarbeit [Federal Minister for Economic Cooperation] (BMZ)

The governments of the Federal Republic lay such stress on their relations with the Third World and on the support of developing countries through economic and technical cooperation, that a separate ministry has been created to undertake duties in this area. Its regulations appear in the *Gemeinsames Ministerialblatt*, and it publishes information on the federal government's policy towards developing countries in the following:

Bericht zur Entwicklungspolitik der Bundesregierung [Report on the federal government's development policy] (Bonn, 1973–). Issued by the Bundesminister für wirtschaftliche Zusammenarbeit; also published as an appendix to the *Verhandlungen des Deutschen Bundestages*

Entwicklungspolitik: Jahresbericht [Development policy: annual report] (Bonn, Bundesministerium für wirtschaftliche Zusammenarbeit, 1969–). Covers the years from 1968; the name of the issuing body frequently changes

Informationsdienst Entwicklungspolitik [Development policy information service] (Bonn, Bundesministerium für wirtschaftliche Zusammenarbeit, 1983–). Monthly

Forschungsberichte des Bundesministeriums für wirtschaftliche Zusammenarbeit [Research reports of the Federal Ministry for Economic Cooperation] (Munich, Weltforum Verlag, 1980–)

Wissenschaftliche Schriftenreihe des Bundesministeriums für wirtschaftliche Zusammenarbeit [Research publications series of the Federal Ministry for Economic Cooperation] (Baden-Baden, Nomos Verlagsgesellschaft, 1965–). Initially published by Klett, Stuttgart

Journalisten-Handbuch Entwicklungspolitik [Development policy handbook for journalists] (Bonn, Bundesministerium für wirtschaftliche Zusammenarbeit, 1975–). Annual.

Bundesminister für Raumordnung, Bauwesen und Städtebau [Federal Minister for Regional Planning, Building and Town Planning] (BMBau)

The official announcements of the Ministry appear partly in the *Gemeinsames Ministerialblatt* and partly in the *Ministerialblatt des Bundesministers der Finanzen und des Bundesministers für Wirtschaft* [Ministerial gazette of the Federal Minister of Finance and the Federal Minister for the Economy]. Other serials issued by the Ministry are:

Bundesbaublatt: Zeitschrift für Wohnungswesen, Städtebau, Raumordnung, Baurecht und Bauforschung [Federal construction gazette: journal for housing, town planning, regional policy, construction law and building research] (Wiesbaden, Bauverlag, 1952–). Monthly; issued by the Ministry in collaboration with the principal *Länder* authorities concerned with construction, housing and development

Die Bauverwaltung: vereinigt mit 'Bauamt und Gemeindebau' und 'Baurechtliche Mitteilungen': Organ des Deutschen Verdingungsausschusses für Bauleistungen [Building administration: incorporating 'The surveyor's office and municipal building' and 'construction law information': organ of the German Contracting Committee for Construction Services] (Hanover, Vincentz, 1952–). Monthly

Raumordnungsbericht [Regional policy report] (Bonn, Bundesministerium für Raumordnung, Bauwesen und Städtebau, 1963–). Previously entitled *Raumordnungsbericht der Bundesregierung* [Regional policy report of the Federal government]; also published as an appendix to the *Verhandlungen des Deutschen Bundestages*

Schriftenreihe des Bundesministers für Raumordnung, Bauwesen und Städtebau [Publications series of the Federal Minister for Regional Policy, Building and Town Planning] (Bonn, the Ministry, 1973–). The series is divided into seven sub-series: 01, *Versuchs- und Vergleichsbauten und Demonstrativmassnahmen* [Experimental and comparative buildings and demonstration measures]; 02, *Stadtentwicklung* [Urban development]; 03, *Städtebauliche Forschung* [Town planning research]; 04, *Bau- und Wohnforschung* [Building and housing research]; 05, *Wettbewerbe* [Competitions]; 06, *Raumordnung* [Regional policy]; 07, *Wohnungsmarkt und Wohnungspolitik* [Housing market and housing policy].

The ministry supports the Bundesforschungsanstalt für Landeskunde und

Raumordnung [Federal Research Institute for Area Studies and Regional Policy] (BfLR) at Bonn. The Institute's research results are published in:

Raumforschung und Raumordnung [Regional research and regional policy] (Cologne, Heymann). Currently published six times per year; issued by the Bundesforschungsanstalt and the Akademie für Raumforschung und Landesplanung [Academy for Regional Research and Area Planning], Hanover. Continues a publication of the earlier Institut für Raumforschung [Institute for Regional Research], first issued in 1936

Informationen zur Raumentwicklung [Information on regional development] (Bonn, Bundesforschungsanstalt für Landeskunde und Raumordnung, 1974–). Monthly

BfLR-Mitteilungen: Raumordnung und Städtebau [BfLR publications: regional policy and town planning] (Bonn, the Institute, 1980–). 10 issues per year

Arbeitsbericht [Report of activities] (Bonn, Bundesforschungsanstalt für Landeskunde und Raumordnung). Traceable as an annual publication since 1976

Seminare, Symposien, Arbeitspapiere [Seminars, symposia, working papers] (Bonn, Bundesforschungsanstalt für Landeskunde und Raumordnung, 1981–)

Forschungsdokumentation Raumordnung, Städtebau, Wohnungswesen [Research documentation on regional policy, town planning and housing] (Bonn, Bundesforschungsanstalt für Landeskunde und Raumordnung, 1978-). Annual; issued by the Institute and the Informationszentrum Raum und Bau der Fraunhofer-Gesellschaft [Region and Building Information Centre of the Fraunhofer Society]. From 1968 to 1977, subdivided into *Forschungsdokumentation Stadt- und Regionalforschung* [Research documentation on urban and regional research] and *Dokumentation laufender Forschungsarbeiten zur Raumentwicklung* [Documentation on regional development research work in progress]

Forschungen zur Raumentwicklung [Research in regional development] (Bonn, Bundesforschungsanstalt für Landeskunde und Raumordnung, 1975–). Continues *Mitteilungen des Instituts für Raumforschung* [Publications of the Institute for Regional Research], first published in 1953

Referateblatt zur Raumentwicklung [Papers on regional development] (Bonn, Bundesforschungsanstalt für Landeskunde und Raumordnung, 1969–). Quarterly.

Bundesminister für Innerdeutsche Beziehungen [Federal Minister for Intra-German Relations] (BMB)

The belief, embodied in the preamble to the constitution, that 'the entire German people' should be 'urged to achieve, by free self-determination, the unity and freedom of Germany', obliges the governments of the Federal Republic to do all in their power to maintain the unity of the nation in spite of the partition of Germany after the Second World War. In order to fulfil this obligation, a separate ministry is maintained. The Bundesministerium für Innerdeutsche Beziehungen publishes information on the problems of relations between the Federal Republic and the German Democratic Republic, and on the Intra-German policy of the federal government, and promotes the development of those areas on the border with the GDR. Its regulations appear in the *Gemeinsames Ministerialblatt*. The more important of its serial publications are:

Informationen [Information] (Bonn, Bundesministerium für Innerdeutsche Beziehungen, 1971–). Issued twice monthly by the Ministry, in collaboration with the Gesamtdeutsches Institut [Intra-German Institute] of the Bundesanstalt für Gesamtdeutsche Aufgaben [Federal Institute for Intra-German Affairs]. It has a supplement entitled *Staats- und Parteiapparat der DDR* [State and party apparatus of the GDR], and occasional special supplements are also issued

Jahresbericht [Annual report] (Bonn, Bundesministerium für Innerdeutsche Beziehungen, 1970–). A separately published extract from the *Jahresbericht der Bundesregierung* [Annual report of the federal government]

Bericht der Bundesregierung zur Lage der Nation im geteilten Deutschland [Report of the federal government on the state of the nation in divided Germany] (Bonn, Bundesministerium für Innerdeutsche Beziehungen, 1971–). The report is presented annually to the Bundestag by the Federal Chancellor, and is therefore first published as an appendix to the *Verhandlungen des Deutschen Bundestages*. It is the most important document on the aims and objectives of the government of the day in respect of relations between the two Germanies. From a bibliographical point of view, the report is elusive, as its title constantly changes: the best reference source is the *Parlamentsspiegel* (*see* section 2.2.)

Texte zur Deutschlandpolitik [Texts on Intra-German policy] (Bonn, Deutscher Bundes-Verlag). Issued by the Bundesministerium für Innerdeutsche Beziehungen, in three series: 1 (1966–1973), 2 (1973–1982), 3 (1982–)

Dokumente zur Deutschlandpolitik [Documents on Intra-German policy] (Frankfurt am Main, Metzner). Issued by the Bundesministerium für Innerdeutsche Beziehungen; the official collection has been published since 1961 in five chronologically arranged series

Zahlenspiegel: Bundesrepublik Deutschland, Deutsche Demokratische Republik, ein Vergleich [Mirror of figures: Federal Republic of Germany, German Democratic Republic, a comparison] (Bonn, Bundesministerium für Innerdeutsche Beziehungen, 1970–). New editions appear irregularly.

Bundesminister für Forschung und Technologie [Federal Minister for Research and Technology] (BMFT)

The constitution does not provide for federal legislative competence in the areas of culture, education and science; only with regard to the principles of university education is the federal government empowered to issue regulations (Rahmenvorschriften) in accordance with article 75, para. 1a of the constitution. As however federal governments since the beginning of the 1970s have been particularly concerned to encourage scientific research, two ministries have been allocated responsibilities in this field. The first is the Bundesministerium für Forschung und Technologie. It is principally concerned with the promotion of innovative research. The results of research which it publishes are thus of particular significance for the technological development of the Federal Republic. In addition to the regulations appearing in the *Gemeinsames Ministerialblatt*, the Minister issues the following serials:

Bundesbericht Forschung [Federal research report] (Bonn, Bundesministerium für Forschung und Technologie, Referat Presse und Öffentlichkeitsarbeit, 1975–).

Continues the *Forschungsbericht der Bundesregierung* [Research report of the Federal government], first published in 1966

Faktenbericht . . . zum Bundesbericht Forschung: eine Information des BMFT [Data report for the Federal research report: a bulletin from the BMFT] (Bonn, the Ministry, Referat Presse und Öffentlichkeitsarbeit, 1977–)

Statistische Informationen [Statistical bulletins] (Bonn, Bundesministerium für Forschung und Technologie, 1980–). Continues a publication of the Bundesminister für Bildung und Wissenschaft [Federal Minister for Education and Science] entitled *Ausgaben des Bundes für Wissenschaft, Forschung und Entwicklung* [Federal expenditure on science, research and development], first published in 1970

Jahresbericht [Annual report] (Bonn, Bundesministerium für Forschung und Technologie, 1973–). Often also entitled *BMFT-Jahresbericht* [BMFT annual report]

BMFT-Journal: Mitteilungen aus dem BMFT [BMFT journal: communications from the BMFT] (Bonn, the Ministry, 1983–). Continues *BMFT-Mitteilungen* [BMFT communications], first published in 1974

BMFT-Förderungskatalog [BMFT sponsorship catalogue] (Bonn, the Ministry, 1971–). Annual; originally entitled simply *Förderungskatalog*.

Research results are published in the following series:

Forschungsbericht [Research report] (Bonn, Bundesministerium für Forschung und Technologie, 1971–). Available from the Fachinformationszentrum Energie, Physik, Mathematik [Energy, Physics and Mathematics Information Centre], Eggenstein-Leopoldshafen. Originally issued by the Bundesminister für Bildung und Wissenschaft. The following series are currently published: *Datenverarbeitung* [Data processing] (BMFT-FB-DV); *Humanisierung der Arbeitswelt* [Humanization of the working environment] (BMFT-FB-HA); *Information und Dokumentation* [Information and documentation] (BMFT-FB-ID): *Kernforschung* [Nuclear research] (BMFT-FB-K); *Meeresforschung* [Marine research] (BMFT-FB-M); *Technologische Forschung und Entwicklung* [Technological research and development] (BMFT-FB-T); *Luft- und Raumfahrt* [Air and space travel] (BMFT-FB-W). An annual *Gesamtverzeichnis* [General index] is compiled by the Fachinformationszentrum Energie, Physik, Mathematik; it was previously entitled *Verzeichnis der Forschungsberichte* [Index of research reports]

Reihe Berichte und Dokumentation [Reports and documentation series] (Bonn, Bundesministerium für Forschung und Technologie, 1978–)

Schriftenreihe Humanisierung des Arbeitslebens [Humanization of working life series] (Frankfurt am Main, Campus Verlag, 1981–). Issued by the Bundesministerium für Forschung und Technologie

Schriftenreihe Technologie und Beschäftigung [Technology and occupation series] (Düsseldorf, Econ, 1980–) Issued by the Bundesministerium für Forschung und Technologie

Schriftenreihe Statusberichte [State-of-the-art reports series] (Cologne, Verlag TüV Rheinland, 1978–). Issued by the Bundesministerium für Forschung und Technologie; published in six unnumbered sub-series, each devoted to a particular theme.

Bundesminister für Bildung und Wissenschaft [Federal Minister for Education and Science] (BMBW)

The Bundesministerium für Bildung und Wissenschaft was created in the 1960s from the former Bundesministerium für wissenschaftliche Forschung [Federal Ministry for Scientific Research]. After the creation of a separate Bundesministerium für Forschung und Technologie, which took over many of its serial publications, the Ministry remained responsible only for educational planning and research, educational advancement (Ausbildungsförderung), vocational education and university education. Its regulations appear in the *Gemeinsames Ministerialblatt*; it also publishes the following serials:

> *Informationen, Bildung, Wissenschaft* [Information on education and science] (Bonn, Bundesministerium für Bildung und Wissenschaft, 1970–). Monthly
> *Grund- und Strukturdaten* [Basic and structural data] (Bonn, Bundesministerium für Bildung und Wissenschaft, 1974–). Annual
> *Rahmenplan für den Hochschulbau nach dem Hochschulbauförderungsgesetz* [Framework plan for university construction in accordance with the Law for the promotion of university construction] (Bonn, Bundesministerium für Bildung und Wissenschaft, Planungsausschuss für den Hochschulbau, 1972–). Published annually, with supplements relating to individual Länder.

Following the creation of the Bundesministerium für Forschung und Technologie, the series issued by the Bundesministerium für Bildung und Wissenschaft were rearranged, and some ceased publication. Two series are still published:

> *Bildung, Wissenschaft aktuell* [Education and science today] (Bonn, Bundesministerium für Bildung und Wissenschaft, 1984–)
> *Grundlagen und Perspektiven für Bildung und Wissenschaft* [Foundations and prospects for education and science] (Bonn, Bundesministerium für Bildung und Wissenschaft, 1984–).

Bundesminister für Umwelt, Naturschutz und Reaktorsicherheit [Federal Minister for the Environment, Nature Conservation and Nuclear Safety]

The former responsibilities of the Federal Minister of the Interior for environmental protection, safety of nuclear installations and radiation protection were transferred in June 1986 to this newly established ministry. Its series *Umweltbrief* [Environment letter] is wholly devoted to environment matters, such as pollution damage and reactor safety. It was first published in 1973. A very important agency comes under it.

UMWELTBUNDESAMT [FEDERAL ENVIRONMENT AGENCY] (UBA)

In 1974, an Umweltbundesamt was set up in Berlin to support and advise the Bundesminister des Innern on environmental matters. The published work of this office appears in series entitled *Berichte* [Reports] (1975–), *Materialien* [Data] (1975–)

and *Texte* [Texts] (1981–). One of its main tasks is to make environmental data available in an information and documentation system, *UMPLIS Informations- und Dokumentationssystem Umwelt* [UMPLIS: environment information and documentation system] (Berlin, E. Schmidt Verlag). This serves as source material for other publications, and includes items such as the *Umweltforschungskatalog* [Environment research catalogue] (1981–) and the *Literatur-Informationsdienst Umwelt* [Environment literature information service] (1976–), which is divided into sections on the waste industry, noise abatement and air purification. With the exception of UMPLIS, all publications are available direct from the Umweltbundesamt.

2.4. Other official agencies of the federal government

It is a peculiar feature of the constitutional and administrative organization of the Federal Republic that the term 'official body' should include not only ministries, public authorities and their agencies, but also foundations, institutes and bodies 'in public law' (des öffentlichen rechts). This applies both at the federal and the Länder level.

One important directly-accountable state foundation (bundesunmittelbare Stiftung) is the Stiftung Preussischer Kulturbesitz [Prussian Cultural Foundation] in Berlin (West). This comprises a number of museums and those parts of the former Preussische Staatsbibliothek [Prussian State Library] remaining in the Federal Republic after World War II. Important 'institutes in public law' are the radio broadcasting authorities of the Länder, which are brought together in the Arbeitsgemeinschaft der Rundfunkanstalten [Working Group of Radio Authorities]. Among the 'bodies in public law', some of which operate at the federal level, are the churches, which in the Federal Republic have the privilege of having the contributions of their members collected by the financial authorities by means of a tax.

All these institutions produce a vast quantity of publications, in particular programmes, exhibition catalogues, library catalogues, information documents and documents intended for ecclesiastical use.

A final significant category of publications emanates from the major research institutions (Grossforschungseinrichtungen) which, although they are constituted as private bodies—registered associations (eingetragene Vereine) or limited companies (Gesellschaften mit beschränkter Haftung)—, are for the most part financed from public funds. Since the end of the 1960s, these have developed into a class of their own within the scientific world of the Federal Republic, and represent an intermediate point between university research and industrial research which is carried out for purely commercial ends. There are currently 15 such institutions:

Stiftung Alfred-Wegener-Institut für Polarforschung [Alfred Wegener Institute Foundation for Polar Research] in Bremerhaven
Stiftung Deutsches-Elektronen-Synchrotron [German Electron Synchrotron Foundation] in Hamburg
Deutsche Forschungs- und Versuchsanstalt für Luft- und Raumfahrt e.V. [German Research and Experimentation Institute for Air and Space Travel] in Cologne
Deutsche Gesellschaft für Mineralölwissenschaft und Kohlechemie e.V. [German Society for Mineral Oil Science and Coal Chemistry] in Hamburg
Stiftung Deutsches Krebsforschungszentrum [German Cancer Research Centre Foundation] in Heidelberg

Gesellschaft für Biotechnologische Forschung [Society for Biotechnological Research] in Braunschweig
GKSS-Forschungszentrum GmbH [GKSS Research Centre] in Geesthacht (research in radiation and radiation protection)
Gesellschaft für Mathematik und Datenverarbeitung [Society for Mathematics and Data Processing] in St. Augustin
Gesellschaft für Reaktorsicherheit [Society for Reactor Safety] in Cologne
Gesellschaft für Strahlen- und Umweltforschung m.b.H. [Society for Radiation and Environmental Research] in Neuherberg
Gesellschaft für Schwerionenforschung [Society for Heavy Ion Research] in Darmstadt
Hahn-Meitner-Institut für Kernforschung [Hahn-Meitner Institute for Nuclear Research] in West Berlin
Max-Planck-Institut für Plasmaphysik [Max Planck Institute for Plasma Physics] in Garching, near Munich
Kernforschungsanlage Jülich GmbH [Jülich Nuclear Research Establishment] in Jülich
Kernforschungszentrum Karlsruhe GmbH [Karlsruhe Nuclear Research Centre] in Karlsruhe.

3. MANNER OF PUBLICATION

In the Federal Republic there is no statutory regulation of official publishing, nor a central printing office or state publishing house. The ministries, authorities and institutes are therefore free to publish what they want in the way that they want. The sole condition attaching to publishing derives from a 1977 judgement of the Bundesverfassungsgericht [Federal Constitutional Court], which established that the constitution requires that a basic consent should at all times obtain between citizens and government. The government therefore has a permanent obligation to provide information about its work and its plans: the only prohibition is against electoral advertising on behalf of the governing party. One of the consequences of this freedom is that the government itself decides what it should publish: thus there remains a large number of official documents which, although they are not classified, are restricted to internal departmental use only. The government's obligation to enlist the public's support for their policies leads, on the other hand, to ever more comprehensive publishing activity.

If one applies the IFLA definition of official publications to the Federal Republic and evaluates the *Deutsche Nationalbibliographie* [German national bibliography] in terms of it, one obtains the following result. Of an annual output of approximately 56,000 new publications which are available through the book trade, roughly 18,000 —i.e. one-third—emanate from official bodies. Another 29,000 publications are issued annually outside the book trade, half of them (14,500) by official bodies at federal, Länder or municipal level. Overall, this gives a proportion of about 38% of official publications in the total number of publications issued.

This high proportion, together with the fact that official publications have extraordinarily high print runs, has provoked criticism of the Federal Republic's publishing industry. The industry commissioned an investigation, and in 1984 published the results in a brochure, entitled *Verlegerische Betätigung der öffentlichen*

Hand: Ergebnisse eines Untersuchungsauftrags des Börsenvereins des Deutschen Buchhandels e.V. [Publicly funded publishing activity: results of an investigation commissioned by the German Publishers' Association] (Frankfurt am Main, 1984). An interesting result of this investigation is the finding that scientific literature of various kinds accounts for 45% of all official publishing. Informational and advisory literature represent 23% of the total, statutes and regulations 14%, surveys and catalogues 7%, reports of conferences 6%, and statistics 2%.

It is true that the Federal government maintains a Bundesdruckerei [Federal Printing Office] in Berlin. But the very fact that it is subordinate to the Bundesminister für das Post- und Fernmeldewesen indicates the restricted nature of its functions. It is the state printing office, and thus is principally engaged in performing those tasks which must absolutely be performed by the state, such as the printing of the *Bundesgesetzblatt* and the *Gemeinsames Ministerialblatt*, etc., and of banknotes and postage stamps. In addition, individual federal authorities may place printing orders with the Bundesdruckerei. Even some foreign states place orders with it, on account of its special technical capacity.

The majority of publications issued by the offices and authorities themselves are produced by private printing firms, and frequently distributed directly, as directed by the commissioning body, to other public institutions which then distribute them to the general public. Members of the public may however apply directly to the issuing body, which is often the only source of information as to whether or not the publication in question is available without charge. Occasionally, a 'Kommissionsverlag' will be used: that is, a publishing firm which, for a fee, produces and distributes a publication on behalf of a client. Publications produced by commercial publishers are distributed through normal book trade channels. In such cases, the price will be negotiated between the publisher and the issuing body, and is generally determined by the commercial assessment of the publisher. Sometimes, however, a state subsidy will be used to keep the retail price low.

4. BIBLIOGRAPHIC CONTROL

4.1. Bibliographies of official publications

As the list of official publications which is issued by the Deutsche Bibliothek [German National Library] in Frankfurt am Main begins only in 1957, for the early years of the Federal Republic one must refer to *German Federal Republic: official publications 1949–1957, with inclusion of preceding Zonal official publications: a survey* prepared by James B. Childs (Washington, Library of Congress, Reference Department, Serial Division, 1958) 2 vols. The bibliography is arranged by corporate body, and lists only publications at federal level. Each section begins with a description of the body in question, then lists its serial publications, followed by its monographs. For each serial, the corresponding publications of the German Reich and the zonal governments, which it continues, are indicated. Publications not held by the Library of Congress are marked by an asterisk. The bibliography has no index.

A brief survey of federal publications to 1957 is provided by *Das amtliche Schrifttum der Bundesrepublik* [Official publications of the Federal Republic] 2. Aufl. (Ende März 1957) (Bonn, Deutscher Bundesverlag, 1957). This was issued by the Presse- und Informationsamt der Bundesregierung [Press and Information Office of the Federal government]. It is a short-title bibliography arranged by corporate body, with no index.

For officially published periodicals, one must also refer to the *Deutsche Bibliographie, Zeitschriften. 1945-1952. 1953-1957. Bibliographie der in Deutschland erscheinenden periodischen Veröffentlichungen sowie der deutschsprachigen Periodica Österreichs, der Schweiz und anderer Länder* [German national bibliography, periodicals. 1945-1952. 1953-1957. Bibliography of periodical publications appearing in Germany, as well as the German-language periodicals of Austria, Switzerland and other countries] (Frankfurt am Main: Buchhändlervereinigung, 1958). Compiled by the Deutsche Bibliothek, this is arranged by subject, with indexes of titles, issuing bodies, publishers, corporate bodies and firms, subjects and keywords.

From 1957 to 1982, a separate bibliography of official publications was published, entitled: *Deutsche Bibliographie, Verzeichnis amtlicher Druckschriften: Veröffentlichungen der Behörden, Körperschaften, Anstalten und Stiftungen des öffentlichen Rechts sowie der wichtigsten halbamtlichen Institutionen in der Bundesrepublik Deutschland und im Lande Berlin* [German national bibliography, list of official publications: publications of the authorities, corporate bodies, institutes and foundations in public law, as well as those of the most important semi-official institutions in the German Federal Republic and the Land Berlin] (Frankfurt am Main, Buchhändlervereinigung, 1963-1984). This was compiled and issued by the Deutsche Bibliothek; each issue covered a two-year period. It lists separately the publications of federal, Länder, municipal and Church authorities, each title being entered under the name of the issuing body. There are indexes of authority names, of place names (i.e. of those places where the bodies are located), and a combined author, title and keyword index. There is no subject index.

The *Verzeichnis amtlicher Druckschriften* does not include the following types of publication: maps; exhibition catalogues; official forms; internal documents; publications in which official bodies are involved only as initiators, supporters or sponsors; publications of academies, universities and schools; publications of the lower administrative level; and the publications of Municipalities with less than 100,000 inhabitants. On the other hand, it does include the publications of private organizations which are closely connected with the official domain, such as federations of public-law bodies and regional associations which are constituted as registered associations (eingetragene Vereine). The publications of those bodies not covered by the *Verzeichnis amtlicher Druckschriften* are listed only in the *Deutsche Bibliographie* itself.

The Deutsche Bibliothek has announced that the *Verzeichnis amtlicher Druckschriften* ceased publication with effect from 1984, and thus does not cover publications after 1982. From 1986, those publications which would have been included in the *Verzeichnis* will be identified in the national bibliography by the symbol §.

4.2. The national bibliography

The national bibliography of the Federal Republic is entitled *Deutsche Bibliographie: Amtsblatt der Deutschen Bibliothek* [German national bibliography: official gazette of the German National Library] (Frankfurt am Main, Buchhändler-Vereinigung). It is published in the following way.

A *Wöchentliches Verzeichnis* [Weekly list] is issued in three series: Reihe A,

Erscheinungen des Verlagsbuchhandels [Publications available through the book trade]; Reihe B, *Beilage: Erscheinungen ausserhalb des Verlagsbuchhandels* [Supplement: publications not available through the book trade]; and Reihe C, *Karten* [Maps] (the latter, despite the title, is only issued quarterly). Series A and B use a classified subject arrangement based on the (UDC) Decimal Classfication. They have a separately published index of authors, titles, keywords and subjects, with an ISSN/ISBN index, which cumulates monthly. Series A also has a non-cumulating index of publishers. Series C arranges the maps in an alphabetical sequence, with indexes of publishers, ISSNs and ISBNs, and a combined author, title and keyword index.

The entries in Series A, B and C are combined in a *Halbjahresverzeichnis* [Half-yearly list], which is issued in two parts: Teil 1, *Alphabetisches Titelverzeichnis* [Alphabetical list] and Teil 2, *Schlagwort- und Stichwortregister mit systematischer Übersicht der Schlagwörter* [Subject and keyword index, with a systematic survey of subject headings].

Series A entries cumulate again in a *Fünfjahresverzeichnis* [Five-yearly list], also in two parts: Teil 1, *Alphabetisches Titelverzeichnis* and Teil 2, *Schlagwort- und Stichwortregister*.

University publications are listed in the main bibliography only if they are issued by commercial publishers. The remainder are announced in the monthly *Hochschulschriften-Verzeichnis, Reihe H* [University publications list, Series H]. This is arranged in 65 classes based on the Decimal Classification, with author, title and keyword indexes.

New periodical titles, and changes of titles, which are listed in Series A and B of the *Deutsche Bibliographie*, also appear in the *Zeitschriftenverzeichnis* [Periodicals list]. Issues of this list cover varying periods. It is arranged in 26 subject classes, and has a combined author, title, keyword and subject index in a separate volume.

Non-book materials are covered by the following:

Musiktonträger-Verzeichnis, Reihe T [Music recordings list, Series T]. Monthly, with an annual cumulation. Arranged in 11 categories, with a company index and an index of artists, titles and keywords

Musikalien-Verzeichnis, Reihe M [Sheet music list, Series M]. Monthly, with the same arrangement and indexes as for Series T.

Series A, B, C and H are all available in magnetic-tape form, as is the *Neuerscheinungs-Sofortdienst CIP, Reihe N* [New titles rapid CIP service, Series N].

A microfiche cumulation of Series A, B, C and H is also available, with the title *Mikro-Katalog 1976–1980* [Micro-catalogue 1976–1980]. The main part of this catalogue is arranged by series, year and issue number. The index is a five-year cumulation of the author, title, keyword and subject indexes.

On-line access to the data-base of the Deutsche Bibliothek is described in section 4.4 below.

4.3. Catalogues and lists of publications

Many German libraries' holdings of officially published serials are recorded in the Zeitschriftendatenbank [Periodicals data-base], compiled at the Deutsches Bibliotheksinstitut [German Library Institute] in Berlin. The contents of the data-base are available on microfiche, which are published half-yearly with monthly cumulating supplements. Some 350,000 titles are currently listed.

For publications issued in Bavaria and Lower Saxony, one should also refer to the *Bayerisches Zeitschriftenverzeichnis* [Bavarian periodicals list] (Munich, Bayerische Staatsbibliothek) and the *Niedersächsischer Zeitschriftennachweis* [Lower Saxony periodicals inventory] (Göttingen, Staats- und Universitätsbibliothek, Niedersächsischer Zentralkatalog). Both are available on microfiche.

Official bodies in the Federal Republic seldom issue lists of their own publications; those that are issued are mostly in effect sales catalogues of currently available titles and thus of little bibliographical value. However, the lists prepared by the Statistisches Bundesamt [Federal Statistical Office] and the statistical offices of the Länder are important sources of information which facilitate access to the specialized statistical series.

4.4. Data-bases

Series A, B, C, H and N of the *Deutsche Bibliographie* since 1966 are available on Biblio-Data (Nationalbibliographische Datenbank der Deutschen Bibliothek) [National bibliographic data-base of the German National Library]. This data-base is operated by Informationssystem Karlsruhe [Karlsruhe Information System], part of the Fachinformationssystem Energie, Physik, Mathematik [Energy, Physics and Mathematics Information System] based at Eggenstein-Leopoldshafen. It uses the GRIPS retrieval system.

The Zeitschriftendatenbank [Periodicals data-base], the *Zeitschriftenkatalog der Bayerischen Staatsbibliothek* [Periodicals catalogue of the Bavarian State Library] and the *Niedersächsischer Zeitschriftennachweis* [Lower Saxony periodicals inventory] are available on-line at the Deutsches Bibliotheksinstitut [German Library Institute] in Berlin.

Other data-bases which are devoted to official publications, or which contain a high proportion of officially published material, are:

DIP. Dokumentations- und Informationssystem für Parlamentsmaterialien [Documentation and information system for parliamentary materials] (Bonn, Deutscher Bundestag). Uses the GOLEM retrieval system

GESTA. Stand der Gesetzgebung des Bundes [Current state of Federal legislation] (Bonn, Deutscher Bundestag). Accessible via the teletext (Bildschirmtext) system of Deutsche Bundespost

JURIS. Juristisches Informationssystem des Bundes [Legal information system of the Federal government] (Bonn, Bundesminister der Justiz, Abteilung Z). Uses the GOLEM retrieval system. Coverage: judgements of the Bundesverfassungsgericht [Federal Constitutional Court] and the high courts of the Federal Republic since their inception; legal journal articles since 1977; social and taxation law literature since 1945

POLDOK. Politische Dokumentation [Political documentation] (West Berlin, Freie Universität, Informationssystem Politik und Massenkommunikation). Accessible through the Satz-Rechen-Zentrum Berlin; uses the GOLEM retrieval system

STATIS-BUND. Statistisches Informationssystem des Bundes [Statistical information system of the Federal government] (Wiesbaden, Statistisches Bundesamt). Intermittent coverage of material since 1950

UFORDAT. Umweltforschungsdatenbank [Environmental research data-base]

(West Berlin, Umweltbundesamt). Accessible through Data-Star Marketing, Bracknell, Berks, UK. Uses the BRS/SEARCH retrieval system

ULIDAT. Umweltliteraturdatenbank [Environmental literature data-base] (West Berlin, Umweltbundesamt). Access as for UFORDAT.

Some of these are available in-house only.

5. LIBRARY COLLECTIONS AND AVAILABILITY

5.1. The national library and legal deposit of official publications

In the Federal Republic, there is no national library which both collects copyright copies of the country's publishing output and acquires the most significant foreign publications. The Deutsche Bibliothek [German National Library] in Frankfurt am Main is the central archival library for post-1945 publications from Germany or in the German language, for translations of German works into other languages and for foreign-language works on Germany. It was originally founded in 1952 by the Land of Hesse and the city of Frankfurt am Main, and in 1969 was established as an 'independent federal agency in public law' (bundesunmittelbare Anstalt des öffentlichen Rechts). The two largest archival libraries for German and foreign publications are the Bayerische Staatsbibliothek [Bavarian State Library] in Munich, and the Staatsbibliothek Preussischer Kulturbesitz [State Library of the Prussian Cultural Foundation] in Berlin. The latter is the West German successor to the former Preussische Staatsbibliothek [Prussian State Library], which was split as a result of World War II. The Federal Republic and the German Democratic Republic have as yet been unable to reach agreement on the question of who, from the point of view of international law, is the legal successor to the Prussian cultural estate.

As a consequence of this complicated library structure, combined with the constitutional independence of the Länder in cultural, and therefore also in library, matters, the legal deposit of official publications is also arranged in a fairly complex manner. Paragraph 18, section 3 of the *Gesetz über die Deutsche Bibliothek* [Law on the German National Library]—the statute which regulates the legal deposit of publications in general at the Deutsche Bibliothek—lays down that publications 'of official content' (amtlichen Inhalts) do not fall within the terms of the depository obligation. In order to safeguard the preservation and public accessibility of its publications, however, the Federal government in 1958 issued an instruction that one copy of every publication issued by all federal authorities and departments (including the 'independent federal bodies, institutes and foundations in public law') should be supplied without charge to the Deutsche Bibliothek, the Staatsbibliothek Preussischer Kulturbesitz, the Bayerische Staatsbibliothek and the library of the Bundestag. Exceptions are classified material, offprints without their own title page, patents (which are only available at the Deutsches Patentamt [German Patent Office] in Munich) and forms.

The terms of this arrangement are laid down in the *Erlass der Bundesregierung über die Abgabe amtlicher Drucksachen an öffentliche Bibliotheken* [Federal government decree on the deposit of official publications with public libraries] of 11 May 1958, amended 17 March 1961. (*See* the *Gemeinsames Ministerialblatt*, 1958, pp. 209-210, and 1961, p. 235.) The Länder governments subsequently issued similar regulations.

5.2. Availability

Given this legal situation, one must proceed on the assumption that these four libraries have holdings of federal and Länder official publications which are as nearly complete as possible. The Municipalities, on account of their administrative autonomy, could not be instructed by the Länder to deposit their publications also with the four libraries. They have however been recommended to do so, both in the regulations issued by the various Länder and through a recommendation (dated 30 May 1960) of their parent body, the Deutscher Städtetag [German Municipalities' Federation].

The holdings of the Deutsche Bibliothek are available for use *in situ* by the general public, but are loaned only in cases where the required publication is not held by any other German lending library. The holdings of the library of the Bundestag are not available for loan, and are accessible to the public only exceptionally and subject to special permission.

The Staatsbibliothek Preussischer Kulturbesitz and the Bayerische Staatsbibliothek, on the other hand, are normal lending libraries. The former has moreover a special role in the public provision of official publications: the Deutsche Forschungsgemeinschaft [German Research Association] has assigned it a special collecting priority for parliamentary publications, as it already has old and extensive collections of such material. In addition, the Staatsbibliothek Preussischer Kulturbesitz conducts the international exchange of official publications on behalf of the federal government, through its Abteilung Amtsdruckschriften und Tausch [Official Publications and Exchange Department]. In the context of the supra-regional supply of publications within the Federal Republic, it is therefore the central clearing-house for orders for domestic and foreign official publications.

The libraries of the federal and Länder parliaments and authorities, and the libraries of the high courts, all naturally have particularly large collections of official publications, but none of them is a lending library. Subject-oriented libraries with significant holdings of official publications include the library of the Institut für Weltwirtschaft [World Trade Institute] in Kiel, the Technische Informationsbibliothek [Technical Information Library] in Hanover, and the libraries of the federal and Länder research institutes and the major research institutions (*see* section 2.4 above).

As almost half the Federal Republic's official publications are published by the issuing bodies themselves, and therefore have to be ordered individually, the acquisition of such material is not very popular with libraries in general. University libraries will usually acquire only those items appropriate to the specialisms of the university in question. The public libraries for the most part hold only that material which is made available free of charge by the Bundeszentrale für Politische Bildung [Federal Centre for Political Education] and the corresponding Länder institutions. Only very large public libraries provide public access perhaps to parliamentary publications or statistical reports.

In other countries, the Abteilung Amtsdruckschriften und Tausch [Official Publications and Exchange Section] of the Staatsbibliothek Preussischer Kulturbesitz has exchange arrangements with 30 foreign countries. A list of these appears in the appendix to this chapter. The Library of the Bundestag in Bonn and the Library of the Statistisches Bundesamt in Wiesbaden also have some exchanges.

6. PUBLICATIONS OF THE LÄNDER, DISTRICTS AND MUNICIPALITIES

According to article 28 of the constitution, the constitutional arrangement of the Länder of the Federal Republic must correspond, like that of the nation as a whole, to the principles of a republican, democratic and constitutional state. At all structural levels of government, therefore, there are representative assemblies elected on a basis of universal, direct, free, equal and secret suffrage. The Municipalities must have the right to be themselves responsible for regulating the affairs of the local community. As a result of this constitutional arrangement, the federal administrative structure is repeated at the levels of the Länder, the Districts (Landkreise or Kreise) and the Municipalities (Gemeinden). Each Land, including West Berlin, thus has its own parliamentary publications, official gazettes, governmental and ministerial information gazettes, research institute publications, etc. There is no standardized form of title for the official gazettes, which differ from one Land to another. Bibliographically, these are most easily accessible under the name of the issuing body. The Zeitschriftendatenbank [Periodicals data-base] is the best source of information in this respect (*see* section 4.3 above).

The Länder and the Municipalities are solely responsible for the administration of cultural matters: schools, universities, academies, museums, galleries and libraries are, with very few exceptions, under local rather than national government control. Such institutions are particularly given to producing publications, which helps to explain the high proportion of official publications in the Federal Republic's publishing output as a whole.

The particular form of independence and autonomy enjoyed by the Länder and the Municipalities, and the consequent restriction of the possibilities for central planning, make it necessary for the federal, Länder and municipal authorities to come together in supra-regional committees and commissions for specific planning purposes. This results in the publication of reports of meetings, findings, supporting documents, generated by various conferences and municipal and regional associations, some of which are permanently established. The Kultusministerkonferenz [Conference of Education Ministers] is one such: among other duties, it has the task of elaborating comparable legal provisions for school and university education in the different Länder. (Because of the constitutional rights of the Länder, these provisions can only be classified as 'recommendations'.) Regional associations are principally concerned with large-scale transport planning, regional planning, water supply, electricity supply, and the protection of landscape and environment.

Each Land has its own law of legal deposit and its own regulations on the deposit of official publications: these provide at least for the supply of free copies to the main regional library and often to other libraries also. The Landesbibliothek generally issues a regional bibliography which covers not only the publications produced in the particular Land, but also publications relating to the Land. These regional bibliographies occasionally also contain official publications which have not been deposited with the Deutsche Bibliothek, and which consequently have not been listed in the *Deutsche*

Bibliographie. Most of the bibliographies are considerably in arrears, however. A survey of them is provided by: Oberschelp, Reinhard. *Die Bibliographien zur deutschen Landesgeschichte und Landeskunde* [Bibliographies on German regional history and regional studies] 2. neubearb. Aufl. (Frankfurt am Main: Klostermann, 1977).

The Deutsches Institut für Urbanistik [German Institute for Urban Studies] in Berlin specializes in research into the problems of the Municipalities. The library of the Senat [Senate] of Berlin (West) specializes in the collecting of literature on the Municipalities and on urban studies, and also collects non-conventional materials relating to urban and regional planning.

7. BIBLIOGRAPHY

System of government and political culture

Behn, Hans Ulrich. *Die Bundesrepublik Deutschland: Handbuch zur staatspolitischen Landeskunde*. Munich, Olzog, 1974. (Geschichte und Staat, 173/174.) 297 p.

Böttcher, Winfried. *Zum politischen System der Bundesrepublik Deutschland*. Ein Arbeitsbuch. Baden-Baden, Nomos, 1977. (Sozialwissenschaftliche Arbeitsmaterialien für Schule und Hochschule, 4.) 238 p.

Democracy in Germany: history and perspectives. Rev. ed. Bonn, Press and Information Service of the Federal Government, 1985. 140 p.

Federal Republic of Germany: a country study. Ed. Richard F. Nyrop. Washington, D.C., Government Printing Office, 1983. (Area handbook series.) 445 p.

Handbuch des politischen Systems der Bundesrepublik Deutschland. Ed. Kurt Sontheimer and Hans H. Röhrig. Munich, Piper, 1977. 761 p.

Handwörterbuch zur politischen Kultur der Bundesrepublik Deutschland: ein Lehr- und Nachschlagewerk. Opladen, Westdeutscher Verlag, 1981. (Studienbücher zur Sozialwissenschaft, 45.) 557 p.

Kistler, Helmut. *Die Bundesrepublik Deutschland: Vorgeschichte und Geschichte 1945-1983*. Bonn, Bundeszentrale für Politische Bildung, 1985. (Schriftenreihe der Bundeszentrale für Politische Bildung, 229.) 448 p.

Pilz, Frank. *Einführung in das politische System der Bundesrepublik Deutschland*. Staatliche, wirtschaftliche und soziale Strukturen und Prozesse. Munich, Beck, 1977. 366 p.

Ploetz, Die Bundesrepublik Deutschland. Daten, fakten, analysen. Freiburg, Ploetz, 1984. 247 p.

Sontheimer, Kurt. *Grundzüge des politischen Systems der Bundesrepublik Deutschland*. 6th ed. Munich, Piper, 1977. 272 p.

Administration

Ämter und Organisationen der Bundesrepublik Deutschland. Dusseldorf, Droste. Each volume is devoted to a particular institution: 63 volumes published to date.

Handbuch für die öffentliche Verwaltung. Einführung in ihre rechtlichen und praktischen Grundlagen. 2 vols. Neuwied, Luchterhand, 1984. 1178, 700 p.

Öffentliche Verwaltung in der Bundesrepublik Deutschland. Baden-Baden, Nomos, 1981. 452 p.

Verwaltungslexikon. Ed. Peter Eichborn. Baden-Baden, Nomos, 1985. 1079 p.

Reference works

Bund transparent. Parlament, Regierung, Bundesbehörden: Organisationen, Gremien, Anschriften, Namen. 2nd rev. ed. Bad Honnef, Bock, 1985. 512 p.

Die Bundesrepublik Deutschland. Staatshandbuch. Cologne, Heymann. Published in 13 parts, covering the federal government, public associations and other institutions, and the governments of the Länder and West Berlin.

Handbuch politischer Institutionen und Organisationen. 1945-1949. Ed. Heinrich Potthoff in collaboration with Rüdiger Wenzel. Düsseldorf, Droste, 1983. (Handbücher zur Geschichte des Parlamentarismus und der politischen Parteien, 1.) 474 p.

Die nicht-ministerielle Bundesverwaltung. Bonn, Bundesministerium des Innern, 1981.

Taschenbuch des öffentlichen Lebens. Bundesrepublik Deutschland und Organisationen der Europäischen Gemeinschaften. Ed. Albert Oeckl. Bonn, Festland Verlag. Annual.

Official publications

Blissenbach, Dieter. Besonderheiten bei der Erwerbung und Bearbeitung von Amtlichen Druckschriften (Bundesrepublik Deutschland und Europäische Gemeinschaft). *Arbeitschilfen für Spezialbibliotheken, 1. Erwerbung.* Ed. Robert Funk. Berlin. Deutsches Bibliotheksinstitut, 1983 (DBI-materialien, 25), pp. 141-152.

Detemple, Siegfried and Stauch, Anita. Amtliche Druckschriften. *Arbeitschilfen für Spezialbibliotheken, 2. Literaturversorgung* (Benutzung). Ed. Robert Funk. Deutsches Bibliotheksinstitut, 1984. (DBI-materialien, 38.) pp. 187-193.

Detemple, Siegfried. Fünfundzwanzig Jahre internationaler amtlicher Schriftentausch an der Staatsbibliothek Preussischer Kulturbesitz. *Jahrbuch Preussischer Kulturbesitz,* XVIII, 1981. Berlin, Mann, 1982. pp. 103-119.

——. Official publishing in the Federal Republic of Germany. A general overview. Paper presented to the IFLA Congress, Munich, 1983. 6 p.

Kaspers, Heinrich. *Die Abgabe amtlicher Drucksachen an die öffentlichen Bibliotheken.* Das Pflichtexemplarrecht für amtliche Druckschriften in Deutschland von seinen Anfängen bis zum gegenwärtigen Stand. Cologne, Greve, 1954. (Arbeiten aus dem Bibliothekar-Lehrinstitut des Landes Nordrhein-Westfalen, 4.) 167 p.

Lansky, Ralph. Die pflichtexemplar- und amtsdrucksachenberechtigten Bibliotheken in der Bundesrepublik Deutschland und in Berlin (West). *Zeitschrift für Bibliothekswesen und Bibliographie,* 1975, pp. 136-142, 464-465; *Mitteilungen der Arbeitsgemeinschaft der Parlaments- und Behördenbibliotheken,* 39, 1975, pp. 47-54.

Stauch, Anita. Amtsdruckschriften in Bibliotheken. *Der Archivar,* 1978, pp. 47-49.

Verlegerische Betätigung der öffentlichen Hand. Ergebnisse eines Untersuchungsauftrages des Börsenvereins des Deutschen Buchhandels. Frankfurt am Main, Börsenverein, 1984. 76 p.

Zehrer, Max. Behandlung von Amtsdruckschriften. *Arbeitsgemeinschaft der Parlaments- und Behördenbibliotheken*. Arbeitshefte, 21. 1967, pp. 34–47.

Zoller-Phillips, Georgette. Official publications of the German Federal Republic. *Aslib proceedings*, 26 (7/8), July/Aug. 1974, pp. 296–303.

APPENDIX

The following is a list of the international exchange partners of the Staatsbibliothek Preussischer Kulturbesitz:

AUSTRALIA
National Library, Canberra

AUSTRIA
Parlamentsdirektion, Vienna

BELGIUM
Bibliothèque Royale Albert 1, Brussels

BULGARIA
Cyril and Methodius National Library, Sofia

CANADA
National Library, Ottawa

CHINA, REPUBLIC OF
National Central Library, Taipei

DENMARK
Danish International Exchange Institute, Copenhagen

FINLAND
Eduskunnan Kirjasto, Helsinki

FRANCE
Bibliothèque Nationale, Paris

HUNGARY
Országos Széchényi Könyvtár, Budapest

INDIA
Lok Sabha Library, Delhi

ISRAEL
State Archives, Jerusalem

ITALY
Library, Camera dei Deputati, Rome

IVORY COAST
Bibliothèque Nationale, Abidjan

APPENDIX

JAPAN
National Diet Library, Tokyo

KOREA, SOUTH
National Assembly Library, Seoul

LUXEMBOURG
Bibliothèque Nationale, Luxembourg

NETHERLANDS
Koninklijke Bibliotheek, The Hague

NORWAY
Universitetsbiblioteket, Oslo

POLAND
Biblioteka Narodowa, Warsaw

PORTUGAL
Biblioteca Nacional, Lisbon

ROMANIA
Biblioteca Centrală de Stat, Bucharest

SOUTH AFRICA
State Library, Pretoria

SWEDEN
Riksdagsbiblioteket, Stockholm

SWITZERLAND
Eidgenössische Parlaments- und Zentralbibliothek, Berne

TANZANIA
University of Dar es Salaam

USSR
Lenin State Library, Moscow

UNITED KINGDOM
British Library, London

USA
Library of Congress, Washington, DC

YUGOSLAVIA
Jugoslavenski Bibliografski Institut, Belgrade

Greece

PANAYOTIS PH. CHRISTOPOULOS

1. INTRODUCTION

According to the constitution of 1975 currently in force (with a few amendments made in 1986), Greece is a parliamentary democracy with an elected president. The prevailing religion is the Eastern Orthodox Church. Legislative power is exercised by Parliament, the executive by the President of the Republic and the judicial power by the law courts. The foundation of the state is popular sovereignty. All forms of authority have their source in the people, 'exist for the nation and are practised as defined by the constitution'. Judicial decisions are also enforced in the name of the Greek people.

The President of the Republic is the regulator of the state and is elected by the Βουλή [Parliament] in a special procedure for a period of five years. The unicameral Parliament comprises 300 members and is elected in a direct, universal ballot for four years. The government must obtain the confidence of the Parliament. The clear distinction of powers into legislative, judicial and executive is theoretical and holds true only up to a point, because the two former have become weaker in comparison with the executive.

The system provides for the functioning of four higher courts. The Αρειος Παγος [Areopagus] is the supreme court of civil and penal law; the Συμβούλιον της Επικρατείας [Council of State] is the highest administrative court; the Ελεγκτικόν Συνέδριον [Audit Office Court] is the highest court controlling public finance in general as well as related matters; and the Ανώτατον Ειδικόν Δικαστήριον [Highest Special Court] is responsible for the resolution of conflicts between decisions of the other higher courts and the adjudication of certain other special cases.

The Church is autonomous, coming under the Oecumenical Patriarchate of Constantinople in dogmatic and spiritual matters. Administrative matters are handled by the Holy Synod, based on the Charter of the Church. Administration is organized according to a decentralized system.

The local authorities, the Municipalities, are elected in secret universal ballot and have administrative autonomy. The state supervises them through the Prefects of the 52 Prefectures into which the country is divided. The Prefects are appointed by the government. An autonomous sector of the country is Mount Athos, which is spiritually under the jurisdiction of the Patriarch of Constantinople and is governed administratively by the Holy Community. This community is composed of representatives of the 20 sovereign monasteries. This special status is defined by the Charter of Mount Athos, which is compiled by the 20 sacred monasteries and is ratified by the Patriarchate and the Greek Parliament.

A large part of state activity is conducted through private enterprise. The idea arose partly from the effort to create flexible units free from the retarding obstacles of bureaucracy. Nowadays, the state controls banks other than the note-issuing Τράπεζα της Ελλάδος [Bank of Greece], as well as businesses in primary industry, secondary industry and the service industries. Some of these units came to be taken over by the state for empirical and historical reasons. For example, the Εθνική Τράπεζα [National Bank] was formerly a note-issuing bank and the state administers it indirectly through bequests which account for the larger part of its shares. Other businesses came into the hands of the state as it carried out its economic policy or for reasons of social or national security. Finally, some businesses which are very important for the national economy were either created by the state from the beginning as joint stock companies (such as the Δημόσια Επιχείρηση Ηλεκτρισμού [Public Power Corporation]) or on other occasions by transforming state services (for example, the Οργανισμός Τηλεπικοινωνιών Ελλάδος [Telecommunications Organization of Greece] or the Ελληνικά Ταχυδρομεία [Greek Postal Services]).

Greece does not have a published manual of government organization.

In the light of this administrative structure and economy, one must look at Greek official publications. In the strict sense, official publications are only the Εφημερίς της Κυβερνήσεως [Government gazette] and the Πρακτικά [Parliamentary minutes], which are printed by the Εθνικόν Τυπογραφείον [National Printing House], as well as a small number of other strictly governmental publications. However, in a broader sense, governmental publications are also those of various services, organizations and businesses which depend directly or indirectly on the government and are supported by the government and serve the goals of the state. There is no generally accepted definition of official publications in Greece. In this chapter, an attempt will be made to provide a simple record of the most important authorities and publications.

2. PRINCIPAL PUBLICATIONS OF CENTRAL GOVERNMENT

2.1. Legislation

The establishment of the present Greek state is a result of the 1821 national revolution. The publication of legislative acts during the revolutionary period was recorded successively in the official newspapers Ελληνική Σάλπιγξ [Greek trumpet], Ο Φίλος του Νόμου [Friend of the law], Γενική Εφημερίς της Ελλάδος [General journal of Greece], Εθνική Εφημερίς [National gazette], and Εφημερίς της Κυβερνήσεως [Government gazette]. The latter has been the definitive title since 1833.[1] Later on, it became necessary to divide the Gazette into several parts, published in parallel series. Each part contains a specific kind of information. Today the Government gazette is issued at regular intervals in the following separate fascicles:

Τεῦχος Πρῶτον [Fascicle one]. In addition to actual laws, this also contains constitutional acts, legislative decrees, international agreements and certain acts of the executive power, such as the appointment of members of the government. It also contains resolutions of the national assemblies.

Τεῦχος Δεύτερον [Fascicle two]. This contains regulatory decisions, official regulations of the state services and their subordinate organizations, and police regulations

Τεῦχος Τρίτον [Fascicle three]. This is reserved for decrees and acts of ministers and other executive authorities concerning appointments, transfers and other changes of government personnel, recorded in brief

Τεῦχος Τέταρτον [Fascicle four]. This publishes the acts of compulsory expropriations and alterations in public property and those creating industrial zones and public forests or concerning town planning

Τεῦχος Παράρτημα [Supplementary fascicle]. This contains everything concerning teachers in institutions of higher education, and some other acts

Δελτίον Ανωνύμων Εταιρειών και Εταιρειών Περιωριμένης Ευθύνης [Bulletin of joint stock companies and limited liability companies]. This contains the information that must by law be published by these companies

Δελτίον Νομικών Προσώπων Δημοσίου Δικαίου [Bulletin of public corporate bodies]. This contains acts and publications concerning these bodies

Δελτίον Εμπορικής και Βιομηχανικής Ιδιοκτησίας [Bulletin of commercial and industrial property]. The contents of this fascicle are self-evident.

Over one-and-a-half centuries, many general and special compilations of laws, classified and indexed, have appeared. The most comprehensive general codification of legislation is the one completed by the editors of the judicial review Θέμις [Themis] for the period from 1821 to 1933. This has been updated regularly since then by the publication of supplements.[2] A systematic overview of the laws in force at any given moment, with detailed subject-indexing, is offered by Raptarchis' Codex.[3]

2.2. Legislative proceedings, debates and documents

The Βουλή [Parliament] is the sole legislative body in Greece, though there have been brief periods (1844-1862 and 1927-1935) when a second, upper chamber, the Γερουσία [Senate] was provided for by the constitutions then in force. The legislative and constitutional texts and documents of the war for independence and of the period of uncertainty which followed have been published by Mamoukas[4] and in the Αρχεία της Ελληνικής Παλιγγενεσίας [Archives of the Greek revival], published by the Parliament in 14 volumes (1857-1981).

The Επίσημα Πρακτικά της Βουλής [Official minutes of Parliament] have been published since 1844. They present parliamentary proceedings in summary form. A parallel series, the Εφημερίς των Συζητήσεων της Βουλής [Journal of Parliamentary debates], started in 1863, and records the debates *in extenso*. Since 1974, the two series have been combined in one, known as the Πρακτικά [Minutes]. It contains the proceedings *in extenso* so that in practice the series of summarized minutes has been abolished. Bills in their final form as approved are included in the Πρακτικά. Documents relevant to the debates and draft bills have been published since 1909 in the Παράρτημα Εφημερίδος της Βουλής [Supplement to the parliamentary journal], which in 1912 was renamed the Αρχείον της Βουλής [Archives of Parliament].

The minutes of the national assemblies (specially elected legislative bodies set up for particular purposes) have also been published in summary form and *in extenso* from 1843 to 1950. The Επιτροπή Νομοθετικής Εξουσιοδοτήσεως [Committee on the Authority for Legislation] functioned from 1946 to 1949 and published only summary minutes; however, the Πρακτικά της Ειδικής Επιτροπής του άρθρου 35 του Συντάγματος [Minutes of the Special Committee on article 35 of the constitution], 1951-1967, were printed in both forms.

The Γερουσία [Senate] published its minutes in summary form from 1845 to 1862 and both synoptically and *in extenso* from 1929 to 1935. During the second period, the Αρχείον Γερουσίας [Archive of the Senate] was published, with contents similar to the equivalent title of the Βουλή [Parliament].

Parliament has also published in special form the minutes of the sessions of special committees for the revision of the constitution (1921-1974) and monographs containing material relevant to its work such as Κρίσιμα κείμενα της πολιτικής ζωής της Ελλάδος *1843-1967* [Significant texts of political life in Greece, 1843-1967], Athens, 1976.[5] Other publications have also been brought out by the Parliament Library.[6]

At the end of each parliamentary session, the various legislative proceedings mentioned here include indexes, which vary in form. In recent years, analytical indexes have been compiled for all parliamentary texts of both Parliament and Senate for the periods 1843-1862, 1862-1909, 1909-1936 and 1946-1967. Multi-volume indexes for the two latter periods have already been printed under the title Ευρετήριον Συζητήσεων του Κοινοβουλίου [Index of parliamentary debates][7] and it is probable that all this material will be put on the computer data-base of the Parliament.

2.3. Publications of the executive agencies of government

Justice

The Υπουργείον Δικαιοσύνης [Ministry of Justice] has published Διαχείρισις της πολιτικής δικαιοσύνης [Management of political justice] and Διαχείρισις της ποινικής δικαιοσύνης [Management of penal justice] since 1857, and the Επετηρίς του Υπουργείου Δικαιοσύνης [Yearbook of the Ministry of Justice] since 1911, together with numerous special collections of laws and codices.

The Αποφάσεις του Αρείου Πάγου [Decisions of the Supreme Court] have been published in self-contained volumes every year since 1840, and the Αποφάσεις του Συμβουλίου της Επικρατείας [Decisions of the Council of State] since 1929. The Ευρετήριον καθ' ύλην των αποφάσεων του Συμβουλίου της Επικρατείας [Subject-index of the decisions of the Council of State] has been published since 1976.

The principal privately-published manuals of jurisprudence are:

Thiveos, P. and Capodistrias, I. Γενικόν Ευρετήριον Νομολογίας *1834-1936* [General index of jurisprudence, 1834-1936], 6 volumes, with supplements up to the present day.

Bacoulas, D. H νομολογία του Αρείου Πάγου [Jurisprudence of the Supreme Court], vol. 1, 1947, etc.

Αρχείον Νομολογίας [Archives of jurisprudence], a monthly review covering public and private law, vol. 1, 1950, etc.

Publications of state institutions are the *Revue héllénique de droit international* [Greek review of international law], vol. 1, 1948, etc., and the Επιθεώρησις Δικαίου του Δημοσίου [State law review], vol. 1, 1984, etc.

The Ινστιτούτο Διενούς Δημοσίου Δικαίου και Διεθνών Σχέσεων [Institute of Public International Law and International Relations] in Salonica publishes the Ελληνική Επιθεώρηση Διεθνών Σχέσεων [Greek review of international relations], Θησαυρός Ακροάσεων [Thesaurus of court hearings], Διεθνής Φιλία [International friendship], and many monographs.

Administration

The Υπουργείον Εσωτερικών [Ministry of the Interior] has published an Επετηρίς [Annual] since 1920 and a Δελτίον Νομοθεσίας [Bulletin of legislation] since 1937. It has also published many collections of special laws and police regulations, popular works, and statistics, particularly demographic and electoral statistics.

As of 1955, all the statistical services were unified in the Εθνική Στατιστική Υπηρεσία της Ελλάδος [National Statistical Service of Greece], which publishes a Μηνιαίον Στατιστικόν Δελτίον [Monthly statistical bulletin], a Στατιστική Επετηρίς [Statistical yearbook of Greece], and a Συνοπτική Στατιστική Επετηρίς [Concise yearbook], in addition to the detailed and analytical statistics covering all aspects of national activity.[8]

Since 1960, the Εθνικόν Κέντρον Κοινωνικών Ερευνών [National Centre for Social Research] has produced publications of wider scope. Besides its periodical Επιθεώρηση Κοινωνικών Ερευνών [Review of social research], vol. 1, 1969, etc., and it has published many monographs on sociology, social anthropology and anthropological geography, demography and population movements, political science, social and economic history, the theory and methods of the social sciences, and so on.[9]

In the local government sector, mention should be made of the Επιθεώρησις της Τοπικής Αυτοδιοικήσεως [Review of local government], vol. 1, 1922, etc., and Στοιχεία συστάσεως και εξελίξεως Δήμων και Κοινοτήτων [Data concerning the foundation and development of the Municipalities], in 50 volumes, 1961/62, one volume for each Prefecture.

The Υπουργείον Προεδρίας της Κυβερνήσεως [Ministry of the Presidency] published the Δελτίον Δημοσίας Διοικήσεως [Bulletin of public administration] from 1976 to 1980 and the General Secretariat of the Press has published information bulletins in many languages, as well as numerous popular works and catalogues of Greek magazines and newspapers in circulation.

Education, culture and religion

The Υπουργείον Εθνικής Παιδείας και Θρησκευμάτων [Ministry of Education and Religion] has published many books for the practical purposes of education and special collections of laws. Since 1900 it has issued an Επετηρίς [Annual].

The Οργανισμός Εκδόσεως Διδακτικών Βιβλίων [Organization for the Publication of Educational Books] has been publishing for half a century, mainly for the first two stages of education, free textbooks and other publications.

The Ακαδημία Αθηνών [Academy of Athens] has published its Πρακτικά [Proceedings] since 1926, and issues some major series, such as Πραγματείαι της Ακαδημίας Αθηνών [Treatises of the Academy of Athens], Εχληνική Βιβλιοθήκη [Greek library], and Μνημεία της Ελληνικής Ιστορίας [Monuments of Greek history]. The research centres of the Academy publish series of publications and the Ιστορικόν Λεξικόν της Νέας Ελληνικής Γλώσσης [Historical dictionary of the modern Greek language]. They also publish specialized periodicals, such as the Λεξικογραφικόν Δελτίον [Lexicographical bulletin], 1939–; Επετηρίς του Κέντρου Ερεύνης της Ελληνικής Λαογραφίας [Annual of the Research Centre for Greek Folklore] (formerly Επετηρίς του Λαογραφικού Αρχείου [Annual of the folklore archives]), 1939–; Μεσαιωνικά και νέα ελληνικά [Mediaeval and modern Greek] (formerly Επετηρίς του Μεσαιωνικού Αρχείου 1939–; Επετηρίς του Κέντρου Ερεύνης του Ελληνικού Δικαίου [Annual of the Research Centre for Greek law] (formerly Επετηρίς του αρχείου ιστορίας του ελληνικού δικαίου [Annual of the archives of the history of Greek law]), 1948–; Φιλοσοφία Επετηρίς του Κέντρου Ερεύνης της Ελληνικής Φιλοσοφίας [Philosophy Yearbook of the Research Centre for Greek Philosophy], 1971–; and the Κέντρον Ερευνών Αστρονομίας και Εφηρμοσμένων Μαθηματικών [Research Centre for Astronomy and Applied Mathematics] has published an *Annual report* since 1960 and *Contributions from the Research Centre for Astronomy and Applied Mathematics*, series I (Astronomy) since 1959.[10]

The Αρχαιολογική Εταιρεία [Archaeological Society] is the main body for scientific research in the area of archaeology. Since 1837, it has published the periodicals Αρχαιολογική Εφημερίς [Journal of Archaeology] and Πρακτικά Αρχαιολογικής Εταιρείας [Proceedings of the Archaeological Society], and since 1954 Το Έργον της Αρχαιολογικής Εταιρείας [Work of the Archaeological Society], and the series Βιβλιοθήκη της εν Αθήναις Αρχαιολογικής Εταιρείας [Library of the Athens Archaeological Society], as well as original monographs, doctoral dissertations and proceedings of international conferences, Αρχαίοι Τόποι και Μουσεία της Ελλάδος [Ancient places and museums of Greece], and other works.[11]

Since 1915, the Archaeological Service has published its main periodical Αρχαιολογικόν Δελτίον [Archaeological bulletin] and a parallel series of dissertations and monographs, and since 1968 it has issued the Αρχαιολογικά Ανάλεκτα εξ Αθηνών [Athens annals of Archaeology] and other publications.

The universities and the independent schools at university level publish scholarly periodicals, series of monographs, doctoral dissertations and essays, administrative yearbooks and calendars.[12] Manuals for students are published by private publishers with a subsidy from the state, and are distributed free of charge. Detailed reference to these university publications would make this list disproportionately long.

The Εθνικό Ίδρυμα Ερευνών [National Research Institute] is productive in research and publishing. The Κέντρο Νεοελληνικών Ερευνών [Modern Greek Research Centre] has numerous publications with special emphasis on bibliographic manuals and the special series Τετράδια Εργασίας [Work notebooks].[13] Since 1966, the Κέντρον Βυζαντινών Ερευνών [Centre for Byzantine Research] has been publishing the periodical Σύμμεικτα [Miscellaneous] and other monographs.[14]

The Γενικά Αρχεία του Κράτους [General state archives] have published a series of monographs with historical texts and documents with indexes.

Since 1951, the Ίδρυμα Κρατικών Υποτροφιών [State Scholarships Foundation] has been publishing an Επετηρίς [Yearbook].

In the cultural field, certain state banks have very important work to present. The Μορφωτικό Ίδρυμα Εθνικής Τραπέζης [Cultural Foundation of the National Bank], with its numerous publications, covers almost all the branches of literature, art and economic history. On the other hand, the Ίδρυμα Έρευνας και Παιδείας της Εμπορικής Τραπεζας [Research and Educational Institute of the Commercial Bank of Greece] is limited to the field of art and archaeology.

There are a number of foundations which function as societies, but which are financially supported by the state. They accomplish admirable work, by publishing high quality scholarly periodicals and series of monographs. Mention should be made here of a characteristic sample of foundations, because there are many of them and they are prolific:

Κέντρο Μικρασιατικών Σπουδών [Centre for Asia Minor Studies]
Ίδρυμα Μελετών Χερσονήσου του Αίμου [Institute of Balkan Studies]
Κέντρο Σπουδών Νοτιοανατολικής Ευρώπης [Centre for Southeast European Studies]
Εταιρεία Μακεδονικών Σπουδών [Society for Macedonian Studies]
Εταιρεία Βυζαντινών Σπουδών [Society for Byzantine Studies]
Η εν Αθήναις Επιστημονική Εταιρεία [The Athens Scientific Society]
Ιστορική και Εθνολογική Εταιρεία της Ελλάδος [Greek Historical and Ethnological Society]
Επιτροπή Ποντιακών Μελετών [Committee for Pontos Studies]
Εταιρεία Ευβοϊκών Σπουδών [Society for Euboean Studies]
Εταιρεία Στερεοελλαδικών Μελετών [Society for Studies on Central Greece]
Εταιρεία Πελοποννησιακών Σπουδών [Society for Peloponnesian Studies]
Εταιρεία Ηπειρωτικών Μελετών [Society for Studies on Epirus]
Χριστιανική Αρχαιολογική Εταιρεία [Christian Archaeological Society]
Ελληνική Λαογραφική Εταιρεία [Greek Folklore Society]
Ιστορική και Λαογραφική Εταιρεία των Θεσσαλών [Historical and Folklore Society of Thessaly]
Εταιρεία Θρακικών Μελετών [Society for Studies on Thrace]
Εταιρεία Κυκλαδικών Μελετών [Society for Studies on the Cyclades]
Εταιρεία Λακωνικών Σπουδών [Society for Studies on Laconia]
Εταιρεία Λογοτεχνικού και Ιστορικού Αρχείου [Society of a Literary and Historical Archive].

Particularly significant is the scholarly and publishing activity of the Ελληνικόν Ινστιτούτον Βυζαντινών και Μεταβυζαντινών Σπουδών [Greek Institute for Byzantine and Post-Byzantine Studies]. Since 1962 in Venice, it has published the periodical Θησαυρίσματα [Accumulated treasures] and a series of important monographs.

The Εκκλησία της Ελλάδος [Orthodox Greek Church] has been publishing since 1922 the periodicals Εκκλησία [Church] and the strictly scholarly Θεολογία [Theology]. As a supplement to the latter, since 1977 it has been publishing the extraordinarily comprehensive Ελληνική Θεολογική Βιβλιογραφία [Greek theological bibliography]. Furthermore, since 1924, it has been publishing the Ημερολόγιον της Εκκλησίας της Ελλάδος [Calendar of the Greek church], which has been modelled on a functional and administrative yearbook, not only for the Greek church, but also for Orthodoxy in general. As a supplement to Εκκλησία [Church], since 1952 it has also published the periodical Εφημέριος [Parish priest]. Since 1976, the bi-monthly newspaper Εκκλησιαστική Αλήθεια [Ecclesiastical truth] has been published. Among the ecclesiastical foundations, the most important to note are as follows. The Αποστολική Διακονία [Apostolic Ministration] publishes very many books ranging from liturgical, scholarly and literary to popular, children's and music titles. It also publishes the missionary quarterly magazine Πάντα τα έθνη [All the nations], as well as records and tapes of ecclesiastical music and the important series of the Πατρολογία (Works of the fathers of the church) (already 65 volumes). The Ίδρυμα Βυζαντινής Μουσικολογίας [Institute of Byzantine Musicology] publishes analytical catalogues of the musical manuscripts of Mount Athos, as well as the series Βυζαντινοί και Μεταβυζαντινοί Μελουργοί [Byzantine and Post-Byzantine Composers of Melody] on records and texts and other related studies.

In the field of theological scholarship, there is an impressively vigorous activity on the part of the Πατριαρχικόν Ίδρυμα Πατερικών Μελετών [Patriarchal Foundation for Patristic Studies], which has its headquarters in Salonica. Since 1969, it has been publishing the periodical Κληρονομία [Heritage], the series of treatises Ανάλεκτα Βλατάδων [Annals of the Vlatádes], special scholarly handbooks of Christian history of literature, theological essays, theological studies, and catalogues of Greek manuscripts of Mount Athos. It is re-printing the valuable periodical of the Oecumenical Patriarchate of Constantinople Εκκλησιαστική Αλήθεια [Ecclesiastical truth], 47 volumes, 1880-1923.

Most of the metropolises in Greece publish popular magazines, which sometimes also print scholarly material. Obviously, it is not possible to mention the names of all these periodicals here.

Finally, in recent years, Mount Sinai has been publishing the series Εκδόσεις Ιεράς Μονής του Θεοβαδίστου Όρους Σινά [Publications of the Sacred Monastery of Mount Sinai]. This includes new essays about the Monastery in the renowned desert, or reprints of old works which are hard to find on the same subject.

Economy

In the sector of primary production (agriculture, forestry, livestock, fishing) the Υπουργείον Παιδείας [Ministry of Agriculture] has published many practical manuals for its personnel and for the public. Since 1901, it has published the Γεωργικόν Δελτίον [Agricultural bulletin]. However, since that date, related periodicals (both scientific and popular) have been multiplying. These cover only certain activities or one important product. Such publications come not only from central services, but also from autonomous organizations, such as the Οργανισμός Βάμβακος [Cotton Organization], the Ινστιτούτο Δασικών Ερευνών [Institute for Forestry Research], the Εθνικός Οργανισμός Καπνού [National Organization for Tobacco], the Ινστιτούτο Ωκεανογραφικών και Αλιευτικών Ερευνών [Institute for Oceanographic and Fishery Research], the Ινστιτούτο Γεωπονικών Ερευνών [Institute for Agricultural Sciences], the Ινστιτούτο Γεωλογικών και Μεταλλευτικών Ερευνών [Institute of Mineral and Geology Exploration], the Ινστιτούτο Αμπέλου [Institute for Vineyards], the Ινστιτούτο Δενδροκομίας [Institute for Arboriculture], the Μπενάκειον Φυτοπαθολογικόν Ινστιτούτον [Benakion Institute for Phytopathology], and others, all state-supported.

The Αγροτική Τράπεζα της Ελλάδος [Agricultural Bank of Greece] has issued many important monographs concerning agricultural economy and various periodicals, of which the Επιθεώρηση Αγροτικών Μελετών [Greek review of agricultural studies] and the Αγροτική [Agriculturist] are still being published.

PRINCIPAL PUBLICATIONS OF CENTRAL GOVERNMENT

The Υπουργείον Εθνικής Οικονομίας [Ministry of the National Economy] (formerly Συντονισμού [Coordination]) has published many composite studies (a large part as of 1950 and afterwards) which cover almost all the branches of production (both primary and secondary) and others of a more general nature, involving demography, environmental research, town planning, market research, as well as hydrological, tourist and educational studies, on a local, regional and national level. At the time of writing, it publishes two periodicals, Τρέχουσες Οικονομικές Εξελίξεις και Προοπτικές της Ελληνικής Οικονομίας/Recent developments and prospects of the Greek economy (a bilingual Greek and English magazine) and Οικονομική Ενημέρωση [Economic information]).

The Υπουργείον Ανοικοδομήσεως [Ministry of Reconstruction], established for a few years after World War II, has issued many similar publications of a general character.

The Υπουργείον Οικονομικών [Ministry of Finance] has published special collections of laws and other material relevant to questions of taxation and tariffs. It also publishes the voluminous annual state accounts and budgets.

The Ελληνικό Κέντρο Παραγωγικότητος [Greek Productivity Centre] has published many monographs, dealing mainly with productivity in industry.

The Εμπορικό και Βιομηχανικό Επιμελητήριο Αθηνών [Athens Chamber of Commerce and Industry] has to its credit an important number of publications. Since 1920, it has been publishing the monthly periodical Δελτίον E.B.E.A. [Bulletin of the A.C.C.I.] and since 1959, the quarterly *Trade with Greece*. A weekly and another monthly bulletin are published by the equivalent Chamber of Commerce and Industry in Salonica, as well as by the Chambers of Commerce in other major cities.

Emphasis is given to everything concerning industry by the publications of the Σύνδεσμος Ελληνικών Βιομηχανιών [Association of Greek Industries], which publishes monographs and the periodical Δελτίον Συνδέσμου Ελληνικών Βιομηχανιών [Bulletin of the Association of Greek Industries].

In the field of commerce, there are the important publications of the Οργανισμός Προωθήσης Εξαγωγών [Organization for the Promotion of Exports], which publishes the monthly periodical Εξαγωγές [Exports].

The Χρηματιστήριον Εμπορευμάτων Πειραιώς [Piraeus Commodity Exchange] has been publishing since 1923 a Ημερήσιον Δελτίον Τιμών [Daily bulletin of prices] and there is an equivalent for Salonica since 1938.

The Υπουργείον Εμπορικής Ναυτιλίας [Ministry of the Merchant Marine] has published a report of its accounts and planning every six months since 1969. In addition, the Ναυτικό Επιμελητήριο Ελλάδος [Hellenic Chamber of Shipping] publishes a quarterly Δελτίον της Ναυτιλίας [Navigation bulletin] and since 1961, it has had an English supplement. Monographs are also published.

The Τεχνικό Επιμελητήριο της Ελλάδος [Technical Chamber of Commerce of Greece] is the technical adviser of the state, provides a documentation unit and has published a significant number of monographs. It also publishes a weekly information bulletin and the periodical Τεχνικά Χρονικά [Technical chronicles] has been published since 1932.

A few technical studies have been printed by the Υπουργείο Συγκοινωνιών [Ministry of Transport] and by the Υπουργείο Δημοσίων Έργων [Ministry of Public Works].

The Κέντρον Προγραμματισμού και Οικονομικών Ερευνών [Centre of Planning and Economic Research] has published a large number of monographs on planning and applied economics. Much of the material is in English.

The Τράπεζα της Ελλάδος [Bank of Greece] has published numerous studies in two main series: *Papers and lectures* and *Series of special research papers*. A great deal of this material is in English. It also publishes a number of serials, such as:

Μηνιαίον Στατιστικόν Δελτίον [Monthly statistical bulletin] 1930–
Νομικόν Δελτίον [Law Bulletin] 1948–
Ημερησία Επισκόπησις Αξιοσημειώτων Οικονομικών Γεγονότων [Daily review of notable economic events] 1958–
Δελτίον Τιμών Ξένων Τραπεζογραμματίων [Price bulletin for foreign bank notes] 1960–
Δελτίον Διεθνών Οικονομικών Ειδήσεων [Bulletin of international financial news] 1962–
Δελτίον Εξωτερικών Συναλλαγών της Ελλάδος [Bulletin of foreign exchange in Greece] 1965–.

Among the remaining state banks the Εθνική Τράπεζα της Ελλάδος [National Bank of Greece] until recently published the Οικονομικαί Εξελίξεις [Economic developments], a monthly financial and statistical bulletin, which began in 1954. The Εμπορική Τράπεζα [Commercial Bank] has been publishing the Οικονομικόν Δελτίον [Financial bulletin] since 1954 and the Ιονική και Λαϊκή Τράπεζα [Ionian and Popular Bank] has published the Μηνιαίον Οικονομικόν Δελτίον [Monthly financial bulletin] since 1959.

The pattern of monetary and financial publications closes with the Χρηματιστήριον Αξιών Αθηνών [Athens Stock Exchange], which every month publishes the Χρηματιστηριακαί Εξελίξεις [Developments on the stock exchange] and the *Athens Stock Exchange*, a monthly statistical bulletin, as well as the *Annual bulletin* and *Yearbook of the Athens stock exchange* (bilingual, in Greek and English).

International relations

The Υπουργείον Εξωτερικών [Ministry of Foreign Affairs] has published many collections of diplomatic documents in different ways. Some other important publications are:

Psyllas, A., Kombotis, A. and Koroneos, A. Νέος Προξενικός Οδηγός [New consular guidebook], a collection of public documents useful for staff of the Greek foreign service, published by order of the Ministry, Athens, 1872
Επετηρίς του επί των Εξωτερικών Υπουργείου [Annual of the Ministry of Foreign Affairs in 1901]. Athens, 1901
Kolokotronis, B. K. Οδηγός Διπλωματικός και Προξενικός [A diplomatic and consular guidebook]. Athens, 1911
Répertoire général des accords internationaux conclus par la Grèce. I. Accords bilatéraux. II. Accords généraux [General repertoire of international agreements signed by Greece. I. Bilateral agreements. II. General agreements]. Ed. A. T. Sgourdeos. Athens, 1938
Γενικόν ευρετήριον συνθηκών· συμβάσεων και συμφωνιών διμερών και Πολυμερών *1832–1956* [General index of treaties, conventions and agreements,

bilateral and multilateral, 1832–1956]. Ed. I. Kouzopoulos. Athens, 1956

Papadakis, B. P. *Éphémérides diplomatiques 1901-1959* [Diplomatic newspapers, 1901–1959]. Athens, 1960. (Two supplements for 1960 and 1961)

Επετηρίδα Υπουργείου Εξωτερικών [Yearbook of the Ministry of Foreign Affairs]. Athens, 1980.

The armed forces

The ministries for the army, navy and air force have published in the past and still do publish regulations, special collections of laws and manuals for the military authorities. Επίσημον Δελτίον του Υπουργείου Στρατιωτικών [Official bulletin of the Ministry of the Army] was printed from 1902 onwards, and the important Ναυτική Επιθεώρησις [Naval review] from 1897, and the historical service of the Army published a large series of volumes concerning the movements of the Greek armed forces during the two world wars.

Labour and social security

The Οργανισμός Απασχολήσεως Εργατικού Δυναμικού [Manpower Employment Organization] publishes important studies and the Ίδρυμα Κοινωνικών Ασφαλίσεων [Social Security Foundation] issues the periodical Επιθεώρηση Κοινωνικής Ασφάλισης [Social security review], which began in 1939, and several other important studies. The Οργανισμός Γεωργικών Ασφαλίσεων [Organization for Agricultural Insurance] has published the Επιθεώρηση Γεωργικών Ασφαλίσεων [Review of agricultural insurance] since 1962. These are the main organizations in the field of social security, and cover the majority of working people.

3. MANNER OF PUBLICATION

Only the Goverment gazette and the Parliamentary minutes are printed exclusively by the Εθνικόν Τυπογραφείον [National Printing House]. The majority of other government publications are printed by private printers or by printing units available in certain services and organizations.

Current issues of the Government gazette can be obtained either on a subscription basis or as single items directly from the Εθνικόν Τυπογραφείον. Older issues are available for the most part on microfilm from the Microform Unit of the Βιβλιοθήκη της Βουλής [Library of Parliament].[15] The Parliamentary minutes of recent years, as well as other publications still in print, are for sale in Parliament. Previous ones are available only on microfilm. Manuals of jurisprudence are sold by commercial publishers. For all others it is necessary to approach the publishing bodies directly. However, the difficulty of acquiring many of these publications should be emphasized, especially when they belong to the category of 'semi-published', 'grey' or 'shadow' literature, of which there are quite a few.

4. BIBLIOGRAPHIC CONTROL

Bibliographic control appears to be impossible. There are no publishers' catalogues for government publications, nor can there be, since in a real sense there is no one government publisher in Greece. A national bibliography of official publications has never existed, and there is not even a current national bibliography[16] where a substantial part of the material might be found. There are a very few organizations and authorities—such as the Academy of Athens, the Archaeological Society, the National Statistical Service of Greece, the National Centre for Social Research, the Institute of Mineral and Geology Exploration, the National Bank of Greece Cultural Foundation and the Patriarchal Foundation of Patristic Studies—which issue a catalogue of their publications at regular intervals. But these are not sufficient. Thus, in the words of W. David Rozkuszka[17] the 'good current bibliographic control' which 'is a sign of hope in acquisition' does not exist in the case of Greece.

5. LIBRARY COLLECTIONS AND AVAILABILITY

The main deposit libraries in Greece are the Εθνικη Βιβλιοθηκη [National Library] and the Βιβλιοθήκη της Βουλής [Library of Parliament], but a large part of the official publications is never deposited in these libraries. The services or organizations which print the publications do not take the trouble to deposit them. They may think that the publications are in part popularizations or are of no interest except to the circles for whom they are specifically produced, or they may consider them as confidential (even after being printed, they are sometimes considered as manuscripts) or grey literature. On the other hand, these two libraries are not particularly sensitive to this material and do not make efforts to collect it with the necessary systematic spirit. Thus it is a problem to locate many of the publications of this kind. Bookshops are not eager to handle them beyond a certain point. The individual or institution interested has a very hard time finding a comprehensive picture of these publications. Small specialized libraries cover only part of the needs of the researcher or scholar, since they offer the material only in fragmentary form according to their specific interests.

NOTES

1. Angelopoulos, G. I. Περί της Εφημερίδος της Κυβερνήσεως κατά την Ελληνικήν Επανάστασιν [Concerning the government gazette during the Greek revolution]. Offprint from Επιθεώρησις Κοινωνικών και Νομικών Επιστημών [Review of social and juridical sciences], vol. 1, (1909), pp. 269–281. See also G. Demakopoulos, in Εφημερίδες της Ελληνικής Επαναστάσεως. Τόμος τέταρτος: Γενική Εφημερίς της Ελλάδος. Έτος Ζ'-1832 [Newspapers of the Greek revolution. Volume 4: General gazette of Greece, 7th year, 1832], Athens, 1973, pp. ε–ιβ where the main bibliography on the subject is to be found.

2. Θέμιδος κώδηξ εκατονταετίας, ήτοι γενική κωδικοποίησις ολοκλήρου της ισχυούσης ελληνικής νομοθεσίας από της συστάσεως του ελληνικού κράτους μέχρι σήμερον, υπό τον τίτλον 'Κώδηξ Θέμιδος 1821-1933'. Εκδ. Οίκος I. N. Ζαχαροπούλου [Themis centenary codex, i.e. general codification of all laws in force from the establishment of the Greek state until today, under the title 'Codex of Themis 1821–1933'. Publishers: I. N. Zacharopoulos]. Athens, 1932–1937, vols. 1–16, supplemented by several later volumes.

3. Raptarchis, Pant. K. Διαρκής κώδιξ της ισχυούσης νομοθεσίας. Πάντοτε ενήμερος κωδικοποίησις νόμων, διαταγμάτων, αποφάσεων κ.λ.π. [Continuous codex of legislation in force. Continuously updated codification of laws, decrees, sentences etc.] Multi-volume publication in loose-leaf. Important for the years 1925 through 1979 is the one volume per annum series published by Const. Sifneos, Πανδέκται νέων νόμων και διαταγμάτων [Digest of new laws and decrees]. To these must be added the following:

NOTES

Πανδέκτης. Διαρκής κώδικας της ισχύουσας νομοθεσίας, εκδιδόμενος από το Υπουργείο Προεδρίας [Digest: continuous codex of the legislation in force]. Published by the Ministry of the Presidency

Πανδέκτης Φορολογικής και Εργατικής Νομοθεσίας [Digest of taxation and labour legislation]. Monthly, since 1975

Κώδικας Επιθεωρήσεως Εργατικού Δικαίου [Codex of labour law review]. Bimonthly

Κώδικας Νομικού Βήματος [Codex of 'law Tribune' review]. Monthly

Κώδικας Ξενοδοχειακής Νομοθεσίας & Νομολογίας [Codex of hotel legislation and jurisprudence]. Quarterly

Κωδικοποίησις Δικαίου Μεταφορών Επιθεώρησης Μεταφορικού Δικαίου. [Codification of transport law by 'transport law review']. Quarterly

Κωδικοποίησις Υπαλληλικού Δικαίου [Codification of employee law]. Quarterly.

4. Mamoukas, A. Τα κατά την αναγέννησιν της Ελλάδος υπό διαφόρων εθνικών συνελεύσεων συνταχθέντα πολιτεύματα [The constitutional texts composed by national assemblies during the revival of Greece period]. Piraeus, 1839. Also by the same compiler: Τα κατά την αναγέννησιν της Ελλάδος, ήτοι συλλογή των περί την αναγεννωμένην Ελλάδα συνταχθέντων πολιτευμάτων, νόμων και άλλων επισήμων πράξεων από του 1821 μέχρι τέλους του 1832. [Concerning the revival of Greece, viz. collection of constitutional texts, laws and other official acts from 1821 to 1832]. Piraeus-Athens, 1839-1852. 11 volumes.

5. A good guidebook to the complex parliamentary publications is the following: Βουλή των Ελλήνων. Πίνακες των υφισταμένων τόμων των επισήμων και των εστενογραφημένων πρακτικών κ.λ.π. των συνεδριάσεων Βουλής, Γερουσίας, νομοθετικών και συνταγματικών επιτροπών. [Charts of the existing volumes of official and stenographed minutes . . . (from 1843 until 1967)]. Athens, 1976.

6. Christopoulos, Panayotis. *The Library of Parliament.* Athens, 1970, pp. 38-40. (In Greek.)

7. Βουλή των Ελλήνων. Ευρετήριον Συζητήσεων του Κοινοβουλίου [Greek parliament index of debates in parliament]. Part III (1909-1936), Athens, 1977-. Part IV (1946-1967), Athens, 1984-.

8. National Statistical Service of Greece. *Price-list of statistical publications.* April 1986.

9. Εθνικό Κέντρο Κοινωνικών Ερευνών. 25 χρόνια λειτουργίας [National Centre for Social Research. 25 years of work]. Athens, 1986.

10. Ακαδημία Αθηνών 1926-1976. Κατάλογος δημοσιευμάτων [Academy of Athens, 1926-1976. Catalogue of publications]. Athens, 1976; and annual catalogues thereafter.

11. It publishes a catalogue of its publications annually.

12. For scholarly periodicals prior to 1968, see *Union Catalogue of scientific periodicals in Greek libraries, Athens area, 1968.* Ed. A. Martin-Papazoglou. Athens, 1971. For current periodicals and magazines, see Επετηρίδα του Ελληνικού Τύπου [Yearbook of the Greek press]. Athens, General Secretariat of the Press, 1985.

13. Centre for Modern Greek Research in the National Research Centre. Έκθεση Εικοσαετίας 1960-1980 [Report on the twenty year period 1960-1980]. Athens, 1980.

14. Byzantine Research Centre. Σύνοψη πεπραγμένων 1960-1980. [A synopsis of

work done between 1960 and 1980]. Athens, 1980.

15. Concerning this unit, see Panayotis Christopoulos, The Library of Parliament in Athens with special reference to its services for microfilming newspapers, in *Parlament und Bibliothek*, international Festschrift für Wolfgang Dietz zum 65 Geburtstag, Herausgegeben von G. Hahn und H. Kirchner, Munich, 1986, pp. 203ff.

16. The most recent attempt to publish one is that of the Βιβλιογραφική Εταιρεία της Ελλάδος [Bibliographical Society of Greece], which edited the *Greek National Bibliography* for 1972, 1973, 1976 and 1977 (annual volumes). Publication postponed because of lack of funds.

17. In *Official Publications of Western Europe*, volume 1. Ed. Eve Johansson. London, 1984, p. 7.

6. BIBLIOGRAPHY

Bulletin analytique de bibliographie Hellenique [Analytical bulletin of Greek bibliography], 1945-.
Includes a considerable proportion of official publications.

Dimaras, C., Koumarianou, C. and Droulia, L. *Modern Greek Culture . A selected bibliography*. 4th ed., Athens, 1974.
In English, French, German and Italian. Bibliography on political, social and economic conditions, pp. 14ff.

Foussaras, G. Βιβλιογραφία των Ελληνικών Βιβλιογραφιών *1791-1947* [Bibliography of Greek bibliographies, 1791-1947]. Athens, 1961.

Kyriakopoulos, El. Τα συντάγματα της Ελλάδος [The constitutions of Greece]. Athens, 1960.

Legg, K. R. *Politics in modern Greece*. 1969.

Markezinis, Sp. Πολιτική ιστορία της νεωτέρας Ελλάδος *1826-1964* [Political history of modern Greece, 1826-1964]. Athens, 1966-. 8 v.

Meynaud, J. *Les forces politiques en Grèce* [Political forces in Greece]. Lausanne, 1965.

New books/Νέα Βιβλία. Athens, 'Hestia' bookshop, 1975-.
Quarterly. A substitute for a national bibliography: a considerable number of official publications can be found in it.

Pipinelis, P. Ιστορία της εξωτερικής πολιτικής της Ελλάδος *1923-1941* [History of the foreign policy of Greece, 1923-1941]. Athens, 1948.

Svoronos, N. Επισκόπηση της νεοελληνικής ιστορίας [A survey of modern Greek history]. Tr. (from French) by A. Asdrachas. 2nd ed., Athens, Themelio, 1976. 338 p.
Includes a bibliographic guide by A. Asdrachas, partly on the government of the country.

Zepos, P. *Greek law*. Athens, 1949. 119 p.

Norway

OLAF CHR. TORP, GERD B. KRAG, HILDE RØDLAND, KJELL FRANK

1. INTRODUCTION

Historical and constitutional background

In this chapter it is only in exceptional circumstances that works dealing with the period prior to 1814 are discussed and described. There are several reasons for this. It is an axiom that Norway's modern history begins in 1814. At that time the 400-year-old union with Denmark was dissolved. During these 400 years Norwegian political history was inextricably bound up with that of Denmark because the ruler of the two kingdoms resided in Copenhagen and the most important government offices were located there. Even though a certain amount of decentralization took place this was an age characterized by royal despotism, and there are therefore few official publications that were specifically Norwegian. The most used and most easily accessible official publications of this period were collections of royal decrees, regulations, circulars and the like published jointly for the two kingdoms and printed in Copenhagen.

Upon its secession from Denmark in 1814 Norway established its first constitution and its own national assembly. This newly won freedom was of short duration, as the country entered into a new union with Sweden, which lasted until 1905. However, the constitution remained in force, even though it was amended and the national assembly, the Storting, has gradually given the country a new body of laws. During the union with Sweden (1814–1905), the day-to-day administration remained with the Norwegian government in Oslo (at that time called Christiania). The king lived in Sweden and held Cabinet meetings relating to matters of common interest with representatives of the Swedish government and a special Norwegian ministerial body in Stockholm. In Oslo the government was led by a viceroy or 'Statholder' (1814–1873) and later by a Prime Minister. All official documents of importance to Norway were printed and published in Norway. For posterity it should only be noted that it took a long time before these publications developed into their final form and were able to satisfy the demands that are made of official publications today.

In the following pages we concentrate on publications issued after 1814. For earlier literature, reference is made to the bibliographies listed in section 7.

Norway is a constitutional monarchy. The Storting [parliament] is responsible for enacting and repealing laws, imposing taxes, raising loans and establishing the budget. The government is responsible to it and may be removed by it upon a vote of censure. Members of the government may not hold a seat in the Storting.

The Norwegian parliament is a unicameral body of a rather unusual form. It is made up of 157 members elected every 4 years by universal adult suffrage. They are elected on a county basis, with 38 representatives from the northern counties, 49 from the south and west, and 70 from the east, of whom 15 are from Oslo. The members themselves elect the upper house, the Lagting, which consists of one quarter of the members and deals with legislative matter, while the remaining 118 constitute the lower house or Odelsting. The Odelsting deals with bills first, and if the two houses are in agreement the act is considered passed. Question-time, interpellations which lead to debate, and debates on domestic and foreign policy are televised, and debates of the full Storting are open to the public. There are also 12 Komiteer [standing committees] whose membership is proportional to the strength of the parties in the Storting, and which are often composed of the parties' representative specialist spokesmen. The standing committees correspond roughly to the departments of central government. They consider all bills and reports to the Storting. Legislation may originate in the government or from a member of the Odelsting.

The Scandinavian institution of the Ombudsman, who is appointed by the parliament to provide a channel for individual complaints against the administration with its growing powers and range of activity, is well known.

Handbooks of government organization

The official handbook and main guide of the Norwegian central government is *Norges statskalender* [Norway's state calendar], which has been issued annually since 1877 with the sole exception of 1946, and dates back in fact to 1815. It describes the function of government agencies and lists the personnel of the civil service. The constitution, decorations and honours, and the functions and activities of most government agencies are included, as are the Municipalities with information on their populations, geographical area and tax rolls.

The following publications are recommended for use with the *Norges statskalender*:

> *Utvalg, styrer, råd m.v.* [Committees, Boards, Councils etc.] issued by the Forbruker- og Administrasjonsdepartementet [Ministry of Consumer Affairs and Government Administration]. It is annual and is published as St. Meld. no. 7. It is an indispensable reference source for permanent government and *ad hoc* working groups.
>
> *Hvem svarer på hva i Staten* [Whom to ask for what in government], published by the Statens Informasjonstjeneste [Central Information Service], 10th ed., 1986. There is an extensive alphabetical index by means of which the user easily finds his way to the solution to his problem.
>
> *Pressekontakter i statsadministrasjonen* [Press contacts in central government], published by the Statens Informasjonstjeneste. Annual.
>
> *Samfunnsboka: hvilke regler gjelder? Hvor henvender man seg?* [The community book: which rules do I follow? To whom do I apply?], published by the Statens

Informasjonstjeneste, 3rd rev. ed., Oslo, 1986. The aim of this book is to simplify contact between the citizen and the authorities.

Statsadministrasjonen [The government administration], ed. Jan Debes and issued by the Forbruker- og Administrasjonsdepartementet [Ministry of Consumer Affairs and Government Administration], Oslo, 1978, 274 p. Not without anecdotes, this book gives a vivid description of the modern government of the country. It is of considerable interest to government officials as well as to the public.

Norske organisasjoner [Norwegian organizations], ed. Abraham Hallenstvedt. 4th rev. ed., Oslo, 1983, xv, 359 p. Since 1975, the *Statskalender* has omitted its lists of organizations. This list therefore is of corresponding importance, and was issued with support from the Norges Almenvitenskapelige Forskningsråd [Norwegian Research Council for Science and the Humanities].

There are also two useful professional registers, issued by the Helsedirektoratet [Directorate of Health]: *Fortegnelse over leger i Norge* [Register of physicians in Norway], issued annually, and *Fortegnelse over tannleger i Norge* [Register of dentists in Norway], which is also annual. *Fortegnelse over veterinærer i Norge* [Register of veterinary surgeons in Norway] is issued annually by the Landbruksdepartementet [Ministry of Agriculture].

Two reference works on regional and local government are *Norges fylkeskommuner og kommuner* [County municipalities and municipalities of Norway], biannual, published by Kommunalforlaget, and *Norges kommunekalender* [The community calendar of Norway], published annually by Økonomisk Literatur.

Three useful historical works of reference are:

Lindstøl, Tallak. *Stortinget og statsraadet 1814-1914*. Oslo, 1914. (B. 1: Biografier.) 1,031 p.

Haffner, Johan Fredrik Vilhelm. *Stortinget og statsrådet 1915-1945*. Oslo, 1949, 2 v. (B. 1: Biografier)

Regjeringer, statsråder og statssekretærer 1945-1986. Oslo, Statsministerens Kontor, 1986. 79 p.

Definition of official publications

No generally accepted definition of offical publications is known to the authors of this chapter. That used for the *Bibliografi over Norges offentlige publikasjoner* [Bibliography of Norwegian official publications] is pragmatic and non-academic. Not all bodies listed in the *Statskalender* are covered, as the *Statskalender* includes quite a lot of semi-official or semi-private bodies. Printed and to some degree mimeographed documents of central government authorities, County authorities, municipal authorities, and institutions and agencies receiving financial support from official bodies are included. This absence of a precise definition reflects a lack of interest in these problems on the part of civil servants: even among librarians there are very few specialists.

2. PRINCIPAL PUBLICATIONS OF CENTRAL GOVERNMENT

2.1. Legislative proceedings

Proceedings of the Storting

Proceedings and documents of the Storting originate in the parliament and in the central government. In a parliamentary democracy the most important decisions and resolutions will be made through the interplay of central government and parliament. The publications resulting from this process are important not only as case documents for the parties concerned, but also as sources of information for contemporary and future use. The form given to such publications is important for their utilization and for the purpose they are to serve and should be given high priority. This was not the case in Norway in 1814. National and political issues dominated the debate, and no one was particularly interested in the form given to these publications which were to become the source material for future generations.

This is the background for the first *Stortingsforhandlinger* (St. forh.) [Proceedings of the Storting].

The Storting began in a special session in 1814, and after 1815 was to meet every third year. Documents were to be issued by a committee of representatives, a task which in reality was left to the Storting's first—and for many years the only—civil servant, the archivist. This was the case in the period 1814–1842. The proceedings from this period were published in a small octavo format and arranged according to the dossier system with all types of documents filed in consecutive chronological order. They run to 83 volumes. A correct use of the Storting's proceedings from this period requires a knowledge of the chronology and it is absolutely necessary to use the subject indexes.

As of 1845 the Storting's proceedings appeared in a new small quarto format, which has been retained ever since. This format makes it possible to print tables, accounts and budgets which had previously been left out or abridged. At the same time the work changed to become a compilation of printed papers of the central government and the Storting arranged systematically by type of paper. In its main features the Storting's proceedings have retained this structure ever since 1845, with some changes introduced in 1871, when the Storting began to convene every year.

The arrangement of the Storting's proceedings reflects the very clear distinction in the Norwegian constitution and political practice between the central government and the Storting. The *Stortingsforhandlinger* divide into 9 parts, of which parts 1–4 are publications of the government and parts 5–9 are publications of the Storting:

> 1 del. [part 1]. *Proposisjoner og Meldinger* (St. prp. 1) [Propositions and reports: proposition 1, the fiscal budget. Includes the Speech from the Throne and report on the state of the nation]
>
> 2 del. [part 2]. *Proposisjoner og Meldinger fremsatt for Stortinget* (St. prp. 2–) [Propositions and reports to the Storting: proposition 2–]
>
> 3 del. [part 3]. *Proposisjoner og Meldinger fremsatt for Stortinget* (St. meld. 1–) [Propositions and reports to the Storting: report 1–]
>
> 4 del. [part 4]. *Proposisjoner og Meldinger fremsatt for Odelstinget* (Ot. prp. 1–, Ot. meld. 1–) [Propositions and reports to the Odelsting: proposition 1–, reports 1–]

5 del. [part 5]. *Dokumenter til Stortinget og dets avdelinger* [Documents of the Storting]

6 del. A [part 6A]. *Innstillinger til Stortinget* (Innst. S) [Recommendations to the Storting]

6 del. B [part 6B]. *Innstillinger til Odelstinget og Beslutninger av Odelstinget* (Innst. O & Besl. O) [Recommendations of the Odelsting, Decisions of the Odelsting]. *Beslutninger av Lagtinget* (Besl. L) [Decisions of the Lagting]

7 del. [part 7]. *Stortingstidende* [Storting gazette, the stenographic report of debates]

8 del. [part 8]. *Forhandlinger i Odelstinget* [Odelsting gazette, the stenographic report of debates]. *Lagtingstidende* [Lagting gazette: debates and statutes]

9 del. [part 9]. *Register* [Index].

Propositions and reports

The central government produces primarily two types of printed matter: propositions and reports.

Propositions (proposisjoner) are bills on legislative matters or appropriations or other matters where the Storting has to adopt a decision. In a proposition the Storting is invited to adopt a specific decision on which a vote is taken.

Reports (meldinger) are all other matters which the central government submits to the Storting for debate. Most of the reports are annual reports from public institutions such as Norges Bank [Bank of Norway] and other state banks, the Norsk Rikskringkasting [Norwegian Broadcasting Corporation], and government commercial operations such as the Postverket [Postal Services Administration] and the Televerket [State Telegraph Administration], or they concern Norway's co-operation in international organizations such as the United Nations, Council of Europe, OECD, NATO, etc. Other reports deal with reforms and plans for the future on which the central government wishes to hear the Storting's opinion before drawing up more detailed proposals. These may refer to matters both of a legislative or of a financial administrative nature. The reports are debated but are not put to the vote.

As background material both for the propositions and for the reports, studies and reports are drawn up by special committees appointed either by the government or by a ministry. These are independent publications issued in a special series, as of 1972 entitled *Norske offentlige utredninger* (NOU) [Norwegian official reports]. They are edited by the Statens trykningskontor [the Government Printing Office], further described in section 3 below, and published by the Universitetsforlaget i Oslo [Norwegian University Press]. The NOUs are numbered consecutively every year, and are given a uniform size and a special colour for the cover each year. They are listed in *Publikasjonsliste fra Storting og Regjering* [List of publications from the Storting and central government], issued by the Forvaltningstjenestene [Government Administration Services] since 1971. Their indexes are described at the end of this section.

If an NOU study results in a matter being submitted to the Storting or in a report, the study will accompany this as a special appendix and thus became a part of the parliamentary publications.

The most important of the central government's regular publications is the Statsbudsjettet [Fiscal budget]. This is called proposition no. 1 to the Storting (St. prp. 1) and constitutes a comprehensive overview which, in text and figures, gives the main features of the budget proposal submitted. This part of the budget proposal has a yellow cover and is usually called the 'Yellow book'. In addition, so-called 'special budgets' are drawn up for each ministry, giving details on amendments and new measures, and include comparisons with the previous fiscal year and appropriations for the current year.

Since 1959 the budget year has been identical with the calendar year. Proposition no. 1 to the Storting (St. prp. 1) is presented by the Finans- og Tolldepartementet [Ministry of Finance] two weeks following the formal opening of the Storting on the first working day in October.

The budget is finally adopted at the last meeting prior to the Christmas Recess (approximately 16 December).

In connection with the Fiscal budget, a so-called 'National budget' is also presented as report no. 1 to the Storting (St. meld. 1). This is a publication of approximately 150 pages which discusses the whole of Norway's economic situation and future prospects. St. meld. 1 is dealt with together with St. prp. 1. It is presented as a report because it is not a proposal on which a vote is to be taken. It is background material for the discussion of the Fiscal budget. A revised 'National budget' is drawn up about six months later.

The titles of the two types of publications which have been mentioned, the propositions and reports, never appear alone, but only with the prefix 'Stortings-' or 'Odelstings-', according to whether the publication is to be discussed by the Storting or the Odelsting.

A special characteristic of the Storting is the division into Komiteer [standing committees]. Immediately following the general election the representatives are placed in one of the 12 standing committees for the whole of the duration of the four-year parliament. All propositions and reports from the government must be dealt with by a standing committee before being taken up by the Storting or the Odelsting. In the final proceedings it is the recommendation from the committee which is entered in the agenda and on which a vote is taken. A unanimous Innstilling [recommendation] very seldom leads to debate, and the recommendation is thus the most reliable source of information on the opinion on the matter in the Storting or the Odelsting, as the case may be.

Recommendations and decisions

The recommendations (Innstillinger) are collected in part 6 of the *Forhandlinger* as set out above, and are usually divided into two volumes, with recommendations to the Storting in part 6A and those to the Odelsting in part 6B.

Part 6A contains three different types of recommendation:

> *Budsjettinnst. S* nr. I–IV [Budget recommendations S nos. I–IV]. These are the recommendations given by the Finanskomiteen [Standing committee on finance] with overall assessments of the government's budget proposal
>
> *Budsjettinnst. S* nr. 1–12 [Budget recommendation S nos. 1–12]. These are the recommendations from all committees on the detail of the government's budget proposal
>
> *Innst. S* no. 1– [Recommendation S no. 1–]. These are the recommendations from all of the standing committees concerning all other matters to be dealt with in plenary session.

Part 6B contains, in addition to the recommendations to the Odelsting (Innst. O), the *Beslutninger* [Decisions] of the Odelsting (Besl. O) and the *Beslutninger* of the Lagting (Besl. L). Besl. O contains the text of the statutes which the Odelsting has adopted and which in the next round is to be adopted by the Lagting. More than ninety per cent of all Besl. O are adopted unchanged. If the Lagting does not assent to the Odelsting's decision, a Besl. L is adopted which specifies wherein the disagreement lies. The matter must then be dealt with again by the Odelsting and the Lagting. If agreement still is not reached, the matter comes up for discussion in plenary session and can only be adopted by a two-thirds majority.

Indexes to the Innstillinger are included in the main index to the *Stortingsforhandlinger*.

It should be emphasized that the Storting makes several types of decision. First, amendments to the constitution must be proposed in one Storting and dealt with by a new Storting. A two-thirds majority is required. Second, statutes (new statutes or amendments to existing statutes) are dealt with by the Odelsting and the Lagting by an ordinary majority. If the two houses cannot agree, the bill must be dealt with in plenary session and a two-thirds majority is required. A statute or act in this context is taken to mean substantive laws, that is to say decisions which set norms and rules and which are decisive for the status of private citizens under the law. Finally, ordinary Storting resolutions are the means by which all other propositions than these are passed. These include all budget resolutions and tax decisions as well as the ratification of treaties and international agreements. These need only a simple majority.

Debates

Stenographic records were kept for the first time in 1857. During the period 1857–1887 these records were published privately. For 1814–1854 there are several publications which record the main points in the debate. They are all entitled *Stortings-Efterretninger* [Storting Intelligences] and were published by different sources. In practice one work is used, the *Storthings-Efterretninger utgitt efter offentlig foranstaltning* [Storting intelligences published at official behest], which were issued in 1874–1911 in two series: 1814–1833 (3 vols.) and 1836–1854 (4 vols.). They are reconstructions on the basis of contemporary published reports, diaries, letters and so on.

In 1888 the stenographic records became an integral part of the comprehensive proceedings of the Storting, forming parts 7 and 8, and entitled *Stortingstidende*, *Odelstingstidende* and *Lagtingstidende* (*tidende* means a gazette). These are the only parts of the proceedings which contain an index. Originally there was both a subject index and an index by name of speaker, but after 1970/71 the subject index was omitted. The index by name of speaker is arranged alphabetically, with both ministers and representatives in one sequence.[1]

Other publications

Dokumenter [Documents] are published by the Storting and include publications not belonging among the recommendations. The most important documents each year are the constitutional annotations, the annual reports of the Ombudsman institutions, and a list of the answers which have been given to proposals that have been sent to the government. Records of debates which had been kept secret and later released are also printed here.

Indexes to the Storting's proceedings

An annual index is found at the end of every edition. The volume containing the index has been part 9 since 1888. It is a subject index with certain special lines of approach. Roughly speaking, the index may be used in the following ways:

for reference by subject. References are plentiful and give all information concerning the proposition or report, the recommendation and the debate

for reference by name of standing committee, though only for matters which have been dealt with by standing committees

for reference by proposition or report number, with an indication of what happened to each proposition or report

for reference by interpellation or question. These are listed under the name of the minister who answered them.

Main indexes have been produced for longer or shorter periods of time. A list follows:

Hovedregister til Stortings-forhandlinger 1814–1870 med Tillæg, inneholdende Register til Komiteindstillinger. Utarb af J. Cappelen. Kristiania, 1885, viii, 724, 194 p.

— *1871–1891.* Utarb af J. Cappelen. Kristiania, 1896. viii, 781 p.

Hovedregister til Stortingsforhandlinger 1892–1899/1900. [Utarb af V. Haffner]. Kristiania, 1905. x, 582 p.

— *1900/01–1910.* Utarb av V. Haffner. Kristiania, 1915. x, 653 p.

— *1911–1924.* Utarb av V. Haffner. Oslo, 1930. xiii, 889 p.

— *1925–1935.* Utarb av V. Haffner. Oslo, 1935, xv, 571 p.

— *1935–1945.* Utarb av A. Gunstrøm. Oslo, 1955. xxi, 404 p.

— *1945/6–1954.* Utarb av A. Gunstrøm. Oslo, 1961. xxix, 776 p.

— *1955–1960/1.* Utarb av Stortingets arkiv. Oslo, 1972, xliv, 747 p.

— *1961/2–1969/70.* Utarb av Stortingets arkiv. Oslo, 1979. xlix, 932 p.

— *1970/1–1980/1.* Utarb av Stortingsarkivet. Oslo, 1984. 1779 p. in 2 parts

Hovedregister til Stortingsforhandlinger valgperioden 1981/2–1984/5. Sakregister. Oslo, Stortingsarkivet, 1986. 8*, 719 p.

— Talerregister. Oslo, Stortingsarkivet, 1986. 12*, 613 p.

All indexes 1814–1980/1 are subject indexes. The first cumulative index by name of speakers was published as the second volume of the *Hovedregister* for 1981/2–1984/5.

All these main indexes are now available on microfiche from Mikromedia AS, P.O. Box 2959 Tøyen, N-0608, Oslo 6. The paper edition is available from the Official Publications Division, Norwegian University Press, P.O. Box 8135 Dep., N-0033, Oslo 1.[2]

The forerunners of the NOU reports, before they became a series in 1972, are listed in:

Haffner, Johan Fredrik Vilhelm. *Innstillinger og betenkninger fra kongelige og parlamentariske kommisjoner, departementale komiteer m.m. 1814–1924.* Oslo, Fabritius, 1925. xlvi, 823 p.

———. *Innstillinger og betenkninger ... 1925–1934. Med tillegg for tidsrummet 1814–1924.* Oslo, Fr. Arnesens Bok- og Aksidenstrykkeri, 1936. xviii, 203 p.

Johansen, Vincent. *Hovedregister til Innstillinger og betenkninger 1935–1971 fra kongelige og parlamentariske kommisjoner, departementale komiteer m.m.* Oslo, Statens Trykningskontor, 1974. xviii, 163 p.

Since 1981 the Library of the Regional College of Nordland has published an annual cumulated index to the NOU reports: *Norges offentlige utredninger 1972/80—. Register over titler/emner og utvalgsledere, samt kronologisk oversikt.* Utg. av Nordland distriktshøgskole.

In 1983 a microfiche version of the three above-mentioned publications, including the NOU list up to 1982, was published by the Norwegian University Press and is for sale through Mikromedia. In addition official reports not appearing in the NOU series for 1972–1982 were listed, and the catalogue cards of the Stortingsbiblioteket covering official reports from 1935 to 1983 were included. The list was published as *Norske utredninger 1814–1983: bibliografier og kataloger over offentlige utredninger pr 1/9 1983.* Red. av Øivind Frisvold. [Norwegian official reports 1814–1983: bibliographies and catalogues to official reports at 1 September 1983. Ed. Øivind Frisvold]. Oslo, Norwegian University Press, 1983. 22 p. + 33 microfiches.[3]

Biographical registers

Important sources are:

Debes, Jan. *Det norske statsråd 1814–1949.* Oslo, Cammermeyer, 1950. 207 p.

Haffner, Johan Fredrik Vilhelm. *Det nye Storthing 1895/7–1898/1900.* Oslo, Haffner & Hille, 1894–1898. 2 v.

———. *Stortinget 1900/3—1954/7.* Oslo, J. G. Tanum, 1900–1954. 16 v.

———. *Stortinget og statsrådet 1915–1945.* Oslo, Aschehoug, 1949. 2 v. I: Biografier. II: De enkelte Storting, av Karl Bjørnstad. 878, 274 p.

Lindstøl, Tallak. *Stortinget og statsraadet 1814–1914.* Oslo, Steenske Bogtrykkeri, 1914–1915. 2 v. I: Biografier. II: De enkelte storting og statsraader.

Nordby, Trond (ed.) *Storting og regjering 1945–1985. Biografier.* Oslo, Kunnskapsforlaget, 1985. 842 p. Biographic articles on members of the Parliament and government.

———. *Storting og regjering 1945–1985. Institusjoner rekruttering.* Oslo, Kunnskapsforlaget, 1985. 332 p. Articles on parliamentary procedure, cabinet work, the electoral system, political parties, the social background of members of Parliament, lists of members of the standing committees of Parliament, and lists of members of the Cabinets.

Torp, Olaf Chr. *Stortinget 1958–1961.* Oslo, Johan Grundt Tanum, 1958. 122 p.

———. *Stortinget 1961/2–1964/5.* Oslo, Johan Grundt Tanum, 1962. 164 p.

———. *Stortinget 1965/6–1968/9.* Oslo, Johan Grundt Tanum, 1966. 173 p.

———. *Stortinget høsten 1969–våren 1973.* Oslo, Universitetsforlaget, 1970. 182 p. 2nd ed., Oslo, 1972. 186 p.

———. *Stortinget høsten 1973–våren 1977.* Oslo, Universitetsforlaget, 1974. 187 p.

———. *Stortinget i navn og tall. Høsten 1977–våren 1981.* Oslo, Universitetsforlaget, 1978. 204 p.

———. *Stortinget i navn og tall. Høsten 1981–våren 1985.* Oslo, Universitetsforlaget, 1982. 218 p.

———. *Stortinget i navn og tall. Høsten 1985–våren 1989.* Oslo, Universitetsforlaget, 1986. 229 p.

2.2. Legislation and secondary legislation

Norway has no official gazette. Information concerning statutes is given in Norway in several ways:

(a) publication of all new statutes and important royal decrees, regulations, circulars and instructions
(b) up-dated compilations of statutes in force at any given time
(c) special reprints of specific texts with amendments
(d) works of commentary on legislation in force in specifically defined areas
(e) various journals from ministries and other branches of the administration.

Norsk Lovtidend (NLT) [Norwegian law gazette] has been published since 1877. It was the successor to *Samling av lover og anordninger* [Collection of acts and ordinances] which was published during the years 1814–1876. *Norsk Lovtidend* is published today by the Statsministerens Kontor [Office of the Prime Minister]. It is issued in two parts, with about 30–40 issues a year in each part. Part 1 includes all new statutes and amendments to existing legislation, the more important resolutions adopted by the Statsråd [Council of State], and circulars and other nation-wide decisions. Part 2 includes local regulations and provisions. Both parts are arranged strictly chronologically, but have very good annual indexes which cumulate every fifth year arranged by subject, ministry and County. The arrangement described is applicable to the period from 1974. During the years 1877–1973 NLT also comprised two parts, the contents of which were in the main identical. During this period Part 1 was a weekly express edition, in which the object was to publish all the provisions as quickly as possible. Part 2 was published quarterly. This was supplied with notes referring to the preparatory proceedings and debates on the acts and had a systematic index. Part 1 had a chronological index. The act regarding NLT (1969) lays down that no statutory texts shall enter into force until one month at the earliest after the text has been printed in NLT.

Individual statutes are published as 'reprints' by the printer which prints NLT, Grøndahl.

Compilations of laws in force have a long tradition in Norway. The most important work of recent date is the *Almindelig norsk lovsamling* [General compilation of Norwegian acts], ed. P. I. Paulsen, J. E. Thomle and C. S. Thomle, and issued during the years 1905–1927 in seven volumes with an index and eight supplementary volumes. It contained statutes in force enacted from 1660 to 1927 as well as the most important royal decrees, circulars, regulations, etc. Today the work is only of historical interest. Beginning in 1930 the Faculty of Law at the University of Oslo has published *Norges Lover* (NL) [Norwegian law compendium] in one volume every other year. NL contains all legislation in force (but not decrees, circulars or secondary legislation) from 1685 to the year of publication. NL is arranged chronologically and has a systematic index and an alphabetical keyword index.[4]

Norwegian laws etc. selected for the Foreign Service is prepared and published in English by the Utenriksdepartementet [Ministry of Foreign Affairs]. It was issued for the first time in 1905 and has since been supplemented repeatedly, most recently in 1963 in a loose-leaf edition with five appendices. A new edition was published in 1981 in one volume. It contains only a selection of the legislation in force, supplemented with other provisions which are of importance to the Foreign Service and for Norwegians resident in foreign countries. It is arranged systematically with an alphabetical keyword index.

Amendments to legislation are also issued as 'reprints' by Grøndahl in a coloured cover. In the case of minor amendments the new text is attached on a special page. In the case of larger amendments the wording of the statute is reprinted and issued in a new edition.

Commentaries on legislation are published privately and will not be discussed in this context.

Journals issued by some of the ministries and the more autonomous directorates also contain texts of statutes and other provisions within their competence, mentioned in section 2.3 below.

There is a useful composite edition of *Norges Lover 1685-1985*, published by Grøndahl in 1986.

An important new publication is *Norges forskrifter* [Regulations of Norway], published by Grøndahl. Eighteen volumes were issued in 1984-1986. It covers the regulations issued by different ministries, arranged in one volume for each ministry and chronologically within each volume. Each has a subject index, an index of the laws under which the regulations are made, and an index to the different departments or offices of the ministry. It is produced by Lovdata, a law data-base owned by private companies and official bodies. New volumes will be published as necessary.

2.3. The executive agencies of government

This section does not aim to present an exhaustive list of Norwegian official publications: the bibliographic sources listed in section 4 should be used for this. What follows is a selection of titles designed to give an impression of the manifold and growing government activity in the field of information.

According to the Norwegian constitution the government shall consist of a Prime Minister and at least seven other members. At present the Regjeringen [Cabinet] consists of the Prime Minister and 16 ministers, each of them heading a ministry in the national administration. The names of the ministries are as follows:

Departementet for Utviklingshjelp [Ministry of Development and Co-operation]
Finans- og Tolldepartementet [Ministry of Finance]
Fiskeridepartmentet [Ministry of Fisheries]
Forbruker- og Administrasjonsdepartementet [Ministry of Consumer Affairs and Government Administration]
Forsvarsdepartementet [Ministry of Defence]
Handelsdepartementet [Department of Trade]
Industridepartementet [Ministry of Industry]
Justis- og Politidepartementet [Ministry of Justice]
Kirke- og Undervisningsdepartementet [Ministry of Church and Education]

Kommunal- og Arbeidsdepartementet [Ministry of Local Government and Labour]
Kultur- og Vitenskapsdepartementet [Ministry of Cultural and Scientific Affairs]
Landbruksdepartmentet [Ministry of Agriculture]
Miljøverndepartementet [Ministry of the Environment]
Olje- og Energidepartementet [Ministry of Petroleum and Energy]
Samferdselsdepartementet [Ministry of Communications]
Sosialdepartementet [Ministry of Health and Social Affairs]
Statsministerens Kontor [Office of the Prime Minister]
Utenriksdepartementet [Ministry of Foreign Affairs].

Communications and navigation

FISKERIDIREKTØREN [DIRECTORATE OF FISHERIES]

Register over merkepliktige norske fiskefarkoster [Register of Norwegian fishing vessels]. Biannual.

KYSTVERKET [COASTAL DIRECTORATE]

Liste over norske seilmerker, 1975 [List of Norwegian navigational markings, 1975]. Oslo, Grøndahl, 1975

Norks fyrliste [Norway's lighthouse list]. Oslo, Kystdirektoratet. Biennial.

LUFTFARTSVERKET [CIVIL AVIATION ADMINISTRATION]

Luftfartsverkets årbok [Yearbook of the Civil Aviation Administration]. Annual.

OLJEDIREKTORATET [NORWEGIAN PETROLEUM DIRECTORATE]

The Continental Shelf. Main acts, regulations and guidelines issued by Norwegian authorities. Ed. and completed by the Norwegian Petroleum Directorate. Stavanger, NPD, 1984. 870 p. This very important collection of bilingual texts is updated to January 1985, and the publisher has promised to keep it up to date

Faste installasjoner. Forskrifter fastsatt av norske myndigheter [Permanent installations. Regulations of Norwegian authorities]. Annual.

POSTDIREKTORATET [POSTAL BOARD]

Gate- og veinavn i Norge, 1983 [Names of streets and roads in Norway, 1983]. 1983. 273 p.

Norges poststeder [Postal stations of Norway]. Annual

Norsk stedsfortegnelse [Norwegian place-names]. Oslo, 1972. 929 p.

Postadressebok [Directory of Post Offices]. Irregular (approximately annual).

SJØFARTSDIREKTORATET [NORWEGIAN MARITIME DIRECTORATE]

Flyttbare oljeplattformer . . . /Mobile drilling platforms [Regulations laid down by Norwegian official control institutions]. Oslo, 1976–. A loose-leaf service with parallel texts in Norwegian and English

Maritime standarduttrykk. Engelsk–norsk [IMCO's standard navigational vocabulary. English–Norwegian]. Oslo, 1977. 64 p.

Norges skipsliste. Fortegnelse over norske orlogs- og handelsfartøyer med kjenningssignaler [List of Norwegian naval and merchant ships to which signal letters have been allotted]. Annual. Parallel texts in Norwegian and English

Sjøveisreglene. Regler til forebygging av sammenstøt på sjøen. Fastsatt 1 Desember 1975. Med kommentarer [Fairway traffic rules. Regulations for preventing collisions at sea. Decreed 1 December 1975. With commentaries]. Oslo, Grøndahl, 1976. 183 p.

STATENS KARTVERK. DIVISJON NORGES SJØKARTVERK
[NORWEGIAN MAPPING AUTHORITY.
HYDROGRAPHIC SURVEY]

Den norske los [The Norwegian pilot]. 4th ed., vols. I–VI, 1980–. A description of the fairway of the entire Norwegian coastline

Den Norske skipskontrolls regler [Norwegian ship control rules]. Oslo, Fabritius. Annual with suppl.

Den Norske skipskontrolls regler, Fiske- og fangstfartøy [Norwegian ship control rules: fishing boats, whaling and sealing vessels]. Oslo, Fabritius. Biennial

Norwegian ship control legislation. Vols. I–III. 1982 ed., with annual suppl.

TELEVERKET [STATE TELEGRAPH ADMINISTRATION]

Norske telestasjoner [Norwegian telephone and telegraph offices]. Annual
Telefonkatalogen. Del. 1–10 [Telephone directory. Parts 1–10]. Annual
Teleks håndbok [Telex handbook]. Annual
Telekskatalog for Norge [Yearbook of subscribers to telex services in Norway]. Annual.[5]

One other long-established publication is *Rutebok for Norge* [Time schedules for Norway], issued eight times a year by Rutebok for Norge publishers in co-operation with the Samferdselsdepartementet [Ministry of Communications]. Published for more than a century, this periodical is a real classic. It contains official timetables for travel by rail, sea, bus, ferry and air, a register of hotels, etc.

International relations and Norwegian foreign policy

UTENRIKSDEPARTEMENTET [MINISTRY OF
FOREIGN AFFAIRS]

The publishing activity of Utenriksdepartmentet covers a range of subjects. Some of its publications are:

Aktuelle spørsmål. FN's Generalforsamling . . . [Topical questions. The UN General Assembly]. 31st sess.–, 1976–. Annual. Issued in advance of the UN General Assembly, it covers the main topics to be discussed

Aktuelle utenrikspolitiske spørsmål [Topical questions for foreign policy]. 1981–. Irregular

Aktuelle økonomiske og handelspolitiske spørsmål [Topical economic and trade questions]. 1975–. Irregular

Liste du corps diplomatique à Oslo [List of the foreign diplomatic representatives in Oslo]. Biannual. Arranged by country

Norges traktater [The treaties of Norway]. 1661–1976. Vols I–IV and index. Oslo, Grøndahl, 1967–1983. A compilation of treaties in force. The index is cumulative, chronological and by subject

Overenskomster med fremmede stater [Agreements with foreign states]. Irregular. Covers new treaties

Stipend til utlandet [Scholarships abroad]. Annual

UD—informasjon [Information from the Ministry of Foreign Affairs]. Mimeographed: irregular. Text and discussions on current foreign policy questions, with a special index of important foreign policy issues from 1966 to 1980

Utenriksdepartementets kalender [Calendar of the Ministry of Foreign Affairs]. Oslo, Grøndahl. Biennial.

Reports regarding the participation of Norway in international organizations are issued regularly as Stortingsmeldinger.

NORSK UTENRIKSPOLITISK INSTITUTT [NORWEGIAN INSTITUTE OF INTERNATIONAL AFFAIRS]

The publishing of the Norsk Utenrikspolitisk Institutt is important. Some of its titles are:

Internasjonal politikk [International politics]. Oslo, 1937–1940, 1947–. Gives documentation and authoritative articles on topics of current interest. Quarterly with summaries in English

NUPI-notat [NUPI notes]. Irregular

NUPI-rapport [NUPI reports]. Irregular

Norsk utenrikspolitisk årbok [Norwegian foreign policy yearbook]. 1973–. Annual. Also includes documentation and articles

Utenrikspolitiske skrifter [Norwegian foreign policy studies]. 1971–. Irregular. Contains mainly monographs in Norwegian and English on essential topics. (*Norsk utenrikspolitisk årbok* appears in this series.)

Judicial decisions

An example of law reports that are officially published in Norway is *Dommer og kjennelser av Arbeidsretten* [Judgements and findings of the Labour Court], issued annually since 1918.

The Norsk Advokatforening [Norwegian Association of Lawyers] issues selections of decisions of the Høyesterett [Supreme Court] and the lower courts in two journals, *Norsk retstidende* [Norwegian case law journal], issued since 1836 with 20–30 issues per year, and *Rettens gang* [Record of lower court proceedings], issued since 1933 with 17 parts per year. It publishes an important collection, *Juridisk Oppslagsbok* [Judicial reference book], which comes in two parts, Del. 1: Privatretten [Part 1: Private law], Oslo, Universitetsforlaget, 15th ed., 1982; Del. 2: Forvaltningretten [Part 2: Administrative law], Oslo, Universitetsforlaget, 15th ed., 1986.

Nordisk domssamling [Scandinavian law reports] has been published since 1959 by Universitetsforlaget. Nordisk skibsrederforening [Northern Shipowners' Association] publishes *Nordiske domme i sjöfartsanliggender* [Collection of maritime law cases from the Scandinavian countries], which is issued seven times a year and began in 1900.

Petroleum: activity, policy and resources

Due to a rapid expansion of interest in this field, a considerable number of official publications concerning petroleum and similar subjects have been issued in recent years. Much of the printed material is translated into English. The majority of these publications appear as Stortingmeldinger or in the NOU series. As this is a relatively new field of activity in Norway, the literature is correspondingly difficult to survey. Most published material should be sought in bibliographies. Two bibliographic tools mentioned in section 4.3. below are recommended: *Norske oljepolitikk* and *Publikasjoner* of the Oljedirektoratet.

Social conditions: medical and health services

HELSEDIREKTORATET [DIRECTORATE OF HEALTH]
  Approved food additives. 1981. 106 p.
  Fortegnelse over leger i Norge [List of physicians in Norway]. Annual
  Fortegnelse over tannleger i Norge [List of dentists in Norway]. Annual.
  Health for all by the year 2000. 1980. 31 p. (This was the Norwegian contribution to an ad hoc meeting on health for all in industrialized countries in Geneva in May 1980.)

KOMITEEN FOR INTERNASJONALE SOSIAL-POLITISKE SAKER [NORWEGIAN JOINT COMMITTEE ON INTERNATIONAL SOCIAL POLICY]
  Health services in Norway. By Karl Evang. 4th ed. 1976. 233 p.
  Labour relations in Norway. 1975. 192 p. Historical as well as current information.[6]

KOMMUNAL- OG ARBEIDSDEPARTEMENTET [MINISTRY OF LOCAL GOVERNMENT AND LABOUR]
  Immigrant in Norway. 1983. 166 p.
  Norsk yrkesleksikon [Dictionary of occupational titles in Norway]. 1974–1980. 3 vols.

LANDBRUKSDEPARTEMENTET [MINISTRY OF AGRICULTURE]
  Fortegnelse over veterinærer [List of veterinary surgeons]. Annual.

RIKSTRYGDEVERKET [NATIONAL INSURANCE INSTITUTION]
  Social insurance in Norway. 1984. 74 p.
  Sosialtrygdene i Norge [Social insurance in Norway]. 1984. 73 p.

SOSIALDEPARTEMENTET [MINISTRY OF HEALTH AND SOCIAL AFFAIRS]
  Sosial trygghet i Norge [Social security in Norway]. 4th ed. Oslo, Universitetsforlaget, 1981. 360 p.
  Sosialkatalogen: oversikt over tjenester og ytelser [The social catalogue: some services and contributions]. Oslo, Universitetsforlaget, c. 1983. 82 p.

STATENS ARBEIDSTILSYN [STATE LABOUR INSPECTORATE]

Immigrant workers in Norway. Equal rights and obligations as other employees. A guide. 1978. 17 p.

The Working environment act and the Annual holidays act—also for non-Norwegians. 1982. 20 p.

Working environment legislation and labour inspection in Norway. 1979. 7 p.

UTENRIKSDEPARTEMENTET [MINISTRY OF FOREIGN AFFAIRS]

Working and living in Norway. A guide for aliens. 1979. 40 p.

State companies and nationalized industries

For information on this type of enterprise, much is to be found in the Stortingsmeldinger [Reports to the Storting], the NOU series described in section 2.1 above, and the NOS series, *Norges offisielle statistikk* [Norway's official statistics], described under the heading 'statistics' below. Annual reports are also issued separately by the individual concerns.

Statistics

STATISTISK SENTRALBYRÅ [CENTRAL BUREAU OF STATISTICS]

The Statistisk Sentralbyrå is the principal but not the only body responsible for issuing official statistics in Norway. It issues about a hundred publications every year, and a selection is listed below. It also issues, irregularly, a *Guide to Norwegian statistics* in English.

Rapporter—RAPP [Reports]. 1979–. Irregular

Samfunnsökonomiske studier—SÖS [Social Economic Studies, SES]. Universitetsforlaget. Irregular. In this series are published the results of studies which are not of a purely statistical nature, such as historical and analytical studies of economic and social problems[7]

Standarder for norsk statistikk [Standards for Norwegian statistics]. 1980–. Irregular

Statistiske analyser—SA [Statistical analyses]. Universitetsforlaget. Irregular. In this series are published comments and analytical surveys for data already published in the NOS series[8]

Norges offisielle statistikk—NOS [Norway's official statistics]. Universitetsforlaget. Irregular. This, the main series, covers annual as well as intermittent publications, and includes subject specialist publications giving detailed information in all fields of statistics and summary publications giving general information from many different subject fields, such as:

Historisk statistikk [Historical statistics]. Decennial
Statistisk årbok [Statistical yearbook of Norway]. Annual
Økonomisk utsyn over året [Annual economic survey]. Annual.[9]

Other important journals are:

Månedsstatistikk over utenrikshandelen [Monthly bulletin of external trade]. Contains detailed monthly data on imports and exports

Statistisk månedshefte [Monthly bulletin of statistics]. Contains current monthly and quarterly statistics, articles and notes on statistical method, on new statistics and on the activities of the Statistisk Sentralbyrå in general.

The publications of the Bureau are provided with preface, table of contents and headings in English as well as English language summaries.

OTHER STATISTICAL SERIES

Other important statistical publications not issued by the Statistisk Sentralbyrå include:

Fengselsstyrets årbok [Yearbook of the Prison Board]. Issued by the Prison Board
Fiskeristatistikk [Fishery statistics]. Published in Bergen by the Fiskeridirektoratet [Directorate of Fisheries]. Now ceased publication
Forsikringsselskaper [Insurance Companies]. Published by the Forsikringsrådet [Insurance Supervisory Board]
Luftfartsstatistikk: Månedsstatistikk [Monthly aviation statistics]. Published by the Luftfartsverket [Civil Aviation Administration]
Norges postverk [Norwegian postal service]. Published by the Postdirektoratet [Postal Board]
Televerket: statistikk [State Telegraph Administration statistics]. Published by the Televerket [State Telegraph Administration]
Yrkesskader i folketrygden [Occupational injuries insurance]. Issued by the Rikstrygdeverket [National Insurance Institution].

Norwegian statistics are also included in the publications of the Nordisk Råd, such as the *Yearbook of Nordic statistics*, and in *International whaling statistics*, published by the Committee for Whaling Statistics of the Norwegian Council on Whaling.

3. MANNER OF PUBLICATION

The most important point to notice about obtaining Norwegian official publications is the fact that no central governmental distribution office exists for the benefit of the public interest in this type of publication.

Statens trykningskontor (STK) [Government Printing Office] is in charge of the coordination and supervision of the printing of official publications, except for some parliamentary proceedings which are the responsibility of the Storting to print. The STK also acts as a consultant on the production and design of special books, pamphlets and other documents. Statens trykksakekspedisjon (STE) [the Government Central Distribution Office] stocks and distributes parliamentary papers, forms and brochures, and provides the civil service with official publications free of charge. Both these organizations come under the Forbruker- og Administrasjonsdepartementet [Ministry of Consumer Affairs and Government Administration]. The Ministry bears the costs of printing for internal distribution but recovers from the individual government ministries the cost of public distribution.

There is also a great variety of publications issued by the ministries and related subsidiary bodies, who are free to print and sell their own publications, and will usually set prices to recover distribution costs but meet production costs out of their own budgets. They are however increasingly using a centralized outlet, the Universitetsforlaget i Oslo [Norwegian University Press in Oslo]. Parliamentary publications and some series of reports are supplied to it free, and the government receives no revenue from the operation. The Universitetsforlaget operates direct mail, subscriptions and a sales point combined with an information counter for the referral of enquiries. However, by no means all government ministries go through the Universitetsforlaget. Private institutions of any kind, foreign or national, may purchase the publications through the Universitetsforlaget, whose address is P.O. Box 8134 Dep., N-0033, Oslo 1,[10] or through their local bookseller.

The greater part of all official publications is printed, although until a few years ago many of the reports leading up to parliamentary proceedings were typescript and impossible for the citizen to identify or obtain. In recent years much effort has been made to make available in microfiche both the parliamentary proceedings and the reports from government committees. The Universitetsforlaget i Oslo began filming parliamentary and government publications in 1981 and publications back to 1970 are now available in microform. Lack of storage space has led to parliamentary proceedings being kept in stock for shorter and shorter periods of time, and also to a reduction in the number of copies printed. Some publications in high demand are out of stock in less than two years following publication, but as a rule publications are kept in stock for the year of publication and for the following two years.

The great demand for information in English on North Sea oil production and related matters has made it necessary to have some bills and official reports translated. Statistical publications are bilingual or with summaries in English.

Those interested in subscriptions to parliamentary proceedings and reports from governmental committees should contact the Official Publications Division of the Universitetsforlaget, P.O. Box 8134 Dep., Oslo 1.[11] Those interested in these publications on microfiche should contact Mikromedia AS, P.O. Box 2959, Töyen, Oslo 0608. Questions about annual subscriptions to the bound editions of *Stortingsforhandlinger* or *Norges offentlige utredninger* (NOU) may be sent direct to Forvaltningstjenestene, Statens Trykningskontor, P.O. Box 8129 Dep., N-0032, Oslo 1.

Publications from minor institutions and directorates have as a rule no central distribution. Nevertheless attention should be drawn to the publications of the Statistisk Sentralbyrå. They may be obtained from booksellers. Subscriptions should be sent direct to the Statistisk Sentralbyrå, P.O. Box 8131 Dep., Oslo 1.

4. BIBLIOGRAPHIC CONTROL

At the beginning of this section we would like to draw attention to a very useful bibliography that includes bibliographies of official publications:

Martens, Johanne and Munthe, Gerhard. *Håndbok over norsk bibliografi. Bibliografisk litteratur i utvalg. De humanistiske fag* [Handbook of Norwegian bibliography. Bibliographical literature in selection. Humanistic studies]. Oslo, Universitetsforlaget, 1965. 61 p.

It covers both national bibliography and subject bibliography within the humanities and social sciences up to 1964. Foreign bibliographies on Norway and Norwegian matters are included. The bibliography is annotated.

Until now this publication, even though published in 1965, was the only bibliography of wide coverage. A very long-felt need was met when the following Nordic bibliography was published in 1984:

> *Guide to Nordic bibliography.* General ed. Erland Munch-Petersen. Issued by the Nordisk ministerråd. Copenhagen, NORD, 1984. 235 p.

The guide was compiled by lecturers from the five Nordic library schools under the auspices of the Nordic cultural fund. The Norwegian part was undertaken by Odd Heide Hald. It presents the national bibliographic systems and the essential subject bibliographies of the Nordic countries to an international forum. The guide is written in English and annotated.

4.1. Government publishers' catalogues

Norway does not so far have a cumulative government publishers' catalogue. There is however a list of parliamentary and government papers in print—*Publikasjonsliste fra Storting og regjering* [List of publications from the Storting and central government]. Oslo, Universitetsforlaget, 1971–. The list appears with 18 numbers during the Storting session and gives half-yearly summaries in numbers 7 and 18, which are the last issues of the autumn and spring sessions. These two cumulated lists have subject and numerical indexes to propositions and reports of the Storting. NOU reports are also listed in numerical order.

Since this is a sales list it should be noted that it is not intended to be complete, and consequently has a limited information value.

From 1981 the list has been published by means of an automated system. This will probably affect both the number of publications registered and the quality of the indexes.

4.2. National bibliography of official publications

The first edition of the Norwegian bibliography of official publications was published in 1957, covering the year 1956. For previous years it is necessary to turn to the *Norsk bokfortegnelse* [Norwegian book index], which to some extent also covers official publications in printed form.

The first special Norwegian book index was compiled by C.C.A. Lange, and it covers the period 1814–1831. This catalogue was later included in Mart. Nissen's *Norsk bokfortegnelse 1814–1847* [Norwegian book index 1814–1847], Oslo, Feilberg & Landmarks Forlag, 1848. The task of compiling the national bibliography was then handed over to Norsk bokhandlerforening [Norwegian Bookseller's Association]. With different editors the association published the index up to 1920, and from 1891 it was published every ten years.

In 1882 the legal deposit Act was passed. It gave to the Universitetsbiblioteket i Oslo [University Library in Oslo], which also serves as the national library, the right to obtain copies of all publications printed by Norwegian printers and publishers who print their publications abroad.

The University Library now started its own *Norsk bogfortegnelse*, published in an annual catalogue since 1883, more complete than the one published by the Norsk bokhandlerforening. In 1920 the two were amalgamated, and the *Årskatalog over norsk litteratur* [Annual catalogue of Norwegian literature] was continued. From 1921 the Universitetsbiblioteket has also issued a five-yearly cumulation.

In 1952 it was agreed that the Universitetsbiblioteket should take over the publishing of the annual catalogue as well as the five-yearly catalogue and the weekly list, which was published as a supplement to the *Norsk bokhandlertidende* [Journal of Norwegian booksellers]. In 1972, however, the weekly list was changed into a monthly one and is now published as a supplement to the journal of the Norsk bokhandlerforening, *Bok og samfunn* [Book and society].

Today Norwegian books from 1971 are recorded in an on-line system in the Universitetsbiblioteket.

From 1956 there is a special bibliography for official publications: *Bibliografi over Norges offisielle publikasjoner*, published by the Universitetsbiblioteket for 1956 onwards. From 1975 the bibliography has been published in two parts. Part 1 lists monographs, serials, annual reports and brochures. Part 2 lists circulars from ministries, directorates and so on. The bibliography covers both printed and mimeographed materials published by various government institutions, public committees, councils, companies, organizations and so on and from institutions based on government grants and their appurtenant bodies.

The indexes to reports in the NOU series and their forerunners before 1972 have been listed in section 2.1 above.

4.3. Publications lists of the executive agencies

Considerations of space make it impossible to mention publications lists from all the Norwegian public institutions. Therefore only a selection is given. Publications lists from educational institutions (such as universities, academies etc.) and museums are not included in the selection. Most of the lists are only available from their publishers. It should be mentioned that many institutions publish their lists of publications only in their annual reports.

Arbeidsdirektoratet [Directorate of Labour]. *Oversikt over yrkesorienterende materiell* [List of vocational guides]. Oslo, 1981. [A new edition will be published in 1986]

Direktoratet for Arbeidstilsynet [Directorate of Labour Inspection]. *Publikasjoner fra Arbeidstilsynet* [Publications from the Labour Inspectorate]. Oslo. Annual

FN-Sambandet og Departementet for Utviklingshjelp/NORAD [United Nations Association of Norway and the Ministry of Development Co-operation/NORAD]. *Katalog* [Catalogue]. Oslo. Annual

Fondet for Markeds- og Distribusjonsforskning [Norwegian Foundation for Market and Distribution Research]. *Publikasjonsliste* [Publications list]. Oslo. Annual

Landbruksteknisk Institutt [Institute of Agricultural Technology]. *En oversikt over publikasjoner fra Landbruksteknisk institutt. Av Torstein Fyhri* [List of publications from . . .]. Ås, 1974. (Later an annual list has been published in the annual report)

Likestillingsrådet [Equal Status Council]. *Publikasjonsliste* [Publications list]. Oslo. Annual

Norges Almenvitenskapelige Forskningsråd [Norwegian Research Council for Science and the Humanities]. *Publikasjonsliste* [Publications list]. Irregular. Latest 1986

Norges Byggforskningsinstitutt [Norwegian Building Research Institute]. *Publikasjoner fra byggforskningen* [Publications from building research]. Oslo. Annual

Norges Geologiske Undersøkelse [Norwegian Geological Survey]. *Foreign dissertations on Norwegian geology. A bibliography 1930-1979.* By Unni Havem Rowell. Trondheim, 1981. 35 p. (Norges geologiske undersøkelse, 361, Bulletin, 58)

———. *Forfatter-, emne- og stedsregister for Norges geologiske undersøokelses publikasjoner nr. 1-315, 1890-1974 (samt småskrifter nr. 1-9).* Av Marit Ryssdal. [Author, subject and place-name index to the NGO's publications nos. 1-315, 1890-1974 (including booklets nos. 1-9). Trondheim, 1976. 132 p. (Norges geologiske undersøkelse, no. 326)

———. *Publikasjoner og kart 1879-1980* [Publications and maps 1879-1980]. Trondheim, 1981. 36 p. Irregular

Norges Landbruksvitenskapelige Forskningsråd [Agricultural Research Council of Norway]. *Liste over Utkomne sluttrapporter* [List of published final reports]. Oslo. Annual. Latest 1974-1986

———. *Publikasjonsliste* [Publications list]. Oslo. 2-3 issues a year

———. *Utredninger avgitt av NLVF* [Studies from the NLVF]. Oslo. Annual. Latest 1952-1986

Norges Landbruksøkonomiske Institutt [Norwegian Institute of Agricultural Economics]. *Oversikt over meldinger utsendt fra Norges landbruksøkonomiske institutt, 1 jan. 1948-31 des. 1972* [List of reports from . . .]. Oslo. 1973. (Since then an annual list has been circulated to those with a specialist interest)

Norges Sjøkartverk og Norsk Polarinstitutt [Hydrographic Office of Norway and Norwegian Polar Institute]. *Katalog over norske sjøkart og nautiske publikasjoner* [Catalogue of Norwegian charts and nautical publications]. Stavanger, 1979. (From 1986 the Norges Sjøkartverk has been incorported in the Statens Kartverk)

Norges Standardiseringsforbund [Norwegian Standards Association]. *Hva leverer NSF?* [What does the NSF do?] Oslo. Irregular. Latest 1985

———. *Katalog over Norsk standard* [Catalogue of Norwegian standards]. Oslo. Annual

———. *Publikasjoner fra NSF* [Publications from the NSF]. Oslo. Annual

Norges Teknisk-Naturvitenskapelige Forskningsråd [Royal Norwegian Council for Scientific and Industrial Research]. *Liste over aktuelle publikasjoner utgitt ved NTNF's sentrale administrasjon* [List of publications of current interest published by the central administration of . . .]. Oslo. Annual. (Also published in the annual report)

———, *FoU indeks over NTNF's forsknings- og utviklingsrapporter*. Utg. av Norsk senter for informatikk. [R & D index of NTNF's research and development reports. Published by the Norwegian Centre for Informatics]. Oslo, 1973–. Published 4 times a year. Also available on-line

Norsk Institutt for By- og Regionforskning [Norwegian Institute for Urban and

Regional Research]. *Eksterne NIBR-publikasjoner 1973-1984* [External NIBR publications 1974-1984]. Oslo, 1984. (NIBR notat 1984: 154)

——. *NIBR publikasjoner til salgs pr. 1/1* . . . [NIBR publications for sale as at . . .]. Oslo. Annual

Norsk Institutt for Luftforskning [Norwegian Institute for Air Research]. *NILU's oppdragsrapporter og tekniske notater 1970-1979*. Av Liv Stenstrømog Frederick Gram [Reports and technical notes from NILU]. Lillestrøm, 1980. (Teknisk notat nr. 4/80)

——. *Rapportliste* [List of reports]. Kjeller. Biannual

Norsk Institutt for Skogforskning [Norwegian Forest Research Institute]. *Annotated bibliography 1974-1980. Sur nedbørs virkning på skog og fisk* [Acid rain. Effects on forest and fish]. By Arne Tollan. Oslo, 1981. 42 p.

Norsk Institutt for Vannforskning [Norwegian Institute for Water Research]. *List of publications*. Oslo, 1979 (+ supplements). Irregular. (Also published in Norwegian)

Norsk oljepolitikk. Bibliografi og stikkordregister. Registrerte offentlige dokumenter om norsk oljevirksomhet [Norwegian oil policy. Bibliography and catchword index. Registered official documents regarding Norwegian oil activity]. Oslo, Mikromedia AS, 1985. 100 p. (This bibliography is produced especially for use in conjunction with a separate full-text edition of all the documents listed, available on microfiche. Annual)

Norsk Polarinstitutt [Norwegian Polar Institute]. *Publications*. Oslo, 1980. (Some later supplements have been published)

Norsk Utenrikspolitisk Institutt [Norwegian Institute of International Affairs]. *Bibliografi: NUPI-rapporter 1970-1980* [Bibliography of NUPI reports and notes, 1970-1980]. Oslo, 1981. 16 p. (NUPI-notat 210)

——. *NUPI-notat og rapport* [NUPI notes and reports]. Annual. Latest 1981-1985

Oljedirektoratet [Norwegian Petroleum Directorate]. *Publikasjoner som utgis av Oljedirektoratet* [Publications from . . .]. Stavanger. Annual

Rikstrygdeverket [National Insurance Institution]. *Liste over Rikstrygdeverkets brosjyrer* [List of brochures from . . .]. Oslo. Annual

Sosialdepartementet [Ministry of Health and Social Affairs]. *Publikasjoner fra Sosialdepartementet og Helsedirektoratet* [Publications from the Ministry of Health and Social Affairs and the Directorate of Public Health]. Oslo. Annual

——. *Sosialdepartementets rundskriftoversikt* [List of circulars from . . .]. Oslo. Annual

Statens Edruskapsdirektoratet [Government Temperance Directorate]. *Opplysningsmateriell. Alkohol. Narkotika. Tobakk* [Information materials. Alcohol. Drugs. Tobacco]. Oslo. Irregular. Latest 1984/5

Statens Forurensningstilsyn [State Pollution Control Authority]. *Oversikt over SFT's rapporter* [List of reports from . . .]. Oslo. Annual

Statens Informasjonstjeneste [Central Information Service]. *Brosjyreoversikten. Brosjyrer utgitt av offtentlige instanser og en del organisasjoner* [List of brochures published by public institutions and some organizations]. Oslo. Latest ed. 1985. 241 p.

——. *Undervisningsmateriell. Brosjyrer og bøker utgitt av offentlige instanser og en del organisasjoner, beregnet for skoler, eller egnet som hjelpemidler for lærere* [Educational material. Brochures and books published by public institutions and some organizations, intended for schools or suitable as teachers' aids]. Oslo. Annual

Statens Institutt for Alkoholforskning [National Institute for Alcohol Research]. *Liste over publikasjoner* [List of publications]. Oslo. Irregular. Latest ed. 1984. (Also published in the annual report)

Statens Institutt for Forbruksforskning [State Institute of Consumer Research]. *Opplysnings- og læremidler* [Educational and teaching aids]. (Published in Forbruker-rapporten)

Statens Kartverk [State Mapping Authority]. *Økonomisk kartverk* [Economic maps]. Hønefoss. Annual

——. *Kartkatalog* [Catalogue for maps.]. Hønefoss. Annual

Statistisk Sentralbyrå [Central Bureau of Statistics]. *Fortegnelse over Norges offisielle statistikk og andre publikasjoner utgitt av Statistisk Sentralbyrå 1828–1976* [Catalogue of Norwegian official statistics and other publications published by the Central Bureau of Satistics 1828–1976]. Oslo, 1978. 196 p. (Norges offisielle statistikk, A 957)

——. *Månedens publikasjoner fra Statistisk Sentralbyrå* [Publications of the month from . . .]. Oslo. Monthly

——. *Publications from the Central Bureau of Statistics*. Oslo. Annual. (Also published in Norwegian)

Teledirektoratet [Norwegian Telecommunications Administration]. *Liste périodique des publications éditées par l'Administration.* Oslo. Annual

Transportøkonomisk Institutt [Institute of Transport Economics].
TØI-bibliografi. En systematisk fortegnelse over publikasjoner fra TØU og TØI 1958–1976 [TOI bibliography. A systematic list of publications from TOU and TOI 1958–1976]. Oslo, 1978. 267 p.

——. *TØI-bibliografi* [TOI bibliography]. Oslo. Annual

——. *Tverrsnittsbibliografi 1958–1976* [Selected bibliography of publications 1958–1976]. Oslo, 1977. 29 p.

Utenriksdepartementet [Ministry of Foreign Affairs]. *Publications on Norway and conditions in Norway.* Oslo. Annual. (Also published in Norwegian, French, German, Dutch, Spanish and Portuguese)

Vegdirektoratet [Directorate of Roads]. *Håndbøker. Oversikt over utgitte håndbøker fra Vegdirektoratet* [Handbooks. List of handbooks from . . .]. Oslo. Irregular. Latest ed. 1986

——. *Rundskriv. Oversikt over gjeldende rundskriv fra Vegdirektoratet* [Circulars. List of circulars in force . . .]. Oslo. Irregular. Latest ed. 1985.

5. PUBLICATIONS OF REGIONAL AND LOCAL GOVERNMENT

5.1. Regional government

Administratively Norway is divided into 20 Fylker [Counties]. They are Akershus, Aust-Agder, Buskerud, Finnmark, Hedmark, Hordaland including Bergen, Møre og Romsdal, Nord Trøndelag, Nordland, Oppland, Oslo, Rogaland, Sogn og Fjordane, Sør Trøndelag, Telemark, Troms, Vest Agder, Vestfold and Ostfold.

The elected governing body of the County is the Fylkesting [County Council] whose members are elected for four years. The County Councils are particularly concerned with hydroelectric development schemes and matters relating to schools, health and transport and communications. The County administrations produce a substantial number of studies, reports and plans, in addition to the documents purely related to proceedings in the County Council. These publications have only a minor circulation. They are largely regarded as procedural documents for the benefit of the local government administration and the elected councillors. Some of these documents are only available to the general public when the printed reports or minutes of the County Councils are published. Reports vary a great deal from County to County as to their extent, format and design. On average they constitute one or two volumes per County each year, and they are not for sale. They are distributed by the publisher to public authorities and libraries within the County. Proceedings of the County Councils are not registered in the *Bibliografi over Norges offentlige publikasjoner* and have hitherto not been mentioned in *Norsk bokfortegnelse*.

5.2. Local government

The Counties are sub-divided into urban and rural Kommuner [Municipalities], except for Oslo which forms a separate County. In 1986 Norway had 454 Kommuner. Their elected bodies are the Kommunestyrer [Municipal Councils]. With effect from 1 January 1964 the Municipalities in a County have also been grouped together into Fylkeskommuner [County Municipalities] in order to facilitate the carrying out of tasks which they have in common. The County Municipalities have their own elections and administration.

The Municipal Councils produce large quantities of documents, but only the largest cities and a few major rural Municipalities publish printed reports of the Municipal Council's proceedings. There is no common norm, and each Municipality solves its own information problems in its own way. Most of these documents are only available in limited numbers, often in the form of stencil or offset prints. They are not for sale and are not registered in any bibliography.

The Statens Informasjonstjeneste [Central Information Service] has in the last few years run a pilot programme with a view to facilitating public access to official information. In some pilot Municipalities they are trying to activate local public libraries and integrate them in this work by among other things making documents in the Municipal decision-making process available in the Municipal libraries.

6. LIBRARY COLLECTIONS AND AVAILABILITY

It is the responsibility of libraries to make official publications available to the public. In accordance with Act no. 2 of 9 June 1939 relating to the mandatory deposit of printed matter to public libraries, the Universitetsbiblioteket i Oslo [University Library in Oslo], which also functions as the national library, receives all printed material published by the government and the various government bodies. The library can therefore assume that its collections of Norwegian official publications are complete. They are not kept as a separate collection, but are included as part of the holdings of the Norske Avdeling [Norwegian Department]. All printed publications above a certain size are catalogued, the remainder being kept in a 'systematisk samling' [systematic collection] and not catalogued.

Even though the reader services at the University Library are well developed, it may be difficult to find the publication wanted. Some users will therefore prefer to go to a specialized library to get a more individual service. The collections of official publications in special libraries will be limited primarily to their specialist fields. But virtually all the libraries will aim to have the more general publications, such as the proceedings of the Storting and official yearbooks and collections. Among the special libraries it is natural to mention first of all the Stortingsbiblioteket [the Library of parliament], where both the collections and the services are fully developed. In addition, the libraries of the Utenriksdepartementet [Ministry of Foreign Affairs] and the Statistisk Sentralbyrå [Central Bureau of Statistics] deserve mention, as does that of the Nobel Institute. Details will be found in *Norske vitenskapelige og faglige biblioteker* [Norwegian research and special libraries], published by the Riksbibliotektjenesten [National Office for Research and Special Libraries], 5th ed., 1984.

Norway extends over a large geographical area and has a scattered population. It will be understood that under these conditions it is difficult to offer all citizens a satisfactory service for official publications. The best collections outside Oslo are to be found in Bergen and Trondheim where the university libraries, through the act relating to the mandatory deposit of printed matter in public libraries, have a right of requisition for all Norwegian publications they might need. The newest university library, in Tromsø, has not so far been given this right of requisition, but it is expected to be included in a forthcoming new act.

Public libraries are established in all the Municipalities, but only the bigger ones have collections of any importance. The 20 County libraries have built up collections which in most cases will meet the local demand for official publications.

In Norway the exchange of official publications is not centralized except for a few countries, for instance the USA, with whom total exchange agreements have been established. These agreements are managed by the Exchange Department of the Universitetsbiblioteket i Oslo, which also takes care of the exchange of scientific publications.

Parliamentary proceedings from Norway are used in the exchange between the Stortingsbiblioteket and a number of parliamentary and university libraries all over the world (see below). It is difficult to say how complete these collections are, but most of the exchange agreements go back to the last century. Some of the libraries receive the microfiche version and there is reason to believe that within a short time this version will be sent to the majority of the exchange partners.

Stortingsforhandlinger can be found in the following libraries:

Europe:
Altingsbiblioteket, Reykjavik, Iceland
Bibliothek des Nationalrates, Vienna, Austria
British Library, London, UK
Deutscher Bundestags Bibliothek, Bonn, Federal Republic of Germany
Folketingets Bibliotek, Copenhagen, Denmark
Göteborgs Universitetsbibliotek, Sweden
Kungliga Biblioteket, Stockholm, Sweden
Lenin State Library of the USSR, Moscow
Lunds Universitetsbibliotek, Sweden
Riksdagsbiblioteket, Helsingfors, Finland
Riksdagsbiblioteket, Stockholm, Sweden
Service de la Documentation Etrangère de l'Assemblée Nationale, Paris, France

State M. E. Saltykov-Shchedrin Public Library, Leningrad, USSR
Statsbiblioteket i Århus, Denmark
Tweede Kamer der Staten-Generaal, The Hague, Netherlands
United Nations Library, Geneva, Switzerland
Uppsala Universitetsbibliotek, Sweden

Outside Europe
National Library of Australia, Canberra
Library of Congress, Washington, DC, USA
Luther College, Decorah, Iowa, USA
New York Public Library, USA
University of Minnesota Libraries, Minneapolis, USA.

Not so much is known about the exchange of other official publications. Some agencies, like the Statistisk Sentralbyrå, belong to international networks of related institutions and exchange publications all over the world. Other types of official publications, like reports from governmental committees or law gazettes, will be found in the larger national and parliamentary libraries.

NOTES

Since this chapter was prepared, many changes have occurred. Details of titles of publications and names of ministries in the text have been brought up to date, but the following notes are intended to update other information.

1. This index can be found in part 7 (for the Storting) and in part (for the Odelsting and the Lagting) up to 1984/5. From 1985/6 these indexes are included in part 9 with the annual subject index.

Cumulative indexes by name of speakers started in 1981 with an index for the 1977/78–1980/81 parliament. From 1981/2 this index is published in a separate volume as part of the *Hovedregister*.

2. Until 1987 Universitetsforlaget through its Official Publications Division was the main distributor of official publications to the general public. From 1988 all functions of this division have been transferred to a new firm of booksellers, Akademika AS at the same address.

3. An updated version was due for publication in 1987.

4. From the 1985 edition an index referring to all regulations pursuant to law is included. All the texts referred to are to be found in *Norges forskrifter*.

5. A new title published by the Televerket is *Telefaxkatalog for Norge* [Telefax directory Norway]. Biannual.

6. From MEDLEX, Norsk Helseinformasjon (Norwegian health information) a very useful work has been published: *Helserett 86: Lover, forskrifter, rundsktiv for helsetjenesten* [Acts, regulations and circulars for the health service]. Oslo, MEDLEX, 1986. 6 v.

7. From 1987 *Sosiale og økonomiske studier*.
8. From 1987 merged with *Sosiale og økonomiske studier*.
9. From 1985 published in *Statistiske analyser*.
10. See note 2.
11. See note 2.

7. BIBLIOGRAPHY

In addition to publications already mentioned in the text, attention should be drawn to the following works:

Andenæs, Johs. *Statsforfatningen i Norge.* 6th rev. ed. Oslo, Tanum/Norli, 1986. 562 p.
   A very up-to-date work on the development and functioning of the Norwegian constitution.

Andenæs, Mads T. and Wilberg, Ingeborg. *Grunnloven. Kommentarutgave.* Oslo, Universitetsforlaget, 1983. 185 p.
   Text of the present constitution and commentary.

Castberg, Frede. *Norges statsforfatning.* 3rd ed. Oslo, Universitetsforlaget, 1964. 2 v.
   A comprehensive work on the constitution of Norway.

Catalogue of Norwegian official statistics and other publications published by the Central Bureau of Statistics 1828–1976. Oslo, 1978. 196 p. (Norges offisielle statistikk, A 957.)
   A complete bibliography with title and subject indexes.

The constitution of the kingdom of Norway . . . as laid down on 17 May 1814 . . . with subsequent amendments. Oslo, Utenriksdepartementet, 1981. 12 p. (Norway information, LOV.001/81.)

Debes, Jan. *Det norske statsråd 1814–1949.* Oslo, Cammermeyer, 1950. 207 p.

Eliassen, Kjell A. and Pedersen, Mogens N. *Nordiske politiske fakta: Nordic political facts.* Oslo, Tiden, 1985. 194 p.

Grunnloven vår 1814 til 1985. Ed. Tønnes Andenæs. 10th ed. Oslo, Universitetsforlaget, 1985. 193 p.
   Text edition of the constitution and other constitutional and historical documents of great importance.

Heidar, Knut. *Norske politiske fakta 1884–1982.* Oslo, Universitetsforlaget, 1983. 404 p.

Husadvokaten. Ed. Tore Bråthen. Oslo, Aschehoug, 1986–87. 3 v.
   This popular handbook is planned in three volumes with two supplementary volumes. It gives a commentary on most aspects of the law that concern people in general.

Knophs oversikt over Norges rett. 8th ed. by Birger Stuevold Lassen. Oslo, Universitetsforlaget, 1981. 1,065 p. Suppl. 1980–84, pp. 1,067–1,147.
   A commentary on more than 25 important aspects of Norwegian law written by experts in their field. Subject index.

Kuhnle, Stein. *Velferdsstaten.* Oslo, Universitetsforlaget, 1983. 140 p.
   About Norwegian social insurance policy; mostly in tables and diagrams.

Lægreid, Per and Roness, Paul G. *Sentraladministrasjonen.* Oslo, Tiden, 1983. 237 p.
   Facts about government administration in Norway: bibliographic review, pp. 221–229.

Mjeldheim, Leiv. *Politiske prosessar og institusjonar.* 3rd ed. Oslo, Universitetsforlaget, 1979. 210 p.

Det Norske samfunn. 3rd ed. by Lars Allden, Natalie Rogoff Ramsøy and Mariken Vaa. Oslo, Gyldendal, 1986. 424 p.

A standard work on most aspects of Norwegian society: bibliography at the end of each chapter.

Nygren, Rolf (ed.) *Handbok i Nordiskt parlamentstryck.* Stockholm, Nord, 1984 [1985]. 149 p.

Sentraladministrasjonens historie. Vols. 1, 2, 4 and 5. Oslo, Universitetsforlaget, 1979–80

This standard work describes the history of the Norwegian government administration from 1814 to the present day. Planned to be published in six volumes.

The Storting, the Norwegian Parliament. Rules of procedure. Oslo, 1984. 36 p.

Svåsand, Lars. *Politiske partier.* Oslo, Tiden, 1985. 195 p.

Torp, Olaf Chr. Stortingsforhandlinger. *Bibliotek og forskning,* 12 (1963), pp. 257–293.

Portugal

ROBERT HOWES

1. INTRODUCTION

Portugal is the oldest country in Europe within its present borders, which it attained during the course of the 13th century. In the 15th century the Portuguese explorers founded a seaborne empire which stretched to India, the Far East, Brazil and Africa. Following the independence of the last colonies in 1975, Portugal is now a mainland European country, together with the Atlantic islands of the Azores and Madeira. As a legacy of this empire, however, Portuguese has become one of the world's major languages.

Modern history

Modern Portuguese history begins in 1807 with the Napoleonic invasion of the country which ushered in several decades of war, economic distress, civil war between liberals and absolutists, and general political instability. In the second half of the 19th century, however, a viable political system consisting of a liberal constitutional monarchy with a parliamentary system of government based on a restricted franchise and manipulated elections was established.

The monarchy was overthrown by an armed uprising in 1910 and replaced by a republic. In its later years the First Republic was beset by political instability and financial chaos leading to a military coup on 28 May 1926. The military installed an economics professor from the University of Coimbra, António de Oliveira Salazar, as Minister of Finance in 1928 and Prime Minister in 1932. Salazar achieved financial and governmental stability at the cost of a stultifying authoritarian dictatorship. By the time his successor, Marcello Caetano, tried to liberalize and modernize the dictatorship, Portugal was embroiled in the colonial wars in Africa which eventually led a group of junior army officers to overthrow the regime on 25 April 1974.

There ensued a remarkable 18-month period of frenetic but largely bloodless political activity in which a variety of centre, moderate and extreme left-wing parties and revolutionary movements vied for power with factions of the military. Free elections were held, however, on 25 April 1975 leading to the installation of a Constituent

Assembly which drew up the present constitution, promulgated on 2 April 1976. Since then Portugal has had a democratic parliamentary regime. On 1 January 1986 Portugal, together with its neighbour Spain, joined the European Communities.

Government and administration

Portugal is a small, homogeneous nation without ethnic, linguistic or religious divisions. At the last census in 1981, the total resident population was 9,833,014, of whom 9,336,760 lived in mainland Portugal and the rest in the islands.

The main institutions of the national government are the Presidente da República [President of the Republic], who is elected by direct popular suffrage; the Assembleia da República [Assembly of the Republic], a single-chamber parliament elected by a system of proportional representation; the Primeiro-Ministro [Prime Minister] and the Conselho de Ministros [Council of Ministers or Cabinet], who run the government departments; and the courts of justice.

For administrative purposes, mainland Portugal is divided into 18 Distritos [Districts], each headed by a civil governor, together with the two Regiões Autónomas [Autonomous Regions] of the Azores and Madeira. The country is further divided into Concelhos [Municipalities] and Freguesias [Parishes]. As of 1984–1985, there was a total of 305 Concelhos, composed of 4,050 Freguesias; of these 275 Concelhos and 3,848 Freguesias respectively were in mainland Portugal. The effective administration of local government in the municipalities is carried out by the Câmara Municipal [Municipal Chamber].

The judicial system distinguishes between civil, commercial, criminal (penal), administrative, labour and fiscal law, with specified lower courts, courts of appeal and the supreme court in Lisbon for each branch of law. For civil and criminal cases the country is divided into Comarcas [judicial Districts], each having one or more lower courts depending on the importance of the area.

Constitutions

Since the beginning of the 19th century Portugal has had six constitutions which have been in force for varying periods, reflecting changes in the political regime. The first was the constitution of 1822, a radical liberal democratic document which was in force from 23 September 1822 to 2 June 1823 and again from 10 September 1836 to 4 April 1838. It was followed by the much more conservative *Carta Constitucional* [Constitutional charter] of 1826 which was in force initially from 29 April 1826 to 10 September 1836, with a break between 1828 and 1834. The constitution of 1838, which was something of a compromise between the first two constitutions, lasted from 4 April 1838 to February 1842, when it was replaced by the restored Constitutional charter of 1826 which then remained in force until the overthrow of the monarchy on 5 October 1910. Amendments were incorporated by additional acts in 1852, 1885, 1895–1896 and 1907.

The constitution of 1911 was drawn up by the Assembleia Nacional Constituinte [National Constituent Assembly] which met following the declaration of the republic in 1910 and remained in force from 21 August 1911 until the end of May 1926. It consecrated the republican regime and the doctrine of the three powers, while emphasizing the role of the legislature or Congresso [Congress], which was divided into a Câmara dos Deputados [Chamber of Deputies] and a Senado [Senate], elected by direct suffrage; Church and State were separated and religious freedom guaranteed. The

INTRODUCTION

authoritarian constitution of 1933 was drawn up by the Salazar regime and approved by a national plebiscite. It maintained the republican system of government and established an Assembleia Nacional [National Assembly] elected by a restricted franchise and a Câmara Corporativa [Corporative Chamber] representing economic and social interests. The Presidente da República [President of the Republic] continued to be head of state, although effective power was concentrated in the hands of the Presidente do Conselho de Ministros [President of the Council of Ministers or Prime Minister], Salazar. This constitution came into force on 11 April 1933 and lasted until 25 April 1974, with amendments passed in 1935–1938, 1945, 1951, 1959 and 1971.

The present constitution was drawn up by the Assembleia Constituinte [Constituent Assembly] which was elected on 25 April 1975 and began its deliberations during the most agitated part of the revolutionary period of 1974–1975. It was promulgated on 2 April 1976. In reaction to the excesses of the Salazar regime, the constitution of 1976 contained many guarantees for personal freedoms and rights, incorporated a range of economic and social measures intended to improve living conditions and develop a socialist economy, and assigned an active political role to the military through the Conselho da Revolução [Council of the Revolution].

In 1982 a major revision of the constitution was carried out. This abolished the Conselho da Revolução [Council of the Revolution] and removed the last vestiges of direct military participation in the political process, reduced the powers of the Presidente da República [President of the Republic] and cut out many of the references to socialism. The revised version of the Constitution of 1976 was published in the *Diário da República, I Série* [Daily journal of the Republic, Series I], no. 227, of 30 September 1982.

As amended, the constitution of 1976 now declares that

> The Portuguese Republic is a democratic state of law, based on popular sovereignty, on respect for and the guarantee of the fundamental rights and freedoms, and on pluralism of democratic expression and political organization, which has as its objective to assure the transition to socialism through the achievement of economic, social and cultural democracy and the strengthening of participatory democracy. (Article 2)

It declares that the state is unitary and respects the principles of autonomy of local bodies and democratic decentralization of public administration, while the people exercises political power through universal, equal, direct, secret and periodical suffrage.

Part I of the constitution defines the Fundamental Rights and Duties, including the rights, freedoms and guarantees of the individual, and those of political participation and of organization and association for the workers. Under the heading of Economic, social and cultural rights and duties are listed measures relating to employment, working conditions, private enterprise and cooperatives, private property, social security, health care, housing, protection of the environment, family life, parenthood, children, youth, the disabled, the old, education, culture and science. Part II, Economic Organization, covers state intervention in the economy, structures of ownership of the means of production, planning, agricultural policy and agrarian reform, the financial and fiscal system, trade and consumer protection.

Part III, Organization of Political Power, states that the organs of sovereignty are the

Presidente da República [President of the Republic], the Assembleia da República [Assembly of the Republic], the Governo [Government] and the Tribunais [Courts]. The Presidente da República [President of the Republic] is elected by universal, direct and secret ballot for five years and can be re-elected for one further term. He appoints the Primeiro-Ministro [Prime Minister] after consulting the parties represented in the Assembleia da República [Assembly of the Republic] and appoints other members of the government as proposed by the Primeiro-Ministro [Prime Minister]. He can dissolve the Assembleia da República [Assembly of the Republic] and call elections, dismiss the government and the Primeiro-Ministro [Prime Minister], and veto laws in certain circumstances. A consultative Conselho de Estado [Council of State] acts as an advisory body to the President.

The Assembleia da República [Assembly of the Republic] consists of between 240 and 250 Deputados [Deputies] elected by proportional representation in multi-member constituencies. Members of the government cannot be deputies. Bills can be introduced by deputies, parliamentary groups or the government. The Governo [Government] is formed of the Primeiro-Ministro [Prime Minister], Ministros [Ministers], Secretários de Estado [Secretaries of State] and Subsecretários de Estado [Sub-secretaries of State], whilst the Primeiro-Ministro [Prime Minister] and Ministros [Ministers] form the Conselho de Ministros [Council of Ministers or Cabinet]. Once appointed by the Presidente da República [President of the Republic], the Primeiro-Ministro [Prime Minister] has within 10 days to present his government's programme of action to the Assembleia da República [Assembly of the Republic] for approval; if the programme is rejected by an absolute majority of deputies, the government falls. Failure to win approval of a motion of confidence or the approval of a motion of censure at other times also leads to the fall of the government. The constitution then goes on to define the political, legislative and administrative responsibilities of the Governo [Government], the Conselho de Ministros [Council of Ministers], the Primeiro-Ministro [Prime Minister] and the Ministros [Ministers]. Article 122 lists the measures which have to be published in the official gazette.

The following sections of the constitution cover the Tribunais [Courts], including the judges and public prosecutors; the Regiões Autónomas [Autonomous Regions] of the Azores and Madeira, with provisions for regional assemblies and governments; local government; public administration; and national defence. Part IV is headed Guarantee and Revision of the Constitution and lays down measures dealing with the safeguarding of constitutionality, the Tribunal Constitucional [Constitutional Court] and revision of the constitution. The text ends with the final transitional measures.

2. PRINCIPAL PUBLICATIONS OF CENTRAL GOVERNMENT

2.1. Legislation

Diário da República [*Daily journal of the Republic*]

Major legislation begins as bills introduced into the Assembleia da República [Assembly of the Republic]. These are first published as *propostas de lei* and *projectos de lei* in the *Diário da Assembleia da República, II Série* [Daily journal of the Assembly of the Republic, Series II]. After being discussed and approved by the Assembleia da República [Assembly of the Republic] and promulgated by the Presidente da República [President of the Republic] they are published as laws in the official gazette, the *Diário da República, I Série* [Daily journal of the Republic, Series I]. This is published daily except for Sundays and public holidays by the Imprensa Nacional-Casa da Moeda [National Printing Office-Mint] and contains various categories of subordinate legislation issued by the different branches of government as well as the laws passed by parliament. The main classes of legislation are laws (lei/-s), decrees (decreto/-s), decree-laws (decreto-lei/-s), regulatory decrees (decreto/-s regulamentar/-es), resolutions (resolução/-ões), regulations (portaria/-s), ministerial decisions (despacho/-s normativo/-s), declarations (declaração/ões), notices (aviso/-s), plus regional legislative decrees (decreto/-s legislativo/-s regional/-ais) and regional regulatory decrees (decreto/-s regulamentar/-es regional/-ais) for the Azores and Madeira. The different types of legislation are numbered consecutively in separate annual series (e.g. 1/85, 2/85, etc). Quarterly indexes to the *Diário da República, I Série* [Daily journal of the Republic, Series I] arranged in numerical order by type of legislation are published some time in arrears.

Other compilations

For many years beginning in the early 19th century there was an annual (later six-monthly) compilation of legislation which was published under the title *Colecção oficial de legislação portuguesa* [Official collection of Portuguese legislation]. This contained laws, decrees, regulations and other miscellaneous government orders. It appears, however, to have ceased publication in the late 1950s.

Another regular official source is the *Boletim do Ministério da Justiça* [Bulletin of the Ministry of Justice] which has a supplement devoted to legislation: *Boletim do Ministério da Justiça. Legislação. Suplemento ao Boletim no. . . .* [Bulletin of the Ministry of Justice. Legislation. Supplement to the Bulletin no. . . .]. This appears monthly or bi-monthly (double issues) and contains the texts of a select number of laws and regulations issued during the month to which the *Boletim* refers; it is published nearly a year in arrears. There are two indexes in each issue of the supplement, one of legislation published in the supplement and the other of legislation not published in it, arranged chronologically by type of legislation. There are also annual chronological and subject indexes to the *Boletim* which appear several years in arrears.

The armed forces and the national police force reprint legislation affecting them in the *Ordem do Exército* [Order of the Army], *Ordens da Marinha* [Orders of the Navy], *Ordem à Força Aérea* [Order to the Air Force] (formerly *Ordem à Aeronáutica* [Order to the Aeronautics]) and *Ordem à Guarda* [Order to the National Republican Guard]. So do some other government bodies such as the Comando-Geral da Guarda Fiscal [General Command of the Customs and Excise] which publishes a monthly *Boletim oficial da Guarda Fiscal* [Official bulletin of the Customs and Excise] and Correios e Telecomunicações de Portugal [Posts and Telecommunications of Portugal] which publishes a loose-leaf *Boletim oficial. Ficha de legislação* [Official bulletin. Legislation notes], together with monthly indexes.

Law codes and reports

Besides these serial publications, the Imprensa Nacional-Casa da Moeda [National Printing Office-Mint] publishes important laws and codes as separate monographs. The Ministério da Cultura [Ministry of Culture] has from time to time published compilations of legislation affecting cultural matters. A few law reports are published officially, notably the *Acordãos do Tribunal Constitucional* [Decisions given on appeal by the Constitutional Court], which replaced the *Pareceres da Comissão Constitucional* [Opinions of the Constitutional Commission], and the *Colecção de acordãos* [Collection of decisions given on appeal] of the Supremo Tribunal Administrativo [Supreme Administrative Court] which appear as appendices to the *Diário da República* [Daily journal of the Republic] (*see* section 2.2. below). Finally there is, of course, a great deal of commercial publishing of legal texts.

2.2. The official gazette

The official gazette is now known as the *Diário da República* [Daily journal of the Republic]. It traces its origins back to the early 18th century, appearing for the first hundred years under the title *Gazeta de Lisboa* [Lisbon gazette]. The title *Diário do Governo* [Daily journal of the Government] was first used from 16 October 1820 to 10 February 1821. There then followed a series of changes of title reflecting the political instability of the 1820s and 1830s: *Diário da Regência* [Daily journal of the Regency], *Diário do Governo* [Daily journal of the Government], *Gazeta de Lisboa* [Lisbon gazette], *Crónica constitucional de Lisboa* [Constitutional chronicle of Lisbon], *Gazeta oficial do Governo* [Official gazette of the Government] and *Gazeta do Governo* [Government gazette], before returning to *Diário do Governo* [Daily journal of the Government] again from 1 January 1835 to 31 October 1859. The title changed to *Diário de Lisboa* [Lisbon daily journal] from 1 November 1859 to 31 December 1868 and then reverted to *Diário do Governo* [Daily journal of the Government] from 2 January 1869 to 9 April 1976. The present title, *Diário da República* [Daily journal of the Republic], was introduced with issue no. 86 of 10 April 1976 which contained the text of the Presidential decree approving the constitution of 1976; some of the supplements continued to appear with the title *Diário do Governo* [Daily journal of the Government] for some time after that date. The *Diário da República* [Daily journal of the Republic] is published by the Imprensa Nacional-Casa da Moeda [National Printing Office-Mint].

During the course of the 20th century, the *Diário do Governo/Diário da República* [Daily journal of the Government/Republic] was divided into three series with a number of appendices. The three series appear daily except for Sundays and public holidays, and frequently include supplements. The *Diário da República, I Série* [Daily journal of the Republic, Series I] contains the texts of laws, decrees, regulations and miscellaneous government orders (*see* section 2.1 above). The *Diario da República, II Série* [Daily journal of the Republic, Series II] contains regulations for appointments to public employment, announcements of competitions and of appointments to public posts, miscellaneous notices concerning public bodies and the texts of opinions, judgements and decisions by certain courts such as the Tribunal Constitucional [Constitutional Court] and the Procuradoria Geral da República [Attorney General's Office]. The *Diário da República, III Série* [Daily journal of the Republic, Series III] contains notices about municipal employment and other matters, notices about the registration of companies, cooperatives and associations, announcements of competitive tenders to supply goods and services to the public sector, and details of exemptions from rates and taxes.

The *Apêndice ao Diário da República. Boletim da Propriedade Industrial* [Appendix to the Daily journal of the Republic. Bulletin of industrial property] appears monthly and gives details of patents and trade marks. The *Apêndice ao Diário da República*.

Ministério das Finanças e do Plano, Secretaria de Estado do Orçamento, Direcção-Geral do Tribunal de Contas [Appendix to the Daily journal of the Republic. Ministry of Finance and Planning, Secretariat of State for the Budget, Directorate-General of the Court of Accounts] is published irregularly and contains the auditors' decisions on public and municipal accounts.

Finally, the *Apêndice ao Diário da República. Supremo Tribunal Administrativo. Acordãos proferidos . . .* [Appendix to the Daily journal of the Republic. Supreme Administrative Court. Decisions given on appeal . . .] reports the decisions of the Supremo Tribunal Administrativo [Supreme Administrative Court]. It appears in five parts: *Acordãos proferidos pelo Tribunal pleno* [Decisions on appeal given by the full Court]; *Acordãos proferidos pela 1a Secção (contencioso administrativo)* [Decisions on appeal given by the 1st Section (administrative disputes)]; *Acordãos proferidos pela 2a. Secção (contencioso tributário-aduaneiro)* [Decisions on appeal given by the 2nd Section (tax disputes—customs duties)]; *Acordãos proferidos pela 2a Secção (contencioso tributário—contribuições e impostos)* [Decisions on appeal given by the 2nd Section (tax disputes—taxes and duties)]; *Acordãos proferidos pela 3a Secção (contencioso do trabalho e previdência social)* [Decisions on appeal given by the 3rd Section (labour and social security disputes)]. Each issue covers one quarter of a year and they appear several years in arrears. A title-page entitled *Colecção de acordãos* [Collection of decisions given on appeal] is issued together with an alphabetical subject index and a summary of the decisions.

2.3. Legislative proceedings

In spite of political vicissitudes and changes in regime, Portugal has had some form of representative assembly which has met continuously with only a few gaps since the first half of the 19th century. All the assemblies have published official records of their proceedings.

The earliest was the *Diário das Cortes Gerais e Extraordinárias da Nação Portuguesa* [Daily journal of the General and Extraordinary Parliament of the Portuguese Nation], January 1821–January 1822, continued as the *Diário das Cortes Gerais, Extraordinárias e Constituintes da Nação Portuguesa* [Daily journal of the General, Extraordinary and Constituent Parliament of the Portuguese Nation], January–November 1822, and *Diário das Cortes da Nação Portuguesa* [Daily journal of the Parliament of the Portuguese nation], November 1822–May 1823. During the first period in which the Constitutional Charter was in force from 1826 to 1828, debates were published under the title *Diário da Câmara dos Senhores Deputados da Nação Portuguesa* [Daily journal of the Chamber of Deputies of the Portuguese Nation]. This was followed by the *Diário das Cortes Gerais e Constituintes da Nação Portuguesa* [Daily journal of the General and Constituent Parliament of the Portuguese Nation], 1837, which became the *Actas das Sessões da Câmara dos Deputados* [Proceedings of the Sessions of the Chamber of Deputies], December 1838–July 1839.

The political system settled down in the middle of the 19th century and from then until 1910, the Cortes or Parliament was divided into two chambers, the Câmara dos Deputados [Chamber of Deputies] and the Câmara dos Pares [Chamber of Peers]. The two bodies published their proceedings separately, both in a verbatim and a somewhat abbreviated summary form. The verbatim proceedings of the Câmara dos Deputados [Chamber of Deputies] appeared under the title *Diário da Câmara dos Deputados* [Daily journal of the Chamber of Deputies] while that of the Câmara dos Pares [Chamber of

Peers] was variously entitled *Anais* [Annals] or *Diário* [Daily journal] at different times. Both summaries were entitled *Sumário*.

Following the overthrow of the monarchy in 1910, the Cortes [Parliament] were replaced by an Assembleia Nacional Constituinte [National Constituent Assembly] which met between June and August 1911 to draw up the first republican constitution. Its proceedings were recorded in both a verbatim *Diário da Assembleia Nacional Constituinte* [Daily journal of the National Constituent Assembly] and an abbreviated *Sumário* [Summary]. The First Republic maintained the two-chamber legislature, now called the Congresso [Congress], which published its proceedings between 1911 and 1926 in two separate publications: *Diário da Câmara dos Deputados* [Daily journal of the Chamber of Deputies] and *Diário do Senado* [Daily journal of the Senate]. The *Sumários* [Summaries] continued to be published up to 1917.

The last session of the First Republic's Congress took place on 31 May 1926, following which it was closed as a result of the military coup which had started on 28 May. The authoritarian constitution of 1933 provided for an Assembleia Nacional [National Assembly] and a Câmara Corporativa [Corporative Chamber] which first met in 1935. Their proceedings are recorded in the *Diário das sessões, Assembleia Nacional* [Daily journal of the sessions, National Assembly], 1935-1974, the *Anais da Assembleia Nacional e da Câmara Corporativa* [Annals of the National Assembly and the Corporative Chamber], 1935-1963/64, and the *Actas da Câmara Corporativa* [Proceedings of the Corporative Chamber], 1954-1974. Both bodies ceased to exist following the Revolution of 25 April 1974.

The present chapter in Portuguese parliamentary history opened with the elections for the Assembleia Constituinte [Constituent Assembly] which met between June 1975 and April 1976 to draw up the Constitution of 1976. Its proceedings were recorded in the *Diário da Assembleia Constituinte* [Daily journal of the Constituent Assembly], 3 June 1975 to 3 and 21 April 1976. Following the promulgation of the new constitution, this became the *Diário da Assembleia da República* [Daily journal of the Assembly of the Republic], which has appeared regularly since 1976. It is published by the Imprensa Nacional-Casa da Moeda [National Printing Office-Mint].

The *Diário da Assembleia da República* [Daily journal of the Assembly of the Republic] for the first session of the 1st Legislature (1976-1977) was published in a single series. Since 1977 it has been divided into two series, *I Série* [Series I] and *II Série* [Series II]. Both series are published several times a week while the Assembly is sitting. Both are numbered according to Legislature, Legislative Session, Series, issue number and date, e.g. III Legislatura, 1.a Sessão Legislativa (1983-1984), I Série, Número 98, Sexta-feira 27 de Abril de 1984. The numbering of issues and the pagination begin anew at the start of each legislative session. The *Diário da Assembleia da República, I Série* [Daily journal of the Assembly of the Republic, Series I] contains a summary of each day's proceedings; lists of deputies present, absent and who came in during the session, arranged by party; a verbatim record of the debates on the floor of the Assembly (*Reunião Plenária*); a verbatim report of the meetings of the Comissão Permanente [Permanent Commission] which meets when the full Assembly is not in session; the results of votes on bills; statements in which deputies justify the way they voted; and the reports and opinions of the Comissão de Regimento e Mandatos [Commission on Procedure and Mandates] sent to the Table for publication.

The *Diário da Assembleia da República, II Série* [Daily journal of the Assembly of the Republic, Series II] contains the texts of the government programme; bills presented by the government and by the deputies (*propostas de lei* and *projectos de lei*); draft amendments (*ratificações*); decrees passed by the Assembleia da República [Assembly of the Republic]; written questions from deputies (*requerimentos*) and written answers from ministers (*respostas a requerimentos*); draft resolutions; resolutions; demands for parliamentary inquiries and the terms of constitution, reports and proceedings of parliamentary commissions, including the proceedings of the Comissão de Economia, Finanças e Plano [Commission on the Economy, Finance and Planning] published in supplements; and other miscellaneous documents.

Besides the *Diário*, the Assembleia da República [Assembly of the Republic] also publishes a number of other publications to facilitate its work including the *Organização da Assembleia e relação nominal dos deputados* [Organization of the Assembly and list by name of the deputies] (1978, 1985), which lists its permanent specialized commissions, parliamentary groups and deputies grouped by party; *Regimento e legislação interna da Assembleia* [Procedure and internal legislation of the Assembly] (1982); *Regimento da Assembleia da República e Estatuto dos deputados* [Procedure of the Assembly of the Republic and Statute of the deputies] (1985); *Regulamento dos serviços* [Regulations on services] (1980); *Estatuto jurídico do pessoal da Assembleia da República* [Juridical statute of the staff of the Assembly of the Republic] (1980); and *Resumo histórico da Biblioteca, do Arquivo e do Museu da Assembleia da República* [Historical résumé of the Library, Archive and Museum of the Assembly of the Republic], by Maria das Dores Lopes da Silva (1977). From time to time, the Imprensa Nacional-Casa da Moeda [National Printing Office-Mint] issues important parliamentary publications such as the programme of new governments, white papers and reports of commissions, and miscellaneous publications relating to elections as separate monographs.

The address of the Assembly of the Republic is: Assembleia da República, Palácio de S. Bento, 1296 Lisboa Codex.

2.4. Publications of the executive

Statistics

The collection, processing and publication of statistics is centralized in the Instituto Nacional de Estatística [National Statistics Institute (INE)]. The INE was established in 1935, taking over the statistical functions exercised by the Direcção Geral de Estatística [General Directorate of Statistics], established in 1911, and its predecessors, which went back to 1841. The INE operates under the guidance of the Conselho Nacional de Estatística [National Statistics Council], presided over by the Prime Minister or his delegate, and the Comissões Consultivas de Estatística [Consultative Commissions on Statistics] which liaise with the various branches of government. The INE is based in Lisbon with regional offices in Oporto and Evora and semi-independent regional statistical services in the Azores and Madeira. Attached to the INE are two specialized research bodies, the Centro de Estudos Demográficos [Centre for Demographic Studies] and the Centro de Estudos Económicos [Centre for Economic Studies]. The INE publishes the censuses and a wide range of serial publications at monthly, quarterly and annual intervals. It has begun to make some statistics available on microfiche and is planning to set up an online database.

The INE acts as its own publisher, although many of its publications are printed by the Imprensa Nacional-Casa da Moeda [National Printing Office-Mint]. Most of the

INE's publications contain a list of all its serial publications at the back. Further information about the INE and its publications can be found in a booklet issued to mark its 50th anniversary: *Instituto Nacional de Estatística. Cinquentenário, 1935-1985* [National Statistics Institute. Fiftieth anniversary, 1935-1985], Lisboa, 1985. The INE's address is: Instituto Nacional de Estatística, Avenida de António José de Almeida 5, P-1078 Lisboa Codex.

CENSUSES

The first population census organized on a scientific basis according to international statistical recommendations was taken on 1 January 1864. The results were published in 1868 by the Imprensa Nacional under the title *Estatística de Portugal. População. Censo no 1.o de Janeiro 1864* [Statistics of Portugal. Population. Census on the 1st of January 1864]. The 1864 census gave details of the actual population in the Distritos, Concelhos and Freguesias according to urban or rural residence, sex, marital status, age and compared with the population with rights of residence. The introduction warned that the other statistics gathered were largely inaccurate.

The next population census was taken on 1 January 1878 and from then on censuses were carried out regularly at approximately 10-year intervals in 1890, 1900, 1911, 1920, 1930, 1940, 1950, 1960, 1970 and 1981, with a special census of Lisbon and Oporto in 1925. Of these the 1890 census was particularly noteworthy for the efficiency with which it was carried out and for the use of mechanical processing of the results. The 1940 census, the first to be carried out by the INE, benefitted from strong government backing, including an advertising campaign to increase public awareness of the census. The preliminary results of the 1970 census based on a 20% sample were published soon after the census was taken but the publication of the full results was delayed by internal problems. The first census of housing was taken at the same time as the 1970 population census.

The 12th population census was carried out on 16 March 1981, together with the second census of housing. The results were published by the Instituto Nacional de Estatística, Serviços Centrais [National Statistics Institute, Central Services], with the title *Recenseamentos da população e da habitação, 1981* [Censuses of population and housing, 1981]. There are 16 volumes giving results for the individual districts and the Autonomous Regions of the Azores and Madeira, one volume giving results for the whole country [*Total do país*] and another which describes earlier censuses, methodology and concepts [*Antecedentes, metodologia e conceitos*]. The results include tables giving a summary of the total population, buildings, dwellings, families, family nuclei and the resident population of individuals broken down by size of population centre, age, year of birth, socio-economic group, level of education, sex, place of birth, nationality, geographical mobility, marital status, religion, working status, means of livelihood, occupation and unemployment, plus women by number of children and resident foreigners. In connection with the 1981 censuses, the INE also issued a *Boletim informativo dos XII Recenseamento geral da população e II Recenseamento geral da habitação* [Information bulletin on the XII General census of population and the II General census of housing].

Details of individual census volumes can be found in the back of the annual volume of the *Estatísticas demográficas* [Demographic statistics], and in the University of Texas Population Research Center, *International population census bibliography: Europe* (Austin, University of Texas, Bureau of Business Research, 1967) and its revised edition, *The international population census bibliography: revision and update, 1945–1977*, compiled by Doreen S. Goyer (New York, Academic Press, 1980).

Besides the population and housing censuses, the INE also conducts censuses and surveys of various branches of the economy. The most recent of these are:

Recenseamento agrícola do Continente [Agricultural census of the mainland] (1979)
Inquérito às receitas e despesas familiares [Survey of family income and expenditure] (1980/81)
Inquéritos integrados ao sector dos transportes [Integrated surveys of the transport sector]: *Recenseamento às empresas do sector dos transportes* [Census of undertakings in the transport sector] (1982) and *Inquérito ao transporte rodoviário de mercadorias* [Survey of freight transport by road] (1983)
Recenseamento industrial [Industrial census] (1984/85)
Recenseamento à distribuição e serviços [Census of distribution and services] (1977).

STATISTICAL SERIES

In the first year of existence in 1935, the INE published a monthly statistical bulletin and five annual series. By 1985, half a century later, it was publishing six monthly, four quarterly and 21 annual series, as well as various irregular publications. These are listed in each annual volume and a more detailed contents list of the main statistical series is given in the *Anuário estatístico* [Statistical yearbook]. The statistical series published by the INE are:

Monthly

Boletim mensal de estatística [Monthly bulletin of statistics]
Boletim mensal das estatísticas do comércio externo [Monthly bulletin of foreign trade statistics]
Estado das culturas e previsão de colheitas [State of the crops and forecast of harvests]
Indices de produção industrial [Indexes of industrial production]
Indices de preços no consumidor [Indexes of consumer prices]

Quarterly

Inquérito ao emprego [Survey of employment]
Inquérito trimestral de conjuntura à indústria transformadora, relatório de síntese [Quarterly survey of the state of processing industry, summary report]
Inquérito trimestral de conjuntura ao comércio [Quarterly survey on the state of trade]

Annual

Anuário estatístico [Statistical yearbook]
Contas nacionais [National accounts]
Estatísticas agrícolas [Agricultural statistics]
Estatísticas do comércio externo [Foreign trade statistics]
Estatísticas da construção e da habitação [Building and housing statistics]

Estatísticas das contribuições e impostos [Statistics on taxes and duties]
Estatísticas da cultura, recreio e desporto [Statistics on culture, recreation and sport]
Estatísticas demográficas [Demographic statistics]
Estatísticas da educação [Education statistics]
Estatísticas da energia [Energy statistics]
Estatísticas das finanças públicas [Statistics on public finances]
Estatísticas industriais [Industrial statistics]:
  Volume I: Indústrias extractivas, electricidade, gaś, água [Volume I: Extractive industries, electricity, gas, water]
  Volume II: Indústrias transformadoras [Volume II: Processing industries]
Estatísticas da justiça [Justice statistics]
Estatísticas monetárias e financeiras [Monetary and financial statistics]
Estatísticas da pesca [Fishing statistics]
Estatísticas da saúde [Health statistics]
Estatísticas de segurança social, associações sindicais e patronais [Statistics on social security, trades unions and employers' associations]
Estatísticas das sociedades [Company statistics]
Estatísticas dos transportes e comunicações [Statistics on transport and communications]
Estatísticas do turismo [Tourism statistics]
Portugal [Statistical synopses in English and French]
Principais sociedades [Main companies]

The INE also publishes the following publications on statistics at irregular intervals:

Série Divulgação [Factsheet series]
Série Documentos [Documents series]
Série Estatísticas regionais [Regional statistics series]
Série Estimativas provisórias [Provisional estimates series]
Série Estudos [Studies series]
Série Legislação [Legislation series]
Série Normas (CAE—V Parte) [Standards series (CAE—V Part)]
Série Retrospectiva [Retrospective series]
Portugal e a CEE em números [Portugal and the EEC in figures]
Revista do Centro de Estudos Demográficos [Review of the Centre of Demographic Studies]
Revista do Centro de Estudos Económicos [Review of the Centre of Economic Studies]
Cadernos do Centro de Estudos Demográficos [Notes of the Centre of Demographic Studies].

The foreign trade statistics in the *Estatísticas do comércio externo* [Foreign trade statistics] are drawn up according to the Nomenclatura Estatística das Mercadorias do Comércio Externo (NEMCE) [Statistical Nomenclature of Foreign Trade Goods], which is similar to the NIMEXE nomenclature used by the European Economic Community. They are also laid out according to the sections, divisions and groups of the Standard International Trade Classification (SITC), 2nd revision.

PRINCIPAL PUBLICATIONS OF CENTRAL GOVERNMENT

The *Estatísticas da cultura, recreio e desporto* [Statistics on culture, recreation and sport] contains statistics on the press, libraries, museums, the film industry, radio and television broadcasting, sports and the Casas do Povo [Houses of the People] recreation centres. The 1984 edition of the *Estatísticas de segurança social, associações sindicais e patronais* [Statistics on social security, trades unions and employers' associations] contains, besides the statistics on social security and trades union and employers' associations, a detailed account of the recent development of the Portuguese social security system and a list of the most important legislation relating to social security, employers' associations and trades unions in force in Portugal.

An exception to the general rule that the publication of statistics is carried out centrally by the INE is the *Estatística das instalações eléctricas em Portugal (Continente e Açores)* [Statistics on electrical installations in Portugal (Mainland and Azores)], which is published by the Ministério da Indústria e Energia, Direcção-Geral de Energia [Ministry of Industry and Energy, Directorate-General of Energy]. The 1983 edition was published in three volumes. From 1983, the *Estatísticas da justiça* [Justice statistics], previously published by the INE, became a publication of the Gabinete de Estudos e Planeamento do Ministério da Justiça [Office of Studies and Planning of the Ministry of Justice], which was classified as a delegated body of the INE.

Many of the statistical series have a long pedigree, reaching back in some cases into the 19th century, albeit with some lack of continuity and the inevitable changes of title. For example, the first issue of the *Anuário estatístico* [Statistical yearbook] appeared in 1875 but then there followed a gap of nine years before the next issue appeared in 1884. The foreign trade statistics have been published since 1843 with the following titles: *Mapas gerais do comércio de Portugal* [General maps of the trade of Portugal] (1843, 1848, 1856, 1861, 1865–1867), *Estatística geral do comércio de Portugal* [General statistics on the trade of Portugal] (1868–1879), *Estatística do comércio de Portugal* [Statistics on the trade of Portugal] (1880–1896), *Comércio e navegação* [Trade and shipping] (1897–1920), *Estatística comercial* [Trade statistics] (1921/22–1928/29, 1930–1937), *Comércio externo* [Foreign trade] (1938–1966), *Estatísticas do comércio externo* [Foreign trade statistics] (1967–).

The demographic statistics have been published since 1862, with the following titles: *Mapas estatísticos dos baptismos, casamentos e óbitos que houve no Reino de Portugal e Ilhas Adjacentes—Ano de 1862* [Statistical tables of the baptisms, marriages and deaths which occurred in the Kingdom of Portugal and Adjacent Islands—Year 1862], *Movimento da população. Estado civil. Emigração* [Population changes. Marital status. Emigration] (1887–1890, 1891/93, 1894/96), *Tabelas do movimento fisiológico da população de Portugal* [Tables of the physiological changes in the population of Portugal] (1901/10), *Emigração portuguesa* [Portuguese emigration] (1901–1912), *Movimento da população. Resumo* [Population changes. Summary] (1907/11, 1908/12), *Estatística demográfica. Movimento da população* [Demographic statistics. Population changes] (1909/13–1917/21), *Estatística do movimento fisiológico da população de Portugal* [Statistics on the physiological changes in the population of Portugal] (1913–1925), *Anuário demográfico. Estatística do movimento fisiológico da população de Portugal* [Demographic yearbook. Statistics on the physiological changes in the population of Portugal] (1929–1940), *Anuário demográfico. Estatística do movimento da população de Portugal* [Demographic yearbook. Statistics on population changes in Portugal] (1941–1966), *Estatísticas demográficas* [Demographic statistics] (1967–1975, 1976/79, 1980/82, 1983–).

The above details are taken from a table in the most recent volume of each series which lists the titles and dates of earlier volumes in the same series or containing statistics on the same subject. The INE's practice of including these tables at the back of most annual volumes is an invaluable aid in tracing statistics over a large number of years.

Other publications of the executive

Many other government bodies also issue publications. Examples are the monographs on employment and wages published by the Departamento de Estudos e Planeamento, Ministério do Trabalho [Department of Studies and Planning, Ministry of Labour] in the *Colecção Estudos* [Studies Collection] series, and the *Boletim* [Bulletin] of the Comissão da Condição Feminina [Commission on the Condition of Women], which is responsible to the Presidência do Conselho de Ministros [Cabinet Office].

Examples of research and cultural journals published by government bodies are the *Revista do Instituto Geográfico e Cadastral* [Review of the Geographical and Survey Institute], which appears annually; *Studia* [Studia], a twice-yearly journal published by the Centro de Estudos Históricos Ultramarinos da Junta de Investigações Científicas do Ultramar [Centre for Overseas Territories Historical Studies of the Board of Scientific Research on the Overseas Territories], which contains articles on the history of the Portuguese empire, and *Estudos contemporâneos* [Contemporary studies], which is published annually in Oporto by the Ministério da Cultura, Delegação Regional do Norte, Centro de Estudos Humanísticos [Ministry of Culture, Regional Delegation of the North, Centre of Humanistic Studies] and contains articles on various aspects of Portuguese culture and social life.

The Banco de Portugal [Bank of Portugal] publishes a well-produced and up-to-date *Boletim trimestral/Quarterly bulletin*. It contains an overview of recent developments in the Portuguese economy in Portuguese, with an English summary, and detailed statistical tables, with headings in Portuguese and English. Amongst publications on a more popular level there are serials such as the *Jornal do Exército* [Army journal], a monthly magazine for soldiers, and booklets such as *Eleições para a Assembleia da República, 83* [Elections for the Assembly of the Republic, 83], published by the Direcção-Geral da Comunicação Social [General Directorate of Social Communication] to mark the 1983 parliamentary elections.

The following are the main publications issued by government departments:

Acordos de Portugal com outros países e organizações internacionais dentro da área económica/Direcção-Geral do Comércio Externo [Agreements of Portugal with other countries and international organizations in the economic area/Directorate-General of Foreign Trade]

Anuário da Administração Pública/Direcção-Geral da Administração e Função Pública [Yearbook of public administration/Directorate-General of Public Administration and the Civil Service]

Bibliografia especializada/Junta Nacional de Investigação Científica e Tecnológica [Specialized bibliography/National Board for Scientific and Technological Research]

Boletim/Secretaria de Estado da Marinha Mercante [Bulletin/Secretariat of State for the Merchant Navy]

Boletim bibliográfico/Direcção-Geral dos Serviços de Informática. Ministério da

Justiça [Bibliographical bulletin/Directorate-General of Information Technology Services. Ministry of Justice]
 Boletim bibliográfico/Centro de Estudos Judiciários. Ministério da Justiça [Bibliographical bulletin/Centre for Judicial Studies. Ministry of Justice]
 Boletim bibliográfico/Polícia Judiciária. Ministério da Justiça [Bibliographical bulletin/Criminal Investigation Police. Ministry of Justice]
 Boletim bibliográfico/Secretaria Geral do Ministério da Justiça [Bibliographical bulletin/Secretariat General of the Ministry of Justice]
 Boletim DGQ/Direcção-Geral da Qualidade [DGQ Bulletin/Directorate-General of Quality]
 Boletim da Administração Penitenciária e dos Institutos de Criminologia/Direcção-Geral dos Serviços Prisionais. Ministério da Justiça [Bulletin of the Prison Administration and the Institutes of Criminology/Directorate-General of Prison Services. Ministry of Justice]
 Boletim da Direcção-Geral dos Registos e do Notariado/Direcção-Geral dos Registos e do Notariado [Bulletin of the Directorate-General of Registers and Notaries/Directorate-General of Registers and Notaries]
 Boletim de Documentação/Secretaria de Estado do Comércio Externo. Direcção-Geral do Comércio Externo [Bulletin of documentation/Secretariat of State for Foreign Trade. Directorate-General of Foreign Trade]
 Boletim de minas/Direcção-Geral de Minas e Serviços Geológicos [Bulletin of mines/Directorate-General of Mines and Geological Services]
 Boletim de sumários/Direcção-Geral das Indústrias Transformadoras e Ligeiras. Ministério da Indústria, Energia e Exportação [Bulletin of abstracts/Directorate-General of Processing and Light Industries. Ministry of Industry, Energy and Exports]
 Boletim de sumários/Direcção-Geral dos Serviços de Informática. Ministério da Justiça [Bulletin of abstracts/Directorate-General of Information Technology Services. Ministry of Justice]
 Boletim de sumários/Centro de Estudos Judiciários. Ministério da Justiça [Bulletin of abstracts/Centre for Judicial Studies. Ministry of Justice]
 Boletim do Ministério da Justiça/Ministério da Justiça [Bulletin of the Ministry of Justice/Ministry of Justice]
 Boletim do Ministério da Justiça. Legislação/Ministério da Justiça [Bulletin of the Ministry of Justice. Legislation/Ministry of Justice]
 Boletim do trabalho e emprego/Ministério do Trabalho [Bulletin of labour and employment/Ministry of Labour]
 Boletim dos Registos e Notariado/Direcção-Geral dos Registos e do Notariado [Bulletin of registers and notaries/Directorate-General of Registers and Notaries]
 Boletim informativo/Ministério da Educação [Information bulletin/Ministry of Education]
 Boletim informativo do Gabinete de Apoio Técnico-Legislativo/Gabinete de Apoio Técnico-Legislativo. Ministério da Justiça [Information bulletin of the Office of Technical and Legislative Support/Office of Technical and Legislative Support. Ministry of Justice]
 Boletim informativo dos Serviços Judiciários/Direcção-Geral dos Serviços Judiciários [Information bulletin of the Judicial Services/Directorate-General of Judicial Services]

Boletim JAE/Ministério do Equipamento Social [JAE Bulletin/Ministry of Social Equipment]

Boletim oficial da Guarda Fiscal/Ministério das Finanças [Official bulletin of the Customs and Excise/Ministry of Finance]

Boletim oficial do Ministério da Justiça/Ministério da Justiça [Official bulletin of the Ministry of Justice/Ministry of Justice]

Cadernos de ciência e técnica fiscal/Centro de Estudos Fiscais. Ministério das Finanças [Notes on fiscal science and techniques/Centre for Fiscal Studies. Ministry of Finance]

Ciência e técnica fiscal/Centro de Estudos Fiscais. Ministério das Finanças [Fiscal science and technique/Centre for Fiscal Studies. Ministry of Finance]

Comunicação social. Legislação/Direcção-Geral da Comunicação Social [Social communication. Legislation/Directorate-General of Social Communication]

Comunicações/Direcção-Geral de Geologia e Minas [Communiqués/Directorate-General of Geology and Mines]

Conta geral do Estado/Direcção-Geral da Contabilidade Pública. Ministério das Finanças [General accounts of the State/Directorate-General of Public Accountancy. Ministry of Finance]

Contas/Junta do Crédito Público [Accounts/Board of Public Credit]

Difusão de legislação/Secretaria de Estado da Reforma Administrativa [Legislation circular/Secretariat of State for Administrative Reform]

Difusão de textos seleccionados/Centro de Informação Científica e Tecnológica da Reforma Administrativa [Selected texts circular/Centre for Scientific and Technological Information on Administrative Reform]

Documentação e direito comparado/Gabinete de Documentação e Direito Comparado. Ministério da Justiça [Documentation and comparative law/Office of Documentation and Comparative Law. Ministry of Justice]

Empresas públicas sob tutela de Ministérios/Direcção-Geral do Comércio Externo [Public undertakings under the care of Ministries/Directorate-General of Foreign Trade]

Estudos, notas e trabalhos/Direcção-Geral de Geologia e Minas [Studies, notes and papers/Directorate-General of Geology and Mines]

Folha bibliográfica/Secretaria Geral do Ministério da Educação [Bibliographical newsletter/Secretariat General of the Ministry of Education]

ICALP Revista/Ministério da Educação. Instituto de Cultura e Língua Portuguesa [ICALP Review/Ministry of Education. Institute of Portuguese Culture and Language]

Infância e juventude/Direcção-Geral dos Serviços Tutelares de Menores. Ministério da Justiça [Childhood and youth/Directorate-General of the Guardianship Services for Minors. Ministry of Justice]

Informação bibliográfica/Secretaria de Estado da Segurança Social [Bibliographical information/Secretariat of State for Social Security]

Informação bibliográfica/Junta Nacional de Investigação Científica e Tecnológica [Bibliographical information/National Board for Scientific and Technological Research]

Jornal da Polícia Judiciária/Polícia Judiciária [Journal of the Criminal Investigation Police/Criminal Investigation Police]

PRINCIPAL PUBLICATIONS OF CENTRAL GOVERNMENT

Jornal do Exército/Estado Maior do Exército [Army journal/General Headquarters of the Army]

Legislação sobre comércio externo/Direcção-Geral do Comércio Externo [Legislation on overseas trade/Directorate-General of Foreign Trade]

Legislação sobre empresas desintervencionadas/Direcção-Geral do Comércio Externo [Legislation on undertakings returned to private enterprise/Directorate-General of Foreign Trade]

Legislação sobre empresas com intervenção do Estado/Direcção-Geral do Comércio Externo [Legislation on undertakings taken over by the State/Directorate-General of Foreign Trade]

Legislação sobre empresas nacionalizadas/Direcção-Geral do Comércio Externo [Legislation on nationalized undertakings/Directorate-General of Foreign Trade]

Legislação sobre empresas para as quais foi requerida falência/Direcção-Geral do Comércio Externo [Legislation on undertakings which have called in the receivers/Directorate-General of Foreign Trade]

Legislação sobre empresas públicas/Direcção-Geral do Comércio Externo [Legislation on public undertakings/Directorate-General of Foreign Trade]

Legislação sobre falências de empresas/Direcção-Geral do Comércio Externo [Legislation on bankruptcies/Directorate-General of Foreign Tade]

Legislação sobre fusão de empresas/Direcção-Geral do Comércio Externo [Legislation on mergers/Directorate-General of Foreign Trade]

Orçamento/Ministério da Qualidade de Vida [Budget/Ministry of the Quality of Life]

Orçamento/Secretaria de Estado do Orçamento. Ministério das Finanças [Budget/Secretariat of State for the Budget. Ministry of Finance]

Orçamento geral do Estado/Imprensa Nacional-Casa da Moeda [General budget of the State/National Printing Office-Mint]

Organização e informática/Direcção-Geral da Organização Administrativa [Organization and information technology/Directorate-General of Administrative Organization]

Polícia e justiça/Polícia Judiciária [Police and justice/Criminal Investigation Police]

Relatório anual/Polícia Judiciária [Annual report/Criminal Investigation Police]

Relatório de actividades da Polícia Judiciária/Polícia Judiciária [Report on the activities of the Criminal Investigation Police/Criminal Investigation Police]

Relatório de actividades/Directoria de Lisboa. Polícia Judiciária [Report on its activities/Lisbon Directorate. Criminal Investigation Police]

Relatório de actividades/Escola da Polícia Judiciária. Polícia Judiciária [Report on its activities/School of the Criminal Investigation Police. Criminal Investigation Police]

Relatório de actividades do Gabinete Coordenador de Combate à Droga/Gabinete Coordenador de Combate à Droga. Presidência do Conselho de Ministros [Report on the activities of the Coordinating Office for the Fight against Drugs. Cabinet Office]

Relatório do Provedor de Justiça/Secretaria de Estado da Comunicação Social [Report of the Director of Justice/Secretariat of State for Social Communication]

Relatório e contas da gerência. ADSE/Ministério das Finanças [Report and accounts of the management. ADSE/Ministry of Finance]

Revista da administração pública/Secretaria de Estado da Administração Pública [Review of public administration/Secretariat of State for Public Administration]

Revista de investigação criminal/Directoria do Porto. Polícia Judiciária [Review of criminal investigation/Oporto Directorate. Criminal Investigation Police]

Revista do Centro de Estudos Demográficos/Instituto Nacional de Estatística [Review of the Centre for Demographic Studies/National Statistics Institute]

Revista do Instituto Geográfico e Cadastral/Instituto Geográfico e Cadastral [Review of the Geographical and Survey Institute/Geographical and Survey Institute].

3. MANNER OF PUBLICATION

3.1. Imprensa Nacional-Casa da Moeda

The main official publishing agency is the Imprensa Nacional-Casa da Moeda [National Printing Office-Mint] which prints and publishes the official gazette, the parliamentary papers, texts of legislation and a variety of official series and monographs, as well as non-official publications.

The Imprensa Nacional has a long history reaching back to the 18th century. It was established by a decree dated 24 December 1768 and signed by King José I and his great reforming minister, the Marquis of Pombal. The original name was the Impressão Régia [King's Printing Works] although the designation Régia Oficina Tipográfica [King's Typographic Workshop] was often used on the title-pages of its publications. The initial capital investment came from a loan provided by the University of Coimbra on royal orders. The printing works was given a monopoly over the printing and sale of playing cards, which lasted until 1832, and the profits from this monopoly allowed it to cover the costs of its other printing operations. The press also established a tradition of fine printing which still continues. A total of 1,230 works were published between 1769 and 1801, giving an average of 40 per year.

During the political upheavals of the first half of the 19th century, the Impressão Régia [King's Printing Works] changed its name to the Imprensa Nacional [National Printing Office] between 1820 and 1823 and again definitively in 1833. Thanks to the adoption of modern machinery and working practices, the Imprensa Nacional was an efficient operation, winning prizes at various international exhibitions for the quality of its printing. It produced elaborate catalogues of its typefaces, vignettes and ornaments in 1859 (dated 1858) and 1870 with later less ornate editions in 1912, 1915 and 1933.

The first composing machine was acquired in 1912, by which year the number of staff totalled 513. During the 20th century the Imprensa Nacional suffered various vicissitudes. Its administrator was shot dead outside the building in November 1927. It absorbed a number of other official and academic presses, beginning with that of the Academia das Ciências [Academy of Sciences] in 1910 and then the presses of the Ministério da Agricultura, Comércio e Indústria [Ministry of Agriculture, Commerce and Industry] and the Biblioteca Nacional [National Library] (1933), the Imprensa da Universidade de Coimbra [University of Coimbra Press] (1934), the printing shop of the Instituto Superior de Ciências Económicas e Financeiras [Higher Institute for Economic and Financial Sciences] (1936) and the Imprensa da Armada [Navy Press] (1940). All recruiting of staff and of apprentices was suspended between 1934 and

1940. By the 1950s the Imprensa Nacional was in need of reform but the package of reforms introduced in December 1953 did not turn out to be a success.

Consequently a government decree-law signed on 30 December 1969 turned the Imprensa Nacional into a public enterprise (empresa pública) and granted it greater financial and administrative autonomy, with the aim of giving it greater flexibility and allowing it to adapt more readily to the increasing pace of technological advance. The government, however, retained overall control through the Imprensa Nacional's administrative and fiscal councils over staffing and pay, the distribution of profits, the accounts, the contracting of long-term loans and the disposal of property. Besides its traditional functions, the Imprensa Nacional was also made responsible for training printing apprentices for private industry and improving the technical level of printing in Portugal. A few years later a decree of 4 July 1972 merged the Imprensa Nacional with the Casa da Moeda [Mint] to form a new public enterprise known as the Imprensa Nacional-Casa da Moeda (INCM). The merger was intended to help the Mint resolve its problems in view of the similar and complementary functions of the two bodies.

In the printing sphere the Imprensa Nacional-Casa da Moeda continues its traditional role, printing and publishing both official publications and works of a literary, cultural or historical nature aimed at the commercial market. The INCM does not have a monopoly of official publishing but does print and publish many of the most important official publications. The main publications are the *Diário da República* [Daily journal of the Republic]; the *Diário da Assembleia da República* [Daily journal of the Assembly of the Republic] and other parliamentary publications; the texts of codes and important laws which are issued as separate monographs; other legal publications such as the former *Pareceres da Comissão Constitucional* [Opinions of the Constitutional Commission]; the government accounts, *Conta geral do Estado* [General accounts of the State]; and a variety of monographs and series published on behalf of other official bodies. The INCM also prints publications which are published by other official bodies such as the Instituto Nacional de Estatística [National Statistics Institute].

On the non-official side, the Imprensa Nacional-Casa da Moeda continues its long tradition of fine printing with works such as the catalogue of all its editions, *Imprensa Nacional. Actividade de uma casa impressora* [National Printing Office. Catalogue of a printing house], volume 1 of which, covering the years 1768–1800, was published in 1975. It also publishes the following series and collections of monographs aimed at university students and the educated public: *Biblioteca de Autores Portugueses* [Library of Portuguese Authors]; *Arte e Artistas* [Art and Artists]; *Presenças da Imagem* [Presence of the Image]; *Musarum Officia* [Musarum Officia]; *Estudos e Temas Portugueses* [Portuguese Studies and Themes]; *Pensamento Português* [Portuguese Thought]; *Escritores dos Países de Língua Portuguesa* [Writers from Portuguese-speaking Countries]; *Colecção Essencial* [Essential Collection]; and *Estudos Gerais/Série Universitária* [General Studies/University Series]. The INCM issues a catalogue of its non-official publications. Its address is: Imprensa Nacional-Casa da Moeda, E. P., Rua de D. Francisco Manuel de Melo 5, 1092 Lisboa Codex.

3.2. Departmental publications

Whilst the main legislative, parliamentary and government publications are printed and published through the Imprensa Nacional-Casa da Moeda [National Printing

Office-Mint] acting as a central government printer, there is also a wide range of official publications which are issued directly by government departments, government-funded organizations, research institutes and public enterprises. These vary from publications recording the official activities of the issuing body through research and cultural journals to information leaflets for the general public.

4. BIBLIOGRAPHIC CONTROL

There is no Portuguese bibliography devoted to official publications. Official publications are included in the national bibliography, the *Boletim de bibliografia portuguesa* [Bulletin of Portuguese bibliography], which is published by the Biblioteca Nacional [National Library] in Lisbon, although they are not classified as a separate category. The *Boletim de bibliografia portuguesa* used to be published in monthly parts but in 1981 it was divided into three sections covering monographs, serials and non-textual documents (maps, posters, postcards, etc). The *Boletim de bibliografia portuguesa: Monografias* [Bulletin of Portuguese bibliography: Monographs] is arranged by subject according to the UDC classification and is published quarterly or bi-annually. The entries in the *Boletim de bibliografia portuguesa: Publicações em série* [Bulletin of Portuguese bibliography: Serial publications] are arranged alphabetically by title with indexes by issuing body, subject and place of publication; official publications are not entered separately but can be traced through the index for issuing bodies where they are grouped together under Portugal. The serials section is published annually.

Portuguese official publications can also be found in the British Library's *General catalogue of printed books* and the *National union catalog* published by the U.S. Library of Congress. Earlier Portuguese official serials are entered in the *List of the serial publications of foreign governments, 1815-1931*, edited by Winifred Gregory (New York, Wilson, 1932).

Individual official bodies publish catalogues of their publications occasionally. Bibliographical sources for the publications of the Imprensa Nacional-Casa da Moeda [National Printing Office-Mint] and the Instituto Nacional de Estatística [National Statistics Institute] have been referred to in their respective sections. The former Agência-Geral do Ultramar [General Agency for the Overseas Territories] published a *Catálogo das publicações* [Catalogue of publications] in two volumes: *Didascálico* [By title] (1965) and *Onomástico* [By author] (1966).

5. PUBLICATIONS OF REGIONAL AND LOCAL GOVERNMENT

The Atlantic islands of the Azores and Madeira are both designated as Regiões Autónomas [Autonomous Regions] with regional governments and assemblies which issue publications. In the Azores the *Diário da Assembleia Regional dos Açores, 1.a Série* [Daily journal of the Regional Assembly of the Azores, lst Series] has been published since 20 July 1976. The *Jornal oficial da Região Autónoma dos Açores* [Official journal of the Autonomous Region of the Azores] is published in four series. The *1.a Série* [lst Series] has been published since 2 March 1977; the *2.a Série* [2nd Series] since 16 March 1977; the *3.a Série* [3rd Series] since 31 December 1980 and the *4.a Série* [4th Series] since 16 March 1982. The *Diário da Assembleia Regional da Madeira, 1.a Série*

NOTE

[Daily journal of the Regional Assembly of Madeira, 1st Series] began publication on 19 July 1976. The *Jornal oficial da Região Autónoma da Madeira* [Official journal of the Autonomous Region of Madeira] appears in three series. The *1.a Série* [1st Series] and the *2.a Série* [2nd Series] have been published since 29 November 1977 and the *3.a Série* [3rd Series] since 17 January 1983.

Other regional bodies also issue publications, including *Açores: anuário estatístico* [Azores: statistical yearbook], the first issue of which for the year 1977 was published in 1980; *Madeira: anuário estatístico* [Madeira: statistical yearbook] published by the Instituto Nacional de Estatística, Delegação do Funchal [National Statistics Institute, Funchal Delegation], beginning in 1978; two bulletins both entitled *Informação* [Information] published respectively by the Serviço Regional do Trabalho [Regional Labour Service] in Funchal, Madeira, and the Serviço Regional de Estatística da Madeira [Regional Statistics Service of Madeira]; and two publications entitled *Boletim semestral* [Six-monthly bulletin], published by the Banco de Portugal [Bank of Portugal], Delegação Regional dos Açores [Regional Delegation of the Azores] and Delegação Regional da Madeira [Regional Delegation of Madeira] respectively.

Many of the local authorities produce their own publications. The most important are those of Lisbon, the capital and largest city, which appear under the heading Câmara Municipal de Lisboa [Municipal Chamber of Lisbon] or Município de Lisboa [Municipality of Lisbon]. The *Diário municipal* [Municipal daily journal] publishes legislation, regulations and circulars emanating from the national government and the decisions of the higher courts which affect Lisbon, together with the deliberations of the Câmara Municipal de Lisboa [Municipal Chamber of Lisbon] and the executive orders of the Presidente da Câmara Municipal [President of the Municipal Chamber]. The main items in the *Diário municipal* are included in the *Sumário anual do Diário municipal* [Annual summary of the Municipal daily journal] which is published about two years in arrears in paperback book format; it contains an index.

The *Actas da Câmara Municipal de Lisboa* [Proceedings of the Municipal Chamber of Lisbon] summarizes the speeches of the vereadores [councillors] and gives the results of votes. It is published in paperback book format in several volumes covering a two-year mandate. An annual *Índice das Actas das reuniões* [Index of the Proceedings of the meetings] is published separately several years in arrears; it comprises an alphabetical index by subject, name and measure (in numerical order). Other publications of the Câmara Municipal de Lisboa/Município de Lisboa are the *Orçamento ordinário para o ano económico de* . . . [Budget for the financial year . . .] (plus occasional supplements) and *Contas do ano financeiro de* . . . [Accounts of the financial year . . .], both published annually, and a variety of cultural publications.

Other local authorities issue publications on a smaller scale. For example, there is a *Boletim municipal* [Municipal bulletin] issued by the Câmara Municipal [Municipal Chamber] in Avis, Matosinhos, Miranda do Douro, Palmela and Silves, to name only a few.

NOTE

I am particularly grateful for the invaluable advice and information provided by Sra Natália Nunes Rocha of the library of the Procuradoria Geral da República in Lisbon. She compiled the list of publications of government departments which appears in section 2.4 under the heading 'Other publications of the executive' and supplied details of most of the regional publications in section 5, as well as answering sundry queries with great promptness.

6. BIBLIOGRAPHY

Farinha, Ramiro. *Imprensa Nacional de Lisboa: sinopse da sua história.* [Lisbon, Imprensa Nacional], 1969.

Instituto Nacional de Estatística. Cinquentenário, 1935—1985. Lisbon, Instituto Nacional de Estatística, 1985.

Ribeiro, José Vitorino. *A Imprensa Nacional de Lisboa: subsídios para a sua história, 1768-1912.* [Lisbon], Imprensa Nacional, 1912.

Sweden

LENNART GRÖNBERG, LUCIA MITLID AND ROLF NYGREN

1. INTRODUCTION

Historical introduction

The development of Swedish constitutional practice can be followed through roughly three phases, a medieval period ending with the sixteenth century, then a period marked by a struggle between royal autocracy and popular power, and finally a period when the democratic system of government gradually gained ground until it prevailed totally. The dividing line between the second and third phases of development is usually drawn at the year 1809, but some people would undoubtedly maintain, with good reason, that it should be set at a considerably later date.

Obviously, no printed constitutional publications are encountered during the Middle Ages. The political decisions were made either in the form of royal legislation or jointly by King and people. It is a debatable question when the Herredagar—that is, meeting between the King and people—can be said to have reached the extent and the representational nature that could be regarded as parliamentary. A precursor to the parliament may have been a meeting in 1435 at Arboga, attended by bishops, knights and commoners: there were subsequent meetings, and rules as to their conduct and the arrangement of the four Estates evolved after about 1600. In the course of the fifteenth century it is possible to speak of a rudimentary four Estates system.

Unquestionably the body of laws is the most important set of constitutional documents remaining from the Middle Ages. It is justifiable to discern two phases of development within the history of the law. During the first period each Province principally had its own set of laws, handed down by a Lagman [literally, law-man] and recited by him at the Ting [assembly] of the Province. The assembled freemen then had the opportunity on the one hand of verifying that the Lagman had correctly comprehended the law and on the other of making necessary corrections. These provincial laws are extant in various editions from most Provinces. In the middle of the fourteenth century, however, the development of society had advanced so far that the legal administration needed national uniformity in legislation. Accordingly around 1350 a Landslag [National Rural Law Code] was drawn up, followed 10 years later by a Stadslag [Urban Law Code]. In 1442 the Landslag was considerably revised, but it is indicative of the royal authority's weakness that the provincial laws seem to have been administered in parallel with the Landslag for several decades, and that the revised Landslag did not succeed in definitely ousting the older provincial ones until the end of the fifteenth century.

Besides the various law codes there are a considerable number of royal regulations, Herredags' resolutions, and so on. In so far as this material is printed, it is to be found principally in *Svenskt diplomatarium*, the Swedish series of published medieval original documents.

It is not justifiable to speak of printed constitutional publications in the strict sense of the word until about 1600. With the art of printing it became possible during the sixteenth century to duplicate political and administrative decisions for a wider circle of receivers, but not until some way into the seventeenth century was the possibility of mass production effectively utilized.

The appearance of centrally published constitutional and statutory publications precisely at the beginning of the seventeenth century can probably be explained by two factors. In the first place, the Riksdag, organized into four Estates, presented a firmer structure around 1600: owing to this, a new factor was definitely established in Swedish political life. Second, and more important, central as well as regional administrations developed into new forms. The central administration, divided into five departments, 'Kollegier', handled chancery questions, legislation and administration of justice, naval and military matters, and tax collection. Regionally, the country was divided into Län [Counties] under the administration of a Landshövding [County Governor]. The County as a unit of administration has survived into present times.

It is true that records were kept of the meetings of the four Estates but they were not intended for printing and public distribution as constitutional documents. Principally it was the business of each Estate of the Riksdag to decide on the printing of its own records. However, it was not until much later that such printing was carried out. As far as the seventeenth century is concerned, printed Riksdag records are rather rare.

During the time between 1680 and 1718 the democratic government system, even in much restricted form, was more and more set aside, and between 1693 and 1718 total royal autocracy reigned *de facto*. The disastrous Great Nordic War, which finished with Sweden losing her Baltic possessions, ended the royal autocracy. It was followed by Frihetstiden [the period of liberty]. The pendulum swung over towards parliamentarism. In the wake of the new constitution there followed a political openness fairly unusual at the time, and in 1766 the Tryckfrihetsförordningen [Freedom of the Press Act], the purpose of which was precisely to create the greatest possible publicity around the manifestations of government power and administration. However, substantial parts of the parliamentary proceedings were withheld from view by the secrecy surrounding the proceedings and debates of the Riksdag standing committees. Remarkably enough, this parliamentary development did not bring about any real initiative of having at least the records of the Estates printed. It is possible that the demands of publicity regarding parliamentary work were sufficiently met by the fairly active press and by specially published Riksdag newspapers.

The powerful position of the Riksdag was gradually reduced after the *coup d'état* by King Gustavus III in 1772. By several amendments to the Freedom of the Press Act, the King tried to counter the increasingly louder criticism against his government. But there was one sphere that could not be altered by legislative measures: the liberty to publish in print what had been spoken at the Riksdag sessions. As a consequence, privately published Riksdag records which, word for word, reproduced critical contributions to the debates of the Estates flooded the country as from 1772. Not until 1785, when the King made all printing dependent on royal privilege, which in case of disgrace could be withdrawn, did this production of libels come to an end. In practice, the Swedish freedom of the press was abolished by this means, not to be restored until 1809 by the great reform of the constitution and the Freedom of the Press Act of 1810, by which the country again threw off the royal autocracy after another disastrous war against Russia. Once more, the door was open to a regular parliamentary life, which by and by brought on the beginning of real printed Riksdag records.

At this stage it must be pointed out that the original lack of printed constitutional and statutory publications from earlier times has in due course been amended—especially by revised editions of the proceedings of the King's Council and of the four Estates. Riksdag records exist today in print partly from as far back as the sixteenth century, and for at least two of the four Estates for the whole of the period of liberty.

The royal autocracy was overthrown in 1809. The classic document in the history of the Swedish constitution, the 1809 Regeringsformen [Instrument of Government], was written within a few weeks in the summer of 1809 and was to be formally in force up to 1975. This new Instrument of Government was combined with a separate Riksdag Act, the Tryckfrihetsförordningen [Freedom of the Press Act] and the Successionsordningen [Act of Succession] of 1810, which jointly formed the basis of Sweden's policy from then on. All these laws had the status of constitutional documents and could be made, altered or abolished only by a specially regulated legislative procedure. The new body of constitutional acts was based on the principle of the distribution of power between King, Estates and courts. Power over more important legislation was shared by King and Riksdag. The King alone handled government administration. The Estates were endowed with the financial power and were allotted two special bodies, the Riksdagens Revisorer [Parliamentary Auditors] and the Riksdagens Ombudsman [Parliamentary Ombudsman] charged with the control of government administration and the administration of justice. Judicial power was in the hands of independent courts. This constitutional practice implied a high degree of publicity. A minimum of the parliamentary proceedings was to be kept back from public control and examination, and as from the Riksdag of 1809 all parliamentary papers of any importance have been printed and published at the expense of the Riksdag.

The Swedish constitution

The Swedish constitution consists of the Regeringsformen [Instrument of Government] of 1974, which replaced the 1809 Instrument of Government, the Successionsordningen [Act of Succession] of 1810 and the Tryckfrihetsförordningen [Freedom of the Press Act] revised in 1949. They specify the fundamental rights and freedoms and the conduct of business in the Riksdag. The constitution cannot be amended or repealed except by decision of two parliaments separated by a general election.

Sweden is a constitutional monarchy. The Crown's role (women have been eligible for the succession to the throne only since 1979) is however almost entirely ceremonial.

The monarch opens the sessions of the Riksdag and is the official representative of Sweden in relations with other countries, receives other Heads of State, and holds the highest military rank: the armed forces are however under the control of the Cabinet.

The Riksdag is the highest organ of government. Since 1971 it has one chamber, composed of 349 members elected for a three-year term on a system of partial proportional representation. Just over 310 members are directly elected in the constituencies, but the remaining seats constitute a nationwide pool from which seats are allocated to parties which achieve over four percent of the total vote, so that these are represented in the final total. The Riksdag enacts laws, decides on taxes and on budget allocations, and examines the administration of the country by the executive branch through the Konstitutionsutskottet [Standing Committee on the Constitution], the Riksdagens Revisorer [Parliamentary Auditors] and the Riksdagens Ombudsmän [Parliamentary Ombudsmen]. Parliamentary business is initially dealt with through the standing committees (Utskott), whose members are selected to reflect the balance of the parties in the Riksdag. At present there are 16 standing committees.

The Cabinet is the highest administrative authority, and is responsible to the Riksdag. The Prime Minister is appointed by a recommendation of the Speaker of the Riksdag, which must approve it. The recommendation is accepted unless more than fifty percent of the members vote against. It is thus possible for a Prime Minister to be appointed on the votes of a minority of members, if there are abstentions. He can only be dismissed by the Speaker in a vote of no confidence, or at his own request. The Prime Minister appoints the Cabinet, and if he resigns or dies all the ministers in the Cabinet must resign.

The Cabinet as the executive authority is responsible for drafting policy, and planning and implementing decisions. It initiates legislation, often by instituting a commission of enquiry and presenting its reports and proposals. It issues new laws and ensures that legislation and budget decisions are carried out. It may issue detailed ordinances on the interpretation or application of legislation, or under enabling legislation issue regulations which have the force of law. It is finally responsible for foreign policy and defence. Cabinet meetings are largely formal meetings for the recording of decisions. Discussions on major items of legislation, co-ordination of policy between ministries and conflicts on the budget tend to be decided by the Prime Minister in informal meetings with the relevant ministers.

Within the central government administration, the separate ministries and the Statsrådsberedningen [Cabinet Office] are charged with preparing and carrying out government decisions, policy-making and legislation. Only in exceptional cases do they concern themselves with the day-to-day work of administration. Under them come a number of administrative bodies or 'boards', normally executive agencies, which are peculiar to the Swedish system of government. Executive functions and day-to-day implementation of policy are delegated to them, and they enjoy a marked degree of independence, which is reflected in the constitution. Ministries cannot direct or order the boards how to act in particular circumstances, and can only direct their operations through legislation. There are also a number of special councils and boards for particular questions, and the state companies for quasi-commercial or industrial functions.

The regional subdivisions of central government are the Länsstyrelserna [County Administrative Boards], each headed by a Landshövding [County Governor]. The national defence services are also divided into military districts, each under a military commander.

The elected assembly of the Län [County] is the Landsting [County Council]. There are 24 Counties. The territory is usually the same as that covered by the national government's regional administration unit. The County Councils handle tasks which require a large population base, such as health care and transport. They own almost all hospitals in Sweden.

At the local level there are 284 (in 1983) urban and rural Kommuner [Municipalities]. The elected body is the Kommunfullmäktige [Municipal Council] whose members are elected every three years. Its executive body is the Kommunstyrelse [Municipal Board]. The Municipalities are responsible for education, building, planning and land use, technical services, roads, water and sewage, social services, and leisure and cultural activities.

Definition of official publications

The definition which is employed here is that followed by the Riksdagsbiblioteket [Swedish Parliamentary Library] in compiling the *Sveriges statliga publikationer* [Annual bibliography of Swedish official publications]. Duplicated and mimeograph documents are included, although the same problems are faced as in any country of drawing the line between those which are available for public distribution and those which must be treated as internal documents. The publications of local government and the Counties are by convention included in the broad definition of official publications in Sweden, and a narrower one of 'official government publications' is also used, to distinguish central from local government materials. The annual bibliography of official publications does not list publications of the local authorities. The definition includes the publications of private organizations whose activities are of vital national interest if they are to a large extent financed by central government funds; however, theses and research reports from the state universities are not included.

Government manuals

The government manual of Sweden is the *Sveriges statskalender*, which is annual and has been issued since 1813. It is now published by Allmänna Förlaget. It lists the government ministries and their related boards, private, professional and research associations, banks, the senior officers of the armed forces, and local government officials.

2. LEGISLATION AND LEGISLATIVE PROCEEDINGS

2.1. Legislative proceedings

1809–1866

The constitution of 1809 has already been mentioned. All parliamentary papers of any importance have been printed and published at the expense of the Riksdag since then.

The arrangement of the Riksdag *Protokoll* [Records] was of course determined by the fact that the Riksdag consisted of four Estates. Proposals were submitted either by the government as a proposition ('proposition') or by a member of the Riksdag as a motion ('motion'). Every proposition or motion has to be considered by an Utskott [standing committee] of the Riksdag, the competence of which was laid down by the constitution. The standing committee analysed the proposals and decided if they should be recommended by the Estates or not. The four Estates thus came to pass their resolutions on the basis of the proposals of the committees and not on the original proposal. The support of three Estates was required to achieve approval of a committee's proposal. The system was complicated and hardly made for efficient decision-making. The task of following a proposal in the Riksdag is quite laborious, and requires a good deal of practice.

On the whole, the Riksdag records have retained this fundamental structure in spite of the difference between the era of the four Estates and modern parliamentary life.

Over the period of the four Estates the Riksdag records developed, with an Appendix beginning in 1810, and consisted of the following at the start and the end of the period:

1810

Protokoll Hållna hos Högloflige Ridderskapet och Adeln, vid Lagtima Riksdagen in Stockholm [Proceedings of the nobility at the ordinary session of the Parliament . . .]

Protokoll Hållna hos Högvördiga Prest-Ståndet vid Riksdagen i Stockholm [Proceedings of the Right Reverend Estate of Clergy at the Parliament . . .]

Protocoller Hållna hos Wälloflige Borgare-Ståndet i Stockholm [Proceedings of the Honourable House of Commons at the Parliament . . .]

Hederwårda Bonde-Ståndets Protokoll vid . . . Riksdagen . . . [Proceedings of the Honourable House of the Peasantry at the Parliament . . .]

Bihang till Samtelige Riks-Ståndens Protocoll . . . [Appendix to the Proceedings of the whole Parliament . . .].

1865/66

Protokoll Hållna hos Högloflige Ridderskapet och Adeln, vid Lagtima Riksdagen in Stockholm . . . [Proceedings of the nobility at the ordinary session of the Parliament . . .]

Högvördiga Preste-ståndets Protocoll vid Lagtime Riksdagen i Stockholm . . . [Proceedings of the Right Reverend House of Clergy at the Parliament . . .]

Protocoller Hållna hos Wälloflige Borgare-Ståndet vid . . . Riksdagen . . . [Proceedings of the Honourable House of Commons at the Parliament . . .]

Hederwårde Bonde-Ståndets Protokoll vid . . . Riksdagen . . . [Proceedings of the Honourable House of the Peasantry at the Parliament . . .]

Bihang till Samtelige Riks-Ståndens Protokoll [Appendix to the Proceedings of the whole parliament, in 11 parts, including the Speech from the Throne, written communications ('Berättelse') requested from the government, reports of the Estate's auditors and the Justitieombudsman [Parliamentary Commissioner for the Judicial and Civil Administration], memoranda ('memorial'), decisions ('utlåtanden') and reports ('betänkanden') from standing committees, and motions ('motioner') from the four Estates].

LEGISLATION AND LEGISLATIVE PROCEEDINGS

1867–1970

In 1867 the Riksdag of four Estates was replaced by a bicameral one. The members of the upper house were elected by the County Councils while those of the lower house were directly elected by a system of one-candidate constituencies up to 1911, when proportional representation was first introduced. The novelty of the bicameral system was mainly the fact that classes which were not previously represented in the Riksdag now obtained the right of suffrage—but it was by no means a complete reform in the direction of universal suffrage. Not until the years 1911–1921 were franchise reforms introduced by which the idea of one vote for every legally competent citizen was realized. Women's suffrage in all respects was introduced in 1921. In 1971 the bicameral system was replaced by the present unicameral system.

With the introduction of the bicameral system the Riksdag records became simpler and more clearly arranged than before. On the whole, what could be kept from the previous system was kept. At the beginning and the end of the period of a bicameral Riksdag, the Riksdag records were divided into the following parts:

1867

Riksdagens Protokoll vid Lagtima Riksmötet ... Första Kammaren [Proceedings of the Riksdag at the regular session ... First Chamber]

Riksdagens Protokoll vid Lagtima Riksmötet ... Andra Kammaren [Proceedings of the Riksdag at the regular session ... Second Chamber]

Bihangen [Appendices]:

1 samling 1 afdeling: *Kongl.maj:ts Propositioner och Skrivelser* [Government propositions]

1 saml. 2 afd.: *Motioner, väckta inom första Kammaren* [Motions raised in the First Chamber]

2 saml. 1 afd.: *Års revisionsberättelser samt Justite-Ombudsmannens Berättelse* [Reports from the Government Auditors and Ombudsmen]

2 saml. 2 afd.: *Komité-Betänkande* [Government committee reports]

3 saml.: *Konstitutions-Utskottets Memorial och Utlånden* [Statements etc. of the Standing Committee on the Constitution]

4 saml. 1 afd.: *Stats-Utskottets Memorial och Utlåtanden* [Statements etc. of the committee of State]

4 saml. 2 afd.: *Sammansatta Stats- och Bevillnings-Utskottets Utlåtande* [Decisions of the Committee of State and the Committee of Ways and Means]

5 saml. 1 afd.: *Bevillnings-Utskottets Memorial, Betänkanden och Utlåtanden* [Statements etc. of the Committee of Ways and Means]

6 saml. 1 afd.: *Banko-Utskottets Memorial, Utlåtanden, och Betänkanden* [Statements etc. of the Standing Committee on Banking]

6 saml. 2 afd.: *Sammansatta Banko- och Lag-Utskottets Utlåtande* [Decisions taken jointly by the Standing Committees on Banking and Laws]

7 saml.: *Lag-Utskottets Memorial, Utlåtanden och Betänkanden* [Statements etc, of the Standing Committee on Laws]

8 saml. 1 afd.: *Särskilda Utskottets Memorial, Utlåtanden och Betänkanden* [Statements etc. of the Special Standing Committee]

8 saml. 2 afd. 1 band: *Första Kammarens Tillfälliga Utskotts Memorial, Utlåtanden och Betänkanden* [Statements etc. of the Special Standing Committee of the First Chamber]

8 saml. 2 afd. 2 band: *Andra Kammarens Tillfälliga Utskotts Memorial, Utlåtanden och Betänkanden* [Statements etc. of the Special Standing Committee of the Second Chamber]

9 saml.: *Protokolls-Utdrag från Kamrarne* [Extracts from the records of the Chambers]

10 saml. 1 afd. 1 band: *Riksdagens underdåniga Skrifvelser till Kongl. Maj:t., m.m.* [Written Riksdag communications to the government]

10 saml. 1 afd. 2 band: *Riksdagsbeslutet, Riksstaten, Bevillningsförordningen, Bankens och Riksgälds-kontorets Reglementen* [Resolutions of the Riksdag, the state establishment, Finance Orders, and Regulations of the Offices of the Bank and Royal Mint]

Allmant Register öfver Bihanget till Kamrarnes Protokoll . . . [General index to the Appendices to the proceedings of the Chambers].

1970

Riksdagens Protokoll . . . Första Kammaren [Proceedings of the Riksdag . . . First Chamber] and *Riksdagens Protokoll . . . Andra Kammaren* [Proceedings of the Riksdag . . . Second Chamber]

Bihang till Riksdagens Protokoll [Appendix to the Proceedings of the Riksdag]

1 saml.: *Propositioner* [Propositions] and *Kungl.Maj:ts tal vid riksdagens oppnande löne* [Royal speech at the opening of the Riksdag]

2 saml.: *Riksdagens lönedelegations verksamhet; Riksdagens revisorers berättelse; Riksdagens förvaltningskontors verksamhets berättelse; Justitieombudsmännens ämbetsberättelse* [Annual report of the Committee on Salaries; Reports of the Riksdag Auditors; Annual report of the Riksdag office of administration; Official report of the Parliamentary Commissioner for the Judicial and Civil Administration]

3 saml.: *Motioner Första Kammaren* [Motions of the First Chamber]

4 saml.: *Motioner Andra Kammaren* [Motions of the Second Chamber]

5 saml.: *Utrikesutskottets utlåtanden och memorial; Konstitutionsutskottets utlåtanden och memorial; Sammansatt konstitutions- och banko-utskottets utlåtande* [Decisions and statements of the Standing Committee on Foreign Affairs; Decisions and statements of the Standing Committee on the Constitution; Joint decisions of the Standing Committees on the Constitution and Banking]

6 saml.: *Statsutskottets utlåtanden och memorial* [Decisions and statements of the Standing Committee of State]

7 saml.: *Bevillningsutskottets betänkanden och memorial* [Reports and statements of the Committee of Ways and Means]

8 saml.: *Bankoutskottets utlåtanden och memorial* [Decisions and statements of the Committee on Banking]

9 saml. 1 avd.: *Första lagutskottets utlåtanden och memorial* [Decisions and statements of the First Law Committee]

9 saml. 2 avd.: *Andra lagutskottets utlåtanden och memorial* [Decisions and statements of the Second Law Committee]

9 saml. 3 avd.: *Tredje lagutskottets utlåtanden och memorial* [Decisions and statements of the Third Law Committee]

10 saml.: *Jordbruksutskottets utlåtanden och memorial* [Decisions and statements of the Committee on Agriculture].

[The set also includes parts 11, 12, 13: 1 and 13: 2 which cover respectively the reports of the Standing Committee on Miscellaneous Affairs, reports from the Special Standing Committee, Skrivelser [written communications] of the Riksdag, and a report on the next year's national budget, but it has not been possible to examine these in the editing of this chapter.]

The present day

A report, submitted by the government, usually goes through a circulation process for consideration by parties concerned. The extent of this circulation depends on the importance of the matter. How this procedure of circulation is arranged is a question of what is politically convenient: it is for the government to decide which bodies are to be consulted as well as on the time when their statements must be submitted to the government. If necessary, the considering bodies can consult their own subordinate agencies. The statements of the considering bodies are not published as a whole, but their main points are presented in the government proposition ('proposition') to the Riksdag. Depending on how the government interprets the opinion of the considering bodies, the circulation process may lead to the proposal being abandoned, considerably revised or even subjected to a renewed investigation. Generally, the process of consultation leads to a government proposition that is submitted to the Riksdag for consideration. If the matter is within the government's legislative competence, it can issue a statute that will be included in the *Svensk författningssamling* [Swedish code of statutes] which is described in section 2.2 below.

In the Riksdag, questions can be raised in three different ways—by a government proposition, by a motion or by a report from a standing committee ('Utskott'). Propositions, motions, and reports of standing committees are always printed and included in the Riksdag *Protokoll*. Also the parliamentary agencies, of which the Ombudsmen are the best known, have limited rights to submit proposals to the Riksdag.

Propositions usually concern either legislation or the national budget. There are certain specific rules for their contents and arrangement and for the procedure of signing and submitting them to the Riksdag.

To a government proposition there is usually attached a report of the government's previous proceedings in the matter and also a justification of its reasons. In accordance with the 1974 Instrument of Government, the Head of the Swedish government, the Prime Minister, signs the proposition and the minister of the department responsible for the question countersigns it. To legislative propositions must be attached the comments of the Lagrådet [Law Council]. In the budget proposition, which from 1975/76 is always given the number 100 among propositions, must be included a financial plan and a national budget. The financial plan states the general outlines of the government's financial policies and is attached to the budget proposition as Appendix 1. In a further 20–25 Appendices are presented the budgets for the individual ministries. Thus the budget proposition proper represents only a tabulated survey of calculations of income and budget estimates: explanatory statements are found in the Appendices.

The budget proposition has to be submitted as a preliminary budget proposal on 10 January at the latest. The final budgetary adjustments should be made in the supplementary budget proposition, which should be submitted to the Riksdag before the end of April. The Riksdag is not obliged to receive any proposition of a new or of a

THE LEGISLATIVE PROCESS

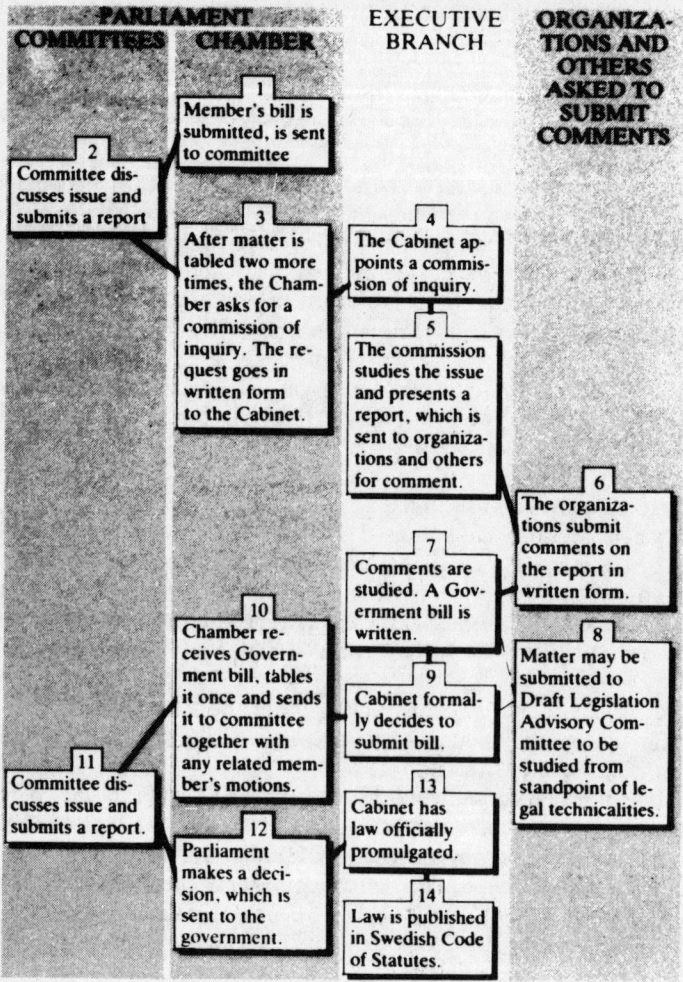

From: Lindström, Eric. *The Swedish parliamentary system.* Stockholm, Swedish Institute, 1982. Reproduced by kind permission of the Swedish Institute.

considerably higher appropriation for the next financial year later than 10 March.

There are fixed time limits also for other propositions than the budget proposition, which the government cannot exceed. The deadline is generally 31 March. The Riksdag is not obliged to consider any proposition submitted thereafter during the current session, but there are certain exceptions from this fundamental rule. Concerning constitutional legislation there is a special rule. All documents concerning constitutional amendments, and also propositions, must be submitted to the Riksdag 10 months before an election, at the latest, unless the Konstitutionsutskottet [Standing Committee on the Constitution] waives the rule with a majority of five-sixths. Amendments to constitutional legislation require the resolution of two Riksdag sessions with an election in between.

Motions can be submitted by one or more members of the Riksdag. There are no special requirements for how a motion should be drafted. Motions are printed and included in the Riksdag *Protokoll*.

There are certain time limits also as to when motions should be submitted to the Riksdag. The following rules are fundamental. Motions concerning any subject may be introduced within 15 days from the day when the budget proposition is submitted. This is called the Allmänna motionstiden [General period for motions]. Furthermore, within 15 days from the date of submission of any government proposition or other government document to the Riksdag, motions on the same subjects may be introduced.

In recent years the number of propositions amounts to about 200 a year, and the number of motions to 2,000 or more. Generally motions are brief, but when they express the views of a political party (party motions) they can be fairly voluminous.

The government also has the possibility of communicating in writing with the Riksdag without submitting a proposition at the same time. This is done by 'skrivelser' [communications]. 'Skrivelser' referring to certain government enterprises for instance make it possible for members of the Riksdag to introduce motions on the matter. The most extensive 'skrivelse' is the so-called *Kommittéberättelsen* [Committee report], which gives an account of the actual situation of the government committees: the *Kommittéberättelse* is nowadays always given the number 103 of the government propositions within the Riksdag *Protokoll*.

A certain limited right to submit proposals to the Riksdag is also exercised by the parliamentary agencies. This is done through 'skrivelser' to the appropriate standing committee. After the usual procedure for consideration (see below) the committee submits the proposal—revised or not—to the Riksdag for resolution. The committee proposal is later included in the Riksdag *Protokoll*, or more precisely in the Appendix of the standing committee concerned. The annual reports of the parliamentary agencies—the most extensive being the one submitted by the Parliamentary Ombudsmen—are also included in the Riksdag *Protokoll*.

Since 1971 the Swedish Riksdag operates with 16 established standing committees, each with a precisely fixed sphere of authority. All standing committees prepare both legislative and financial matters. Propositions, communications, motions and proposals of the parliamentary agencies must all be considered by a standing committee. It is on the committee's proposal, based on the Riksdag one, that the Riksdag passes a resolution. All questions introduced have to be considered by a standing committee: in other words, it is impossible for a standing committee to suppress a proposal that has been submitted. It has all power to modify proposals and may furthermore initiate proposals of its own. The difference, however, between a considerable alteration to a proposal and a proposal introduced by the standing committee itself may be difficult to determine.

The decision of the standing committee is substantiated in a 'betänkande' [report]. As regards more important questions, the standing committees' reports contain a summary of earlier preparation of the question and a statement of the significance of the proposal. The standing committee defines its decision on each part of the proposal that has been submitted by a more or less extensive justification, ending with a 'kläm' [closing remark]. If a standing committee finds that one of its proposals may be of interest to other standing committees, the latter can be given the opportunity to make an 'yttrande' [written statement]. This kind of statement is accounted for to the Riksdag, but is not part of the basis for a Riksdag resolution.

The Riksdag resolutions are passed by the house and included in the *Protokoll*. The debates in the house are recorded on tape as well as in shorthand. On this basis a printed 'snabbprotokoll' [preliminary record] is produced, in which the members, within certain limits, may correct their own pronouncements. The minutes are then verified and become final. These confirmed minutes are the *Protokoll* and constitute the official resolution documents of the Riksdag.

The resolutions are communicated to the government by the Riksdag 'skrivelser' which constitute instructions to the government to publish the resolutions as statutes in the *Svensk författningssamling* (SFS) [Swedish code of statutes], where the government also publishes its own regulations.

A member of the government may be summoned to the Riksdag to answer questions asked by Riksdag members. Such question times may be originated either by an interpellation ('interpellation') or by 'enkla frågor' [simple questions]. The interpellation procedure allows a debate in which several participants may join: the simple question procedure only permits a brief exchange of words between the minister and the member of the Riksdag who raised the question. The debates arising from interpellations and questions are included in the Riksdag *Protokoll*.

The *Protokoll* amount to about 20,000 pages a year, divided into seven groups:

A. *Protokoll* [Stenographic record of debates]
B. *Propositioner* [Propositions] with *Bilagor* [Supplements, including that on the budget, which is always proposition no. 100]
C.1. *Berättelse . . . riksdag om vad i rikets styrelse sig tilldragit* [Reports requested from the government by the Riksdag]
C.2. *Justitieombudsmännens ämbetsberättelse* [Official report of the Parliamentary Commissioner for the Judicial and Civil Administration]
C.3. *Riksdagens revisorers verksamhetsberättelse* [Annual report of the Riksdag auditors] and *Redogörelse för riksdagens lönedelegations verksamhet* [Annual report of accounts of the Riksdag Committee on Salaries]
C.4. *Framställningar och berättelser* [Accounts and reports]
D. *Motioner* [Motions]
E. [Reports to the chamber from the 16 Standing Committees]

F. *Riksdagsskrivelser* [Riksdag communications].

Up to 1975/76 the *Riksdagens Författningssamling* (RFS) [Riksdag Code of Statutes] was included in the Riksdag proceedings as part G, but it is now published separately.

Indexes by subject and name have been issued since 1809. For the period 1867–1970 there are also 10-year indexes which are quite up to the standard of the annual ones. A 10-year index for the 1970s is in course of preparation.

The following two works may also be useful:

Thyselius, Erik. *Förteckning öfver kommittebetänkanden afgifna under åren 1809–1894, 1895–1903*. Stockholm, Nordiska Bokhandeln, 2 v., 1896–1904. 670, 233 p. This index covers printed and unprinted papers, and has a subject index and an index by name of committee members.

Lindberger, Anders. *Förteckning över statliga utredningar 1904–1945*. Stockholm, Riksdagsbiblioteket, 1953. vi, 1,405 p. It includes both printed and unprinted reports, including those of committees of investigation of government ministries, and is arranged by ministry. There are personal name and subject indexes.

Background documents

Practically all important legislation is prepared by means of government investigations. The number of government working committees amounts to 300–350 a year. A committee can be a working group within the government office or within a government agency. It can also be constituted as a separate committee with members of the Riksdag, experts and representatives from many agencies. Important and exacting subjects of investigation must for practical reasons be left to separate committees.

Government committees publish their results as reports within the series of *Statens offentliga utredningar* (SOU) [Swedish government official reports]. The SOU series started in 1922: earlier the most important reports were published in the Riksdag *Protokoll*.

The SOU reports have the status of a supplementary source of law. The text of the reports generally is a key to the comprehension of the final law text. A report is usually referred to by the year of publication and its series number, for instance SOU 1980: 73, and only in exceptional circumstances by its own title.

The SOU report is the final product of a committee. However, it is not the only material of interest left by the committee: the full amount of its working papers is generally not published in the SOU series. Nowadays it is usual for committees to publish parts of their work as preliminary or interim reports or as contributions to the public debate.

Results of the work of departmental committees are not published in the SOU series but in the DS [departmental stencil] series, and often so are the preliminary reports of government committees, mentioned above. Primarily, the DS reports are a basis for government legislation. They are referred to by the abbreviation of the name of the actual department, the year of publication and the series number, for instance DS U 1981: 3 [Departmental stencil, Utbildningsdepartementet [Ministry of Education and Cultural Affairs], 1981, no. 3].

The parliamentary agencies

The parliamentary agencies, which report direct to the Riksdag, include the Riksbanken [Central Bank], the Riksgäldskontoret [National Debt Office], and the Riksdagens Ombudsmän [Parliamentary Ombudsmen]. The Riksbanken publishes regular information on Sweden's assets and liabilities, instructions concerning the application of the currency laws, and so on. The Riksgäldskontoret produces regular information concerning the national debt. The Ombudsmen deal with complaints about the government administration and the way in which legislation is enforced.

General information on the Riksdag

Riksdagens årsbok, published annually since 1974 through Allmänna Förlaget, provides a summary of the business dealt with by the Riksdag through the year. The following biographical registers are also of use:

Förteckning över Andra Kammarens ledamöter vid lagtima/urtima riksdagen ... 1867-1970. Norstedt. Annual
Förteckning över Första Kammarens ledamöter vid lagtima/urtima riksdagen ... 1867-1970. Norstedt. Annual
Mårtensson, Ludwig. Förteckning över bondeståndets ledamöter vid riksdagarna 1600-1697, 1717-1800. 1950, 1937
Riksdagen 1982-1985. Biografiska uppgifter om ledamöterna. Riksdagens Förvaltningskontor, 1984
Riksdagen. Uppgifter om ledamöter och riksdagsorgan, 1982/83–
Svenskt porträttgalleri, XXV, 1. Riksdagens första kammare 1867-1904. Med biografiska uppgifter av A. Hildebrand. Stockholm, Tullbergs Boktryckeri, 1904. 242 p.
Svenskt porträttgalleri, XXV, 2. Riksdagens andra kammare 1867-1904. Med biografiska uppgifter av A. Hildebrand. Stockholm, Tullbergs Boktryckeri, 1905. 389 p.
Tvåkammarriksdagen 1867-1970. Ledamöter och valkretsar. På riksdagens uppdrag utarbetad av Anders Norberg och Andreas Tjerveld. [Bicameral Parliament 1867-1970. Members and constitution]. In press.

2.2. Legislation and secondary legislation

As in many other countries, the body of constitutional laws in Sweden presents a rather divided picture. There are three groups of legislators: the government, local government and the Allmänna Kyrkomötet [General Church Assembly]. The most important is of course the government, but by way of conclusion we shall also briefly discuss local and ecclesiastical legislation.

The Regeringsformen [Instrument of Government] of 1809 was founded on a very strictly realized distribution of power. All laws were to be made, altered and repealed through decisions made by the government and the Riksdag jointly. Any one of the two governing authorities could initiate legislation and each could refuse to sanction a proposal from the other. The Riksdag alone had financial power, that is the right to decide on taxation. This constitutional dualism was repealed by the 1974 Instrument of Government. The Riksdag retained the financial power and was given the status of supreme legislator. In practice, a strict application of this principle would have meant that every trifling piece of legislation had to be decided by the Riksdag. This of course was absurd, and a paragraph was inserted into the Instrument of Government to enable the government to legislate on its own in certain matters as well as making it possible for the Riksdag to delegate a large number of legislative questions to the government. The government in its turn might delegate legislative power to subordinate authorities. By taking this step, however, the Riksdag did not give up its right to intervene in particular matters. This structure of legislative power has been the origin of not one but several codes of statutes.

New laws are promulgated by the Cabinet and only come into force when issued in *Svensk författningssamling* [Swedish code of statutes] which began in 1825.

Regulations and statutes were consistently published through the seventeenth and eighteenth centuries, until 1833, as the 'Årstrycket', a compilation of laws, decrees and regulations of which the exact title was usually *Förteckning på Kongl. Placater, Resolutioner, Förordningar* ... [List of royal proclamations, resolutions, edicts and statutes ...]. This was not a genuine code of laws but a collection of separate measures, published annually by the printers to the Crown. During the seventeenth century it was already regarded as an integral series and was provided with an annual index. The decrees do not have consecutive numbers but are arranged throughout according to the date of decision by the legislators. The 'Årstryck' volumes may present variations in content, simply because the printers' opinions as to what should be included varied.

The 'Årstryck' volumes contain decrees that can roughly be divided into three groups: first, decisions, laws and statutes imposed by the King (in other words, legislation); second, statutes issued by the executive agencies of government and the Supreme Courts; and third, Riksdag resolutions. Regarding the last group, it should be noted that these resolutions were seldom very elaborate. The precise legislation was published within the first group, the Riksdag sharing law-making power with the King. Within the 'Årstrycket' are also documents of a purely temporary character, for instance regulations for procedure at some specific royal funeral or coronation. Some decrees concerning local government, especially those referring to Stockholm, are also included.

After 1825 the 'Årstrycket' was gradually replaced by the *Svensk författningssamling* (SFS). Its prototype was the French *Bulletin des lois*. It is published by the Statsrådsberedningen [Cabinet Office] and printed and published by Liber Grafiska AB. Statutes were published in fascicles until 1911 and numbering was by year, fascicle and page. From 1876 to 1911 there was also an Appendix, *Bihang till Svensk författningssamling*, for minor legislation. Since 1912 all statutes are individually numbered in consecutive order within the year and a law is usually referred to by its year and number in SFS (for instance, SFS 1980: 100).

For legislation enacted by the Riksdag concerning itself and its own organs there was previously a special serial, *Riksdagens författningssamling*, issued from 1967 to 1982, but since 1983 such statutes have also been published in the SFS.

There is no single codified body of laws along the lines adopted by many of the countries of Europe.

2.3. Local government statutory codes

Local government has always had a dominant position in Sweden and is executed through three different units, the civil and ecclesiastical local authorities and the Landstinge [County Councils]. There are 280 local government units, about 2,500 parishes and 24 County Councils. These local decision-making bodies are endowed with the power to impose taxes but have no power to lay down the rules for taxation. However, decisions on local government planning and regulations in general can be issued under enabling legislation or can be sanctioned by the government through the County administrations and thus assume the status of law. In practice this implies that every local government could publish a code of statutes.

As a result of the expansion of local government activity it has become necessary for many such authorities to do this. They may be issued in the form of stencilled or printed booklets or loose-leaf publications, drawn up on the same lines as SFS. The Länskungörelser [County administrative ordinances] may number between one and four hundred per county per year. Several minor ordinances may be put together as one major ordinance or statute. A substantial number concern questions of appointments, and some are fairly extensive, especially those concerning traffic regulations within the County. There are alphabetical indexes to each volume.

Other local authority publications are not treated as official publications.

2.4. Church Assembly measures

With the reform of representation of the 1860s the Clergy Estate was no longer a legislative body, but the Swedish Church was partly compensated by the creation of the Allmänna Kyrkomötet [General Church Assembly]. This assembly, until now consisting of all the bishops together with elected representatives of the clergy and laymen, has had the position of a third state authority in matters of making, altering and repealing ecclesiastical decrees. However, the legislative status of the General Church Assembly has not been considered to accord with the normative principles of the 1974 Instrument of Government, and was abolished in 1982. Since then it has had the status of a purely ecclesiastical body.

From 1868 to 1982 the Allmänna Kyrkomötet acted as a minor Riksdag and along the same lines of procedure, with proposals put forward through motions from the members and through government communications. All important decisions were printed and drafted in the same manner as the Riksdag records, with minutes, government communications, motions, communications from the central ecclesiastical administration, committee reports and indexes.

2.5. Principal publications of the executive agencies of government

Swedish public administration may be roughly divided into three main categories: central government administration, central government regional administration and local government administration.

Central government regional administration is exercised through Länsstyrelserna [county administrative boards], each headed by a Landshövding [County Governor] for each Län [county administrative district].

The large measure of autonomy which the local authorities enjoy through their parliamentary assemblies (Landstingen) is characteristic of Sweden. The Landstingen and Kommunstyrelserna [Municipal councils] and their administrative bodies are themselves responsible for their official publications, which are not counted as official government publications and not listed in the annual bibliography of official publications (see section 4 below).

The most important publications put out by the ministries have already been discussed in section 2.1. These are the reports and recommendations of government committees of enquiry which are published in the SOU series and the recommendations of internal departmental committees published in the DS series.

Every central government department produces an annual report. These annual reports and a number of publications of minor importance have been omitted in the overview of central government publications which follows. The list is arranged by publishing body with boards, research institutions and related bodies listed with their parent departments.

Arbetsmarknadsdepartementet [Ministry of Labour]

The Ministry of Labour is responsible for questions relating to worker protection, work environment and immigrant questions.

The Arbetsmarknadsstyrelsen [Labour Market Board] oversees the labour market and publishes comprehensive statistics in its *Arbetsmarknadsstatistik*. It issues a handbook, *AMS-handboken*, containing instructions and recommendations in this field. The Board also publishes career information, periodic editions of two publications, *Arbete och Framtid* [Work and the future] and *Nordisk Yrkesklassificering* [Nordic job classification], and reports on job counselling. The Länsarbetsnämnder [County Labour Boards] publish surveys of the labour market situation.

The Arbetarskyddsstyrelsen [National Board of Occupational Safety and Health] publishes several research report series on industrial injuries, the work environment and toxic substances.

The Statens Invandrarverk [State Immigration and Naturalization Board] has a report series on the condition of immigrants and issues brochures on schools, housing, elections, social services and so on in all the immigrant languages. The Arbetslivcentrum [Swedish Centre for Working Life] does research into worker participation, the position of the trade unions, the effect of computerization on working life in different industries, and publishes the results.

Bostadsdepartementet [Ministry of Housing]

The Ministry of Housing deals with national physical planning, and publishes a research report series on this, housing policy and housing subsidies. The Bostadsstyrelsen [Housing Board] issues detailed regulations concerning loans for housing construction, housing supplements, etc., and publishes a housing construction programme once a year.

The Statens Institut för Byggnadsforskning [National Institute for Building Research] and Statens Råd för Byggnadsforskning [National Council for Building Research] have several very extensive series dealing with everything connected with research and rationalization in the building field.

The Statens Lantmäteriverk [National Land Survey Administration] is responsible for the production of maps and has a continuing publication programme for economic, topographical and general maps of Sweden. It also has a series of notices containing regulations applying in the land survey field and a series of technical papers. The Statens Planverk [National Physical Planning Board] publishes Swedish building standards with commentaries and rules for approval, plus a report series dealing with planning in the building field.

Budgetdepartementet [Ministry of the Budget][1]

The Ministry of the Budget is concerned with taxation and appropriations for government authorities, which may be studied in the *Statsliggaren* [State ledger]. The ministry also publishes Swedish taxation agreements with other countries and the government's budget proposals.

The Statskontoret [Swedish Agency for Administrative Development] supervises the administrative activities of government authorities and their rationalization, in particular by means of ADB routines. It publishes a report series in this field.

The Riksrevisionsverket [National Accounting and Audit Bureau] supervises the financial affairs of government authorities and publishes an extensive series of audit reports (*Revisionsrapporter*).

The Riksskatteverket [National Taxation Board] is responsible for tax assessment and publishes yearbooks covering different kinds of tax, ordinances on assessment for property tax, selective taxes, value added tax and so on. The Board also has charge of population census and election matters and publishes various brochures prior to elections.

The Arbetsgivarverket [State Employers' Board] is responsible for negotiating wages and conditions of work between the state and public servants at central level. They publish orders relating to civil service pensions and state-regulated services, both of them in annual series, and collective agreements in various fields.

Finansdepartementet [Ministry of Finance][1]

The Finance Department, which took in the former Ekonomidepartementet [Ministry of Economic Affairs], is concerned with major economic questions. It carries out long-term surveys of the Swedish economy which are followed up every fifth year and publishes the government finance plans.

Under it the Konjunkturinstitutet [National Institute of Economic Research] is responsible for national economic forecasting and publishes a report on the state of the economy annually in three parts. There is an English-language version entitled *The Swedish economy* and *An economic barometer*.

The Statistiska Centralbyrån [Central Bureau of Statistics] is in charge of Swedish official statistics. The SOS series has been published since the middle of the nineteenth century and is the collective series titles of most government statistics. SOS is published either as yearbooks on different subjects, such as *Jordbruksstatistisk Årsbok* [Agricultural statistics yearbook] or *Fiskestatistisk Årsbok* [Fishery statistics yearbook], or as numbers in the series *Statistiska meddelanden* [Statistical monographs]. There is a report series *Levnadsförhållanden: rapporter* [Living conditions: reports]. The best-known but the least specialized yearbook is the *Statistisk Årsbok* [Statistical yearbook], which first appeared in 1914. It presents a statistical survey of every branch of industry and of every field of social life in Sweden. About 60 yearbooks are published each year. There is a complete list of all the statistical titles published in the catalogue *Årets tryck* [Annual catalogue of printing] published by the Central Bureau of Statistics.

The Bankinspektionen [Bank Inspectorate] publishes statistics and circulars.

Försvarsdepartementet [Ministry of Defence]

The Ministry of Defence is responsible for all authorities relating to the national defence. Its Sekretariat för Säkerhetspolitik och Långsiktsplanering inom Totalförsvaret [Secretariat for Security Policy and Long-term Planning within the Total Defence System] publishes several series of reports on defence policy and national and international security policy. The ministry also publishes the annual *Rulla* [Armed forces list], the list of officers and civilian employees within the national defence, an annual *Totalförsvarets författningshandbok* [Statute handbook of the armed forces] and *Värnpliktsförfattningar* [National conscription orders].

The Försvarsstaben [Defence Staff] publishes training material, such as *Soldat-instruktionen* [Instructions to Soldiers], *Perspektivplaner för framtida försvar* [Perspective plans for future defence], the *Handbok i militär rättsvård* [Handbook of military law] etc. The Army, Air Force and Navy Commanders-in-Chief also publish training manuals in their own fields, as does the Försvarets Brevskola [Defence Correspondence College].

The Försvarets Forskningsanstalt [Defence Research Establishment] publishes many different series of research reports, the majority of a technical nature, but also including overviews of the world situation and digests of foreign reports.

The Försvarets Materielverk [Defence Materiel Administration] publishes a very large number of purely technical specifications and catalogues of spare parts for war materiel, as well as the defence service notices.

The Försvarets Rationaliseringsinstitut [National Institute of Defence Organization and Management] publishes reports series relating to defence economy and defence rationalization, particularly on the use of computers.

The Fortifikationsförvaltningen [Fortification Administration] is responsible for defence buildings and installations and publishes technical and administrative reports, service notices and so on.

The Civilförsvarsstyrelsen [Civil Defence Board] is engaged in matters relating to the protection of the civilian population in wartime, principally with questions relating to shelters.

Mention might also be made of the voluntary defence organizations such as the Lottakårerna [Women's Voluntary Defence Corps], the Röda korset [Red Cross], and the Centralförbundet folk och försvar [Central Association for People and Defence], which makes the reports of the Ministry of Defence available to a wider public.

Handelsdepartementet [Ministry of Commerce]

The Ministry of Commerce covers trade policy matters, prices, business, competition and consumer affairs. It publishes the *EG-handboken* [European Community handbook] and an annual report entitled *Sverige och EG* [Sweden and the European Community].

The Kommerskollegium [Board of Commerce], one of the oldest of the Swedish executive agencies, supervises foreign trade and publishes lists of authorized interpreters, translators and accountants.

The Generaltullstyrelsen [Board of Customs] publishes handbooks on customs tariffs, customs legislation, free trade regulations, smuggling of goods and so on which are continuously kept up to date.

The Patent- och Registreringsverket [National Patent and Registration Office] publishes the *Svensk varumärkestidning* [Swedish trade mark gazette], official announcements concerning the approval of new surnames, and the *Svensk Patenttidning* [Swedish Patents Journal].

The Marknadsdomstolen [Market Court] publishes decisions relating to questions of fair business practice.

The Statens Pris- och Kartellnämnd [National Price and Cartel Office] publishes a series of reports, arranged by industry, showing price and competition conditions, and issues an annual report entitled *Fusioner i Svenskt Näringsliv* [Swedish business mergers].

The Komsumentverket [National Consumer Board] publishes advice and reports on goods and services.

The Överstyrelsen för Ekonomiskt Försvar [National Board of Economic Defence] publishes an annual report entitled *Vår Försörjningsberedskap* [Sweden's economic preparedness].

Industridepartementet [Ministry of Industry]

The Ministry of Industry is concerned with industrial and energy policy, questions of natural resources and the management of state-owned industries. It publishes an annual report on the state-owned industries. The Delegationen för Energiforskning [Delegation for Energy Research] comes under this ministry and publishes an extensive series on energy problems.

The Statens Industriverk [National Industrial Board] publishes two reports series dealing with industry and handicrafts, mining, energy supply, etc.

The Statens Geologiska Undersökning [Swedish Geological Survey] publishes geological map sheets and accompanying descriptions.

The Energiforskningsnämnden [Energy Research Commission] issues reports on research on alternative sources of energy.

The Statens Vattenfallsverk [State Power Board], which is a trading agency, administers the hydroelectric and nuclear power plants and publishes statistics and brochures relating to them.

The Styrelsen för Teknisk Utveeking [Technical Development Board] has research reports in various technical fields on projects to which the Board has made grants.

The Statens Provningsanstalt [National Institute for Materials Testing] issues technical reports on the control and testing of weights and measures and a Swedish catalogue of weighbridges.

The Marintekniska Institutet [Maritime Research Institute] issues a reports series on naval construction work and an annual symposium report on international marine engineering.

The Domänverket [Swedish Forest Service] owns large tracts of forest and is a trading agency. It publishes brochures about the national parks and statistics (*Domänverket: driftsstatistik*).

The national defence factories are also a trading agency and publish technical specifications of the military materiel they manufacture on behalf of the armed forces.

Jordbruksdepartementet [Ministry of Agriculture]

The Ministry of Agriculture is reponsible for agriculture, forestry, fisheries and the care of the environment.

The Sveriges Lantbruksuniversitet [Swedish University of Agriculture] comes under this ministry, unlike other universities and higher institutes of education. It publishes research series in all fields with which it deals.

The Lantbruksstyrelsen [Board of Agriculture] has a series of notices on agriculture in different areas, the encouragement of horse-breeding, the activities of the agricultural marketing boards, etc. It also publishes general advice concerning the rationalization of agriculture, rules on the protection of flora and veterinary regulations.

The Skogsstyrelsen [Board of Forestry] publishes statistics, the annual reports of the forestry protection boards, and advice on pests and vermin.

The Fiskeristyrelsen [Board of Fisheries] publishes report series from freshwater and salt-water laboratories with research findings concerning fish stocks, acidification of water and oceanographical information.

The Statens Jordbruksnämnd [Agricultural Marketing Board] publishes Sweden's foreign trade in foodstuffs in tabular form and issues notices of different kinds relating to the rural economy.

The Statens Naturvårdsverk [Nature Conservancy Board] has several different series dealing with air and water conservancy, noise, air and water purification, the nature reserves, and conditions in the waterlands, mountain regions and so on. The Produktkontrollnämnden [Product Control Board] also comes under the Nature Conservancy Board and publishes an annual list of pesticides and insecticides.

The Koncessionsnämnden för Miljöskydd [National Franchise Board for Environmental Protection] publishes decisions relating to permits to carry on activities potentially dangerous to the environment.

The Statens Strålskyddsinstitut [National Institute of Radiation Protection] investigates the radioactive content of the environment and publishes its findings.

Justitiedepartementet [Ministry of Justice]

The Ministry of Justice deals with matters relating to the public courts of law, the police and public prosecutors and the national correctional administration.

The supreme authority for the various courts of law is the Domstolsverket [National Courts Administration] which publishes annual volumes of cases and case reports from the Arbetsdomstolen [Labour Court], the Bostadsdomstolen [Housing Court], and the Kammarrätterna [Administrative Courts of Appeal]. The National Courts Administration also publishes handbooks on certain legal matters such as estate and trust inventories. The Swedish *Skeppsregistret* [Register of Shipping] is also published by the National Courts Administration.

The Brottsförebyggande Rådet [Swedish National Council for Crime Prevention] does research into criminality, including economic crime, abuse of narcotics and criminal offences, and publishes a report series entitled *Rapporter från brottsförebyggande rådet* [Reports from the Swedish National Council for Crime Prevention] and a series of papers.

The Rikspolisstyrelsen [National Police Board] produces the *Polisunderrättelser* [Police gazette], list of stolen vehicles and boats etc., which are confidential. It also publishes police training manuals and maintains a computer register of passports, vehicles etc.

The Kriminalvårdsstyrelsen [National Prisons and Probation Administration] publishes *Rapporter från kriminalvårdsstyrelsens forsknings- och utvecklingsenhet*, a series of research papers primarily devoted to investigations of the prison population, level of literacy, and so on.

The Centralnämnden för Fastighetsdata [Central Board for Real Estate Data] is engaged on a far-reaching project concerning the collation of property and registration records, and publishes occasional reports on these matters.

The Datainspektionen [Data Inspectorate] was set up to protect the privacy of the individual in respect of computer information, and exercises surveillance over Swedish files of information about individuals held in machine-readable form.

Kommundepartementet [Ministry of Local Government][2]

The Ministry of Local Government is responsible for central government activities at local level. It publishes an annual guide and monographs. The Länsstyrelserna [County Administrative Boards], which are 24 in number, publish a very large corpus of administrative and nature conservancy material, and each produces its own collection of administrative orders.

Under it, the Statens Brandnämnd [National Fire Protection Council] publishes a small series on fire protection.

The Länsstyrelsernas Organisationsnämnd [County Administrative Boards Organizational Council] publishes papers on regional administration and rationalization, and manuals for the use of county administrative board personnel.

Kommunikationsdepartementet [Ministry of Communications]

The Ministry of Communications covers transport by land, sea and air as well as post and telecommunications.

The Postverket [Post Office] publishes statistics and a comprehensive range of administrative orders, instructions and handbooks in this field. The Post Office has the character of a trading agency, as do the following three agencies. The Televerket [Telecommunications Board] publishes statistics, administrative orders, *Telefonkataloger* [Telephone directories], and *Telexkataloger* [Telex directories]. The Statens Järnvägar [State Railways] and the Luftfartsverket [Board of Civil Aviation] publish large collections of administrative orders regulating their activities, as well as statistics and traffic instructions.

The Sjöfartsverket [Board of Shipping] is an ordinary executive agency, and publishes *Underrättelser för sjöfarande* [Notices to seafarers], charts and nautical publications, such as the *Svensk lots* [Swedish pilots' list] and the *Svensk fyrlista* [Swedish lighthouses list]. There are also administrative orders relating to navigation signs, signals, and so on.

The Statens Vägverk [Swedish National Road Administration] publishes a handbook about road and bridge construction work, reports on road planning in general, and traffic orders.

The Statens Trafiksäkerhetsverk [National Road Safety Board] is engaged in road safety propaganda, and publishes brochures, posters and so forth as well as handbooks for the inspection of motor vehicles. It keeps the central registers of motor vehicles and driving licences.

The Statens Väg- och Trafikinstitut [State Road and Traffic Institute] publishes a large range of research reports dealing with road transport of different kinds, driving in winter conditions, studded tyres and so on.

The Transportrådet [Board of Transport] and Transportforskningsdelegationen [Transport Research Delegation] publish reports on the transport of goods, persons and dangerous materials, and on old people in traffic.

The Sveriges Meteorologiska och Hydrologiska Institutet [Swedish Meteorological and Hydrological Institute] issues monthly surveys of weather conditions and a yearbook, *Sveriges meteorologiska och hydrologiska instituts årsbok*, containing information on precipitation, temperatures, height of water etc. There is also a series of research reports on hydrology and oceanography and another on climatology and meteorology.

The Statens Haverikommission [State Accidents Commission] publishes the results of enquiries into accidents on land and at sea.

Socialdepartementet [Ministry of Health and Welfare]

The Ministry of Health and Welfare deals with questions of public health and medical care, pharmaceuticals, social welfare, social insurance, and care of the disabled. The Socialstyrelsen [Board of Health and Welfare] comes under this ministry and publishes a good many series of reports on these subjects as well as a purely scientific series relating to pharmaceuticals, administrative orders etc. The Board of Health and Welfare has under it a number of boards such as the Statens nämnd för Adoptionsfrågor [National Board for Overseas Adoptions], which publish brochures and short reports. In the social insurance field there is the Försäkringsöverdomstolen [Higher Insurance Court] and the insurance courts at regional level, whose decisions are public but are not collected into annual published volumes. The Allmänna Pensionsfonden [Public Pensions Fund] only produces annual reports. The Riksförsäkringsverket [National Insurance Board] publishes statistical reports and investigations into pension conditions and industrial injuries, and the *Pensionshandboken* [Pensions handbook].

The Statens Bakteriologiska Laboratorium [State Bacteriological Laboratory] publishes weekly surveys of infectious diseases and epidemics, entitled *Veckorapporter*.

The Statens Handikappråd [National Council for the Disabled] issues general advice for disabled persons, information about study opportunities and so on, and publishes reviews of new legislation in the field. The Handikappinstitutet [Institute for the Disabled] publishes catalogues of technical aids for the disabled.

Utbildningsdepartementet [Ministry of Education]

The Ministry of Education is responsible for all education at universities and comprehensive schools and for 'cultural manifestations' in general. The Riksarkivet [National Archives] which come under it publish a series of notices on the care of archives. The Riksantikvarieämbetet och statens historiska museer [Central Office of National Antiquities and the State Historical Museums] have a report series on archaeology and the care of the national monuments, and publish monographs, particularly in connection with the work of the Statens Historiska Museum, the Myntkabinettet [Royal Cabinet of Coins and Medals] and the Medelhavsmuseet [Museum of Mediterranean and Near Eastern Antiquities]. The Statens Konstmuseer [National Art Museums] publish a series of notices concerning the art collections belonging to the state, as well as exhibition catalogues.

The Kungliga Biblioteket [Royal Library] issues a document series containing biographies of writers and personalities in the world of culture. Its Bibliografiska Institutet [Institute of Bibliography] is responsible for the *Nationalbibliografin*

[National bibliography], which is made up of the *Svensk bokförteckning* [Swedish book list], the *Svensk bok-katalog* [Catalogue of Swedish books], which comes out every five years, the *Svensk tidskriftsförteckning* [Swedish journals list], *Svensk musikförteckning* [Swedish music list], and the *Suecana extranea*. It also oversees LIBRIS, the computerized system which links the Swedish research libraries.

The Universitets- och Högskoleämbetet [National Board of Universities and Colleges] publishes a research report series relating to the reform of Swedish higher education in various educational fields, and draws up study plans.

The Skolöverstyrelsen [Board of Education] publishes a report series on educational research at comprehensive and upper secondary level, school curricula and notices on education.

The Statens Kulturråd [Swedish Cultural Council] publishes a report series on cultural policy.

Utrikesdepartementet [Ministry of Foreign Affairs]

The Ministry of Foreign Affairs' sphere of activity is of course Sweden's relations with foreign powers. The ministry publishes a number of series, including documents containing reports of meetings of the UN General Assembly and special conferences, such as the law of the sea conferences, and *Documents on Swedish foreign policy* (in English and Swedish). The ministry also issues *Sveriges Traktater med främmande magte*, the Swedish treaty series.

Styrelsen för Internationell Utveckling [the Swedish International Development Authority] comes under the aegis of this ministry and publishes reports on aid activities and the recipient countries. The Nordiska Afrikainstitutet [Nordic Africa Institute] publishes monographs on conditions in African countries: these often take the form of doctoral theses. The Svenska Institutet [Swedish Institute] publishes information about Sweden in all the major world languages in several factual series.

Stiftelsen Stockholms Fredforskningsinstitut [the Stockholm International Peace Research Institute (SIPRI)] produces a yearbook on *World armaments and disarmament* and monographs in English on disarmament questions.

3. MANNER OF PUBLICATION

The greater part of Swedish official publications for sale is handled by Liber Grafiska AB. Liber Grafiska is a state-owned company whose Allmänna Förlaget (part of its General Publishing Division) runs 'government publishing and bookselling on the back of a much wider commercial operation. It accepts material for publication from government departments either at its own risk or on an agency basis' (Cherns, J. J. *Official publishing: an overview*. Oxford, Pergamon, 1979. Guides to official publications, 3) and it can commission publications. It co-ordinates the distribution of free printed material, has one retail outlet, is responsible for marketing to the book trade and the public, and is the agent for the publications of international organizations.

Allmänna Förlaget is a unique organization. It has no public or official function and the relationship between it and the originating departments is a purely contractual one. The Liber group of companies was set up by statute in 1969 as a result of long-standing parliamentary concern at the lack of co-ordination of, and the financing of, government publishing, going back as far as a 1949 report of the Committee for Social Information (SOU 1949: 31). Previously there was no central publishing organ or control, though a small office for printing procurement, the Statens Tryckerisakkunniga, was set up in 1921 within the Ministry of Finance, and gradually enlarged its authority. Allmänna Förlaget absorbed this office.

Public authorities are virtually obliged by decrees of 1969 and 1974 to use the services of Allmänna Förlaget, and in practice the central government departments and boards all use it. The state companies are obliged to consult it. Sweden has thus achieved a substantial and effective degree of central co-ordination, exceptional in Europe. Pricing is on a 'commercial' basis, though the costs of non-commercial publications are thrown back on the originating departments by Allmänna Förlaget using the 'agency' arrangement.

The Parliamentary printing is carried out by private contractors, and although all parliamentary documents are obtainable from Liber Grafiska they are also for sale at the Riksdag's own sale point and there is a separate subscription scheme. They are heavily subsidized through the parliamentary budget.

The SOU reports are published by Liber Grafiska in accordance with special agreements with the Swedish state. There are some other exceptions. The *Svensk Författningssamling* is published by the Statsrådsberedningen [Cabinet Office]. The DS series is published by the respective ministries. The administrative office of the Riksdag publishes for the Allmänna Kyrkomötet [Church of Sweden Synod].

Local authorities and county councils are responsible for their own printing and publishing arrangements.

4. BIBLIOGRAPHIC CONTROL

A bibliography of Swedish government publications has been published by the Riksdagsbiblioteket [Parliamentary library] since 1931. In that year the government issued a decree which charged the state administration to deliver a deposit copy of every printed official document to the parliamentary library. The bibliography was entitled *Bibliografi över Sveriges offentliga publikationer* from 1931/33 to 1975/76 and *Sveriges statliga publikationer* from 1976/77 to the present. Duplicated material has also been listed since 1968. The original decree on legal deposit was replaced by a new statute in 1978.

The Swedish state administration has been steadily growing, during the last decade at an accelerating pace. Thus in the first volume of the *Bibliografi över Sveriges offentliga publikationer* the total number of authorities listed was 191, while in the last edition they totalled 535. Naturally this is also reflected in the number of titles listed. The unpretentious size of the early volumes contrasts with the voluminous bibliographies of later years.

Some selectivity has been necessary. As has been mentioned in the introduction, the official publications of county councils and local authorities are not included in the annual bibliography, nor are dissertations and research reports, although publications issued by private organizations whose activities are of vital national interest and are to a large extent financed by government funds are included. Publications put out by the state research councils, learned and professional academies and the universities receive special treatment. Their administrative publications are listed but their research report series are summarily recorded without separate cataloguing of each volume. They are however listed in full in the main national bibliography, *Svensk bokförteckning*. Publications resulting from the trading and commercial activities of the state are not all included. Those of the railways, the post office and the telecommunications authorities are listed but those of the state-owned industries such as Apoteksbolaget AB, the pharmaceuticals company, or Tobaksmonopolet, the tobacco monopoly, are not. About 6,000 titles a year are included in *Sveriges statliga publikationer*.

Publications sent to the parliamentary library are promptly taken care of and arranged according to publishing authority. They are almost immediately available for loan. From the newly arrived material slightly more than twenty-five percent is selected to form part of a list of acquisitions, which is generally published once a week. These lists of acquisitions are distributed to all members of parliament and to several libraries of government departments and authorities, research libraries and so on. The same bibliographical information also reaches a large number of readers, as the official journal, *Från riksdag och departement* [From Parliament and ministries], published in about 20,000 copies, reproduces the lists. This often has an immediate effect on demand for the publications concerned.

In the past the annual bibliography was produced in a conventional manner. From 1983 however the bibliography and the weekly list have been fed into the LIBRIS system used by Swedish research libraries. With the extension of co-operation in the exchange of bibliographic data between countries it should also be possible to scan the list of Swedish government publications internationally. The printed edition of the annual bibliography will however continue to be published in the future, as the majority of interested parties are not linked to LIBRIS.

The annual bibliography is distributed to Swedish state institutions and public libraries. Copies are sent abroad as gifts and on an exchange basis; they are also available for purchase.

5. LIBRARY COLLECTIONS AND AVAILABILITY

The Riksdagsbiblioteket has an almost complete collection of all central government publications. They are catalogued in detail and are in principle available to all interested parties—members of the Riksdag, civil servants, local government officials, researchers and so on. Material can be lent to other libraries through the traditional system of inter-library lending in Sweden. Loans to Nordic neighbour countries are not usual, and there is nothing to prevent loans to libraries outside the Scandinavian countries. Loan requests for official government documents can almost always be carried out on the day of receipt. Loan periods are always short, and photocopies of short documents are supplied. Editorial staff also have to answer enquiries about material of current interest—a mission that is usually carried out promptly.

The Kungliga biblioteket [Royal Library], the Swedish national library, and the university libraries are archival libraries for Swedish literature. They have large collections of official publications, but some gaps in holdings of minor publications, and parts of their collections are catalogued only summarily.

NOTES

1. The Budgetdepartementet was merged with the Finansdepartementet in 1983, after preparation of this text.

2. The Kommundepartementet's functions were taken over by the Civildepartementet in 1983, after preparation of this text.

6. BIBLIOGRAPHY

Andersson, Hans G. *Riksdagens funktioner och arbetssätt*. 2nd ed. Lund, Student litteratur, 1972. 97 p.

Andrén, Nils Bertel Einar. *Svensk statskunskap*. 5th rev. ed. Stockholm, Utbildningsförlaget Liber, 1972. 397 p.

Bring, Samuel Ebbe. *Bibliografisk handbok till Sveriges historia*. Stockholm, Norstedt, 1934. 980 p. Cap. III-V, pp. 38-126.

——. *Svenskt boklexikon 1700-1829*. Uppsala, Svenska Litteratur, 1958-1961. (Skrifter utgivna av Svenska Litteratursällskapet, 32: 1, 2). 259, 226 p.

Constitutional documents of Sweden. The instrument of government, the Riksdag act, the Act of Succession, the Freedom of the Press act. Stockholm, Riksdag, 1981. 164 p.

Ekholm, Sverker and Runström, Lena. *Statsskicket i Sverige*. Lund, Studentlitteratur, 1981. 292 p.

Elder, Neil, C. M. *Government in Sweden: the executive at work*. Oxford, Pergamon, 1970. ix, 210 p. (Commonwealth and International Library.)

Fact sheets on Sweden. Stockholm, Swedish Institute, irregular.
See particularly 'Law and justice in Sweden', 'Constitutional protection of rights and freedoms in Sweden' and 'Local government in Sweden'.

Gustafsson, Agne. *Local government in Sweden*. Stockholm, Swedish Institute, 1983. 138 p.

Holmberg, Erik and Stjernquist, Nils. *Grundlagarna med tillhörande författningar*. Stockholm, Norstedt, 1980. xiv, 1,017 p.

Lindström, Eric. *Riksdagslexikon. Om folksrepresentationens ställning, uppgifter och arbetssätt i Sverige*. Stockholm, Liber Förlag, 1981. 94 p.

——. *Riksmöte pågår. En bok om riksdagens arbete*. Stockholm, LT's förlag, 1975. 103 p.

——. *The Swedish parliamentary system*. How responsibilities are divided and decisions are made. Stockholm, Swedish Institute, 1982. 98 p.

Local government in Sweden. Stockholm, Kommundepartementet, 1983. 64 p.

Nygren, Rolf et al. *Handbok i Nordiskt parlamentstryck*. Stockholm, Nord, 1984. [1985]. 149 p.

Petrén, Gustaf and Ragnemalm, Hans. *Sverige grundlagar och tillhörande författningar med förklaringar*. 12th ed. Stockholm, Liber Förlag, 1980. 255 p.

Strömholm, Stig (ed.) *Introduction to Swedish law*. Stockholm, Norstedt, 1981. 436 p.

Vinde, Pierre and Petri, Gunnar. *Swedish government administration*. 2nd ed. Stockholm, Swedish Institute, 1978. 91 p.

Weibull, Jörgen, Palmstierna, Carl-Fredrik and Tarras-Wahlberg, Björn. *The monarchy in Sweden*. Stockholm, Swedish Institute, 1981.

Switzerland

INGUNN RÜFENACHT

Translated by Stephen Hanger

1. INTRODUCTION

Constitution and government

The legislative authority of Switzerland is the parliament, the Bundesversammlung/Assemblée Fédérale/Assemblea Federale [Federal Assembly], which is bicameral, consisting of the Nationalrat/Conseil National/Consiglio Nazionale [National Council] of 200 members elected by universal direct suffrage, and the Ständerat/Conseil des États/Consiglio dei Stati [States Council] of 46 members, which represents the Cantons. The Bundeskanzlei/Chancellerie Fédérale/Cancelleria Federale [Federal Chancellery] which comes under the Federal Assembly is responsible for its secretarial business. The Chancellor is elected by the Federal Assembly for a term of four years.

The executive authority is the Bundesrat/Conseil Fédéral/Consiglio Federale [Federal Council], which consists of seven Bundesräte [Federal Councils]. Each of these administers a department. The seven present departments of the federal government are:

Eidgenössisches Departement für Auswärtige Angelegenheiten/Département Fédéral des Affaires Étrangères/Dipartimento Federale degli Affari Esteri [Federal Department of Foreign Affairs]

Eidgenössisches Departement des Innern/Département Fédéral de l'Intérieur/Dipartimento Federale dell'Interno [Federal Department of the Interior]

Eidgenössisches Justiz- und Polizeidepartement/Département Fédéral de Justice et de Police/Dipartimento Federale di Giustizia e Polizia [Federal Dipartment of Justice and Police]

Eidgenössisches Militärdepartement/Département Militaire Fédéral/Dipartimento Militare Federale [Federal Army Department]

Eidgenössisches Finanzdepartement/Département Fédéral des Finances/Dipartimento Federale delle Finanze [Federal Department of Finance]

Eidgenössisches Volkswirtschaftsdepartement/Département Fédéral de l'Économie Publique/Dipartimento Federale dell'Economia Pubblica [Federal Department of the Economy]

Eidgenössisches Verkehrs- und Energiewirtschaftsdepartement/Département Fédéral des Transports, des Communications et de l'Énergie/Dipartimento Federale dei Trasporti, delle Comunicazioni e delle Energie [Federal Department for Transport, Communications and Energy].

Each department has a general secretariat and a varying number of Bundesämter/Offices Fédéraux/Uffici Federali [Federal Offices]. The seven members of the Bundesrat are elected by the Bundesversammlung, and presided over by a President whose powers are nominal. The Bundesrat is responsible for foreign affairs, security, international treaties, public works, national highways, railways, telecommunications, coinage, weights and measures, copyright, patents, bankruptcy, and atomic energy. Its authority is specified in the constitution. It is also entrusted with the execution of the legislature's decisions and normally issues the rules and regulations required to bring new legislation into force. These rules and regulations are steadily increasing in number. The Bundesrat is accountable to the Bundesversammlung through the mechanism of the 'interpellation' or written questions.

There are 23 Cantons, each with its unicameral assembly the Kantonrat, which is elected by universal suffrage and has the functions of a parliament except that in many Cantons the machinery of the referendum is extensively used for questions of finance, constitutional revisions, agreements with other Cantons, and new legislation generally. Each Canton has its own constitution. The cantonal governments consist of a governing board of between five and eleven members. The Cantons are responsible for all matters not specifically assigned to the federal authorities and for the enforcement of most legislation, though the Bundesrat exercises a general supervisory power over them in this respect.

At the level below the Cantons are the Districts and Communes.

The administration of justice is primarily a function of the Cantons. The only federal court is the Bundesgericht/Tribunal Fédéral/Tribunale Federale [Federal Tribunal] which serves as a court of appeal in civil and criminal cases and has the power to review decisions of cantonal courts.

Definition of official publications

The Schweizerische Landesbibliothek [National Library of Switzerland] uses a definition of an official publication as one which is issued by a public authority or office. All those which appear in the *Eidgenössischer Staatskalender* [Federal government manual] are taken into account, as are publications of cantonal authorities which are listed in their respective government manuals. The publications of universities, institutes and associations are not included. The Eidgenössische Drucksachen- und Materialzentrale [Federal Printing and Supply Centre] (see section 3 below) considers as official publications all which are produced at government expense.[1] This includes forms, driving licences, posters, the highway code and technical instruction manuals.

Manuals of government organization

The *Eidgenössischer Staatskalender/Annuaire fédérale/Annuario federale* [Federal government manual] has been published since 1850 in German, French and Italian. It lists the addresses of the federal offices.

Languages

German, French, Italian and Romansch are recognized as the national languages but German, French and Italian are the official languages. All federal laws and statutes are published in these languages, although the Italian version is a translation made after the passage of the legislation, and all these language groups must be represented on the Bundesgericht.

German is the most frequent language of publication. Some items are published in German only, some in German and French in separate language editions, a small number in an Italian edition as well, and there are a few bilingual or trilingual titles. This chapter follows the precedent of others in giving all three language versions of the names of organizations and all the language versions in which a publication appears at the first mention in the text of the organization or title, and an English translation appears in square brackets. Thereafter if it is referred to again the name is given in German only.

2. PRINCIPAL PUBLICATIONS OF THE FEDERAL GOVERNMENT

2.1. Legislation and subordinate legislation

Legislation is published in the *Sammlung der eidgenössischen Gesetze/Recueil des lois fédérales/Raccolta delle leggi federali* [Collection of federal laws] 1849–, which is issued several times a year. It has an alphabetical index and appears in German, French and Italian. New laws appear as they are published in the *Bundesblatt/Feuille fédérale/Foglio federale* [Federal gazette] (described in section 2.2. below).

2.2. Legislative proceedings, debates and documents

Legislation is usually initiated by the Bundesrat, though the Nationalrat and the Ständerat can also originate it through the mechanism of Die Anregung [the initiative], and Cantons may by correspondence (Korrespondenz). Bills originate as departmental drafts (Departementsentwurfen) which are sent to the Bundesversammlung with a report or message (Botschaft) after a wide-ranging consultation with experts, interested bodies, and the Cantons. They are presented as a final draft (Bereinigung) and normally steered through both Chambers to their conclusion by a Federal Councillor. The Nationalrat and Ständerat decide together at the beginning of each session which bills will go to which Chamber first. In each Chamber a bill is debated in committee and on the floor of the whole house.

Bills are published in the *Bundesblatt*. The *Bundesblatt* is essentially the record of the business of the Bundesrat. It has been published since 1848 and appears weekly in German, French and Italian. There is an alphabetical index. It includes the budget report and national accounts, reports of the Bundesrat on major issues, messages, arrêtés (orders made by the Federal Council either under powers delegated to it by the constitution or under statute), circulars to Cantons, departmental guide-lines having the authority of statute, and notices of new publications of the federal departments.

The verbatim account of proceedings in the Bundesversammlung is the *Amtliches Bulletin der Bundesversammlung/Bulletin officiel de l'Assemblée Fédérale* [Official bulletin of the Federal Assembly] which has been published since 1891. It is issued four times a year in two parts, Teil 1 for the Nationalrat and Teil 2 for the Ständerat, and it has a subject and name index. It includes the stenographic report of debates on messages and propositions, initiatives, petitions, etc., with the result of the vote, and answers to questions. A summary, *Übersicht über die Verhandlungen der Bundesversammlung/Résumé des délibérations de l'Assemblée Fédérale*, is published four times a year as an annexe to the *Amtliches Bulletin*.

2.3. Publications of the executive agencies of government

The reports of the business of the Bundesrat and of the seven departments and their Federal Offices are published in the *Bericht des Bundesrates über seine Geschäftsführung/Rapport du Conseil Fédéral sur sa gestion* [Report of the Federal Council on the conduct of its business] which is annual and appears in German and French editions. An annual summary, *L'administration fédérale: ses tâches et son activité* [The federal government: its functions and work] is also issued free.

Publishing by the federal government of Switzerland is not extensive, and tends to concentrate on serials, of which the 1976 supplement to the *Bibliographie der schweizerischen Amtsdruckschriften* (see section 4.2. below) lists 140. Most departments issue an annual report. Their pattern of publishing is relatively stable, though a growing number of reports on issues of current interest is published, and all departments issue leaflets and publicity material. A selective list of the principal serial titles follows:

Bundesamt für Geistiges Eigentum/Office Fédéral de la Propriété Intellectuelle/Ufficio Federale della Proprietà Intellettuale [Federal Office for Intellectual Property]

Schweizerisches Patent-, Muster- und Markenblatt/Feuille suisse des brevets, dessins et marques/Foglio svizzero dei brevetti, disegni e marchi [Swiss patent, design and trademark gazette].

Bundesamt für Statistik/Office Fédéral de la Statistique/Ufficio Federale di Statistica [Federal Statistical Office]

Eidgenössische Volkszählung/Recensement fédéral de la population [Federal census of population] e.g. 1980. Issued every ten years since the census of 1860.

Quellenwerke der Schweiz/Statistique de la Suisse [Swiss statistics], issued since 1862 in several parts per year.

PRINCIPAL PUBLICATIONS OF THE FEDERAL GOVERNMENT

Bundesamt für Zivilschutz/Office Fédéral de la Protection Civile/Ufficio Federale della Protezione Civile [Federal Civil Defence Office]

Mitteilungsblatt des Zivilschutzes/Feuille officielle de la protection civile/Foglio d'informazione della protezione civile [Civil defence official gazette], published since 1964. There is an index for 1964–1969.

Bundesbahnen/Chemins de Fer Fédéraux Suisses/ Ferrovie Federali Svizzere [Swiss Railways]

Eisenbahn-Amtsblatt/Feuille officielle des chemins de fer/Foglio ferroviario ufficiale [Official railway gazette], issued weekly since 1902.

Bundesgericht/Tribunal Fédéral/Tribunale Federale [Federal Tribunal]

Bundesgericht/Rapport du Tribunal Fédéral suisse [Report of the Federal Tribunal], issued annually since 1855.

Entscheidungen des Schweizerischen Bundesgerichtes . . . Amtliche sammlung/Arrêts du Tribunal fédéral suisse . . . Recueil officiel [Orders of the Federal Tribunal . . . Official collection], which has appeared annually in five parts from 1875 to 1898 and since 1972. There are annual and five-yearly indexes.

Eidgenössisches Militärdepartement/Département Militaire Fédéral/Dipartimento Militare Federale [Federal Army Department]

Militäramtsblatt/Feuille officielle militaire/Foglio ufficiale militare [Official military gazette], in four or five issues per year.

Eidgenössische Oberzolldirektion/Direction Générale des Douanes/Direzione Generale delle Dogane [Directorate of Customs]

Jahresstatistik des Aussenhandels der Schweiz/Statistique annuelle du commerce extérieur de la Suisse [Annual statistics of the foreign trade of Switzerland] (a bilingual publication).

Monatsstatistik des Aussenhandels der Schweiz/Statistique mensuelle du commerce extérieur de la Suisse [Monthly statistics of the foreign trade of Switzerland] (also bilingual editions).

Postdepartement/Département de la Poste/Dicastero della Posta [Post Office]

Post-, Telephon- und Telegraphen-Amtsblatt/Feuille officielle des postes, téléphones et télégraphes [Postal, telephone and telegraph gazette], issued weekly since 1922.

SWITZERLAND

Schweizerische Landesbibliothek/Bibliothèque Nationale Suisse/Biblioteca Nazionale Svizzera [National Library of Switzerland]

Bericht für das Jahr/Rapport pour l'année [Annual report].

Schweizerische Nationalbank/Banque Nationale Suisse/Banca Nazionale Svizzera [National Bank of Switzerland]

Geld, Währung und Konjunktur/Monnaie et conjoncture [Money supply and competition], issued quarterly since March 1985.
Geschäftsbericht/Rapport de gestion [Annual report], published since 1907/08.
Monatsbericht/ Bulletin mensuel [Monthly bulletin], published since 1926.

Schweizerische Unfallversicherungsanstalt/Caisse Nationale Suisse d'Assurances en cas d'Accidents/ Istituto Nazionale di Assicurazione contro gli Infortuni [National Fund for Accident Insurance]

Schweizerische Blätter für Arbeitssicherheit/Cahiers suisses de la sécurité du travail/ Rivista svizzera sulla sicurezza nel lavoro [Notes on safety at work], issued irregularly since 1956.

There are growing numbers of duplicated or 'semi-published' materials, often intended for internal use only.

2.4. Publications of the judiciary

The principal series are issued by the courts themselves:

Bundesgericht/Tribunal fédéral/Tribunale federale [Federal Tribunal]
Entscheidungen des Schweizerischen Bundesgerichtes. Amtliche sammlung/Arrêts du Tribunal fédéral suisse. Recueil officiel [Decisions of the Swiss Federal Tribunal]. Teil 1a: Staatsrecht/Droit public [Public law]. Teil 1b: Verwaltungsrecht/Droit administratif [Administrative law]. Teil 2: Zivilrecht/Droit civil [Civil law]. Teil 3:
Betreibungs- und Konkursrecht/Poursuites et faillite [Prosecutions and bankruptcy]. Teil 4: Strafrecht/Droit pénal [Penal law]. Teil 5: Sozialversicherungsrecht/Droit des assurances sociales [Social security law].

Militärkassationsgericht/Tribunal militaire de cassation/Tribunale militare di cassazione [Military Court of Appeal]
Entscheidungen/Arrêts/Sentenze [Decisions].

Cantonal courts

Aargau. Obergericht. *Aargauische Gerichts- und Verwaltungsentscheide* [Judicial and administrative rulings]. Published with varying titles since 1901.

Baselland. Obergericht. *Amtsbericht des Obergerichts* [Bulletin of the High Court]. Published annually since 1880. Includes extracts and decisions.

Fribourg. Tribunal Cantonal. *Extraits des principaux arrêts rendus par les diverses sections du Tribunal cantonal de l'État de Fribourg* [Extracts of the main decisions of the sections of the Cantonal Tribunal of Fribourg]. Published since 1903.

Graubünden. Kantonsgericht. *Die Praxis des Kantonsgerichtes von Graubünden PKG* [The jurisprudence of the Cantonal Tribunal of Graubünden]. Published since 1942.

Luzern. Obergericht. *Entscheidungen des Obergerichtes des Kantons Luzern und der Anwaltskammer* [Decisions of the Supreme Court of the Canton of Lucerne and of the Chamber of Barristers]. Published with varying titles since 1871/72.

Neuchâtel. Tribunal Cantonal. *Recueil de jurisprudence neuchâtloise* [Collected jurisprudence of Neuchâtel]. 1re. partie: Droit civil [Civil law]. 2me. partie: Droit pénal [Penal law]. 3me. partie: Droit administratif [Administrative law]. Published since 1953/57.

Solothurn. Obergericht. *Solothurnische Gerichtspraxis. Auszüge aus den Entscheiden des Obergerichtes, des Verwaltungsgerichtes und des Versicherungsgerichtes* [Solothurn jurisprudence. Extracts from the decisions of the High Court, the Court of Administration and the Social Security Court]. Published annually since 1974.

Thurgau. Obergericht. *Rechenschaftsbericht des Obergerichtes, der Rekurskommission des Versicherungsgerichtes, des Kriminalgerichtes und der Kriminalkammer* [Statement of account of the High Court, of the Appeal Commission of the Court of Insurance, the Criminal Court and the Criminal Chamber]. Published under different titles since 1839.

Valais. Tribunal Cantonal/Kantonsgericht. *Revue valaisanne de jurisprudence/ Zeitschrift für Walliser Rechtsprechung* [Valais review of jurisprudence]. Published since 1895.

3. MANNER OF PUBLICATION

The Bundeskanzlei runs the Eidgenössische Drucksachen- und Materialzentrale/ Office Central Fédéral des Imprimés et du Matériel/Ufficio Federale degli Stampati e del Materiale [Federal Printing and Supply Centre] (abbreviated to EDMZ), which handles all printing requirements and large issues of publications by the federal government. The publications which have been mentioned in this chapter are all issued by this Centre. Duplicated publications are produced in the individual federal offices, and there are growing amounts of 'semi-published' materials intended mainly for internal use. The volume of Swiss official publishing is not great. The EDMZ is responsible for 60% of all government publications, and the individual offices, publishing through their own information departments, for 40%.

4. BIBLIOGRAPHIC CONTROL

4.1. Government publishers' catalogues

The EDMZ does not publish a catalogue.

4.2. National bibliography of official publications

The *Bibliographie der schweizerischen Amtsdruckschriften/Bibliographie des publications officielles suisses* [Bibliography of Swiss official publications] which has been published since 1946 is issued by the Schweizerische Landesbibliothek/Bibliothèque Nationale Suisse/Biblioteca Nazionale Svizzera [Swiss National Library]. It appears annually, and has an alphabetical name and subject index. Each issue covers the year preceding its publication. It lists the publications of the federal, cantonal and communal governments, and those of the inter-cantonal and inter-communal authorities. The adequacy of its coverage depends on the collecting activity of the Schweizerische Landesbibliothek. Legal deposit does not work automatically, and does not cover 'semi-published' materials intended mainly for internal use. Publications must be identified and actively sought. The *Bibliographie* aims at completeness.

Special issues of the *Bibliographie der schweizerischen Amtsdruckschriften* in 1967 and 1976 have covered officially-published periodicals.

4.3. Other lists

The Bundesamt für Statistik issues a list of its publications which is irregular and free of charge. So also do the Bundesamt für Wohnungswesen/Office Fédéral du Logement/Ufficio Federale per l'Abitazione [Federal Housing Office] and the Bundesamt für Umweltschutz/Office Fédéral de la Protection de l'Environnement/Ufficio Federale per la Protezione dell'Ambiente [Federal Office of Environmental Protection]. Notices of new publications appear in the *Bundesblatt*.

5. LIBRARY COLLECTIONS AND AVAILABILITY

5.1. National library

In the course of fulfilling its legal obligation to collect all publications issued in or pertaining to Switzerland, the Schweizerische Landesbibliothek has built up a collection of Swiss official publications. This extends back to 1848, and includes the official publications of the federal, cantonal and communal governments. These are both regularly published items (such as yearbooks, state calendars, reports of proceedings, collections of laws, official gazettes, annual accounts, annual estimates, court judgements, and statistics) and one-off publications (such as expert reports, histories and information brochures).

Agreements have been made with the EDMZ and with the chancelleries of the various Cantons and of the larger Municipalities for them to deposit one copy of each of their publications with the Landesbibliothek.

5.2. Other principal collections

The official publications of the federal government are also collected by the Eidgenössische Parlaments- und Zentralbibliothek/Bibliothèque Centrale du Parlement et de l'Administration/Biblioteca Centrale del Parlamento e dell'Amministrazione [Federal Parliamentary and Central Library] in Bern. There are also large collections of official publications in the library of the Eidgenössische Technische Hochschule/Ecole Polytechnique Fédérale [Federal Technical University] in Zurich.

Other collections are to be found in the library of the University of Basel, at Zurich and at St. Gallen. The Zentralbibliothek Luzern [Lucerne Central Library] houses the collection of pre-1848 official publications.

5.3. Collections abroad and acquisitions problems

International exchange programmes are of very limited scope and cover only bibliographies. All Swiss official publications may be obtained by overseas libraries from the EDMZ or direct from the government departments themselves, or in the case of the cantonal publications from the chancelleries of the Cantons. Coverage of overseas libraries is impossible to assess, but it is likely that only major libraries such as the Library of Congress and the British Library hold substantial collections.

Requests for inter-library loan may be considered by the Schweizerische Landesbibliothek, case by case, but there are a good many restrictions on the availability of official publications for interlending.

6. PUBLICATIONS OF STATE, REGIONAL AND LOCAL GOVERNMENTS

The state governments of Switzerland are the cantonal governments. They are a vital part of political life. Each Canton issues a collection of its laws, a state calendar, a report of legislative proceedings, accounts, estimates, an official gazette, court judgements and statistics. All these are held by the Schweizerische Landesbibliothek.

The regional governments are the inter-cantonal and inter-communal authorities. There are annual reports of the Erziehungsdirektorenkonferenz/Conférence Suisse des Directeurs cantonaux de l'Instruction Publique/Conferenza Svizzera dei Direttori cantonali della Pubblica Educazione [Conference of Directors of Education], of the Volkswirtschaftsdirektorenkonferenz [Conference of Economic Directors] and of the Justizdirektorenkonferenz/Conférence des Chefs des Départements cantonaux de Justice et de Police [Conference of Directors of Justice], all bodies in which the Cantons co-operate. There are also inter-communal unions formed by several Communes.

Local governments are the communal authorities and municipal administrations and authorities. The Communes publish annual reports, accounts, estimates, collections of regulations, and informational material for their inhabitants.

The cantonal, inter-cantonal, inter-communal and communal publications are also covered by the *Bibliographie der schweizerischen Amtsdruckschriften*.

NOTES

1. I am indebted for this point to Dr. Theresa Schweizer of the Eidgenössische Technische Hochschule in Zurich.

7. BIBLIOGRAPHY

Aubert, Jean François. *Petite histoire constitutionnelle de la Suisse.* Bern, 1974. (Monographies d'histoire suisse, v. 9.) 118 p.

Der Bund kurz erklärt. Annual, in German, French and Italian.

Codding, George Arthur. *The federal government of Switzerland.* London, Cambridge, Mass., 1961. 171 p.

Huber, Hans. *How Switzerland is governed.* Tr. Mary Hottinger. Zurich, 1946. 64 p.

Hughes, Christopher John. *The federal constitution of Switzerland. Translation and commentary.* Oxford, 1954. 218 p.

——. *The Parliament of Switzerland.* London, Hansard Society of Great Britain, 1962. 204 p.

Kerr, Henry H. *Parlement et société en suisse.* Saint-Saphorin, 1981. 310 p.

Switzerland, Bundeskanzlei. *Eidgenössischer Staatskalender/Annuaire fédéral/Annuario federale.* Published by the EDMZ.

Switzerland, Bundesversammlung, Generalsekretariat. *Die schweizerische Bundesversammlung/L'Assemblée fédérale suisse/L'Assemblea federale svizzera/The Swiss federal assembly.* 1984. 47 p.

United Kingdom

EVE JOHANSSON

1. INTRODUCTION

Constitution

The United Kingdom of Great Britain and Northern Ireland is a constitutional monarchy with a parliamentary system of government. It has no written constitution.

The role of the Crown is not solely a ceremonial one. The monarch as Head of State must approve all legislation, opens and dissolves Parliament, appoints ministers, and has the power to conclude treaties, make peace or declare war, acting always on the advice of ministers.

The Parliament is bicameral. The lower house, the House of Commons, is composed of 650 directly elected members, elected on the 'first-past-the-post' system by all adults over the age of 18 years. The life of a Parliament is not more than five years, divided into annual sessions which normally run from early November to October. The upper house, the House of Lords, is non-elective and is composed of over 1,100 members, including 24 bishops, 793 hereditary peers, and 343 members honoured with a peerage for their services to the country in all areas of public life. Either house may initiate legislation, but only the House of Commons may initiate financial measures and the House of Lords has no powers of amendment over these.

The executive consists of the government (the Prime Minister and other ministers), the government departments, local authorities, and some public corporations. The Prime Minister and other ministers are members of Parliament: this includes members of the House of Lords, although in the twentieth century it has been the convention for the Prime Minister to be a member of the House of Commons. The Prime Minister is appointed by the monarch, and will normally be the leader of the majority party in the House of Commons. The Prime Minister advises the monarch on the appointment of other ministers, who are directly accountable to Parliament through the systems of annual reports, questions in Parliament, votes of no confidence, and through the system of Parliamentary Select Committees, formed to monitor the activities of the executive branch. The UK also has an Ombudsman, the Parliamentary Commissioner for Administration, who is responsible for dealing with complaints of maladministration in the implementation of policy or the handling of individual cases.

In 1986 there were 43 ministries or government departments, assisted by a great number of advisory bodies, commissions, committees of enquiry, regulatory bodies, and independent bodies governed by public sector rules of conduct and forms of accountability. The composition of the Cabinet and the number and responsibilities of ministries can vary widely, and are not fixed by law. There are also the boards of the nationalized industries and public corporations. The number of these other organizations has increased greatly since World War II with the extension of government activity into all areas of public life, research and education. The most popular term for such bodies has up to now been 'quangos'—normally taken to be an acronym for 'quasi-autonomous non-governmental organizations', although there are variant interpretations of this. The term was coined at a conference at Ditchley in 1969 (Hague, D. C. and Mackenzie, W. J. M. *Private policy and public interest*. London, Macmillan, 1975). Other terms used are 'fringe bodies' and 'non-departmental public bodies' (NDPBs). The number of such organizations as at April 1985 was given as 1,681 in the 1986 edition of *Britain: an official handbook*. They exist to carry out functions which require public accountability but some degree of independence, and are often not part of the traditional concerns of government. The British Broadcasting Corporation is often considered to be a classic example. The *Report on non-departmental public bodies* (Cmnd. 7797) describes them in three categories: executive bodies carrying out operational or regulatory functions or scientific and cultural activities, advisory bodies, and tribunals. Examples are the Advisory Committee on the Safety of Medicines, the British Library, the Consultative Panel on Badgers and Tuberculosis, the Health and Safety Executive, the Nature Conservancy Council, the Security Council and the Welsh Development Agency.

Central government is responsible for the execution of foreign policy, defence, international relations, taxation and fiscal policy, trade, economic, employment and industrial policy, energy, agriculture and fisheries, home affairs and communications. It also establishes policy overall for health, welfare, education, housing, transport, environmental planning, civil defence, consumer protection, police, fire services, public libraries, and some museums and recreational facilities, though the execution of these policies is largely delegated to the local level.

Local government in England and Wales is composed of 53 County authorities subdivided into 369 District authorities, and below that into Parishes. In metropolitan areas the equivalent of the County authority is the Borough. There is no regional level except in the case of health administration. Local authorities are composed of directly elected Councils, headed by a Chairman or Mayor, and a permanent executive (who are not civil servants). In Scotland there are 9 Regions subdivided into 53 Districts, and in Northern Ireland 26 Districts. Local authorities have the power to raise funds through local taxes (known as the 'rates' and assessed on property) but also receive grants made by central government. Central government has no direct control over the activities of local government except through the sanctions of the level of financial support and statutory controls passed by Parliament. Schools, polytechnics and colleges of further and higher education are the responsibility of this level of government, as are public libraries. The universities however are funded from central government funds, through a quango, the University Grants Committee.

INTRODUCTION

The judiciary is independent of both legislature and executive.

Northern Ireland is a part of the United Kingdom and had its own legislative assembly from 1921 to 1972, when it was suspended and replaced by direct rule by the UK Parliament and government. (There is a Northern Ireland Assembly, elected in 1982 and intended to carry out scrutiny and consultative functions, but a number of its elected members have not taken their seats.) A UK Cabinet minister is currently responsible for the functions formerly exercised by the Northern Ireland government, and directs the work of the six Northern Ireland departments and their related bodies.

The Isle of Man and the Channel Islands are not part of the United Kingdom, but are dependencies of the Crown, and the British government is responsible for their defence and foreign policy. They have their own legislative assemblies, local government and legal systems.

The account of British official publications which follows will concentrate on those of the present day.

Definition of official publications

There is no legal definition of a publication, an official publication nor even government in the UK, and no generally accepted definition in the library literature. UK official publications present the same problems of definition as those of all developed countries, including the proliferation of 'semi-published' material. This chapter will follow the practice that is common in libraries with significant collections, including the British Library, of regarding as published any document that is not actually restricted (hence all 'grey literature'), even if its circulation is small or specialized, and of regarding as official any body that is funded directly by central government or accountable to it. By convention, the publications of the universities are not considered as official, but those of the nationalized industries are.

A helpful definition of official publications has been accepted by the Official Publications Section of IFLA (the International Federation of Library Associations) and by SCOOP (the Standing Committee on Official Publications of the Library Association's Information Services Group). SCOOP is mentioned below. The definition is printed in Appendix 1 of this chapter.

Government organization manuals

The *Civil service yearbook* is the principal manual of government organization. Currently prepared by the Cabinet Office and published by HMSO, it began as the *British imperial calendar and civil service list*, first issued for 1810/15 and annually thereafter. It lists the members of the Royal Household, government departments and some fringe bodies with addresses and the names of senior officials, and salary scales. About 350 bodies are currently included.

Public bodies, prepared by the Management and Personnel Office of the Cabinet Office, provides a different list of non-departmental public bodies as defined in the *Report on non-departmental public bodies* (*see* above) and including the nationalized industries and public corporations. It gives details of their costs, staffing and appointments and includes approximately 400 bodies. It is published annually by Her Majesty's Stationery Office (HMSO).

Britain: an official handbook, an annual, published by HMSO, gives a simple list of the responsibilities of the main government departments.

SCOOP

The Standing Committee on Official Publications of the Information Services Group of the Library Association, already mentioned, is an active group representing interests in the Library Association, users of official publications, other library interests and Her Majesty's Stationery Office. Before 1983 it was the Library Association/HMSO Working Party of the Reference, Special and Information Section of the Library Association, now the Information Services Group. It acts as a useful pressure group, publishes a column of information in *Refer*, the ISG newsletter, among others, and organizes seminars to improve knowledge of the resources listing local authority official publications. In 1985 it published a *Directory of specialists in official publications* which it intends to maintain up-to-date at approximately two-year intervals. *Local authority information sources: a guide to publications, data-bases and services* was published at the end of 1986. SCOOP aims to improve access to and understanding of British official publications among librarians and others with a need to find and use official information.

2. PRINCIPAL PUBLICATIONS OF CENTRAL GOVERNMENT

2.1. Laws and legislation

Laws or statutes of the United Kingdom are classified as *Public general acts and Church Assembly measures*, *Local and personal acts*, and *Private acts*. The first category are the most numerous and are statutes of general application. Local and personal acts are those which concern local interests, and were very voluminous in the nineteenth century, including many permitting the construction of railways. Private acts are rare and are those where Parliament is acting almost in a judicial capacity. They concern most usually divorces and the settlement of estates. The style of their numbering distinguishes them. Public general acts have a number in Arabic numerals, local and personal acts a number in Roman numerals, and private acts a number in italics. The correct description of an act is simply the year and number—1972 c. 54 was the British Library Act. Until 1963 the regnal year of the monarch was used instead of the calendar year—hence 1 & 2 Geo. 5 c. 46 was the Copyright Act of 1911.

All acts are separately published by Her Majesty's Stationery Office (HMSO) and available immediately they have received the Royal Assent. They are also collected into annual bound volumes with indexes. The sets in their official arrangement begin in 1800.

The United Kingdom has no system of codes of law, but a codified version of the *Statutes in force* was begun in 1972 and is being published in loose-leaf form by HMSO. It has an index and printed guide.

Commercial publishing houses, such as Butterworths and Sweet & Maxwell, make an important contribution to the available reference sources through publications such as *Halsbury's statutes* and legal encyclopaedias.

Some older sets of the acts of Parliament are available in microform. The public general acts from 1801 to 1922 are on microfiche, available from Harvester Press. The *Statutes of the Realm* from 1101 to 1713 and the *Acts of the Parliament of*

Scotland have been microfilmed and are available from Microform International Marketing Corporation.

INDEXES TO LEGISLATION

The *Index to the statutes in force* indexes legislation in force in annual cumulations covering the year 1235 to date, and serves as an index to the loose-leaf *Statutes in force*. It is accompanied by a *Chronological table of the statutes in force*, also cumulating annually. They include local and personal acts considered to be of general interest. Both are published by HMSO. LEXIS, the on-line service available through Butterworths, covers public general acts in force, but at the time of writing is not yet comprehensive. POLIS, the on-line system of the House of Commons Library, available to subscribers through the SCICON host, includes all public general acts since 1979 and local and private acts since November 1982.

2.2. Secondary legislation

Secondary legislation is the orders having the force of law made by government bodies under the authority of enabling legislation. Most such orders are called statutory instruments. Like the acts of Parliament, they are published separately by HMSO and are also collected into an official set with an annual index. There is an annual *Index of government orders in force*, and a *Table of government orders in force* (also annual), which explains the orders that have lapsed or been repealed. Both are HMSO publications. *Halsbury's statutory instruments*, published by Butterworths, also provides a complete reference service.

Statutory instruments in force are included (not as yet comprehensively) on the LEXIS data-base and on POLIS since November 1982.

There are other types of government order but they are not so numerous. Examples are the *Circulars* of the Department of the Environment and Department of Transport and regulations for the forces made by the Ministry of Defence. Government orders are not collected into ministerial bulletins as is the case in many countries. It is also important to note that the *London gazette* (*see* section 2.5 below) does not include statutes or secondary legislation, only Orders in Council.

2.3. Parliamentary publications

The principal series of parliamentary publications are the *Journals* of the two houses (the official record of business done), the *Debates* (the stenographic record of what is said and the official record of voting by members), the minutes of proceedings and agenda papers (sometimes called the Daily business papers), and the parliamentary or sessional papers. The first three are records of proceedings internal to Parliament; the latter include bills at all their stages with amendments, and also information from outside sources gathered by Parliament in the course of its work—reports of investigations, regular statistical reports, the annual reports and accounts presented by many bodies to Parliament, and the budget documentation. All of these series are described in greater detail below. They form four distinct series: the UK has never had the tradition of a single official gazette.

There are separate, parallel sets for the two houses. As in many countries, the legislative process means that it may be necessary to use both in order to follow the progress of a piece of legislation. In general all are easy to use, well indexed and readily comprehensible in their arrangement.

The Journals

The *Journals* of the House of Commons from 1547 and the House of Lords from 1510 are the formal record of sittings, business done, bills read, reports received, motions and petitions submitted and the results of votes taken. Since 1834 they have been accepted as the official record of Parliament. They are published, by HMSO, in sessional volumes, appearing usually some time after the end of the parliamentary year. There is an index for each session, and cumulated indexes for the House of Commons for 1547–1714, 1714–1774, 1774–1790, 1790–1800, 1801–1820, 1820–1837, 1837–1852, 1852/53–1865, 1866–1878/79, and then decennial indexes until 1950, and indexes for the House of Lords *Journals* for 1509–1714, 1714–1779, 1780–1819, 1820–1833, 1833–1863, 1864–1873 and then decennial indexes until 1952/53.

The *Journals* of the House of Commons have been microfilmed by Brookhaven Press for 1547–1900 and Readex for 1900–1974; those of the House of Lords for 1509–1931 are available on microfilm from Microform International Marketing Corporation. From 1984/85 the *Journals* are also available on microfiche from Chadwyck-Healey Ltd.

The Debates

The printed verbatim report of the debates in Parliament is popularly known as Hansard: its full title is *Parliamentary debates: House of Commons* (or *House of Lords*) *official report*. It contains the text of speeches and of written or oral replies to questions, and the division lists—the lists of the names of members voting for or against motions or bills (each house 'divides' in voting). Debates in Standing Committee are published in sub-series. The Parliamentary debates are published by HMSO and appear daily while Parliament is in session, with weekly cumulations and bound sets for the full parliamentary year. Members of Parliament do not have the right to amend the record before the weekly cumulations appear, though the editors may make corrections. The House of Lords and House of Commons debates appear in separate volumes and have done so since 1909.

Before 1909, the *Parliamentary debates* were privately published. The ancestors of the series were *Cobbett's parliamentary history of England* (later the *Parliamentary history of England*), covering 1066–1803, and *Cobbett's parliamentary debates* covering 1803/04–1812, and *Hansard's parliamentary debates* after 1811. Before 1803 a number of unofficial and competing reports were published, which are listed in the bibliography by Bond (*see* section 7 below). The nineteenth century saw a good deal of interesting controversy over the right of journalists to report proceedings in Parliament, and there were cases of their being ejected from the gallery.

Indexes to the *Parliamentary debates* appear weekly and at the end of the sessional bound set. There is no cumulated index except for the years 1803–1830. Since November 1981 the indexes are accessible on-line to subscribers to the POLIS database.

The *Parliamentary debates* from 1811 to 1908, including *Cobbett's parliamentary history*, and the House of Lords debates 1909–1982, are available on microfilm from Microform International Marketing Corporation. The House of Commons debates from 1909 to 1977/78 have been microfilmed by Readex. From 1985/86 they are published on microfiche by Chadwyck-Healey Ltd.

The Votes and proceedings *and* Minutes of proceedings

The House of Commons daily minutes of proceedings are entitled the *Votes and proceedings* and are included in a bundle of papers distributed daily to members of Parliament and many government offices: it includes the agenda paper for the day's business, detailed amendments to bills made in Standing Committee, division lists and a number of other categories. They are largely superseded for purposes of research by the *Journals* and *Debates*, and are not heavily used outside Parliament itself except by pressure groups or others following the detail of the passage of a piece of legislation, or for exceptionally detailed analysis of the changes made to a bill.

The equivalent set in the House of Lords is the *Minutes of proceedings*, which are similarly little used outside Parliament.

Parliamentary papers

The parliamentary or sessional papers form physically very substantial sets and since the early nineteenth century have been one of the richest sources of contemporary documentation on all aspects of society and current affairs. They are heavily used by researchers for information on social and economic history, political history, the history of the former colonies, technological development and so on.

The parliamentary papers are printed daily and published immediately while Parliament is in session. All are published by HMSO. The House of Commons papers currently divide into three categories:

(a) bills. These include the first printing, lists of amendments, and periodic amended reprints. They are distinguished by numbering in square brackets
(b) House of Commons papers. These are reports of Select Committees composed of members of Parliament, and are distinguished by numbers in round brackets. The numbering sequence starts anew at the beginning of each parliamentary session
(c) Command papers. These are reports originating outside the House of Commons, including reports of commissions of investigation and many annual reports and accounts of official bodies and regular statistical reports. They are called Command papers because they are presented to Parliament by command of the monarch. Their numbers appear in square brackets, preceded by an abbreviation of the word 'command': Cmd., Cmnd., Cm., and so on. The numbering of these does not start again with each new parliamentary session but runs over many years.

There are several popular terms used to describe the parliamentary or sessional papers, some of them best avoided. 'Blue books' is used to describe the whole set of the parliamentary papers, but is also confusingly applied to some other materials, the trade reports among them. A 'white paper' is a statement of government policy usually for a proposed piece of legislation: white papers are always parliamentary papers. 'Green papers' are always consultative documents but are not always parliamentary papers. The covers of these last two categories are not always white or green!

After the end of the session, the parliamentary papers of the House of Commons are arranged by its Library into an official bound set and indexed. The bound set preserves the three distinct categories of paper. It is available from HMSO.

Before 1980 the papers were arranged in four sequences: bills, reports of committees, reports of commissioners, and accounts and papers. The distinctions between them are no longer significant. The arrangement went back to 1800, before which there was no official set and no complete sets were archived. Five variously incomplete sets were bound up, one of which survives in the British Library. An exhaustive scholarly reprint has been edited by Sheila Lambert (*see* section 7 below).

The indexing does not follow any thesaurus in general use, but has been consistent and readily comprehensible for many years. The indexes give access by paper number, subject, and names of chairmen of committees and authors of reports. They appear some years after publication of the original paper: in the meantime the catalogues of HMSO include them and may reliably be used as indexes. The indexes from May 1979 are also accessible to subscribers to the POLIS data-base. There are cumulated indexes for the years 1800–1852, 1852/53–1899, 1900–1949 and 1950–1959/60, and a number of special indexes, for instance to the trade and colonial reports.

A microfiche edition of the parliamentary papers has been published by Chadwyck-Healey Ltd for the years 1800–1921, and since parliamentary session 1975/76 the current papers are produced on microfiche by the same company, together with a monthly cumulated index.

The House of Lords sessional papers amount to much less in bulk. There are some reports which are unique to the Lords, but bills are the largest category. An official arrangement, similar to that of the Commons set, goes back to 1832. By convention it does not include the papers that are common to both houses. The pattern of indexing is similar but there are cumulated indexes only to the years 1800–1859, 1860–1870 and 1871–1885: after that there are sessional indexes only. The indexes are however on the POLIS data-base from November 1981. A scholarly reprint of all surviving papers to 1859 has been edited by F. W. Torrington (*see* section 7 below).

House of Lords sessional papers from 1984/85 are available on microfiche from Chadwyck-Healey Ltd.

General information on Parliament

A useful, up-to-date summary of parliamentary business is provided by the weekly *House of Commons information bulletin*, edited by the House of Commons Library and published by HMSO. The *Sessional information digest* is published annually by the Public Information Office of the House of Commons. It appears after the end of each session and includes a summary of the business of the session, lists of bills and acts, and lists of reports and documentation received.

The Public Information Office provides a popular and heavily used information service for the general public: details are given in the *Guide to government department and other libraries* listed in section 7 below.

2.4. Non-parliamentary official publications

The great development of the body of non-parliamentary (sometimes called departmental) publications has occurred during the twentieth century. The diversification and growth of government activity, the extension of publishing for public information, and certain changes of practice in the interests of economy have contributed to this. The change is reflected in the reduction in the number of the parliamentary sessional papers after 1922.

For the user and librarian, it is essential to bear in mind the distinction between the parliamentary papers and departmental publications. In a library which keeps the parliamentary papers in the official set, or purchases the microfiche, it will be necessary to have the full details about an item required in order to trace it. There is a further crucial distinction between departmental publications which are published by HMSO and those (a large and growing proportion) which are published by the departments themselves. This problem is discussed further in sections 3 and 4 below. In this section, all publications which are published by HMSO will be indicated: others are published by the originating departments.

Until roughly the time of World War I, very little was published that was not in the category of the parliamentary papers. The principal exceptions are army handbooks, the *Admiralty Pilots* (guides for mariners) and some circulars and forms of the Board of Agriculture and Board of Health. The balance has shifted radically with the setting up of many more official bodies and their involvement in new areas of research, regulation, public advice and provision of services. The tendency has been reinforced by certain economy measures taken by government in ceasing to include in the set of parliamentary papers some important categories of reports. In 1922 the colonial reports and in 1972/73 the annual reports and accounts of a large number of the nationalized industries and other public bodies ceased to be published as parliamentary papers. (The element of economy was that a copy of every parliamentary paper has to be printed for each member of Parliament.)

The volume of non-parliamentary official publications is such that a comprehensive description cannot be given here. The main series published by the largest official bodies and those of particular interest to libraries will be listed and a rough description given of the types of reports, publicity material and so on that each body issues. Fringe bodies and nationalized industries will be listed on their own in the alphabetical sequence and not with the parent body. A comprehensive account useful for selection and reference purposes will be found in the *Directory of British official publications: a guide to sources*, edited by Stephen Richard (*see* section 7 below) and the reader is referred to this for fuller information.

The selection which follows will concentrate on titles currently published.

AGRICULTURAL AND FOOD RESEARCH COUNCIL

The Agricultural and Food Research Council makes grants for research, to the universities and other bodies, and maintains a number of research stations such as the Food Research Institute, the Institute for Research on Animal Diseases, the John Innes Institute and the Plant Breeding Institute. Examples of their publications are reports of trials on plant varieties, technical leaflets giving advice to farmers and growers, and the annual lists of recommended varieties of agricultural and feed crops produced by the National Institute of Agricultural Botany.

ARTS COUNCIL

The Arts Council is responsible for the promotion of the arts generally through the provisions of grants and through its services and publications. It issues an *Annual report and accounts*, some exhibition catalogues, popular booklets, and a monthly magazine, *Arts documentation monthly*.

BANK OF ENGLAND

The Bank of England issues an annual report and accounts, a *Quarterly bulletin*, and a monthly *Banking statistics* which replaces the *Statistical abstract* published formerly. There is also a series of *Discussion papers* on current issues of policy and methodology.

Much Bank of England monetary, financial and banking data is accessible on-line on the Bank of England Databank through CISI-Wharton.

BRITISH BROADCASTING CORPORATION

The *Annual report and handbook* is the principal source of information on matters internal to the BBC, but there is a range of very high quality publications on subjects of popular interest, such as politics and travel, educational teaching materials, and publications based on programmes. The Monitoring Service at Caversham, Reading, which is responsible for monitoring the radio broadcasts of many parts of the world, publishes the fortnightly *Summary of world broadcasts*, and this is also available on-line full-text on the World Reporter data-base.

BRITISH COUNCIL

The British Council works to promote an understanding of Britain in other countries through educational, cultural and training programmes. It publishes an *Annual report* and an annual *Statistics of overseas students in the UK*. *British book news*, monthly, is its best-known periodical publication.

BRITISH LIBRARY

The British Library publishes an *Annual report*. It issues the *British national bibliography* in weekly, four-monthly and annual cumulations. *BNB* forms the basis of the UK-MARC file on the BLAISE data-base maintained and marketed by the British Library. Current catalogues of different parts of the Library are available on microfiche and on the BLAISE system and there are many specialized and general published catalogues, such as the *Catalogue of printed music* and, perhaps best-known, the authoritative *General catalogue of printed books* to 1975. There are series of research reports in library and information science, an *Index to conference proceedings received* (acquired that is by the Document Supply Centre at Boston Spa), a current awareness service for the library and information professions (*Current awareness for British library and information staff* (CABLIS)), and regular newsletters from different parts of the Library. An exhaustive account cannot be given here. Of particular interest for work with official publications are the following: the *Checklist of British official serial publications* (latest ed. 1980); *Current research in Britain*, published by the Document Supply Centre in three parts; and *British reports, translations and theses*, a monthly list of the report literature acquired by the Document Supply Centre. It lists reports of central government and local government bodies and forms the basis for UK input to the SIGLE (System for Grey Literature in Europe) data-base, which is accessible on-line on BLAISE.

A complete publications catalogue is available from the Publications Sales Unit, British Library, Boston Spa, Wetherby, West Yorks. LS23 7BQ, England.

BRITISH TOURIST AUTHORITY

The British Tourist Authority with the regional tourist boards is responsible for the promotion of tourism in the UK both to nationals and to overseas visitors. It issues brochures, magazines, and publicity materials such as lists of hotels and guest-houses, in several languages.

BRITISH WATERWAYS BOARD

British Waterways is the state-owned network of canals and water transport, and is responsible for the provision of recreational as well as transport facilities. Its annual *Report and accounts* is published by HMSO and it issues research report series including *Recreational planning reports* and *Recreational research reports*.

BUILDING RESEARCH ESTABLISHMENT

The BRE issues research reports on new building materials and methods, an annual *Research programme*, an annual *Information directory*, and a bi-monthly *News of construction research*.

CABINET OFFICE

The Cabinet Office issues reports on policy, some consultative papers, and official and military histories. It produces the *Civil service yearbook*, published by HMSO, the quarterly *List of ministerial responsibilities*, and the *Annual review of government funded research and development*, an HMSO publication. Its Management and Personnel Office produces leaflets and guides on career planning and management in the civil service, pamphlets and recruitment literature, circulars, regulations, administrative memoranda, and an annual report. It also prepares an annual list of non-departmental public bodies, published by HMSO as *Public bodies*.

CENTRAL OFFICE OF INFORMATION

The COI issues pamphlets, periodicals, publicity material and reference works on all aspects of government services and contemporary life in the UK, as well as information leaflets on the services it provides to official bodies in the area of marketing and publicity. It is the compiler of *Britain: an official handbook*, which has already been mentioned and is an HMSO publication. There are also a six-monthly list of *Information, press and public relations officers in government departments and public corporations*, and a monthly *Survey of current affairs* and *Economic progress report*. General information on current affairs is provided in a number of languages in magazines such as *Anglia, Brytania* and *Gran Bretana Hoy*. The COI publishes an *Annual report and accounts*.

CENTRAL STATISTICAL OFFICE

The Central Statistical Office is one of the major publishers among government departments in the UK, although many important statistics are published not by it but by the official bodies collecting them. An important, comprehensive guide is the *Guide to official statistics*, prepared by the CSO and published by HMSO. The latest edition, the fifth, was published in 1986. *Government statistics: a brief guide to sources* is a free leaflet describing the principal series, updated annually and available from the CSO.

The titles of the principal series are self-explanatory. They are the *Annual abstract of statistics*, the *Monthly digest of statistics*, *Economic trends*, which is monthly, *Financial statistics*, also monthly, *Regional trends* and *Social trends*, both annual, giving general social statistics, *UK balance of payments*, which is annual, *UK national accounts*, also an annual, and *Studies in official statistics*, an irregular series on statistical method. All CSO titles are published by HMSO.

Much CSO macroeconomic and financial data is available on the Central Statistical Office Databank through CISI-Wharton.

CIVIL AVIATION AUTHORITY

The Civil Aviation Authority is responsible for the economic, technical and operational regulation of civil aviation and for navigational services at some airports. Its principal series are the *Annual report and accounts*, annual statistics of airline traffic, *CAA monthly statistics*, and regulations and civil airworthiness requirements. The *Civil aviation communications handbook* is a loose-leaf publication frequently updated.

COMMISSION FOR RACIAL EQUALITY

The Commission for Racial Equality has the duty of working towards the elimination of discrimination and of promoting equality of opportunity and good relations between the different racial groups. It publishes an *Annual report*, a six-monthly *Calendar of religious festivals* which covers all the religious observances of a multicultural society, and information journals such as *New community*, *Education journal* and *Employment report*, all four-monthly.

COMMONWEALTH AGRICULTURAL BUREAUX

The Commonwealth Agricultural Bureaux publish indexing and abstracting services: examples are *Nutrition abstracts and reviews*, *Animal breeding abstracts* and *Plant breeding abstracts*, but there are many more.

COMPANIES REGISTRATION OFFICE

The Companies Registration Office collects and makes available to the public the statutory documents which have to be deposited by public limited companies. It produces forms and publicity literature and publishes on microfiche an index to all registered companies, which is revised and fully updated monthly. A summary of its work is included in *Companies*, an annual report prepared by the Department of Trade and Industry.

CUSTOMS AND EXCISE

The annual report is published by HMSO and is a command paper. *UK Customs and Excise tariff*, published annually by HMSO, gives tariffs and details of entry procedures, and there are statistical compilations, and some information pamphlets.

DEPARTMENT OF AGRICULTURE AND FISHERIES FOR SCOTLAND

The annual report of the Department is *Agriculture in Scotland*, issued by HMSO as a command paper, and it produces an annual *Economic report on Scottish agriculture*, *Scottish sea fisheries statistical tables*, also annual (both these being published by HMSO), *Animal health* (annual) and *Agricultural research and development* (also annual). There is an irregular series of *Scottish fisheries research reports*, and reports on the inspection and registration of seed potato crops. The Marine Laboratory in Aberdeen comes under the Department: it publishes an *Annual review of research*. The Royal Botanic Gardens in Edinburgh, for which the Department is responsible, publishes an annual report, guides, and *Monthly notes*.

DEPARTMENT OF EDUCATION AND SCIENCE

The DES is one of the largest government departments. Its *Annual report* is published by HMSO. *Education statistics for the UK* and the *Digest of statistics* are published annually by the Department. Other important serial publications are *Current educational research projects supported by the DES*, an annual, and *DES news*, issued irregularly. The Department issues reports series, consultative and policy documents, circulars and memoranda to local education authorities, pamphlets on matters relating to education such as school buildings, and publicity and careers material for students.

DEPARTMENT OF EMPLOYMENT

The Department is responsible for the enforcement of employment legislation, registration of the unemployed, provision of an employment agency service, some aspects of manpower planning and some careers information. It issues an annual report and the very important *Employment gazette*, published monthly by HMSO, and one of the oldest-established official publications (it started life as the *Board of Trade labour gazette* in 1893, and was later the *Ministry of Labour gazette*). Statistics are mainly provided in the *Employment gazette* and in the annual *Family expenditure survey*, an HMSO publication. The former *British labour statistics yearbook* ceased publication in 1976. *Employment news* is monthly, *Employment legislation* irregular, and there are reports series giving the results of research, pamphlets and leaflets such as guides to employment law, circulars and administrative memoranda, and publicity materials. The Department has prepared some major reference works such as *British labour statistics. Historical abstract 1886-1968* (HMSO, 1971) and *Retail price indices 1914-1984* (HMSO, 1985).

The Work Research Unit of the Department publishes irregular *Occasional papers* on research into work organization, and bibliographies on subjects such as stress, job satisfaction, performance appraisal and quality circles.

DEPARTMENT OF ENERGY

The Department issues an annual report, an annual report with statistics on *Development of the oil and gas resources of the UK* (an HMSO publication), and an annual *Digest of UK energy statistics* (also published by HMSO). Its principal journal is the monthly *Energy management*, and its reports series are *Energy papers* and *Offshore technology reports*, both published irregularly by HMSO. Important publicity material and leaflets on energy conservation and guides to good practice are series such as *Making buildings pay* and *Fuel efficiency booklets*. The Department is responsible for publishing the *UK continental shelf oil well records*, issued on microfiche by HMSO, and *UK land oil well records*, also on microfiche. Its Library issues an irregular series of *Energy bibliographies*.

DEPARTMENT OF HEALTH AND SOCIAL SECURITY

The DHSS is another of the largest government departments, having responsibility for all aspects of health care, the social services, social security and nutrition. Its annual report is *The health service in England*, which is published by HMSO. It issues annually *Health and personal social services statistics for England*, published by HMSO (equivalent statistics for the other regions, Wales, Scotland and Northern Ireland are mentioned below under the relevant bodies), and *Social security statistics*, also an HMSO publication. *Mental health statistics* is an annual compilation published by the Department itself. There is an annual *Research and development report and handbook*, published by HMSO, a quarterly periodical, *Health trends*, an irregular series of *Research reports*, published by HMSO, and *Hospital abstracts*, a monthly survey of world literature and another HMSO title. More specialized titles include *Health building notes*, also published by HMSO. There are circulars, letters and notices and memoranda on the application of the law, the *Housing benefits guidance manual*, frequently updated, notes and information for claimants, publicity material for the general public, and reports on major policy issues. HMSO publishes the series of decisions on claims. The Library of the DHSS is responsible for publishing *Social service abstracts*, which is monthly, and an irregular series of bibliographies.

DEPARTMENT OF THE ENVIRONMENT

The Department of the Environment looks after transport, housing, local government, building and building research, regional planning, environmental improvement, reduction of pollution, waste disposal, land use and the rehabilitation of the inner cities. As a publisher it has a wide range. There is an annual report and a *Report on Department of the Environment research and development*, also annual. Statistics are published in *Local housing statistics* quarterly, *Housing and construction statistics* annually, *Transport statistics Great Britain* annually, *Road accidents in Great Britain* annually, *Local government financial statistics in England and Wales* annually, and *Digest of environmental protection and water statistics* annually. All the above are HMSO publications. Reports series include *Waste management papers*, published by HMSO, and a wide range of others. There are circulars and administrative memoranda, such as the irregular *Housing circulars* (published by HMSO), publicity material, information series on area improvement, and traffic regulations. The Library of the Department issues a useful *Library bulletin*, a fortnightly accessions list, and a series of valuable bibliographies.

DEPARTMENT OF TRADE AND INDUSTRY

The remit of the Department includes trade, industry, industrial and regional development, company law, bankruptcy, insurance, weights and measures, the promotion of small business and the encouragement of industrial and office automation, including the application of new technology. The main annual reports are *Companies in . . .* and *Bankruptcy: general annual report*, both HMSO publications. The principal statistical publication is *Overseas trade of the UK*, published annually by HMSO, and the Department's journal is the weekly *British business*, which gives the most up-to-date information and statistics on prices and economic indicators. There are major reports and policy documents, for instance in 1986 on the protection of intellectual property, and a wide range of information for small businesses and exporters.

Its Business Statistics Office conducts the regular censuses of industrial production and of the distributive and service industries, and the series of *Business monitors* publishes the results (through HMSO) monthly, quarterly and annually.

The Library of the Department issues a weekly *Contents of recent economics journals*, and its Statistics and Market Intelligence Library publishes guides to information sources such as the trade statistics and development plans of other countries.

Within the Department of Industry, the Alvey Directorate is responsible for promoting research into and applications of new technology. It issues the *Alvey programme annual report*.

DEPARTMENT OF TRANSPORT

The Department of Transport is responsible for roads, motor vehicle registration and safety, traffic signs, bridges and shipping. It issues an annual report and statistics in *Road accidents in Great Britain* and *Transport statistics*, an annual compilation of time-series over a ten-year period. These are published by HMSO. The Department itself publishes *Quarterly transport statistics* and an annual *National road traffic forecast*.

There are regular surveys of road traffic, travel patterns, and freight transport, and some general publicity and information material for the public, such as leaflets for cyclists or the disabled. Regulations for merchant shipping are published in the *Merchant shipping notices*, published by HMSO.

The Transport and Road Research Laboratory reports to the Department of Transport. It carries out technical research and evaluations and publishes an annual *Transport and road research* and a monthly *Digest of TRRL reports* which includes methodological studies.

DESIGN COUNCIL

The Design Council promotes good design in industry and consumer goods. It has an *Annual report*, a monthly magazine, *Design*, and directories of expertise and lists of courses in design. It has published one major book, *Design policy*, in six volumes, in 1984.

ECONOMIC AND SOCIAL RESEARCH COUNCIL

The ESRC funds research by academic and other bodies. It issues an annual report, a reports series, research reviews, bibliographies, and a house journal.

EQUAL OPPORTUNITIES COMMISSION

The EOC, responsible for promoting equality of opportunity for men and women through publicity and education, is an active publisher. It issues an *Annual report* through HMSO, the quarterly *EOC research bulletin*, codes of practice, and some important news releases.

FOREIGN AND COMMONWEALTH OFFICE

The FCO publishes international agreements and treaties, which appear as command papers in the parliamentary sessional papers. It edits the *Yearbook of the Commonwealth* and the *Diplomatic Service List* (annual), and annual administrative reports on the remaining dependent territories. There is also the *London diplomatic list*, a six-monthly list of the representatives of foreign states and Commonwealth countries in the UK. All of these are published by HMSO. The FCO also edits *Documents on British foreign policy*, a selection of unpublished documents, issued through HMSO, and makes available a series of *Background briefs* which explain current policy issues.

The Arms Control and Disarmament Unit of the FCO has an irregular series of reports entitled *Arms control and disarmament*.

FORESTRY COMMISSION

The Forestry Commission is the national forestry authority, producing timber and advising on forestry and arboriculture. It publishes an *Annual report*, which appears in the parliamentary sessional papers, an annual *Report on forest research*, which is published by HMSO, censuses of woodland trees, *Research information notes*, *Arboriculture research notes*, and, through HMSO, other series of booklets and leaflets. There are also occasional manuals of arboricultural practice and bibliographies.

GENERAL REGISTER OFFICE FOR SCOTLAND

The General Register Office for Scotland carries out the same census and statistical functions for Scotland that the Office of Population Censuses and Surveys does for England and Wales. The *Annual report* is published by HMSO, as are annual

Population estimates. The reports resulting from the decennial census of population have a similar pattern of publication to those issued by the Office of Population Censuses and Surveys (*see below*).

HEALTH AND SAFETY EXECUTIVE

The HSE is responsible for ensuring the observance of the provisions of the Health and Safety at Work Acts, including the inspection of places of work. It issues leaflets, codes of practice, *Guidance notes*, lists of approved products, irregular *Bibliographies*, and occasional *Investigation reports* in the areas of industrial and agricultural health and safety. It publishes annual reports on individual sectors of the economy, such as quarries, manufacturing industry and the service industries. HSELINE is its publicly available on-line data-base, covering its own publications as well as other materials: it is available through ESA-IRS on Pergamon Infoline.

HOME OFFICE

The Home Office has responsibility for penal affairs, police matters, immigration, equal opportunities, broadcasting, fire prevention, and gaming. It publishes an annual report, an important series of *Research studies*, issued by HMSO, and reports and consultative papers on all subjects within its remit. Its Research and Planning Unit publishes *Criminal statistics*, *Prison statistics*, a *Report on the work of the Prison Department*, and *Control of immigration statistics*. All are annual and published by HMSO as command papers. There are also an annual *Statistics of misuse of drugs* and a *Home Office statistical bulletin*, and general information leaflets for the public on fire, crime prevention, nationality law and so on.

INLAND REVENUE

The Inland Revenue is responsible for the administration and collection of personal, corporate and value added tax. Its annual report is published by HMSO as a command paper. Two annual statistical compilations, *Inland revenue statistics* and the *Survey of personal incomes*, are published by HMSO, as are the reports of tax cases before the Court of Appeal, and codified versions of taxation legislation. There is also a series of general information leaflets, IR_x for the public.

LAW COMMISSION

The Law Commission researches proposals for law reform, for instance the updating of the law in the light of changes in society and technology. Its *Annual report* appears in the parliamentary sessional papers and is hence an HMSO publication. HMSO also publishes a series of *Working papers* for the Commission.

MANPOWER SERVICES COMMISSION

The Manpower Services Commission advises government on manpower planning and assists people in finding, applying for and obtaining jobs. It maintains a variety of training schemes. It issues an annual report, a *Review and plan for Scotland* and another of similar title for Wales, and leaflets on the different employment and training schemes.

MEDICAL RESEARCH COUNCIL

The Medical Research Council funds research in the universities and other institutions, and maintains a number of centres for specialist research. It issues an *Annual* report and annual *Handbook*, and the specialist centres such as the Biochemical Genetics Unit, the Leukaemia Unit and the Radiobiology Unit issue annual reports, newsletters and research reports.

METEOROLOGICAL OFFICE

The Meteorological Office prepares and broadcasts weather forecasts and conducts related research. Its *Annual report* and monthly *Meteorological magazine* are published by HMSO, as is the *Monthly weather report* compiled from observations made by official and voluntary observers all over the UK. There is also a series of *Climatological memoranda*, a range of leaflets, popular booklists and lists of the services which the Office provides to many sectors of the community.

MINISTRY OF AGRICULTURE, FISHERIES AND FOOD

The annual report of the Ministry is entitled *Annual review of agriculture* and appears as a command paper. The principal series are the annual *Agricultural statistics: UK*, *Sea fisheries statistical tables*, which is annual, and an annual *Report on wages in agriculture*, all these being published by HMSO. There are also occasional *Research and development reports*, a series on *Current topics*, a *Farm income series* and *Reference books* series, the two latter being published by HMSO, and pamphlets of information for farmers.

The Ministry maintains the Agricultural Development and Advisory Service, which prepares information leaflets. The National Food Survey Committee reports to it and publishes an annual survey of *Household food consumption and expenditure*, which is an HMSO publication. The Ministry maintains a number of research and advisory services, such as the Veterinary Service and the Experimental Husbandry Farms and Experimental Horticulture Stations, which prepare annual reports and reviews of research. The Rothamsted Experimental Station prepares an annual report on the soil surveys for which it is responsible and an irregular *Soil survey bulletin*. The Torry Research Station for marine research has an annual report and a series of *Torry advisory notes*. The Royal Botanic Gardens at Kew also report to the Ministry, and they issue an irregular *Kew bulletin*, published by HMSO, and a monthly *Bibliography*.

MINISTRY OF DEFENCE

The Ministry has a wide range of publications on matters of policy and internal to the running of the army, navy and air force. It issues, through HMSO, the *Air force list* and *Army list*—lists of personnel—as well as regulations for the forces and materials specifications. Its main periodicals are the *Journal of naval science*, which is quarterly, *Soldier*, which is monthly, and *RAF news*, which is fortnightly.

Its many research establishments issue reports, technical memoranda and technical translations and library bulletins. Examples are the *ARE technical reports* of the Admiralty Research Establishment, *Technical memoranda* of the Royal Signals and Radar Establishment, and accessions lists published by their specialist libraries. For a more complete list the reader is referred to the sources mentioned in section 4 below. The Hydrographic Department, which reports to the Ministry of Defence, publishes the *Admiralty Pilots*, one of the longest-established official series, the *Admiralty list of lights*, *Admiralty list of radio signals*, tide tables, notices to mariners, and an annual *Catalogue of Admiralty charts*.

NATIONAL ECONOMIC DEVELOPMENT OFFICE

The NEDO provides a forum for the discussion of matters of economic policy between government, industry and the trade unions. It issues an *Annual report* and two series of occasional discussion documents, *Economic working papers* and *Council papers*. There are also different Economic Development Committees for individual trades and services, and these produce newsletters and reports such as *Construction forecasts* which is published by the Building Economic Development Committee.

NATIONAL PHYSICAL LABORATORY

The NPL issues an annual report and scientific reports on a wide range of areas of research, including computer science, materials science and radiation science.

NATIONAL RADIOLOGICAL PROTECTION BOARD

The Board carries out research into the effects of radiation and publishes advice and information. Its annual *Accounts* are presented to Parliament and published by HMSO, and its *Reports*, *Advice notes* and press releases are important sources of information, for example after an incident.

NATURAL ENVIRONMENT RESEARCH COUNCIL

The NERC funds research done by other institutions and maintains some research stations. It issues an *Annual report* and an annual report on *Research grants awarded*. More detail is included in *Research training supported by the NERC: series A. Research students and fellows* and *series B. Research policy reviews*. There is a quarterly *NERC news journal*.

NORTHERN IRELAND OFFICE

The functions of the Northern Ireland Office are mentioned in sections 1.1 above and 2.7 below. It publishes the annual appropriation accounts for the Northern Ireland departments, which is a House of Commons paper and therefore an HMSO publication. It issues the *Ulster yearbook*, through HMSO, and through its Northern Ireland Information Office pamphlets and information material. Its other principal publication is the annual *Report on the administration of the prison service* (HMSO).

OFFICE OF POPULATION CENSUSES AND SURVEYS

The OPCS is the body responsible for the decennial census of population and for other demographic statistics and regular social surveys and survey research. The reports of the census are published, through HMSO, in a substantial series of reports giving very sophisticated breakdowns, and information on such varied subjects as travel to work, economic activity, housing, language and so on.

Population trends, issued quarterly by HMSO, and the *Registrar General's weekly return* based on returns of births and deaths are the two other general primary sources produced by the OPCS. There are also a number of statistical and research reports on demographic matters, on abortion (with the title AB), mortality (DH1, DH2 and so on to DH5), electoral patterns (EL), birth and family statistics (FM), the General Household Survey (GHS), cancer, communicable diseases and illnesses (MB), migration (MN), population projections (PP) and vital statistics (VS). All are issued irregularly and all are published by HMSO. Research results and methodology are written up in *Studies on medical and population subjects*, an irregular series issued by HMSO.

The Social Survey Division of the OPCS issues a *Reports* series which HMSO publishes. Its library publishes a monthly *Library bulletin*, *Library bibliographies* and reading lists.

OVERSEAS DEVELOPMENT ADMINISTRATION

The ODA is responsible for the administration of overseas aid and related research. It publishes an annual report with statistics entitled *British overseas aid*, a six-monthly journal, *Developments in the European Communities*, a bi-monthly journal, *Overseas development* and *Technical co-operation: a monthly bibliography*. Finally there is a useful series of *Bibliographies*.

PARLIAMENTARY COMMISSIONER FOR ADMINISTRATION

The Parliamentary Commissioner, the British Ombudsman, publishes an *Annual report* and frequent reports on selected cases. Both are HMSO publications and are included in the parliamentary sessional papers.

PROPERTY SERVICES AGENCY

The Property Services Agency looks after the land and accommodation of government buildings and those of some fringe bodies. It issues an *Annual report* and its library publishes *Construction references* and *Current information in the construction industry* (irregular). PICA is its on-line information service, available through Pergamon Infoline. There are also series of specifications and guides to buildings maintenance.

PUBLIC RECORD OFFICE

The Public Record Office publishes an *Annual report of the Keeper of the Public Records*, guides to the records entitled *Handbooks*, and calendars of original documents, all through HMSO.

SCIENCE AND ENGINEERING RESEARCH COUNCIL

The SERC issues an annual *Report* (through HMSO) and the six-monthly *SERC bulletin*. Its specialist committees and research establishments include the Daresbury Laboratory for research in nuclear physics, whose publications include *Daresbury*, an annual report, a newsletter, lists of conferences and numerous research report series; the Royal Greenwich Observatory, which has an *Annual report* and series of *Bulletins* and *Annals*; and the Royal Observatory, Edinburgh, which publishes specialist research reports and an annual list of *Research and facilities*.

SCOTTISH DEVELOPMENT DEPARTMENT

The Scottish Development Department is the counterpart for Scotland of the Department of the Environment. It publishes an annual *Report*, an annual compilation of *Scottish housing statistics* (published by HMSO), *Road accidents Scotland* (annual) and *Scottish transport statistics* (annual). There is a quarterly *Development plan bulletin*, an irregular series of *Planning information notes*, and a series of leaflets on historic buildings and monuments prepared by its Historic Buildings and Monuments Directorate.

SCOTTISH EDUCATION DEPARTMENT

The Department issues an annual *Basic educational statistics (Scotland)*, an irregular *Statistical bulletin*, and *Educational research: a register of current educational projects funded by the SED*, which is annual. It also publishes circulars and administrative memoranda, a guide to student grants, a directory of further education courses, and regular reports on children in care and residential accommodation for children.

SCOTTISH HOME AND HEALTH DEPARTMENT

The Department exercises many of the functions of the Department of Health and Social Security and the Home Office in Scotland. Its annual report is published by HMSO and appears in the parliamentary sessional papers. *Health in Scotland* and *Prisons in Scotland* are two other annual reports, both published by HMSO. The Department issues the *Scottish health services directory*, occasional reports, for instance on contaminated wine, and circulars.

SCOTTISH OFFICE

The Scottish Office exercises some of the functions of the Home Office in Scotland. It is responsible for the annual general compilation of *Scottish statistics*, the *Scottish abstract of statistics*, and a six-monthly *Scottish economic bulletin*, and there are circulars and orders mainly concerning local government in Scotland.

TREASURY

The Treasury prepares most of the Budget documentation, which appears in the parliamentary sessional papers, including the *Supply estimates* and the annual report on the government's expenditure plans and economic forecasts. The Treasury also issues *Civil service statistics* annually through HMSO and an occasional series of *Economic Service working papers*.

UNITED KINGDOM ATOMIC ENERGY AUTHORITY

The UKAEA is responsible for research and development on nuclear power. It issues an *Annual report*, a monthly magazine, *Atom*, and occasional safety reports. Its research stations include the Atomic Energy Research Establishment, which publishes research reports, bibliographies, and an annual *UK nuclear data progress report*, and the Culham Laboratory which publishes an annual report and some research reports.

WELSH OFFICE

The Welsh Office has functions similar to those of several government departments in England, relating to transport, local government and housing, agriculture, health and home affairs. Its principal series are *Local housing statistics*, published quarterly jointly with the Department of the Environment, through HMSO, *Road accidents Wales* (annual), *Welsh local government financial statistics* (annual), the *Digest of Welsh statistics* (annual), *Welsh social trends* (annual), *Welsh agricultural statistics* (annual) and *Farming progress* (quarterly). There are other regular titles specific to Wales in the areas of health, social security, local government and transport, and a wide variety of occasional reports.

THE BUSINESS DATA PACKAGE

Early in 1986, HMSO launched a series of *Business data packages* on floppy disc, formatted for use with a wide range of microcomputers and permitting updating and secondary analysis by the customer. Specific industries can be subscribed to individually. Data are taken from a wide variety of sources, including industry statistics from the *Business monitor* series, *Overseas trade statistics of the UK*, the Health and Safety Executive and the parliamentary debates.

2.5. The *London gazette*

The *London gazette* is the official organ of the Crown in its constitutional role. It includes Orders in Council (subordinate legislation for which the Crown in Privy Council is responsible), statutory notices relating to bankruptcy, notices of promotions and decorations in the armed forces and the award of civilian honours and decorations. It has never included legislation or parliamentary proceedings. It is published three times a week by HMSO and has a quarterly index.

2.6. Publications of the judiciary

A few law reports are published by the courts and tribunals themselves, through HMSO, rather than by professional bodies or commercial publishing houses. They include *Court of Appeal judgments*, which are on microfiche, *Decisions of the Commissioners*, on social security cases, issued by the Department of Health and Social Security, *Awards of the Industrial Court (Northern Ireland)*, the *Rules of the Supreme Court*, and *Immigration appeals* of the Immigration Appeals Tribunal.

2.7. Northern Ireland

Before the suspension of the Northern Ireland Parliament in 1972, the province had a similar pattern of publishing to that of Great Britain. The laws were published as *Public general acts* or (more rarely) *Local and private acts*. Secondary legislation, the *Statutory rules*, and the public general acts were individually published and also available as bound volumes from Her Majesty's Stationery Office in Belfast. The House of Commons and Senate each published *Parliamentary records*, the equivalent of the *Journals*, *Parliamentary debates* in weekly parts and bound volumes, and sets of sessional papers: House of Commons papers, Senate papers, and command papers. The distinction between parliamentary and non-parliamentary papers was the same: government departments also published a certain amount independent of HMSO. The equivalent of the *London gazette* was the *Belfast gazette*.

The pattern of publishing of laws and parliamentary proceedings has altered since 1972. At the time of writing, Northern Ireland has no legislature except for the Parliament of the United Kingdom, and its public general acts have in effect been replaced by Orders in Council or statutory instruments made by the United Kingdom government under the Northern Ireland (Temporary Provisions) Act 1972, or else by the laws passed by the Parliament in London. The Orders in Council and statutory instruments are collected in a loose-leaf publication, *Northern Ireland statutes*, issued by HMSO since 1973. Statutory rules (made by Northern Ireland departments under enabling legislation) continue the same, however, as does the *Belfast gazette*. The Northern Ireland Assembly now issues *Assembly papers*, the reports of its standing committees and consultative papers. They are relatively few in number.

Northern Ireland still has its executive and the publications of the government departments continue. A brief selection of some typical titles follows. The Department of Agriculture issues *Agriculture in Northern Ireland*, its annual report, through HMSO, and an annual *Report on the sea and inland fisheries of Northern Ireland*, also an HMSO publication. The Department of Economic Development publishes the *Companies general annual report*, an annual report on the census of production, and the reports of the Industrial Training Boards. *Education in Northern Ireland* is the annual report of the Department of Education. The Department of the Environment publishes *Northern Ireland housing statistics* (annual), reports on historic buildings, and building regulations. The Department of Finance and Personnel is responsible for the estimates and financial accounts and for the *Northern Ireland statutes revised 1226-1850*, a loose-leaf publication. The Department of Health and Social Security publishes *Northern Ireland social security statistics* annually, and the quarterly and annual returns of the Registrar General. All the above are published by HMSO. It is difficult to establish an overview of the category of non-HMSO publications.

2.8. Channel Islands

The different islands in the group of the Channel Islands are governed by Commanders-in-Chief appointed by the British Crown and have their own legislative assemblies and systems of courts, and broadly similar patterns of publication of acts, secondary legislation, bills and legislative proceedings. There are very few reports or publications of the executive branch (the executive committees of the legislatures). Jersey publishes a *Recueil des lois* [Collection of laws] in bound volumes covering the years 1908/15 onwards (the latest is that for 1975/78) and *Acts* separately as they are approved. Secondary legislation is the *Regulations and orders*, separately published and with continuous numeration. Individual bills are the *Projets de loi*, the official proceedings of the legislative assembly are the *States minutes*, and the nearest equivalents of the parliamentary papers of the UK are the *Reports*, printed separately and unnumbered by the States. There is a monthly publications list issued by the States Greffe (the office of the legislative assembly) as *States of Jersey publications*, traceable back to 1958. It is a simple printer's list and does not carry any information as to the availability of the publications listed or that of the list itself. In Guernsey, bills, *Projets de loi*, are printed in separate fascicles and after receiving the Royal Assent are published as *Orders in Council*, in bound volumes, or as *Ordinances* separately as a supplement to the *Billet d'État* [State bulletin]. There are also bound volumes of the *Recueil d'ordonnances* [Collection of Ordinances] of which vol. xxi for 1977/80 is the latest. Secondary legislation is the *Statutory instruments*, separately published. The *Billet d'État* is an official gazette including the agendas, reports of the executive committees, annual reports, correspondence, budget documentation, the annual economic report, some statistics such as the retail price index, and development plans. It has an annual index. Alderney has a similar pattern with a *Billet d'État* and *Projets de loi*.

3. MANNER OF PUBLICATION

Her Majesty's Stationery Office (HMSO) is known throughout the world as the British government printer and publisher. It was first established in 1786 to organize the supply of stationery and materials to government offices, and took on print procurement in 1810 as a result of a parliamentary scrutiny of the bills presented by printers. Its first sales catalogue appeared in 1836 after a House of Commons resolution that all its documents should be placed on sale to the public. The first catalogue listed 650 House of Commons papers. In 1883 it became the publisher of the parliamentary papers and in 1889 the Queen's printer for acts of Parliament. Later it became the publisher of Hansard and in 1917 acquired its own printing facilities. Its development has been gradual and there is no statutory authority for most of its publishing activity.

HMSO is not however the sole source of British official publications. It publishes all acts of Parliament and all statutory instruments, and all parliamentary papers and debates; however it probably accounts for only 20% of the total output of British government departments. This is the estimate of Stephen Richard in his *Directory of British official publications: a guide to sources* and Diana Marshallsay (*State librarian*, 26(3), 1978). Since World War II increasing numbers of official publications have been published by individual government departments themselves. New methods of reprography have been the critical factor, combined with the expansion of government activity and the appearance of new kinds of publications, such as technical reports, training manuals and consultative documents. There is no centralized control of government publishing and the costs of much printing and publishing are often buried in the budgets of specific programmes. Non-HMSO publications are usually not published or marketed through the channels of the book trade and can be very difficult to identify and obtain. Some are intended for a small circulation and come into the category of grey literature, but many are substantial and worthwhile items of general interest.

The total volume of British official publications is not known, but the number of publications included in the catalogues of Chadwyck-Healey Ltd. (*see* section 6 below) was 7678 in 1985: this figure excludes all parliamentary and all HMSO publications, free material and many minor items such as circulars.

4. BIBLIOGRAPHIC CONTROL

4.1. The national bibliography

The *British national bibliography*, which began publication in 1950, is selective in its coverage of official publications, although it is based on the legal deposit intake of the British Library. The foreword to the annual cumulations gives a profile of the publications that are excluded, such as minor returns to Parliament and publications of an ephemeral nature, but pressure of work has led to much more material being excluded in practice than is suggested and it can be difficult to predict what will be included and what will not. *BNB* is not the first source to which those working with official publications will turn for information about new publications nor for identifying older ones. The UKMARC files on BLAISE are therefore not comprehensive in their coverage.

4.2. The HMSO catalogues

Since 1922 HMSO has established a pattern of daily publications lists and monthly and annual sales catalogues with indexes. There are also lists which provide subject access in different forms, and most new publications are notified on Prestel, the public viewdata service operated by British Telecom. Before 1922 there are a variety of sales catalogues which have been reprinted: details of the reprints are given below. The catalogues are primarily sales tools but their indexing and layout have been practical and consistent over long periods of time.

A wide range of bibliographic services is offered by HMSO, possibly more comprehensive than is offered in any other country. It includes:

(a) monthly and annual printed catalogues. Production of the catalogues is computer-based. The rules used are an adaptation of AACR2 and entries are arranged by corporate body as in the British Library Name Authority file, and there are indexes by subject, name of author, chairman or government department, and

ISBN. Before 1976, entries were arranged by government department in alphabetical order with subsidiary bodies listed under the parent department. The indexes were similar to those of the present day. There are five-yearly cumulations of the indexes taking the user up to the period 1981–1985.

All parliamentary publications and acts of Parliament are included in the catalogues, and the publications of the international organizations for which HMSO acts as a sales agent in the UK are included in the monthly catalogues (though not in the annual: there is a separate annual list entitled *International organizations annual catalogue*). Statutory instruments, of which separate lists are published (*see* section 2.2 above) are not included, nor are statutory rules of Northern Ireland

(b) the daily list. This includes the same materials as the monthly list and also statutory instruments and Northern Ireland statutory rules

(c) the *International organizations annual catalogue*

(d) the sectional lists and subject catalogues. These are the lists which provide a subject approach. The sectional lists include publications in print for particular departments or subjects, such as agriculture and food, energy, industry and trade, fisheries and ancient monuments and historic buildings. Some have indexes and all are revised at intervals varying between six months and two years. They are free and are available from HMSO bookshops and agents. A complete list is included in the monthly and annual catalogues. Useful publicity catalogues are the subject catalogues, a relatively recent departure, which include lists on art books, books for schools and architecture and building. They provide brief abstracts and are also free and regularly updated, although they do not claim to be comprehensive

(e) *List of statutory instruments*. This is produced monthly and cumulates to the *Annual list of statutory instruments*. It includes the statutory rules of Northern Ireland since 1983

(f) *Index to the committee reports published by HMSO, indexed by chairman*. This index is quarterly with annual cumulations, and has appeared since October/December 1982. Prior to that date other indexes were edited by Stephen Richard and Mary A. Morgan (*see* section 7 below).

(g) *HMSO in print*: a list of titles in print, published quarterly on microfiche

(h) the Prestel frames, with lead frame 50040. Publications that are listed are displayed for one week from the day of publication, and can be ordered on Prestel.

Details of all these bibliographic services are given in all issues of the monthly and annual catalogues. The catalogues themselves are available from the Publicity Department, HMSO Books, St. Crispin's, Norwich NR3 1PD, England, who can also supply a free *Guide to publications and services*.

Reprinted editions of older HMSO sales catalogues and lists are:

(a) *The sale catalogues of British government publications 1836–1921*. Dobbs Ferry, Oceana, 4 v., 1977. A slightly reduced photographic reprint of all the surviving lists, with a useful introduction to their history and to the history of HMSO

(b) *Cumulative index to the annual catalogues of Her Majesty's Stationery Office publications 1922–1972*. Washington and Inverness, US Historical Documents Institute, Inc., 2 v., 1976

(c) *Catalogues and indexes of British government publications 1920–1970*. Cambridge, Chadwyck-Healey Ltd., 1974. A photographic reprint in five volumes, of which vol. 1 reprints the consolidated (five-year) indexes of the HMSO catalogues, and vols. 2–5 reprint the annual catalogues for the periods 1920–1935, 1936–1950, 1951–1960, and 1961–1970.

HMSO in Belfast has published monthly and annual catalogues since 1921. At the time of writing they list the reports of the Northern Ireland Assembly and the small numbers of statutory rules and departmental publications.

4.3. Non-HMSO publications

The most important contribution to recording the mass of these publications has been made by a commercial firm, Chadwyck-Healey Ltd., which in 1980 began publication of the *Catalogue of British official publications not published by HMSO*. It is issued bimonthly with annual cumulations, and includes an author and subject index and from 1983 a keyword index on fiche. It excludes the most ephemeral material but has achieved good coverage, listing currently about 8,000 items per year. The catalogue is supported by a document supply service on microfiche.

Many government departments issue their own lists of their departmental publications. This has been a development of relatively recent date and has been much encouraged by the libraries of the government departments, most of which aim to collect comprehensively all publications of the departments they serve. Some lists are published separately, some appear in other sources, such as the annual report of the organization or the *Employment gazette*. A detailed list is not presented here because one is issued free by the British Library Official Publications and Social Sciences Service, Great Russell St., London WC1B 3DG, England.

4.4. Other sources

The British Library publishes a *Checklist of British official serial publications*, of which the latest edition was the 11th., in 1980. It is however intended to keep it up-to-date. Some, but not all, official publications excluded from the *British national bibliography* are catalogued for the catalogues of the Humanities and Social Sciences Division and therefore appear in the published catalogues of holdings after 1975, and can be identified on-line on the DPB files on BLAISE.

An important source, though it is not a bibliography, is the *Directory of British official publications: a guide to sources*, edited by Stephen Richard and listed in the bibliography in section 7.

The POLIS data-base, mentioned in section 2.3 above, includes bills (though not amendments), and selected HMSO and non-HMSO publications. Report literature published by government bodies is listed in *British reports, translations and theses*, published monthly by the British Library Document Supply Centre and listing new report literature taken into the British Library's lending stock. The contents form the basis for the UK input to the SIGLE (System for Grey Literature in Europe) data-base, mentioned in section 2.4 above. A useful guide, though not a bibliographic listing, is *Local government information sources: a guide to publications, data-bases and services*, published by SCOOP in 1986.

UNITED KINGDOM

5. LOCAL GOVERNMENT PUBLICATIONS

Local government publications have not conventionally hitherto been considered by most UK libraries to be government publications, but they are now included in the definition accepted by SCOOP (*see* section 1.2 above) and it may be useful to include a short account of them here. They consist mainly of annual reports, important structural and development plans, some magazines or newspapers mainly designed for publicity, and tourist material and town guides. They can be very difficult to identify and trace and have received a good deal of attention in recent years. Bibliographically they present particular problems and many go unrecorded. *British reports, translations and theses* includes them: 2,000 were listed in 1986. Local government publications are however not separately identified and must be sought among other materials. There is some coverage of local government publications in the regional bibliographies produced by library authorities, such as the *East Anglian bibliography*. The *British national bibliography* lists very few.

6. LIBRARY COLLECTIONS AND AVAILABILITY

The principal library collection in the UK is the legal deposit collection of the British Library (Humanities and Social Sciences), which throughout the twentieth century has been active in enforcing legal deposit of this very difficult body of material. The official publications are collected in a physically separate stock with specialist reference services which can considerably ease the task of the unfamiliar user. The UK legal deposit official publications are not available for loan. The Document Supply Centre (until 1985 the Lending Division) of the British Library stocks all HMSO publications since 1962, and a selection of others with particular emphasis on scientific and technical reports. It can provide them for inter-library loan, including overseas, or can provide photocopies of those that are not protected by copyright. It is also the principal source for photocopies of out-of-print titles since HMSO moved the library from which it formerly provided this service. Registered borrowers can use the usual British Library forms, or they can be bought from HMSO. (Details are given in the back of the HMSO monthly catalogues.)

The Bodleian Library in Oxford is the only other library of legal deposit aiming to collect all UK central government publications, including all non-HMSO titles.

There is no system of depository libraries for official publications, as there is in the USA. Many public libraries however take advantage of the Selective Subscription Service offered by HMSO, whereby for a predetermined annual subscription they can receive all HMSO publications or a selection. A list of 74 libraries which subscribe in this way is included in the HMSO annual catalogues. The catalogue and document supply service of Chadwyck-Healey Ltd. have helped to improve coverage of official publications in libraries generally.

Libraries of government departments and public bodies provide an important service, some of them being fully open to the public without formality. A directory of them is published by the British Library Science Reference and Information Service as the *Guide to government department and other libraries* (latest ed. 1986).

Collections overseas are principally concentrated on the exchange partners of the British Library. There are almost 100 exchanges with 38 countries: a list appears in Appendix 2 of this chapter.

HMSO services are extensive and its publications easy to acquire. There is a range of

HMSO's own bookshops in London, Edinburgh, Belfast, Manchester, Birmingham and Bristol, and HMSO has agents in other towns throughout the UK and in 50 countries overseas: lists are published in the monthly and annual catalogues. A short list of addresses for enquiries about HMSO publications follows:

to ask for free catalogues/information material: Publicity Department, HMSO Books, St. Crispin's, Duke St., Norwich NR3 1PD, England. Tel. (0603) 694498
to make a general publications enquiry: Tel. (01) 211 5656
for standing orders: PC.13/A/1, HMSO Publications Centre, 51 Nine Elms Lane, London SW8 5DR. Tel. (01) 211 0363
for subscriptions: PC.13/A/2, HMSO Publications Centre, 51 Nine Elms Lane, London SW8 5DR. Tel. (01) 211 8667/8668
for bibliographic services: Bibliographic Services Manager, HMSO, 51 Nine Elms Lane, London SW8 5DR. Tel. (01) 211 8655/8656.

Non-HMSO publications present far greater difficulty. Recent materials may be identified in the catalogues published by Chadwyck-Healey Ltd., and ordered on microfiche, but if they have not been included or if the enquirer does not have access to the catalogues non-HMSO publications are very difficult to obtain. The libraries of the relevant government department are usually the most appropriate first port of call, and for older items the British Library Official Publications and Social Sciences Service, Great Russell Street, London WC1B 3DG. Tel. (01) 323 7536.

7. BIBLIOGRAPHY

Constitution

Bagehot, Walter. *The English constitution*. With an introduction by R. H. S. Crossman. London, Collins/Fontana, 1971. 312 p.

Report on non-departmental public bodies. [Chairman, Sir Leo Pliatsky.] Cmnd. 7797. London, HMSO, 1980. 186 p.

Parliamentary procedure

Dod's Parliamentary companion. 1832-. Annual.

Factsheets, 1-. London, House of Commons Library, 1980-.

May, Sir Thomas Erskine. *Treatise on the law, privileges, proceedings and usage of Parliament*. 20th ed., ed. Sir Charles Gordon. London, Butterworths, 1983. 1199 p.

Questions in the House of Commons. London, HMSO, 1979. (House of Commons Library, Public Information Office series, 1.) 17 p.

Vacher's Parliamentary companion. 1831-. Quarterly.

Directories of government organization

Civil service yearbook. London, HMSO. Annual.

Public bodies. London, HMSO. Annual.

Councils, committees and boards. Beckenham, CBD Research Ltd. 6th ed., 1984.

Guides to official publications and government publishing

Access to subordinate legislation. London, HMSO, 1963. (House of Commons Library Document, no. 5.) 38 p.

Acts of Parliament: some distinctions in their nature and numbering. London, HMSO, 1955. (House of Commons Library Document, no. 1.) 8 p.

Bibliographic sources of British official publications not published by HMSO. London, British Library Official Publications and Social Sciences Service. Irregular. Latest ed. 1983

A bibliography of Parliamentary debates of Great Britain. London, HMSO, 1956. (House of Commons Library Document, no. 2.) 62 p.

Bond, Maurice F. *Guide to the records of Parliament.* London, HMSO, 1971. 352 p.

Bradfield, Valerie J. (ed.) *Proceedings of the conference on British government publishing.* London, Library Association/HMSO Services Working Party, [1983]. 93 p.

Butcher, David. Catalogue of British official publications not published by HMSO: a review. *Refer,* 1(4), 1981. pp. 10–13.

———. *Official publications in Britain.* London, Clive Bingley, 1983. 161 p.

Checklist of British official serial publications. London, British Library. Irregular. Latest ed. 1980. 102 p.

Circle of State Librarians conference on government publications. *State librarian,* 27(1), 1979, pp. 4–8.

Englefield, Dermot. *Parliament and information.* London, Library Association, 1981. 132 p.

Ford, P. and Ford, G. *A guide to Parliamentary papers.* 3rd ed. Shannon, Irish University Press, 1972. 87 p.

Foreman, Lewis. HMSO catalogue developments: a personal account. *State librarian,* 29(3), 1981, pp. 35–36.

———. HMSO assesses the way ahead for its bibliographical services. *Vine,* 41, Dec. 1981, pp. 27–31.

Guide to official statistics. 5th ed. London, HMSO, 1986, 192 p.

Hamilton, Geoffrey. Official publications. In *British librarianship and information work, 1981–1985.* London, Library Association, forthcoming.

Handover, P. M. *A history of the London Gazette 1665–1965.* London, HMSO, 1965. 95 p.

[Hansard, John Henry]. *The Hansards: printers and publishers.* Shannon, Irish University Press, 1970. 12 p.

Howard, Bridget. Government publications SCOOP'd. *Library Association record,* 87(5), May 1985, pp. 183, 185.

Johansson, Eve. Bibliographic control of official publications. *Catalogue and index*, 50, autumn 1978, pp. 5–6.

——. *Current British government publishing*. London, Association of Assistant Librarians, South East Division, 1978. 64 p.

——. Official publications. In Taylor, L. J. (ed.) *British librarianship and information work 1976–1980*. London, Library Association, 1983, pp. 69–81.

Kemp, Betty. *Votes and standing orders of the House of Commons: the beginning*. London, HMSO, 1971. (House of Commons Library Document, no. 8.) 47 p.

Lambert, Sheila. *Bills and acts. Legislative procedure in eighteenth century England*. Cambridge, Cambridge University Press, 1971. 246 p.

McShane, P. C. (ed.) *United Kingdom statistical sources: a selection guide for libraries*. 4th ed. London, Library Association, Reference, Special and Information Section, 1985. 24 p.

Mallaber, Kenneth A. The House of Lords sessional papers. *Journal of librarianship*, 4(2), 1972, pp. 106–114.

Marshallsay, Diana. Catalogue of British official publications not published by HMSO. *State librarian*, 29(3), 1981, pp. 38–39, 42.

——. Departmental publications: some problems. *State librarian*, 26(3), 1978, pp. 37–40.

Menhennet, David. *The Journals of the House of Commons. A bibliographical and historical guide*. London, HMSO, 1971. (House of Commons Library Document, no. 7.) 96 p.

Nurcombe, Valerie J. *Whitehall and Westminster: proceedings of the seminar on official publications, London 21 March 1984*. London, Library Association, Reference, Special and Information Section, 1984. 57 p.

Official publications. London, HMSO, 1958 (repr. 1963). 20 p.

Ollé, James G. *An introduction to British government publications*. 2nd ed. London, Association of Assistant Librarians, 1973. 175 p.

Pemberton, John. *British official publications*. Oxford and New York, Pergamon Press, 1973. xii, 328 p.

——. Government green papers. *New library world*, lxxi, no. 830, 1969.

Richard, Stephen. *British government publications: an index to chairmen*. Vol. 1 1800–1899. London, Library Association, 1981. 186 p. Vol. 2 1900–1940. London, Library Association, 1974 (repr. 1981). 174 p. Vol. 3 1941–1978. London, Library Association, 1981. 152 p. Vol. 4 1979–1982. London, Library Association Publishing, 1984. 95 p.

——. *Directory of British official publications: a guide to sources*. 2nd ed. London, Mansell, 1984. xxxvi, 431 p.

——. The publications of British national paragovernmental organizations. *Government publications review*, 5(4), 1978, pp. 399–407.

Rodgers, Frank. *A guide to British government publications*. New York, H. W. Wilson, 1980. xviii, 750 p.

Smith, Barbara E. British official publications. I. Scope and substance. *Government publications review*, 4(3), 1977, pp. 201–207.

——. British official publications. II. Publication and distribution. *Government publications review*, 5(1), 1978, pp. 1–12.

——. British official publications. III. Accessibility and use. *Government publications review*, 6(1), 1979, pp. 11–18.

Toase, Charles A. Official reports: indexes to chairmen of committees. *Refer*, 2(1), 1982, pp. 10–12.

Trewin, J. C. and King, E. M. *Printer to the House. The story of Hansard*. London, Methuen, 1952. 272 p.

Guides to law reports

Guide to law reports and statutes. 4th ed. London, Sweet and Maxwell, 1962. 143 p.

Reprinted and microfiche collections of parliamentary papers

House of Commons Appendices to the Votes and Proceedings 1817–1890 and Reports of the Select Committee on Public Petitions 1833–1900. Ed. F. W. Torrington. (Index for 1833–1852.) Cambridge, Chadwyck-Healey Ltd.

House of Commons Division lists 1836–1909. Ed. F. W. Torrington. (Index for 1836–1875.) Cambridge, Chadwyck-Healey Ltd.

House of Commons parliamentary papers 1801–. Cambridge, Chadwyck-Healey Ltd., 1980–.

House of Commons sessional papers of the eighteenth century. Ed. Sheila Lambert. Wilmington, Delaware, Scholarly Resources Inc., 1975. 147 v. (Vols. 1–2 are Introduction and list.)

House of Lords sessional papers. Ed. F. W. Torrington. [Paper copy photographic reprint 1714–1805; microfilm 1806–1859.] Dobbs Ferry, Oceana, 1972–1978.

Indexes to parliamentary papers

Di Roma, Edward and Rosenthal, Joseph A. *A numerical finding list of British command papers published 1833–1961/62*. New York, New York Public Library and Arne Press Inc., 1971. 148 p.

Gabiné, P. L. *A finding-list of British Royal Commission reports 1860–1935*. Cambridge, Mass., Harvard University Press, 1935. 66 p.

Lambert, Sheila. *List of House of Commons sessional papers, 1701–1754*. 1968 (List and Index Society special series, vol. 1.) Distributed to subscribers. 155 p.

McBride, Elizabeth A. *British command papers: a numerical finding-list 1962/63–1976/77*. Atlanta, Georgia, Emory University, 1982. 35 p.

Rodgers, Frank. *Serial publications in the British parliamentary papers 1960-1968. A bibliography.* London, Library Association, 1971. 146 p.

Temperley, H. and Penson, L. M. *A century of British diplomatic blue books 1814-1914.* Repr. London, Frank Cass, 1966. xvi, 600 p.

Vogel, Robert. *Breviate of British diplomatic blue books 1919-1939.* Montreal, McGill University Press, 1963. xxxv, 474 p.

Catalogues and indexes of official publications

Catalogue of British official publications not published by HMSO. Cambridge, Chadwyck-Healey, Ltd., 1980-. Bi-monthly with annual cumulations. Keyword index on microfiche since 1983.

Chadwyck-Healey, Charles. Commercial sources of non-conventional literature: the Catalogue of British official publications not published by HMSO and Business and government. *Aslib proceedings,* 34 (11-12), 1982, pp. 487-492.

——. Microfilming and cataloguing British official publications: problems and possibilities. In *Proceedings of the 29th. annual study group, Library Association, Reference, Special and Information Section, Newcastle-upon-Tyne, April 1981.*

Consolidated indexes to British government publications 1936-1970 (vol. 1) and *Annual catalogues of British government publications* 1920-1935, 1936-1950, 1951-1960, 1961-1970 (vols. 2-5). Bishops Stortford, Chadwyck-Healey Ltd., 1974.

Cumulative index to the catalogues of Her Majesty's Stationery Office 1922-1972. 2 v. Washington, D.C. and Inverness, Historical Documents Institute, 1976. 567, 583 p.

HMSO/Oriel seminar on changes in cataloguing of British official publications. *Government publications review,* 5(3), 1978, pp. 269-271.

House of Commons sessional papers. Monthly index. Microfiche. Cambridge and Alexandria, Va., Chadwyck-Healey Ltd., 1985/86-.

The sale catalogues of British government publications 1836-1921. [Photographic reprint.] 4 v. Dobbs Ferry, Oceana, 1977.

Tolley, Paul. The Catalogue of British official publications under scrutiny. *Refer,* 2(3), 1983, pp. 4-6.

Scotland and Northern Ireland

Hamilton, Geoffrey (ed.) Great Britain and Northern Ireland. *Government publications review,* 12(6), 1985, pp.597-607.

Maltby, Arthur. *The government of Northern Ireland 1922-1972. A catalogue and breviate of parliamentary papers.* Dublin, Irish University Press, 1974. xxii, 235 p.

Local government publications

Butcher, David. Tracing local government publications. *Refer,* 3(3), 1985, p. 19.

Capital Planning Information. *Access to local government documentation.* British Library, Research and Development Department, 1981 (BLR & D report no. 5619). 82 p.

Grayson, Lesley. British local government documentation. *Government publications review*, 3(3), 1976, pp. 203-211.

Kennington, Don. Access to local government documentation. *Interlending review*, 9(4), 1981, pp. 118-121.

Local government information sources: a guide to publications, data-bases and services. SCOOP Publications. Over, Winsford, Cheshire, 1986.

Nurcombe, Valerie J. (ed.) *Access to local authority official publications: proceedings of a seminar, London 14 March 1985.* London, Library Association, Reference, Special and Information Section, 1985.

Nuttall, Barry S. Local government information: a grey area. *Aslib proceedings*, 34 (11-12), 1982, pp. 473-479.

——. Problems of local government publications. *Aslib proceedings*, 33(5), 1981, pp. 202-209.

Sturges, R. P. and Dixon, D. *An investigation of local publications.* Loughborough University, Department of Library and Information Studies, 1983. (BLR & D report no. 5645). 66 p.

Library collections

Guide to government department and other libraries. London, British Library, Science Reference and Information Service, 1986. 107 p.

Howard, Bridget and Nurcombe, Valerie J. *Directory of specialists in official publications.* 1985. Published by Standing Committee on Official Publications, 8 Kingfisher Drive, Over, Winsford, Cheshire.

Johansson, Eve. The Official Publications Library of the British Library. *State librarian*, 25(1), 1977, pp. 6-7.

——. The reference work of the British Library Official Publications Library. *Government publications review*, 3(4), 1976, pp. 271-276.

Johnson, David G. The BLLD and British official publications. *Government publications review*, 3(4), 1976, pp. 277-283.

Wood, D. N. and Ekers, A. Official publications at the British Library Lending Division. *Interlending and document supply*, 11(1), 1983, pp. 17-20.

Channel Islands

Le Herissier, R. G. *The development of the government of Jersey, 1771-1972.* [St. Helier], States of Jersey, [1974]. 251 p.

APPENDIX 1

The following definition of official publications was adopted by the International Federation of Library Associations, Official Publications Section, August 1983.

1. An official publication is any item produced by reprographic or any other method

issued by an organization that is an official body, and available to an audience wider than that body.
2. An official body is:
   (i) any legislature of a state, or federation of states, or of a province (state) or regional, local or other administrative sub-division;
   (ii) any executive agency of the central government of such a state or federation of states or of a province (state) or regional, local or other administrative sub-division;
   (iii) any court or judicial organ;
   (iv) any other organization which was set up by an official body as in (i), (ii) and (iii) above, and maintains continuing links with that body whether through direct funding or through its reporting mechanisms or its accountability;
   (v) any organization of which the members belong to any of the above four categories, including intergovernmental organizations
   provided that the body is considered to be official in the country concerned.
3. An official publication is defined by the status of the issuing source regardless of the subject-matter, content or physical form.

Notes

(i) For the purposes of this definition, the term 'official publication' is comparable to terms used in some countries, such as 'government publication' and 'government document'.

(ii) The following bodies:
universities
learned societies and academies
industrial and trade associations and chambers of commerce
libraries, museums and art galleries
independent research institutes not direct recipients of public funds
will be included as official bodies according to the practice of the individual country.

(iii) Political parties will not normally be considered as official bodies unless in the practice or constitution of a particular country there is reason to do so.

(iv) Nationalized enterprises and banks, public corporations and other statutory bodies set up to carry out industrial or other productive activity will be considered as official bodies according to the practice of the individual country. However, state majority ownership of capital and heavy direct state subsidy in enterprises that are otherwise nominally independent will not cause those enterprises to be considered as official bodies.

(v) Publications originating in official bodies but published by or with the co-operation of commercial firms, universities or independent research institutes, or any other non-official bodies, will normally be considered as official publications.

APPENDIX 2

The following is a list of the exchange partners of the British Library (Humanities and Social Sciences). HMSO publications and the British Library's own publications are exchanged: non-HMSO publications are not. The libraries marked with an asterisk(*)

receive the set of the parliamentary papers (often on microfiche) as well as other material.

AUSTRALIA
Library Board of Western Australia, Perth
Monash University, Clayton, Victoria
National Library, Canberra, ACT*
Parliament Library, Brisbane, Queensland*
Parliament Library, Adelaide, South Australia
Parliament Library, Hobart, Tasmania
Parliament Library, Melbourne, Victoria*
State Library, Sydney, New South Wales*
State Library, Brisbane, Queensland
State Library, Adelaide, South Australia*
State Library, Hobart, Tasmania
State Library, Melbourne, Victoria

AUSTRIA
Bundesministerium für Justiz, Vienna
Nationalbibliothek, Vienna

BULGARIA
Cyril and Methodius National Library, Sofia
National Information Office, Sofia

CANADA
Assemblée Nationale, Quebec*
Boreal Institute, Edmonton
Legislative Library, Manitoba
National Library, Ottawa
Parliament Library, Ottawa*
University Library, Edmonton

CHINA, PEOPLE'S REPUBLIC
National Library, Beijing

CHINA, REPUBLIC OF
National Central Library, Taipei

CZECHOSLOVAKIA
State Library, Prague

DENMARK
Danish International Exchange Institute, Copenhagen*
Folketinget, Copenhagen*

FIJI
University of the South Pacific, Suva

FINLAND
Exchange Centre for Scientific Literature, Helsinki
Helsinki University Library

APPENDIX 2

FRANCE
Assemblée Nationale, Paris*
Bibliothèque Nationale, Paris

GENERAL AGREEMENT ON TARIFFS AND TRADE, GENEVA

GERMAN DEMOCRATIC REPUBLIC
Deutsche Staatsbibliothek, Berlin

GERMANY, FEDERAL REPUBLIC OF
Deutscher Bundestagbibliothek, Bonn
Hessischer Landtag, Wiesbaden
Landtag von Baden-Wurttemberg, Stuttgart
Schleswig-Holsteiner Landtag, Kiel
Staatsbibliothek Preussischer Kulturbesitz, Berlin*
Statistische Landesamt Nordrhein-Westfalen, Dusseldorf

HUNGARY
Economic Institute of the Hungarian Academy of Sciences, Budapest
Magyar Orszagos Leveltár
National Library, Budapest*

INDIA
Parliament Library, New Delhi

ISRAEL
State Archives, Jerusalem

ITALY
Chamber of Deputies, Rome*
Senate, Rome*

JAPAN
Institute of Developing Economies, Tokyo
Mitsubishi Research Institute, Tokyo
National Diet Library, Tokyo*

KOREA, SOUTH
National Assembly Library, Seoul
National University Library, Seoul

LIECHTENSTEIN
Informationsamt, Vaduz

MALAYSIA
University of Malaya, Kuala Lumpur

NETHERLANDS
Royal Library, The Hague
Staten-Generaal, The Hague*
Tekniske Hogeschool, Enschede

NEW ZEALAND
General Assembly Library, Wellington*

NIGERIA
National Library, Lagos
University of Lagos Library

NORWAY
Norges Tekniske Høgskøle, Trondheim
Statistisk Sentralbyrå, Oslo
University of Olso Library*

PHILIPPINES
National Library, Manila

POLAND
Akademia Polnicza, Warsaw
Biblioteca Sejmowa, Warsaw*
Central Statistical Library, Warsaw

ROMANIA
Central State Library, Bucharest

SINGAPORE
National Library

SWEDEN
Riksdagsbiblioteket, Stockholm*
Statistiska Centralbyrån, Stockholm

THAILAND
National Library, Bangkok

TRINIDAD AND TOBAGO
University of the West Indies, Port of Spain

USSR
Academy of Sciences, Moscow
Kirghiz Academy, Frunze
Lenin State Library, Moscow*
Saltykov-Shchedrin Public Library, Leningrad
State Library, Minsk
State Library, Tashkent

UNITED NATIONS
Dag Hammarskjöld Library, New York

USA
Kansas State Library, Topeka
Kansas Supreme Court, Topeka
Library of Congress, Washington, DC*
New Hampshire State Library, Concord
New York State Library, Albany
Pennsylvania State Library, Harrisburg
Temple of Justice, Washington, DC

VIETNAM
Thu Vien Khoa Xa Hoi

APPENDIX 2

YUGOSLAVIA
National Library of Macedonia, Skopje
National Library of Slovenia, Ljubljana

ZIMBABWE
National Archives, Harare

Indexes

Where a page reference relates to a particular country, that country is indicated by the following abbreviated forms:

Austria	Au	Greece	Gr	Switzerland	Swi
Belgium	Be	Norway	No	United Kingdom	UK
Federal Republic of Germany	Ge	Portugal	Po		
		Sweden	Swe		

Where a country uses more than one official language, the following practice has been adopted:

> Belgium: French   Switzerland: German

Greek titles and organizations where the capital letter corresponds to the Roman have been filed under that letter. Otherwise the order of the Greek alphabet has been observed.

The Bibliography sections of the text are indexed by subject only, and not by author or title or sponsoring body.

Titles of major publications are given both in the original language and in English. Limitations of space prevent the inclusion by title of minor works and minor statistics, but most of them may be found under their subject or under the subject heading 'statistics'.

Notes and appendices have not been indexed.

Organizations and Titles Index

ABOS (Algemeen Bestuur van de Ontwikkelingssamenwerking)   Be 33
AGCD (Administration Générale de la Coöpération au Développement)   Be 33
Abgeordnetenhaus   Ge 55
Abteilung für Auswärtige Kulturpolitik   Ge 66
Abteilung Wissenschaftliche Dokumentation   Ge 61
Academy of Athens   Gr 111–12, 118
Acordãos do Tribunal Constitucional   Po 154
Açores: anuário estatístico   Po 169
Act of Succession   Swe 173
Actas da Câmara Municipal de Lisboa   Po 169
Acts of the Parliament of Scotland   UK 212–13
Administration de l'Énergie   Be 34, 35
Administration fédérale, L'   Swi 202
Administration Générale de la Coöpération au Développement   Be 33
Administrations de l'Industrie, du Commerce, des Mines   Be 34–5
Administrative and judicial yearbook of Belgium   Be 27
Administrative Courts of Appeal   Swe 191
Admiralty Pilots   UK 217
Advisory Committee on the Safety of Medicines   UK 210
Agência-Geral do Ultramar   Po 168
Agricontact: le courrier du Ministère de l'Agriculture   Be 38

Agricultural and Food Research Council   UK 217
Agricultural Bank of Greece   Gr 114
Agricultural Marketing Board   Swe 191
Αγροτική Τράπεζα Της Ελλάδος   Gr 114
Ακαδημία Αθηνών   Gr 111–12, 118
Alfred Wegener Institute Foundation for Polar Research   Ge 93
Algemeen Bestuur van de Ontwikkelingssamenwerking   Be 33
Allgemeines Bürgerliches Gesetzbuch   Au 12
Allmänna Förlaget   Swe 194–5
Allmänna Kyrkomötet   Swe 184, 186, 195
Allmänna Pensionsfonden   Swe 193
Almanach royal officiel   Be 28, 32–3
Almindelig norsk lovsamling   No 130
Alvey Directorate   UK 222
Amt der Landesregierung   Au 14–15
Amtliche Sammlung wiederverlautbarter österreichischer Rechtsvorschriften   Au 5
Amtliche Schrifttum der Bundesrepublik, Das   Ge 95
Amtliches Bulletin der Bundesversammlung   Swi 202
Amtliches Handbuch des Deutschen Bundestages   Ge 62
Amtsblatt der österreichischen Justizverwaltung   Au 7
Annales de la Faculté de Droit, d'Économie et des Sciences Sociales de Liège   Be 31
Annales parlementaires   Be 30, 31
Annuaire administratif et judiciaire de

ORGANIZATIONS AND TITLES INDEX

Belgique Be 27, 50
Ανώτατον Ειδικόν Δικαστήριον
    Gr 107
Anuário estatístico Po 159
Anzeiger des österreichischen Buchhandels
    Au 13
Aperçu de l'évolution économique Be 34
Approved food additives No 135
Arbeitsgemeinschaft der
    Rundfunkanstalten Ge 93
Arbeitsmarkt, Der Au 8
Arbetarskyddsstyrelsen Swe 187
Arbetsdomstolen Swe 191
Arbetsgivarverket Swe 188
Arbetslivcentrum Swe 187
Arbetsmarknadsdepartementet Swe 187
Arbitration Court Be 23
Archaeological Society Gr 112, 118
Αρχαιολογική Εταιρεία Gr 112, 118
Αρχεία της Ελληνικής Παλιγγενεσίας
    Gr 109
Αρχείον Γερουσίας Gr 110
Αρχείον της βουλής Gr 109
Archive of the Senate Gr 110
Archives et bibliothèques de Belgique
    Be 46
Archives Générales du Royaume Be 33,
    45-6, 48
Archives of Parliament Gr 109
Archives of the Greek revival Gr 109
Αρειος Παγος Gr 107
Areopagus Gr 107
Arresten van het Hof van Cassatie Be 31
Årskatalog over norsk litteratur No 140
Årstrycket Swe 185
Arte e Artistas Po 167
Arts Council UK 217
Assembleia Constituinte Po 151, 156
Assembleia da República Po 150, 152,
    156-7
Assembly of the Republic Po 150, 152,
    156-7
Association of Greek Industries Gr 115
Athens Chamber of Commerce and
    Industry Gr 115
Athens Stock Exchange Gr 116
Audit Office Au 3, 6, 12
Audit Office Court Gr 107
Aus Politik und Zeitgeschichte Ge 62
Austrian official yearbook Au 3, 8, 18
Austrian State Printing Office Au 3, 5,
    11-13, 18
Auswärtiges Amt Ge 66-7

BBH (*Berichten over de Buitenlandse
    Handel*) Be 38
BLAISE UK 218, 231, 233
*BMI-Mitteilungen: Informationen des
    Bundesministeriums des Innern*
    Ge 68
Balance of the federal accounts of the
    Republic of Austria Au 6
Banco de Portugal Po 162
Bank Inspectorate Swe 188
Bank of England UK 217-18
Bank of Greece Gr 108, 116
Bank of Norway No 125
Bank of Portugal Po 162
Bankinspektionen Swe 188
Banque Nationale Be 36-7
Bayerische Staatsbibliothek Ge 99, 100
Bayerisches Zeitschriftenverzeichnis Ge 98
Beiträge zur österreichischen Statistik Au 8
Belfast gazette UK 229
Belges au ..., Les Be 33
Belgian codes of law Be 29
Belgian Parliament, The Be 31
Belgian Royal Folklore Commission Be 44
Belgique: économie et technique Be 37
Belgium at the heart of Europe Be 32
*Bericht des Bundesrates über seine
    Geschäftsführung* Swi 202
Berichte und Dokumentationen Ge 65, 67
Berichten over de Buitenlandse Handel Be 38
Bezirkshauptmannschaft Au 15
Biblio-Data (Nationalbibliographische
    Datenbank der Deutschen
    Bibliothek) Ge 98
*Bibliografi över Norges offentlige/offisielle
    publikasjoner* No 123, 140
*Bibliografi över Sveriges offentliga
    publikationer* Swe 195
Bibliographia Belgica Be 47
Bibliographic Society of Greece Gr 120
Bibliographie de Belgique Be 45, 46
*Bibliographie der schweizerischen
    Amtsdruckschriften* Swi 202, 206, 207
*Bibliographie der verstaatlichten
    Industrie* Au 11
*Bibliographie rétrospective des publications
    officielles de la Belgique* Be 47, 50
Bibliographien Ge 63-4
*Bibliographien zur deutschen Landesgeschichte
    und Landeskunde, Die* Ge 102
Bibliography of Norwegian official
    publications No 123
Bibliography of Swiss official

ORGANIZATIONS AND TITLES INDEX

publications Swi 202, 206, 207
Biblioteca de Autores Portugueses Po 167
Biblioteca Nacional Po 168
Bibliothèque Africaine Be 51
Bibliothèque Centrale 'Fonds Quetelet' du Ministère des Affaires Économiques Be 51
Bibliothèque du Parlement Be 51
Bibliothèque Royale Albert I Be 45, 51
Βιβλιοθήκη της Βουλής Gr 117, 118
Billet d'État (Guernsey) UK 230
Biographical handbook of the National Council and Federal Council of the Republic of Austria Au 6
Biographical notices Be 31
Biographisches Handbuch des Nationalrates und des Bundesrates der Republik Österreich Au 6
Board of Agriculture Swe 191
Board of Civil Aviation Swe 192
Board of Commerce Swe 189
Board of Customs Swe 189
Board of Education Swe 194
Board of Fisheries Swe 191
Board of Forestry Swe 191
Board of Public Credit Po 164
Board of Shipping Swe 192
Board of Transport Swe 193
Bodleian Library, Oxford UK 234
Bok og samfunn No 140
Boletim de bibliografia portuguesa Po 168
Boletim do Ministério da Justiça Po 153
Bonner Almanach Ge 65
Bostadsdepartementet Swe 187-8
Bostadsdomstolen Swe 191
Βουλή των Ελλήνων Gr 119
Βουλή Gr 107, 109-10
Brabant Provincial Council Be 21
Britain: an official handbook UK 210, 211, 219
British Broadcasting Corporation UK 210, 218
British Council UK 218
British Library Po 168; Swi 207; UK 210, 211, 218, 233, 234
British national bibliography UK 218, 231
British reports, translations and theses UK 233, 234
British Tourist Authority UK 218
British Waterways Board UK 218-19
Brottsförebyggande Rådet Swe 191
Budget économique de . . . Be 34
Budgetdepartementet Swe 188

Building Research Establishment UK 219
Bulletin de l'administration pénitentiaire Be 34
Bulletin de liaison de l'Office de la Protection de la Jeunesse Be 34
Bulletin de statistique Be 38, 41
Bulletin des adjudications Be 29
Bulletin des arrêts de la Cour de Cassation Be 31
Bulletin des questions de Messieurs les senateurs et représentants et réponses de Messieurs les Ministres Be 30
Bulletin of commercial and industrial property Gr 109
Bulletin of joint stock companies and limited liability companies Gr 109
Bulletin of Portuguese bibliography Po 168
Bulletin of public corporate bodies Gr 109
Bundesamt für Geistiges Eigentum Swi 202
Bundesamt für Statistik Swi 202, 206
Bundesamt für Umweltschutz Swi 206
Bundesamt für Wohnungswesen Swi 206
Bundesamt für Zivilschutz Swi 203
Bundesanstalt für Arbeit Ge 77
Bundesanstalt für Materialprüfung Ge 73-4
Bundesanzeiger Ge 57, 58-9, 63, 64, 70
Bundesarbeitsgericht Ge 56
Bundesarchiv Ge 69-70
Bundesbahnen Swi 203
Bundesblatt Swi 201-2, 206
Bundesdruckerei Ge 95
Bundesfinanzhof Ge 56, 70
Bundesforschungsanstalt für Landeskunde und Raumordnung Ge 88-9
Bundesgericht Swi 200, 203
Bundesgerichtshof Ge 56, 70
Bundesgesetzblatt Au 4-5, 12, 17; Ge 55, 57-8, 60, 66, 70
Bundesgesundheitsamt Ge 86-7
Bundeskammer der gewerblichen Wirtschaft Au 11
Bundeskanzler Au 2, 4, 8; Ge 56, 65; Swi 199
Bundesminister der Finanzen Ge 71-2
Bundesminister der Justiz Ge 57, 59, 70-1
Bundesminister der Verteidigung Ge 84-5
Bundesminister des Auswärtigen Ge 66
Bundesminister des Innern Ge 66, 67-8
Bundesminister für Arbeit und Sozialordnung Ge 75-8

Bundesminister für Bildung und Wissenschaft Ge 92
Bundesminister für das Post- und Fernmeldewesen Ge 82-3
Bundesminister für Ernährung, Landwirtschaft und Forsten Ge 74-5
Bundesminister für Forschung und Technologie Ge 90-1
Bundesminister für Innerdeutsche Beziehung Ge 89-90
Bundesminister für Jugend, Familie, Frauen und Gesundheit Ge 85-7
Bundesminister für Raumordnung, Bauwesen und Städtebau Ge 88-9
Bundesminister für Umwelt, Naturschutz und Reaktorsicherheit Ge 92
Bundesminister für Verkehr Ge 78
Bundesminister für Wirtschaft Ge 72-3, 74
Bundesminister für wirtschaftliche Zusammenarbeit Ge 87-8
Bundesministerium für Auswärtige Angelegenheiten Au 2
Bundesministerium für Bauten und Technik Au 2
Bundesministerium für Familie, Jugend und Konsumentschutz Au 2
Bundesministerium für Finanzen Au 2, 8; Ge 58
Bundesministerium für Gesundheit und Umweltschutz Au 2, 7, 8
Bundesministerium für Handel, Gewerbe und Industrie Au 2
Bundesministerium für Inneres Au 2, 7
Bundesministerium für Justiz Au 2
Bundesministerium für Landesverteidigung Au 2
Bundesministerium für Soziale Verwaltung Au 2, 7, 8
Bundesministerium für Unterricht, Kunst und Sport Au 2, 7
Bundesministerium für Verkehr Au 2, 7, 8; Ge 57
Bundesministerium für Wissenschaft und Forschung Au 2, 7
Bundespatentgericht Ge 70
Bundespolizeidirektion Au 8
Bundespräsident Au 2; Ge 56, 64
Bundesrat Au 1, 2, 4; Ge 55, 56, 64; Swi 199-200, 201, 202
Bundesrat. Bericht über . . . Ge 64
Bundesrat: Drucksachen Ge 64
Bundesrechnungsabschluss der Republik Österreich Au 6, 12
Bundesregierung Ge 56, 57, 66
Bundesrepublik Deutschland: Staatshandbuch Ge 57
Bundessozialgericht Ge 56
Bundesstelle für Aussenhandelsinformation Ge 73
Bundestag Ge 55, 56, 60-4
Bundesverfassungsgericht Ge 56, 67, 94
Bundesversammlung Au 2, 4; Ge 56, 64-5; Swi 199, 200, 202
Bundesverwaltungsgericht Ge 56, 70
Bundeswehr Ge 84
Bundeszentrale für politische Bildung Ge 62, 69, 100
Bureau du Plan Be 35-6
Bürgerservice Ge 66
Business Data Package UK 228

CABLIS UK 218
Cabinet Be 26; No 131; Po 150; Swe 174; UK 210, 219
Câmara Municipal Po 150, 169
Carte géologique détaillée de la Belgique Be 35
Catálogo das publicações Po 168
Catalogue of British official publications not published by HMSO UK 233
Catalogue of Swedish books Swe 194
Ce qu'il faut savoir de . . . Be 32
Central Bank Be 36-7
Central Board for Real Estate Data Swe 192
Central Bureau of Statistics No 136-7, 138, 145; Swe 188
Central Commission on Statistics Be 39
Central Economic Council Be 35
Central Information Service No 144
Central Office of Information UK 219
Central Statistical Office Au 8; UK 219
Centralnämnden för Fastighetsdata Swe 192
Centre d'Étude de la Population et de la Famille Be 42
Centre for Byzantine Research Gr 112
Centre for the Study of Population and the Family Be 42
Centre of Planning and Economic Research Gr 115-16
Chadwyck-Healey Ltd UK 231, 233, 234
Chamber of Deputies Ge 55
Chamber of Representatives Be 20, 30
Chambre des Représentants Be 20, 30

ORGANIZATIONS AND TITLES INDEX

Checklist of British official serial publications UK 233
Chiefs of state and cabinet members of foreign governments Be 28
Chronik: Debatten, Gesetze, Kommentare Ge 63
Civil Aviation Administration No 132
Civil Aviation Authority UK 219-20
Civil service yearbook UK 211, 219
Coastal Directorate No 132
Cobbett's parliamentary history of England UK 214
Code of commercial law Au 12
Codes belges, Les Be 29
Codes Larcier, Les Be 29
Colecção Essencial Po 167
Colecção oficial de legislação portuguesa Po 153
Collection of federal laws Swi 201
Comissão da Condição Feminina Po 162
Comité Ministériel de la Région Bruxelloise Be 26
Commercial Bank Gr 116
Commission Centrale de Statistique Be 39
Commission for Racial Equality UK 220
Commission on the Condition of Women Po 162
Commission Royale Belge de Folklore Be 44
Commission Royale de Toponymie et Dialectologie Be 44-5
Commission Royale des Monuments et des Sites Be 45
Commission on the Authority for Legislation Gr 110
Commonwealth Agricultural Bureaux UK 220
Community calendar of Norway No 123
Companies Registration Office UK 220
Compte rendu analytique Be 30, 49
Compte rendu intégral Be 48
Conference of Directors of Education Swi 207
Conference of Directors of Justice Swi 207
Conference of Economic Directors Swi 207
Conference of Education Ministers Ge 101
Conseil Central de l'Économie Be 35
Conseil Communal Be 27
Conseil de la Communauté Française Be 24, 49
Conseil National de la Politique Scientifique Be 33, 34
Conseil Provincial Be 26

Conseil Régional Wallon Be 25, 49
Conseil Supérieur des Bibliothèques Be 45
Conselho de Estado Po 152
Conselho de Ministros Po 150, 152
Conselho Nacional de Estatística Po 157
Constituent Assembly Be 19; Po 151, 156
Constitutional Court Au 3, 9, 10-11; Po 152
Continental Shelf, The No 132
Contributions to Austrian statistics Au 8
Council of Europe No 125
Council of State Au 1-2; Gr 107; No 130; Po 152
County Administrative Boards Swe 174, 186
County administrative ordinances Swe 186
County Council No 144; Swe 175, 185
County Governor Swe 172, 174
County Municipalities No 144
County municipalities and municipalities of Norway No 123
Cour de Cassation Be 22, 23, 31
Cours d'Appel Be 22, 23
Cours d'Assises Be 22, 23
Court and State Printing Office Au 11
Court of Administration Au 3, 9-10
Criminal Investigation Police Po 164, 165, 166
Cultural Foundation of the National Bank Gr 112, 118
Customs and Excise UK 220

DIP (Dokumentations- und Informationssystem für Parlamentsmaterialien) Ge 98
Daily journal of the Assembly of the Republic Po 156-7, 167
Daily journal of the Republic Po 151, 152-3, 154-5, 167
Data Inspectorate Swe 192
Datainspektionen Swe 192
Δελτίον Ανωνύμων Εταιρειών και Εταιρειών Πεωρισμένης Ευθύνης Gr 109
Δελτίον Εμπορικής και Βιομηχανικής Ιδιοκτησίας Gr 109
Δελτίον Νομικών Προσώπων Δημοσίου Δικαίου Gr 109
Departementet for Utviklingshjelp No 131
Department of Agriculture and Fisheries for Scotland UK 220
Department of Education and Science UK 220-1

253

Department of Employment UK 221
Department of Energy UK 221
Department of Health and Social
  Security UK 221-2
Department of the Environment UK 222
Department of Trade No 131
Department of Trade and Industry
  UK 222
Department of Transport UK 222-3
Députation Permanente Be 26
Design Council UK 223
*Deutsche Bibliographie: Amtsblatt der
  Deutschen Bibliothek* Ge 96-7
*Deutsche Bibliographie, Verzeichnis amtlicher
  Druckschriften* Ge 96
Deutsche Bibliographie, Zeitschriften Ge 96
Deutsche Bibliothek Ge 70, 95-6, 99, 100
Deutsche Bundesbahn Ge 80-1
Deutsche Bundespost Ge 82-3
Deutsche Forschungs- und Versuchsanstalt
  für Luft- und Raumfahrt e.V. Ge 93
Deutsche Forschungsgemeinschaft Ge 100
Deutsche Gesellschaft für
  Mineralölwissenschaft und
  Kohlechemie e.V. Ge 93
Deutsche Nationalbibliographie Ge 94
Deutscher Bundestag see Bundestag
Deutscher Städtetag Ge 100
Deutscher Wetterdienst Ge 79-80
Deutscher Zolltarif Ge 58
Deutsches Archäologisches Institut Ge 66
Deutsches Bibliothekinstitut Ge 97, 98
Deutsches Hydrographisches Institut
  Ge 78-9
Deutsches Institut für Urbanistik Ge 102
Deutsches Patentamt Ge 71, 99
Deutschland heute Ge 66
Diário da Assembleia Constituinte Po 156
Diário da Assembleia da República
  Po 156-7, 167
*Diário da Assembleia Regional da
  Madeira* Po 168-9
Diário da Assembleia Regional dos Açores
  Po 168
Diário da República Po 151, 152-3, 154-5,
  167
Diário municipal Po 169
*Dictionnaire des services publics relevant de
  l'État* Be 28
Diet Au 2, 4, 14
Dimension 3 Be 33
Δημόσια Επιχείρηση Ηλεκτρισμού
  Gr 108

Diplomatic Service List UK 223
Direcção-Geral da Administração e Função
  Pública Po 162
Direcção-Geral da Comunicação Social
  Po 164
Direcção-Geral da Organização
  Administrativa Po 165
Direcção-Geral da Qualidade Po 163
Direcção-Geral de Minas e Serviços
  Geológicos Po 163, 164
Direcção-Geral do Comércio Externo
  Po 162, 163, 164, 165
Direcção-Geral dos Registos e do
  Notariado Po 163
Direction Générale des Études et de la
  Documentation Be 34
Directorate of Customs Swi 203
Directorate of Fisheries No 132
Directorate of Health No 123, 135
Directorate-General of Administrative
  Organization Po 165
Directorate-General of Foreign Trade
  Po 162, 163, 164, 165
Directorate-General of Mines and
  Geological Services Po 163, 164
Directorate-General of Public
  Administration and the Civil
  Service Po 162
Directorate-General of Quality Po 163
Directorate-General of Registers and
  Notaries Po 163
Directorate-General of Social
  Communication Po 164
Directory of British official publications
  UK 217, 231, 233, 237
*Directory of specialists in official
  publications* UK 212
Documents of the Storting No 127-8
Documents parlementaires Be 30
Dokumentation an der Bibliothek des
  Verwaltungsgerichtshofes Au 6
Dokumentation Parlamentsspiegel Ge 62
Dokumentationsstelle der parlamentarischen
  Materialien der
  Parlamentsdirektion Au 6
Dokumenter No 127-8
Domänverket Swe 190
Dommer og kjennelser av Arbeidsretten
  No 134
Domstolsverket Swe 191

*EPZ—EPC—CPE, 1969-1978. Phraseologie
  der Europäischen Politischen*

ORGANIZATIONS AND TITLES INDEX

Zusammenarbeit Ge 67
Economic and Social Research
 Council UK 223
Economic Institute for Agriculture Be 38
Économie belge en . . . , L' Be 34
Εφημερίς της Κυβερήσεως Gr 108-9
Εφημερίς των Συζητήσεων της Βουλής
 Gr 109
Eidgenössische Drucksachen- und
 Materialzentrale (EDMZ) Swi 200,
 205, 206, 207
Eidgenössische Oberzolldirektion Swi 203
Eidgenössische Parlaments- und
 Zentralbibliothek Swi 206
Eidgenössische Technische
 Hochschule Swi 206
Eidgenössische Staatskalender Swi 200-1
Eidgenössisches Departement des
 Innern Swi 199
Eidgenössisches Departement für
 Auswärtige Angelegenheiten Swi 199
Eidgenössisches Finanzdepartement
 Swi 199-200
Eidgenössisches Justiz- und
 Polizeidepartement Swi 199
Eidgenössisches Militärdepartement
 Swi 199, 203
Eidgenössisches Verkehrs- und
 Energiewirtschaftsdepartement
 Swi 200
Eidgenössisches
 Volkswirtschaftsdepartement Swi 200
Ευρετήριον Συζητήσεων του
 Κοινοβουλίου Gr 110
Εκκλησία της Ελλάδος Gr 113
*Élections législatives: résultats des élections
 du . . .* Be 33
Ελεγτικόν Συνέδριον Gr 107
Ελληνικά Ταχυδρομεία Gr 108
Ελληνική Σάλπιγξ Gr 108
Ελληνικό Κέντρο Παραγωγικότητος
 Gr 115
Ελληνικόν Ινστιτούτον βυζαντινών και
 Μεταβυζαντινών Σπουδών
 Gr 113
Employment gazette UK 221, 233
Εμπορική Τράπεζα Gr 116
Εμπορικό και βιομηχανικό Επιμελητήριο
 Αθηνών Gr 115
Energiforskningsnämnden Swe 190
Energy Research Commission Swe 190
Enquête socio-économique Be 41
*Entreprises industrielles et commerciales en
 Belgique* Be 34
Επίσημα Πρακτικά της Βουλής Gr 109
Επιτροπή Νομοθετικής
 Εξουσιοδοτήσεως Gr 110
Equal Opportunities Commission UK 223
Erziehungsdirektorenkonferenz Swi 207
*Escritores dos Países de Língua
 Portuguesa* Po 167
Estatísticas demográficas Po 158
Estudos e Temas Portugueses Po 167
Estudos Gerais/Série Universitária Po 167
Εθνική Βιβλιοθηκη Gr 118
Εθνική Εφημερίς Gr 108
Εθνική Στατιστική γπηρεσία της
 Ελλάδος Gr 111, 118
Εθνική Τράπεζα της Ελλάδος Gr 108, 116
Εθνικό Ιδρυμα Ερευνών Gr 112
Εθνικόν Κέντρον Κοινωνικών Ερευνών
 Gr 111, 118
Εθνικόν Τυπογραφείον Gr 108, 117
Études et documents budgétaires Be 36
Études statistiques Be 38, 41
European Communities Be 37; Ge 57;
 Swe 189
Exécutif de la Région Wallonne Be 25

FNRS (Fonds National de la Recherche
 Scientifique) Be 44
Federal Administrative Court Ge 56, 70
Federal Agency for Materials Testing
 Ge 73-4
Federal Archive Ge 69-70
Federal Armed Forces Ge 84
Federal Army Department Swi 199, 203
Federal Assembly Au 2, 4; Ge 55, 56,
 60-4; Swi 199, 200, 202
Federal Centre for Political Education
 Ge 62, 69
Federal Chancellor Au 2, 4, 8; Ge 56, 65;
 Swi 199
Federal Civil Defence Office Swi 203
Federal Constitutional Court Ge 56, 67, 94
Federal Convention Ge 56, 64-5
Federal Council Au 1, 2, 4; Ge 55, 56, 64;
 Swi 199-200, 201, 202
Federal Court of Justice Ge 56, 70
Federal Department for Transport,
 Communications and Energy Swi 200
Federal Department of Finance
 Swi 199-200
Federal Department of Foreign Affairs
 Swi 199

Federal Department of Justice and
  Police   Swi 199
Federal Department of the Economy
  Swi 200
Federal Department of the Interior
  Swi 199
Federal Employment Agency   Ge 77
Federal Environment Agency   Ge 92–3
Federal Fiscal Court   Ge 56, 70
Federal gazette   Ge 57, 58–9, 63, 64, 70;
  Swi 201–2, 206
Federal government   Ge 56, 57, 66
Federal government manual   Swi 200–1
Federal Government Press and Information
  Office   Ge 65
Federal Health Office   Ge 86–7
Federal Housing Office   Swi 206
Federal Labour Court   Ge 56
Federal law gazette   Ge 55, 57–8, 60, 66,
  70
Federal legislation finding list   Ge 59
Federal Minister for Defence   Ge 84–5
Federal Minister for Economic
  Cooperation   Ge 87–8
Federal Minister for Education and
  Science   Ge 92
Federal Minister for Employment and
  Social Affairs   Ge 75–8
Federal Minister for Food, Agriculture and
  Forestry   Ge 74–5
Federal Minister for Foreign Affairs   Ge 66
Federal Minister for Intra-German
  Relations   Ge 89–90
Federal Minister for Posts and
  Telecommunications   Ge 82–3
Federal Minister for Regional Planning,
  Building and Town Planning   Ge 88–9
Federal Minister for Research and
  Technology   Ge 90–1
Federal Minister for the Economy
  Ge 72–3, 74
Federal Minister for the Environment,
  Nature Conservation and Nuclear
  Safety   Ge 92
Federal Minister for Youth, the Family,
  Women and Health   Ge 85–7
Federal Minister of Finance   Ge 71–2
Federal Minister of Justice   Ge 57, 59
Federal Minister of the Interior   Ge 66,
  67–8
Federal Minister of Transport   Ge 78
Federal Ministry for Building and
  Engineering   Au 2

Federal Ministry for Education and the
  Arts   Au 2, 7
Federal Ministry for External Affairs   Au 2
Federal Ministry for Finance   Au 2, 8
Federal Ministry for Health and
  Environmental Protection   Au 2, 7, 8
Federal Ministry for Home Affairs   Au 2, 7
Federal Ministry for Justice   Au 2
Federal Ministry for National Defence
  Au 2
Federal Ministry for Science and
  Research   Au 2, 7
Federal Ministry for the Family, Youth and
  Consumer Affairs   Au 2
Federal Ministry for Trade, Business and
  Industry   Au 2
Federal Ministry for Transport   Au 2, 7, 8
Federal Ministry for Welfare   Au 2, 7, 8
Federal Office for Intellectual
  Property   Swi 202
Federal Office of Environmental Protection
  Swi 206
Federal Parliamentary and Central
  Library   Swi 206
Federal Physico-Technical Agency   Ge 73
Federal Police Directorate   Au 8
Federal President   Ge 56, 64; Swi 200
Federal Printing and Supply Centre
  Swi 200, 205, 206, 207
Federal Research Institute for Area Studies
  and Regional Policy   Ge 88–9
Federal Social Court   Ge 56
Federal Statistical Office   Ge 68–9, 98;
  Swi 202, 206
Federal Technical University   Swi 206
Federal Tribunal   Swi 200, 203
Fernmeldetechnisches Zentralamt   Ge 82
Finances de l'État en . . . , Les   Be 36
Finans- og Tolldepartementet   No 126,
  131
Finansdepartementet   Swe 188
Fiscal budget   No 125–6
Fiskeridepartementet   No 131
Fiskeridirektøren   No 132
Fiskeristyrelsen   Swe 191
Flemish Community   Be 24, 49
Fonds de la Recherche Fondamentale
  Collective   Be 44
Fonds de la Recherche Scientifique
  Médicale   Be 44
Fonds National de la Recherche
  Scientifique   Be 44
Forbruker- og

ORGANIZATIONS AND TITLES INDEX

Administrasjonsdepartementet No 131, 137
Foreign and Commonwealth Office UK 223
Foreign Office Ge 66–7
Forestry Commission UK 223
Forsvarsdepartementet No 131
Försvarsdepartementet Swe 189
Från riksdag och departement Swe 196
Freedom of the Press Act Swe 172, 173
French Community Be 24, 49
Friend of the law Gr 108
From Parliament and ministries Swe 196
Fundstellennachweis über die Bundesgesetzgebung Ge 59–60
Fylkesting No 143

GESTA (Stand der Gesetzgebung des Bundes) Ge 63, 98
GKSS-Forschungszentrum GmbH Ge 94
Gemeinden Ge 56, 100, 101–2
Gemeindeordnungen Au 15–16
Gemeinderat Au 16
Gemeinsames Ministerialblatt Ge 66, 67–8
General Agency for the Overseas Territories Po 168
General catalogue of printed books Po 168
General Church Assembly Swe 184, 186
General code of civil law Au 12
General Directorate for Surveys and Documentation Be 34
General journal of Greece Gr 108
General Register Office for Scotland UK 223–4
General state archives Gr 112
Generaltullstyrelsen Swe 189
Γενικά Ἀρχεῖα τοῦ Κράτους Gr 112
Γενική Ἐφημερίς τῆς Ἑλλάδος Gr 108
Geographical and Survey Institute Po 166
German Community Be 24, 49
German Federal Republic: official publications 1949 1957 Ge 95
German Hydrographic Institute Ge 78–9
German Municipalities Federation Ge 100
German National Library Ge 70, 95–6
German Postal Service Ge 82–3
German State Railways Ge 80–1
German Weather Service Ge 79–80
Γερουσία Gr 109–10
Gesellschaft für Biotechnologische Forschung Ge 94
Gesellschaft für Mathematik und Datenverarbeitung Ge 94
Gesellschaft für Reaktorsicherheit Ge 94
Gesellschaft für Schwerionenforschung Ge 94
Gesellschaft für Strahlen- und Umweltforschung Ge 94
Gesetz über die Deutsche Bibliothek Ge 99
Gesetz über die Sammlung des Bundesrechts Ge 59
Government gazette Gr 108–9
Government Printing Office No 137
Greek Institute for Byzantine and Post-Byzantine Studies Gr 113
Greek Postal Services Gr 108
Greek Productivity Centre Gr 115
Greek trumpet Gr 108
Grundgesetz Ge 55
Guide des Ministères: revue de l'administration belge Be 27, 50
Guide to government department and other libraries UK 216, 234, 240
Guide to Nordic bibliography No 139
Guide to Norwegian statistics No 136
Guide to official statistics UK 219

HMSO (Her Majesty's Stationery Office) UK 211, 212, 230–3, 234–5
HMSO in print UK 232
Hahn-Meitner-Institut für Kernforschung Ge 94
Halsbury's statutory instruments UK 212, 213
Håndbok over norsk bibliografi No 138
Handbuch des Bundesrates Ge 64
Handelsdepartementet No 131; Swe 189–90
Handelsgesetzbuch Au 12
Handikappinstitutet Swe 193
Hansard UK 214, 236
Health and Safety Executive UK 210, 224
Hellenic Chamber of Shipping Gr 115
Helsedirektoratet No 123, 135
Her Majesty's Stationery Office UK 211, 212, 230–3, 234–5
Highest Special Court Gr 107
Hof- und Staatsdruckerei Au 11
Home Office UK 224, 228
Hoover Institution Be 51
House of Commons UK 209
House of Commons information bulletin UK 216
House of Lords UK 209, 216
Housing Court Swe 191
Hovedregister til Stortings-forhandlinger No 128–9

Høyesterett No 134
Hvem svarer på hva i Staten No 122

ICE (Informations du commerce extérieur) Be 37
IEA (Institut Économique Agricole) Be 38
IFLA (International Federation of Library Associations) Ge 94; UK 211, 240
INBEL (Institut Belge d'Information et de Documentation) Be 32, 46, 48
INCM (Imprensa Nacional-Casa da Moeda) Po 153, 165, 166–7
INE (Instituto Nacional de Estatística) Po 157–8, 159–60, 166, 167
Ἴδρυμα Ερευνας και παιδείας της Εμπορικής Τράπεζας Gr 113
Ἴδρυμα Κοινωνικών Ασφαλίσεων Gr 117
Ἴδρυμα Κρατικών Υποτροφιών Gr 112
Imprensa Nacional Po 167
Imprensa Nacional-Casa da Moeda Po 153, 165, 166–7
Index of government orders in force UK 213
Index of parliamentary debates Gr 110
Index to the committee reports published by HMSO UK 232
Industridepartementet No 131; Swe 190
Information guide 1981 Be 32
Informations parlementaires Be 29
Informationsführer: Bibliotheken und Dokumentationsstellen Österreichs Au 17
Inland Revenue UK 224
Institut Belge d'Information et de Documentation Be 32, 46, 48
Institut Économique Agricole Be 38
Institut Économique et Social des Classes Moyennes Be 38
Institut für Weltwirtschaft Ge 100
Institut Géographique National Be 48
Institut Interuniversitaire des Sciences Nucléaires Be 44
Institut National de Statistique Be 34, 38–41, 46, 48
Institut pour l'Encouragement de la Recherche Scientifique dans l'Industrie et l'Agriculture Be 44
Institute of Mineral and Geology Exploration Gr 114, 118
Instituto Geográfico e Cadastral Po 166
Ινστιτούτο Γεωλογικών και Μεταλλευτικών Ερευνών Gr 114, 118
Instituto Nacional de Estatística Po 157–8, 159–60, 166, 167

Instrument of government Swe 173, 184
International Council on Archives Be 45
International Federation of Library Associations UK 211, 240
International organizations annual catalogue UK 232
International whaling statistics No 137
Interparlamentarische Arbeitsgemeinschaft Ge 61
Ionian and Popular Bank Gr 116
Ιουική και Λαϊκή Τράπεζα Gr 116

JURIS (Juristisches Informationssystem des Bundes) Ge 98
Jahresbericht der Bundesregierung Ge 65
Jordbruksdepartementet Swe 190–1
Jornal oficial da Região Autónoma da Madeira Po 169
Jornal oficial da Região Autónoma dos Açores Po 168
Journal of Norwegian booksellers No 140
Journal of Parliamentary debates Gr 109
Journal officiel (of the European Communities) Be 37
Journals (of British Parliament) UK 213–14
Judgements and findings of the Labour Court No 134
Judicial reference book No 134–5
Junta do Crédito Público Po 164
Junta Nacional de Investigação Científica e Tecnológica Po 162, 164
Juridisk Oppslagsbok No 134–5
Juristisches Informationssystem des Bundes Ge 98
Justis- og Politidepartementet No 131
Justitiedepartementet Swe 191–2
Justizdirektorenkonferenz Swi 207

Kammarrätterna Swe 191
Kammer der gewerblichen Wirtschaft Au 11
Kammer für Arbeiter und Angestellte Au 11
Kantonrat Swi 200
Κέντρο Νεοελληνικών Ερευνών Gr 112
Κέντρον Βυζαντινών Ερευνών Gr 112
Κέντρον Προγραμματισμού και Οικονομικών Ερευνών Gr 115–16
Kernforschungsanlage Jülich GmbH Ge 94
Kernforschungszentrum Karlsruhe GmbH Ge 94

ORGANIZATIONS AND TITLES INDEX

Kirke- og Undervisningsdepartementet
   No 131
Komiteen for Internasjonale Sosial-Politiske
   Saker No 135
Komiteer No 122, 126
Kommerskollegium Swe 189
Kommittéberättelsen Swe 181
Kommunal- og Arbeidsdepartementet
   No 132, 135
Kommundepartementet Swe 192
Kommuner No 144; Swe 175
Kommunestyrer No 144
Kommunfullmäktige Swe 175
Kommunikationsdepartementet Swe 192-3
Kommunstyrelsen Swe 175, 186
Komsumentverket Swe 190
Koncessionsnämnden för Miljöskydd
   Swe 191
Konjunkturinstitutet Swe 188
Konstitutionsutskottet Swe 174
Kriminalvårdsstyrelsen Swe 191
Kultur- og Vitenskapsdepartementet
   No 132
Kultusministerkonferenz Ge 101
Kungliga Biblioteket Swe 193, 196
Kystverket No 132

LEXIS UK 213
LIBRIS Swe 194, 196
Labour Court Swe 191
Labour market, The Au 8
Lagrådet Swe 179
Lagting No 122
Lagtingstidende No 127
Län Swe 172, 174-5, 185-6
Landbruksdepartementet No 123, 132, 135
Länder Ge 56, 60, 101-2
Landesbibliothek Ge 101
Landesgesetzblätter Au 14
Landshövding Swe 172, 174
Landslag Swe 172
Landsting Swe 175, 185, 186
Landtag Au 2, 4, 14
Landwirtschaftskammer Au 11
Länskungörelser Swe 186
Länsstyrelserna Swe 174, 186, 192
Lantbruksstyrelsen Swe 191
Larcier codes of law Be 29
Law Commission UK 224
Law Council Swe 179
Law on the digest of federal law Ge 59
Legislative Library of Quebec Be 52
Liber Grafiska AB Swe 194-5

Library Association UK 212
Library of Congress Be 51; Po 168;
   Swi 207
Library of Parliament Gr 117, 118;
   No 145
List of publications from the Storting and
   central government No 125
List of statutory instruments UK 232
*List of the serial publications of foreign
   governments, 1815-1931* Po 168
Local government information sources
   UK 212, 233
London gazette UK 213, 229
Lovdata No 131
Lucerne Central Library Swi 207
Luftfartsverket No 132; Swe 192

Madeira: anuário estatístico Po 169
Manpower Employment Organization
   Gr 117
Manpower Services Commission UK 224
Marintekniska Institutet Swe 190
Maritime Research Institute Swe 190
Market Court Swe 190
Marknadsdomstolen Swe 190
Materialien Ge 63
Max-Planck-Institut für Plasmaphysik
   Ge 94
Medelhavsmuseet Swe 193
Media Law Au 4, 11, 12, 13
Medical Research Council UK 224-5
Mediengesetz Au 4, 11, 12, 13
Memo from Belgium Be 32
*Mémorial administratif de la province
   de...* Be 50
Meteorological Office UK 225
Militärgeschichtliches Forschungsamt
   Ge 85
Military History Research Office Ge 85
Miljøverndepartementet No 132
Ministère de la Défence Nationale Be 34
Ministère de la Justice et des Réformes
   Institutionnelles Be 33
Ministère de la Prévoyance Sociale Be 42
Ministère de la Région Bruxelloise et des
   Classes Moyennes Be 26, 36, 38
Ministère de la Santé et de la Famille
   Be 41
Ministère de l'Éducation Nationale et de la
   Culture Française Be 33, 43, 48
Ministère de l'Emploi et du Travail Be 42
Ministère de l'Intérieur Be 28, 33
Ministère des Affaires Économiques Be 34,
   48

ORGANIZATIONS AND TITLES INDEX

Ministère des Affaires Sociales et des Réformes Institutionnelles   Be 41
Ministère des Classes Moyennes   Be 38
Ministère des Colonies   Be 48
Ministère des Finances et du Commerce Extérieur   Be 36, 48
Ministère des Relations Extérieures   Be 32, 43
Ministère du Budget, de la Politique Scientifique et du Plan   Be 36
Ministerie van Nationale Opvoeding en Nederlandse Cultuur   Be 33, 43
Ministério da Cultura   Po 153, 162
Ministério da Educação   Po 163, 164
Ministério da Indústria, Energia e Exportação   Po 163
Ministério da Justiça   Po 153, 162-3, 164
Ministério da Qualidade de Vida   Po 165
Ministério das Finanças   Po 164, 165
Ministério do Equipamento Social   Po 164
Ministério do Trabalho   Po 162, 163
Ministry for Employment and Labour   Be 42
Ministry for the Colonies   Be 48
Ministry of Agriculture   Gr 114; No 123, 132, 135; Swe 190-1
Ministry of Agriculture, Fisheries and Food   UK 225
Ministry of Church and Education   No 131
Ministry of Commerce   Swe 189-90
Ministry of Communications   No 132, 133; Swe 192-3
Ministry of Consumer Affairs and Government Administration   No 131
Ministry of Cultural and Scientific Affairs   No 132
Ministry of Culture   Po 153, 162
Ministry of Defence   No 131; Swe 189; UK 225
Ministry of Development and Cooperation   No 131
Ministry of Economic Affairs   Be 34
Ministry of Education   Po 163, 164; Swe 193-4
Ministry of Education (French and Dutch)   Be 25
Ministry of Education and Religion   Gr 111-12
Ministry of External Relations   Be 32, 43
Ministry of Finance   Gr 115; No 126, 131; Po 164, 165; Swe 188
Ministry of Finance and External Trade   Be 36
Ministry of Fisheries   No 131
Ministry of Foreign Affairs   Gr 116-17; No 131, 132, 133-4, 136, 145; Swe 194
Ministry of Health and Social Affairs   No 132, 135
Ministry of Health and Welfare   Swe 193
Ministry of Housing   Swe 187-8
Ministry of Industry   No 131; Swe 190
Ministry of Industry, Energy and Exports   Po 163
Ministry of Justice   Ge 57, 59; Gr 110-11; No 131; Po 153, 162-3, 164; Swe 191-2
Ministry of Justice and Institutional Reform   Be 33
Ministry of Labour   Po 162, 163; Swe 187
Ministry of Local Government   Swe 192
Ministry of Local Government and Labour   No 132, 135
Ministry of National Defence   Be 34
Ministry of Petroleum and Energy   No 132
Ministry of Public Health and the Family   Be 41
Ministry of Public Works   Gr 115
Ministry of Reconstruction   Gr 115
Ministry of Social Affairs and Institutional Reform   Be 41
Ministry of Social Equipment   Po 164
Ministry of Social Security   Be 42
Ministry of the Brussels Region and Middle Classes   Be 26, 36, 38
Ministry of the Budget, Science Policy and Planning   Be 36
Ministry of the Environment   No 132
Ministry of the Interior   Be 28, 33; Gr 111
Ministry of the Merchant Marine   Gr 115
Ministry of the Middle Classes   Be 38
Ministry of the National Economy   Gr 115
Ministry of the Presidency   Gr 111
Ministry of the Quality of Life   Po 165
Ministry of the Transport   Ge 57; Gr 115
Minutes of Proceedings   UK 215
Modern Greek Research Centre   Gr 112
Moniteur belge   Be 28-9, 30, 32, 33, 37, 39, 46, 48
Μορφωτικό Ιδρυμα Εθνικής Τραπέζης   Gr 112, 118
Municipal Chamber   Po 150
Municipal Council   Au 16; No 144; Swe 175, 186
Musarum Officia   Po 167
Myntkabinettet   Swe 193

ORGANIZATIONS AND TITLES INDEX

NATO (North Atlantic Treaty Organization) No 125
NEMCE (Nomenclatura Estatística das Mercadorias do Comércio Externo) Po 160
NIMEXE Po 160
NL (Norges Lover) No 130-1
NOS (*Norges offisielle statistikk*) No 136, 137
NOU (*Norges offentlige utredninger*) No 125, 129, 135, 136, 138
National Accounting and Audit Bureau Swe 188
National Archives Swe 193
National Assembly No 121, 124-30
National Bank of Greece Gr 108, 116
National Bank of Switzerland Swi 204
National bibliography Swe 193-4, 195
National Board for Scientific and Technological Research Po 162, 164
National Board of Economic Defence Swe 190
National Board of Occupational Safety and Health Swe 187
National Board of Universities and Colleges Swe 194
National Centre for Social Research Gr 111, 118
National Consumer Board Swe 190
National Council Au 2, 3, 4; Swi 199, 201
National Council for Science Policy Be 33, 44
National Council for the Disabled Swe 193
National Courts Administration Swe 191
National Debt Office Swe 184
National Economic Development Office UK 226
National Fire Protection Council Swe 192
National Franchise Board for Environmental Protection Swe 191
National Fund for Accident Insurance Swi 204
National gazette Gr 108
National Industrial Board Swe 190
National Institute for Building Research Swe 187
National Institute for Materials Testing Swe 190
National Institute of Economic Research Swe 188
National Institute of Radiation Protection Swe 191
National Insurance Board Swe 193
National Insurance Institution No 135
National Land Survey Administration Swe 187
National Library Gr 118; Po 168; Swi 200, 204, 206, 207
National Library of Canada Be 52
National Patent and Registration Office Swe 189-90
National Physical Laboratory UK 226
National Physical Planning Board Swe 187
National Police Board Swe 191
National Price and Cartel Office Swe 190
National Printing House Gr 108, 117
National Printing Office-Mint Po 153, 165, 166-7
National Prisons and Probation Administration Swe 191
National Radiological Protection Board UK 226
National Research Institute Gr 112
National Road Safety Board Swe 191
National Rural Law Code Swe 172
National Statistical Institute Be 34, 38-41, 46, 48
National Statistical Service of Greece Gr 111, 118
National Statistics Institute Po 157-8, 159-60, 166, 167
National Taxation Board Swe 188
National union catalog (LC) Po 168
Nationalbibliografin Swe 193-4
Nationalrat Au 2, 3, 4; Swi 199, 201
Nationalrat und Bundesrat Au 6
Natural Environmental Research Council UK 226
Nature Conservancy Board Swe 191
Nature Conservancy Council UK 210
Ναυτικό Επιμελητήριο Ελλάδος Gr 115
New York Public Library Be 51
Niedersächsischer Zeitschriftennachweis Ge 98
Nobel Institute No 145
Nomenclatura Estatística das Mercadorias do Comércio Externo (NEMCE) Po 160
Nordic Africa Institute Swe 194
Nordisk Skibsrederforening No 134
Nordiska Afrikainstitutet Swe 194
Norges Bank No 125
Norges fylkeskommuner og kommuner No 123
Norges forskrifter No 131

ORGANIZATIONS AND TITLES INDEX

Norges kommunekalender No 123
Norges Lover (NL) No 130-1
Norges offisielle statistikk (NOS) No 136
Norges statskalender No 134
Norsk Advokatforening No 134
Norsk bokfortegnelse No 139-40
Norsk bokhandlertidende No 140
Norsk Rikskringkasting No 125
Norsk Lovtidend (NLT) No 130
Norsk Utenrikspolitisk Institutt No 134
Norske offentlige utredninger (NOU)
 No 125, 129, 135, 136, 138
Norske oljepolitikk No 135
Norske organisasjoner No 123
*Norske vitenskapelige og faglige
 biblioteker* No 145
Northern Ireland Assembly UK 211, 229
Northern Ireland Office UK 211, 226
Northern Shipowners' Association No 134
Norwegian Association of Lawyers No 134
Norwegian book index No 139
Norwegian Broadcasting Corporation
 No 125
Norwegian Institute of International
 Affairs No 134
Norwegian Joint Committee on
 International Social Policy No 135
Norwegian law compendium No 130-1
Norwegian law gazette No 130
*Norwegian laws etc. selected for the Foreign
 Service* No 131
Norwegian Mapping Authority.
 Hydrographic Survey No 133
Norwegian Maritime Directorate
 No 132-3
Norwegian official reports No 125
Norwegian Petroleum Directorate No 132
Notices biographiques Be 31

OECD (Organization for Economic
 Cooperation and Development)
 No 125
Ο Φίλος του Νόμου Gr 108
Oberste Gerichtshof Au 9
Oberste Rückerstattungsgericht Ge 70
Odelsting No 122
Odelstingstidende No 127
Oecumenical Patriarchate of
 Constantinople Gr 107-8
Office Belge du Commerce Extérieur
 Be 37
Office National d'Allocations Familiales
 pour Travailleurs Salariés Be 42

Office National de la Sécurité Sociale
 Be 42
Office of External Trade Be 37
Office of Population Censuses and
 Surveys UK 226-7
Office of the Prime Minister No 130, 132
Official bulletin of the Federal
 Assembly Swi 202
Official collection of Portuguese
 legislation Po 153
Official collection of re-promulgated
 Austrian legal regulations Au 5
Official gazette Be 28-9, 30
Official minutes of Parliament Gr 109
*Official publications of European
 governments* Be 47
Official publishing: an overview Swe 194
Offical record of the Austrian National and
 Federal Councils Au 5
Olje- og Energidepartementet No 132
Oljedirektoratet No 132, 135
Ombudsman No 122, 128
Οργανισμός Απασχολήσεως Εργατικόν
 Δυναμικού Gr 117
Οργανισμός Γεωργικών Ασφαλίσεών
 Gr 117
Οργανισμός Εκδόσεως Διδακτικών
 Βιβλίων Gr 111
Οργανισμός Προωθήσης Εξαγωγών
 Gr 115
Οργανισμσς Τηλεπικοινωνιών Ελλάδος
 Gr 108
*Organização da Assembleia e relação nominal
 dos deputados* Po 157
Organization for Agricultural Insurance
 Gr 117
Organization for the Promotion of
 Exports Gr 115
Organization for the Publication of
 Educational Books Gr 111
Orthodox Greek Church Gr 113
Österreich-Bericht Au 8
Österreichische Nationalbibliographie Au 13
Österreichische Nationalbibliothek Au 13,
 16
Österreichische Staatsdruckerei Au 3, 5,
 11-13, 18
Österreichischer Amtskalender Au 3, 18
Österreichischer Arbeiterkammertag
 Au 11
Österreichisches Jahrbuch Au 8, 18
Österreichisches Statistisches
 Zentralamt Au 8, 12

Ouvrages de référence Be 45
Overseas Development Administration UK 227
Överstyrelsen för Ekonomiskt Försvar Swe 190

POLDOK (Politische Dokumentation) Ge 98
POLIS (Parliamentary On-line Information Service) UK 213, 233
Pareceres da Comissão Constitucional Po 154, 167
Parlament: die Woche im Bundeshaus, Das Ge 62
Parlamentarischer Rat Ge 55, 60
Parlamentsspiegel Ge 61-2
Parlement belge, Le Be 31
Parliament Gr 107, 109-10; No 121-2, 124-30; Swe 172-3, 174, 175-84; UK 209, 213-16, 235
Parliamentary Auditors Swe 173, 174
Parliamentary Commissioner for Administration UK 209, 227
Parliamentary Council Ge 55, 60
Parliamentary Debates UK 213, 214
Parliamentary minutes Gr 108, 109
Parliamentary Ombudsmen Swe 173, 174, 184
Parliamentary Select Committees UK 209
Pasicrisie: recueil général de la jurisprudence Be 31
Pasinomie: Collection complète des lois, décrets, arrêtés et règlements généraux Be 29, 32
Patent- och Registreringsverket Swe 189-90
Patriarchal Foundation for Patristic Studies Gr 114, 118
Πατριαρχικόν Ἴδρυμα Πατερικῶν Μελετῶν Gr 114, 118
Pensamento Português Po 167
Periodika-Zentralkatalog der Universitätsbibliothek Wien Au 13
Perspectives de population Be 41
Physikalisch-Technische Bundesanstalt Ge 73
Piraeus Commodity Exchange Gr 115
Planning Bureau Be 35-6
Polícia Judiciária Po 164, 165, 166
Post Office No 125; Swe 192; Swi 203
Post- und Telegraphenverordnungsblatt Au 7
Postal Board No 132
Postal Services Administration No 125

Postdepartement Swi 203
Postdirektoratet No 132
Postlexicon der Republik Österreich Au 8, 18
Posttechnisches Zentralamt Ge 82
Postverket No 125; Swe 192
Πρακτικά Gr 108, 109
Präsidentenkonferenz de Landwirtschaftskammern Österreichs Au 11
Presenças da Imagem Po 167
President Au 2; Gr 107; Po 150, 151, 152; Swi 200
Presidente da República Po 150, 151, 152
Presse- und Informationsamt der Bundesregierung Ge 65
Pressekontakter i statsadministrasjonen No 122
Preussische Staatsbibliothek Ge 93
Prime Minister No 121, 131; Po 150, 152; Swe 179; UK 209
Primeiro-Ministro Po 150, 152
Product Control Board Swe 191
Produktkontrollnämnden Swe 191
Projets de coöpération entre la Belgique et ... Be 33
Projets de loi (Channel Islands) UK 230
Property Services Agency UK 227
Protokolle Au 5-6, 14
Provincial Council Be 26
Prussian Cultural Foundation Ge 93
Public bodies UK 211, 219
Public Pensions Fund Swe 193
Public Power Corporation Gr 108
Public Record Office UK 227
Publications périodiques éditées par les services centraux des Ministères, Les Be 47
Publications scientifiques de l'État Be 47
Publikasjonsliste fra Storting og Regjering No 125, 139

Quid Be 32

Rat der Deutschen Kulturgemeinschaft Be 24, 49
Recensement Be 39
Rechnungshof Au 3, 6, 12
Rechtsüberleitungsgesetz Au 1
Recommendations of Storting No 126-7
Recueil des actes des princes belges Be 29
Recueil des anciennes coutumes de la Belgique Be 29
Recueil des lois UK 230
Recueil des lois, décrets et arrêtés Be 29, 32

Recueil des ordonnances des anciens Pays-Bas Be 29
Recueil des pièces imprimées par ordre de la Chambre de Représentants Be 30
Recueil des traités et conventions concernant le royaume de Belgique Be 33
Recueil d'ordonnances (Channel Islands) UK 230
Refer UK 212
Regeringsformen Swe 173, 184
Regiões Autónomas Po 150, 152, 168
Register of Shipping Swe 191
Register zu den Verhandlungen des Deutschen Bundestages Ge 61
Regjeringen No 131
Règlement Be 31
Regulations of Norway No 131
Répertoire de l'information 1981 Be 32
Répertoire des périodiques paraissant en Belgique Be 47
Répertoire des thèses de doctorat Be 33
Repertorium van de voorlichting 1981 Be 32
Report on non-departmental public bodies UK 210, 211
Research and Educational Institute of the Commercial Bank of Greece Gr 113
Revue de la presse Be 38
Revue du travail Be 42
Riksantikvarieämbetet och statens historiska museer Swe 193
Riksarkivet Swe 193
Riksbanken Swe 184
Riksdag Swe 172-3, 174, 175-84
Riksdag Code of Statutes Swe 183, 185
Riksdag *Protokoll* Swe 175-83
Riksdagens årsbok Swe 184
Riksdagens Författningssamling (RFS) Swe 183, 185
Riksdagens Ombudsmän Swe 173, 174, 184
Riksdagens Revisorer Swe 173, 174
Riksdagsbiblioteket Swe 175, 195, 196
Riksförsäkringsverket Swe 193
Riksgäldskontoret Swe 184
Rikspolisstyrelsen Swe 191
Riksrevisionsverket Swe 188
Riksskatteverket Swe 188
Rikstrygdeverket No 135
Royal Library Swe 193, 196
Royal Library of Albert I Be 45, 51

SCICON UK 213
SCOOP (Standing Committee on Official Publications of the Library Assocation's Information Services Group) UK 211, 212, 233
SIGLE (System for Grey Literature in Europe) UK 218, 233
SITC (Standard International Trade Classification) Po 160
STATIS-BUND (Statisches Informationssystem des Bundes) Ge 98
STE (Statens trykksakekspedisjon) No 137
STK (Statens trykningskontor) No 137
Samferdselsdepartementet No 132, 133
Samfunnsboka No 122
Samling av lover og anordninger No 130
Sammlung der eidgenössischen Gesetze Swi 201
Schriftenreihe des Bundesministeriums des Innern Ge 68
Schweizerische Landesbibliothek Swi 200, 204, 206, 207
Schweizerische Nationalbank Swi 204
Schweizerische Unfallversicherungsanstalt Swi 204
Science and Engineering Research Council UK 227
Scottish Development Department UK 227
Scottish Education Department UK 227-8
Scottish Home and Health Department UK 228
Scottish Office UK 228
Secretaria de Estado da Reforma Administrative Po 164
Secretaria de Estado da Segurança Social Po 164
Secrétariat d'État aux Affaires Européennes et à l'Agriculture Be 36, 38
Secretary of State for European Affairs and Agriculture Be 36, 38
Security Council UK 210
Sénat Be 20
Senat Ge 102
Senate Be 20; Ge 102; Gr 109, 110
Serial publications of foreign governments Be 47
Service Belge des Échanges Internationaux Be 52
Services d'information et de relations publiques, Les Be 32
Services de Programmation de la Politique Scientifique du Premier Ministre Be 44

Sessional information digest   UK 216
Sjøfartsdirektoratet   No 132-3
Sjöfartsverket   Swe 192
Shoppsregistret   Swe 191
Skogsstyrelsen   Swe 191
Skolöverstyrelsen   Swe 194
Social and Economic Institute for the Middle Classes   Be 38
Social Security Foundation   Gr 117
Socialdepartementet   Swe 193
Sosialdepartementet   No 132, 135
Staatsbibliothek Preussischer Kulturbesitz   Ge 57, 70, 99, 100
Staatsdruckereigesetz   Au 12
Staatsgesetzblatt   Au 1, 5
Staatsvertrag   Au 1
Stadslag   Swe 172
Stand der Gesetzgebung des Bundes ....   Ge 63
Standard International Trade Classification (SITC)   Po 160
Ständerat   Swi 199, 201
Standing Committee on Official Publications of the Library Association's Information Services Group   UK 211, 212
Standing Committee on the Constitution   Swe 174
Stanford University   Be 52
State Accidents Commission   Swe 193
State Bacteriological Laboratory   Swe 193
State Employers Board   Swe 188
State Immigration and Naturalization Board   Swe 187
State Labour Inspectorate   No 136
State law gazette   Au 1
State ledger   Swe 188
State Library of the Prussian Cultural Foundation   Ge 57, 70, 99, 100
State Power Board   Swe 190
State Railways   Swe 192
State Road and Traffic Institute   Swe 192
State Scholarships Foundation   Gr 112
State Telegraph Administration   No 125, 133
State Treaty   Au 1
Statens Arbeidstilsyn   No 136
Statens Bakteriologiska Laboratorium   Swe 193
Statens Brandnämnd   Swe 192
Statens Geologiska Undersökning   Swe 190
Statens Handikappråd   Swe 193
Statens Haverikommission   Swe 193

Statens Historiska Musem   Swe 193
Statens Informasjonstjeneste   No 144
Statens Institut för Byggnadsforskning   Swe 187
Statens Invandrarverk   Swe 187
Statens Järnvägar   Swe 192
Statens Jordbruksnämnd   Swe 191
Statens Kartverk. Divisjon Norges Sjøkartverk   No 133
Statens Konstmuseer   Swe 193
Statens Kulturråd   Swe 194
Statens Lantmäteriverk   Swe 187
Statens Naturvårdsverk   Swe 191
Statens offentliga utredningar (SOU)   Swe 183, 195
Statens Planverk   Swe 187
Statens Pris- och Kartellnämnd   Swe 190
Statens Provningsanstalt   Swe 190
Statens Strålskyddsinstitut   Swe 191
Statens Trafiksäkerhetsverk   Swe 192
Statens trykksakekspedisjon (STE)   No 138
Statens trykningskontor (STK)   No 137
Statens Väg- och Trafikinstitut   Swe 192
Statens Vägverk   Swe 192
Statens Vattenfallsverk   Swe 190
States Council   Swi 199, 201
States Greffe   UK 230
States of Jersey publications   UK 230
Statistical yearbook   Po 159
Statistisches Bundesamt   Ge 68-9, 98
Statistisk Sentralbyrå   No 136-7, 138, 145, 146
Statistiska Centralbyrån   Swe 188
Statsadministrasjonen   No 123
Statsbudsjettet   No 125-6
Statskontoret   Swe 188
Statsliggaren   Swe 188
Statsministerens Kontor   No 130, 132
Statsråd   No 130
Statsrådsberedningen   Swe 174, 195
Statutes in force   UK 212-13
Statutes of the Realm from 1101 to 1713   UK 212
Stenographische Berichte (of Federal Council)   Ge 64
Stenographische Berichte (of Parliamentary Council)   Ge 60, 61
Stenographische Protokolle   Au 5-6, 17
Stiftelsen Stockholms Fredforskningsinstitut (SIPRI)   Swe 194
Stiftung Alfred-Wegener Institut für Polarforschung   Ge 93

ORGANIZATIONS AND TITLES INDEX

Stiftung Deutsches-Elektronen
  Synchroton   Ge 93
Stiftung Deutsches
  Krebsforschungszentrum   Ge 93
Stiftung Preussischer Kulturbesitz   Ge 93
Stockholm International Peace Research
  Institute (SIPRI)   Swe 194
Storting   No 121-2, 124-30
Storting Intelligences   No 127
Stortings-Efterretninger   No 127
Stortingsbiblioteket   No 145
Stortingsforhandlinger   No 124-5, 126-7,
  128-9, 138, 145-6
Stortingsmeldinger   No 125, 135, 136
Stortingstidende   No 127
Styrelsen för Internationell Utveckling
  Swe 194
Styrelsen for Teknisk Utveeking   Swe 190
Successionsordningen   Swe 173
Suecana extranea   Swe 194
Supreme Court   Be 22, 23, 31; No 134
Supreme Court of Justice   Au 9
Supreme Court of Restitution   Ge 70
Συμβούλιον της Επικρατείας   Gr 107
Σύνδεσμος Ελληνικών Βιομηχανιών
  Gr 115
Svensk bok-katalog   Swe 194
Svensk bokförteckning   Swe 194, 195
Svensk författningssamling (SFS)   Swe 179,
  182, 185, 195
Svensk musikförteckning   Swe 194
Svensk tidskriftsförteckning   Swe 194
Svenska Institutet   Swe 194
Svenskt diplomatarium   Swe 172
Sveriges Lantbruksuniversitet   Swe 190-1
Sveriges Meteorologiska och Hydrologiska
  Institutet   Swe 193
Sveriges statliga publikationer   Swe 175,
  195, 196
Sveriges statskalender   Swe 175
Swedish Agency for Administrative
  Development   Swe 188
Swedish book list   Swe 194
Swedish Central Bank   Swe 184
Swedish Centre for Working Life   Swe 187
Swedish code of statutes   Swe 179, 182, 185
Swedish Cultural Council   Swe 194
Swedish Forest Service   Swe 190
Swedish Geological Survey   Swe 190
Swedish government official reports
  Swe 183
Swedish Institute   Swe 194
Swedish International Development
  Authority   Swe 194
Swedish journals list   Swe 194
Swedish Meteorological and Hydrological
  Institute   Swe 193
Swedish music list   Swe 194
Swedish National Council for Crime
  Prevention   Swe 191
Swedish National Road
  Administration   Swe 192
Swedish Parliamentary Library   Swe 175,
  195, 196
Swedish University of Agriculture
  Swe 190-1
Swiss Railways   Swi 203

Table of government orders in force   UK 213
Technical Chamber of Commerce of
  Greece   Gr 115
Technical Development Board   Swe 190
Τεχνικό Επιμελητήριο της Ελλάδος
  Gr 115
Technische Informationsbibliothek   Ge 100
Telecommunications Organization of
  Greece   Gr 108
Televerket   No 125, 133; Swe 192
Textes et documents   Be 32
Themis   Gr 109
θέμις   Gr 109
Third dimension   Be 33
Ting   Swe 171
Transitional constitutional Law   Au 1
Transitional justice law   Au 1
Transportrådet   Swe 193
Τράπεζα της Ελλάδος   Gr 108, 116
Treasury   UK 228
Tribunais   Po 152
Tribunal Constitucional   Po 152
Tryckfrihetsförordningen   Swe 172, 173

UFORDAT
  (Umweltforschungsdatenbank)   Ge 98
ULIDAT (Umweltliteraturdatenbank)
  Ge 99
*Übersicht über den Stand der
  Gesetzgebung*   Ge 63
Ulster yearbook   UK 226
Umweltbundesamt   Ge 92-3
United Kingdom Atomic Energy
  Authority   UK 228
United Nations   No 125
Universitets- och Högskoleämbetet
  Swe 194
Universitetsbiblioteket i Oslo   No 140, 145

ORGANIZATIONS AND TITLES INDEX

Universitetsforlaget i Oslo   No 138
University Grants Committee   UK 210
University Library of Graz   Au 17
University Library of Innsbruck   Au 17
University Library of Linz   Au 17
University Library of Salzburg   Au 17
University Library of Vienna   Au 16, 17
University of Basel   Swi 207
University of California at Berkeley   Be 52
Urban Law Code   Swe 172
Utbildningsdepartementet   Swe 193–4
Utenriksdepartementet   No 131, 132, 133–4, 136, 145
Utrikesdepartementet   Swe 194
Utvalg, styrer, råd m.v.   No 122

Verfassungsgerichtshof   Au 3, 9, 10–11
Verfassungsüberleitungsgesetz   Au 1
Verhandlungen des Deutschen Bundestages   Ge 61
Verhandlungen des Hauptausschusses   Ge 60
Verlegerische Betätigung der öffentlichen Hand   Ge 94
Vermittlungsausschuss   Ge 57
Verordnungsblatt des Landesschulrates   Au 7
Verordnungsblatt des Stadtschulrates in Wien   Au 7
Verträge der Bundesrepublik Deutschland   Ge 66
Verwaltungsgerichtshof   Au 3, 9–10
Vlaamse Gemeenschap   Be 24, 49
Vlaamse Raad   Be 24
Volksanwaltschaft   Au 12
Volkswirtschaftsdirektorenkonferenz   Swi 207
Votes and Proceedings   UK 215
Vox: hebdomadaire militaire   Be 34
Vu par les Belges   Be 32

Walloon Region   Be 49, 50
Welsh Development Agency   UK 210
Welsh Office   UK 228
Wiederverlautbarungsgesetz   Au 4
Wiener Zeitung   Au 12, 13
Woche im Bundestag: Parlamentskorrespondenz   Ge 62
Working and living in Norway   No 136
World Trade Institute   Ge 100

Χρηματιστήριον Αξιών Αθηνών   Gr 116
Χρηματιστήριον Εμπορευμάτων Πειραιώς   Gr 115

Yearbook of Nordic statistics   No 137
'Yellow book'   *see* Statsbudsjettet
Υπουργείο Δημοσίων Εργων   Gr 115
Υπουργείο Συγκοινωνιών   Gr 115
Υπουργείον Ανοικοδομήσεως   Gr 115
Υπουργείον Δικαιοσύνης   Gr 110
Υπουργείον Εμπορικής Ναυτιλίας   Gr 115
Υπουργείον Εσωτερικών   Gr 111
Υπουργείον Εθνικής Οικονομίας   Gr 115
Υπουργείον Εθνικής Παιδείας και Θρησκευμάτων   Gr 111–12
Υπουργείον Εξωτερικών   Gr 116–17
Υπουργείον Οικονομικών   Gr 115
Υπουργείον Παιδείας   Gr 114
Υπουργείον Προεδρίας της Κυβερνήσεως   Gr 111

Zeitschriftendatenbank   Ge 97, 98, 101
Zeitschriftenkatalog der Bayerischen Staatsbibliothek   Ge 98
Zeitschriftenliste   Au 13
Zentralbibliothek Luzern   Swi 207
Zur Sache: Themen parlamentarischer Beratung   Ge 63

Subject Index

Aargau Swi 205
academies Au 7; Gr 111
accidents Swe 193; Swi 204; UK 222, 227
act of parliament *see* statutes
administrative reform Po 164
African studies Swe 194
agreements *see* treaties
agriculture Au 11; Be 36, 38; Ge 74–5; Gr 114; No 135; Po 159; Swe 188, 190–1; UK 217, 220, 225, 229
  see also forestry
air force *see* armed forces
alcoholism Ge 86; No 143
Alderney UK 230
ancient monuments Be 45
  see also archaeology
archaeology Ge 66; Gr 112; Swe 193
  see also ancient monuments; history
archives
  local and specialized Gr 109, 110
  national Be 33, 45–6, 48; Ge 69–70; Gr 112; Swe 193
armed forces Be 34; Ge 84; Gr 117; Po 153, 165; Swe 189; Swi 199, 203; UK 217, 225
  see also defence; military affairs
arms control UK 223
arts Au 2, 7; Be 43–4; Gr 111–14; Po 167; Swe 193; UK 217
associations Ge 96; Gr 115; UK 211, 212, 240
  see also societies
astronomy Gr 112
atomic energy UK 228
  see also energy
audit, public Au 3, 6, 12; Gr 107
Austria Au 1–18

Autonomous Regions Po 152, 168–9
aviation No 132; Swe 192; UK 219–20
Azores Po 152, 168–9

bankruptcies Ge 58; Swi 200; UK 229
banks
  commercial Gr 116
  national Be 36–7; Gr 108, 116; No 125; Po 162; Swe 188; Swi 204; UK 217–18
Baselland Swi 205
Belgium Be 19–54
benefits, social *see* social security
Berlin (West) Ge 55–6, 64, 101, 102
bibliography, national *see* national bibliography
bibliography, regional *see* regional bibliographies
bills Au 6; Be 30; Ge 57; Gr 109; No 125; Po 152; Swe 175–82; Swi 201; UK 215, 230
biography Au 6; Be 28, 31; No 129–30; Swe 184
biology Ge 75
'blue books' *see* parliament, documents
books Au 18; Be 46–8; Ge 95–9, 102–4; Gr 118; No 139–40; Po 167–8; Swe 194; Swi 206–7; UK 231–3
  see also yearbook
boroughs UK 210
Britain *see* United Kingdom
broadcasting Ge 93; No 125; UK 218, 224
  see also media; radio; telecommunications
Brussels Region Be 19, 25–6, 49, 50
budget Au 6; Be 25, 36; Ge 71; No 126; Po 165; Swe 179, 188; UK 228
  see also finance

SUBJECT INDEX

building Au 2; Ge 88-9; Po 159;
   Swe 187-8; UK 219, 230
   see also construction; housing
Burgenland Au 1, 16
business Au 2; Be 34, 38; Gr 108;
   Swe 190; UK 228
   see also commerce; industry; trade
Byzantine studies Gr 113

Canada Be 52
cantons Swi 200, 205, 207
careers Ge 77; No 140
Carinthia Au 1, 16
catalogues *see* government printers,
   catalogues; ministries, catalogues of
   publications
census Au 8; Be 39; Po 158-9; Swi 202;
   UK 223-4, 226-7
   see also population
chamber of commerce Au 11; Gr 115
Channel Islands UK 211, 230, 240
churches Ge 93; Gr 107, 113-14; Swe 184,
   186
civil aviation *see* aviation
civil code *see* law, code of
civil service Au 2-3, 6-9; Be 21-8;
   Ge 56-7; Gr 107-8; No 122, 131-2;
   Po 152, 162; Swe 174-5, 185-6, 188;
   Swi 199-200, 207; UK 209-11, 219,
   228, 230
coasts No 132
colonies Be 48
command papers *see* parliament,
   documents
commerce Be 35; Gr 115; Swe 189-90
   see also business; trade
commercial code *see* law, code of
committees
   minutes Gr 110
   parliamentary Au 6
   reports Swe 181
   select UK 209
   standing Be 29-31; Ge 57, 62; No 122,
      126; Swe 174, 175, 177-9, 181;
      UK 211, 212, 214, 215
Commonwealth UK 220, 223
communes Swi 200
   see also local government
communications No 132; Swe 192-3;
   Swi 200
Communities Be 24-6, 48-50
companies Be 28; Gr 109; Po 154, 160;
   UK 222

registration UK 220
reports (Northern Ireland) UK 229
   see also state enterprises
computers *see* data bank/base
conference Ge 101; Swi 207
conservation Ge 92; Swe 191
   see also environment; nature
constitution Au 1; Be 19, 20; Ge 55-6, 60;
   Gr 107; No 121-2; Po 150-2;
   Swe 173-5; Swi 199-200; UK 209-11,
   235
   see also under courts; law
construction Ge 88; UK 227
   see also building; housing
consumer affairs Au 2; No 143
copyright Ge 99; UK 234
Council of State Au 1-2; Ge 55, 56, 64;
   Gr 107; No 130; Po 152; Swi 199-200,
   201, 202
counties No 143-4; Swe 172, 174-5,
   185-6; UK 210
   see also local government
courts Au 3, 9; Be 31; Ge 56; Gr 107;
   No 134; Po 150, 152, 154; Swe 191;
   Swi 200, 204-5; UK 229
   see also justice
   administrative Au 3, 9-10; Ge 56;
      Gr 107; Swe 191; Swi 204
   appeal Be 22, 23; Po 150; UK 229
   arbitration Be 23
   assize Be 22, 23
   cantonal Swi 205
   civil Swi 204
   constitutional Au 3, 9, 10-11; Ge 56;
      Po 152, 154
   decisions Au 10-11; Po 155; Swi 204
   federal Swi 200, 204
   fiscal Ge 56; Gr 107
   immigration appeal UK 229
   industrial UK 229
   labour Ge 56; No 134; Swe 191
   military Swi 204
   national Swe 191
   penal Swi 204
   social Ge 56; Swi 204; UK 229
   special Gr 107
   supreme Au 9; Be 22; Gr 107; No 134;
      Po 150, 154; UK 229
crime Au 8; Swe 191; UK 224, 226
Crown Be 20-1, 23; Swe 172-3; UK 209
cultural affairs Be 43-5; Ge 93;
   Gr 111-14; No 132; Po 153, 160, 162,
   164; Swe 193-4; UK 218

SUBJECT INDEX

current affairs Ge 66
customs and excise Ge 58, 73; Po 153, 164; Swe 189; Swi 203; UK 220

data bank/base Au 13; Ge 98–9; No 131; Swe 192, 196; UK 213, 219, 233
decrees Be 29; Ge 57–60; Gr 109; No 130; Po 153, 154; Swe 185
  see also secondary legislation
defence Au 2; Ge 59, 84–5; No 131; Swe 189; Swi 203; UK 225
  see also armed forces
definition (of official publications) Au 4; Ge 57, 94; Gr 108; No 123; Swe 175; Swi 200; UK 211
demography see census; population
Denmark No 121
department, government see subject for which responsible
deposit see legal deposit
design Swi 202; UK 223
developing countries Be 33; Ge 87–8; UK 227
development Be 33; Ge 87–8, 89; UK 210, 227
directory Be 32
  government organization UK 235
  official publications Be 47; UK 212, 217, 231, 233, 237
  see also government, organization manuals
disabled, the Swe 193
dissertations see theses, doctoral
district Au 15; Ge 56, 101–2; Po 150; Swi 200; UK 210
  see also local government
doctoral theses see theses, doctoral
drugs Au 8; Po 165; UK 224
Dutch language Be 19–20

economic affairs Be 34–6; Ge 72–3; Gr 114–16; Po 151; Swi 200, 207; UK 223, 226
economic cooperation Ge 87–8
education Au 7–8; Be 25, 43; Ge 92; Gr 111–12; Po 160, 163, 164; Swe 193–4; Swi 207; UK 220–1, 227–8, 229
  see also schools; teaching; universities
elections
  administrative Au 2
  local Ge 56; Swe 175; UK 210
  municipal Au 3; Swe 175
  parliamentary Be 20–1, 33; Ge 61, 64; Gr 107; No 122; Po 152; Swe 174; Swi 200; UK 209
  presidential Gr 107
  provincial Au 1–2; Be 26; UK 211
  register Ge 61
  see also suffrage
electricity Be 35
employers' associations Po 160
employment Be 42; Ge 75–8; Po 159, 163; UK 221, 224
  see also labour
energy Au 9; Be 35; Po 160; Swe 190; Swi 200; UK 221
  see also atomic energy; electricity; gas
engineering Au 2; UK 227
enterprise see private enterprise; state enterprises
environment Au 2, 7, 8; Ge 92–3; Swe 191; Swi 206; UK 222, 226, 229–30
equality No 141; UK 220, 223, 224
European Communities Be 37; Ge 57; Swe 189
exchange (of publications) Au 17; Be 52; Ge 100–1, 104–5; No 145–6; Swe 196; Swi 207; UK 234, 241–5
executive branch see ministries
exploration Ge 93
exports Ge 73, 74; Gr 115
  see also trade

family Au 2; Be 41–2; Ge 85–7
Federal Republic of Germany Ge 55–105
finance Au 2, 8; Be 36–7; Ge 71; Gr 115; No 126, 131; Po 160, 164, 165; Swe 188; Swi 199–200; UK 228
  see also budget; treasury
fire Swe 192; UK 224
fisheries Gr 114; No 132; Po 160; Swe 188, 191; UK 220, 225, 229
Flanders Be 19
folklore Be 44; Gr 112, 113
food Ge 74–5; No 135; UK 217, 225
foreign affairs Au 2; Be 32–4; Ge 66–7; Gr 116–17; No 133–4, 136; Swe 194; Swi 199; UK 223
  see also international affairs; trade
foreign trade Po 159, 162, 163, 165
forestry Ge 74–5; Gr 114; Swe 190, 191; UK 223
  see also agriculture
freedom of the press Swe 172, 173
French language Be 19–20; Swi 201

SUBJECT INDEX

Fribourg Swi 205
'fringe bodies' No 123; Swe 174; UK 210

gaming UK 224
gas UK 221
gazettes, official *see* official gazettes
geography Po 166
geology Po 163, 164; Swe 190
German language Be 19; Swi 201
Germany, Federal Republic of Ge 55–105
government
  aspects of *see* subject
  departments *see* ministries *and* subjects for which responsible
  gazettes *see* official gazettes
  guides to Be 53–4
  organization manuals Au 3; Be 27–8; Ge 57; No 122–3; Swe 175; Swi 200, 201; UK 211, 235
  printer *see* government printers
  structure of Au 1–3; Be 20–4; Ge 56, 102; Gr 107, 109; No 131–2; Po 149–52; Swe 173–4, 186; Swi 199–200; UK 209–10
  see also local government
government departments *see* ministries *and* subjects for which responsible
government printers Au 11–13; Be 46; Ge 94–5; Gr 108, 117; No 137–8; Po 166–7; Swe 194–5; Swi 200, 205; UK 230–1
  bookshops Be 46; No 138; Swe 194; UK 235
  catalogues Au 13; Po 167; Swi 205; UK 231–3
government publishing house *see* government printers
Graubünden Swi 205
Great Britain *see* United Kingdom
Greece Gr 107–20
'green papers' *see* parliament, documents
grey literature Gr 117–8; UK 211, 218, 233
Guernsey UK 230

handicapped, the *see* disabled, the
health Au 2, 7, 8; Be 41–2; Ge 75, 85–7; No 135; Po 160; Swe 193; UK 221–2, 228
health and safety UK 224
highways *see* roads
historic buildings *see* ancient monuments
history Au 1; Be 19–20; Ge 55; Gr 107; No 121; Po 149–51; Swe 171–3; UK 210, 211
home affairs *see* interior affairs
housing Be 39; Ge 88–9; Po 159; Swe 187–8; Swi 206; UK 221, 222, 227, 230
  see also building; construction
hydrography Ge 78–9; No 133, 141; UK 225

immigration Be 41; Swe 187; UK 224, 229
incomes UK 224
industrial property *see* patents
industry Au 2, 11; Be 35; Ge 71; Gr 108, 115; No 136; Po 159, 160, 163; Swe 190, 196; UK 222
information policy Ge 65; UK 219
information technology Po 163, 165
insurance, national *see* social security
intellectual property Swi 202
  see also copyright; patents
inter-library loan *see* libraries
interior affairs Au 2, 7; Ge 67–8, 89–90; Swi 199
international affairs Gr 116–17; No 133–4
  see also foreign affairs
international social policy No 135
investment Be 35
Ireland, Northern *see* Northern Ireland
Isle of Man UK 211
Italian language Swi 201

Jersey UK 230
judicial system *see* courts; justice
judiciary Au 9–11; Be 21–3; Ge 56; No 134; Po 150; Swi 204–5; UK 211, 229
  see also courts
jurisprudence Gr 110–11
justice Au 2–3; Ge 57, 59, 70–1; Gr 110–11; No 131; Po 153, 162–3, 164; Swe 191–2; Swi 199, 200
  see also courts

king *see* Crown

labour Gr 117; No 135, 136; Po 163; Swe 187
  see also employment
labour market organizations *see* trade unions
land UK 227

SUBJECT INDEX

language(s) Be 19-20; Gr 112; Po 164;
  Swi 201
law
  administrative Au 3, 9; Ge 59, 70;
    Gr 107; Po 150; Swi 204
  bulletin Be 29, 31
  cantonal Swi 200, 205
  civil Au 12; Ge 59, 70; Gr 107; Po 150;
    Swi 204
  code of Be 29; Po 153-4; Swe 172, 179,
    182-3, 185
  collection Be 29; Ge 59; No 130-1;
    Po 152-4; Swe 185; Swi 201;
    UK 212-13
  commercial Au 12; Ge 59; Po 150
  compendium of No 130
  constitutional Au 1, 3, 4-5, 9-11; Be 23,
    28; Ge 56, 59, 70; Po 153-4;
    Swe 171-2, 173, 184-5; UK 213, 229
  criminal Au 12; Be 34; Ge 59; Gr 107;
    Po 150; Swi 204
  ecclesiastical Swe 184, 186
  fiscal Ge 56; Gr 107; Po 150
  gazette Au 14, 15-16; Ge 57-8;
    Gr 108-9; No 130; Swi 201
  industrial Ge 70
  international Be 28
  labour Ge 56, 59; No 134; Po 150;
    Swe 191
  local Swe 185-6; UK 212
  media Au 4, 11, 12, 13
  municipal Au 15-16
  penal see law, criminal
  provincial Swe 171
  reform UK 224
  reports No 134; Po 153-4; Swe 179;
    UK 238
  social security Swi 204
  system of Ge 70; Swe 179-82
  see also bills; courts; justice; secondary
    legislation; statutes
lawyers Au 11
  see also notaries
legal code see law, code of
legal deposit Au 13, 16; Be 45, 46-7, 51;
  Ge 99-100, 101; Gr 118; No 139;
  Swe 195-6; Swi 206; UK 234
legislation
  proposals for see bills
  secondary see secondary legislation
  see also law; statutes
legislative instruments see secondary
  legislation

legislative proceedings see parliament,
  legislative process
legislature see parliament
lexicography Gr 112
libraries Au 16-18; Be 45, 51-2;
  Ge 99-101; Gr 118; No 144-6; Po 168;
  Swe 193-4, 196; Swi 204, 206-7;
  UK 234-5, 240
  administrative Au 16
  associations Ge 94; UK 211, 212, 240
  catalogue Be 51; No 144; Swe 194, 196;
    UK 218
  colonial Be 51
  economic Be 51
  guide to Au 17
  ministerial Au 17; UK 234
  national Au 16; Be 45, 51; Ge 99-100;
    Gr 118; No 144; Po 168; Swe 193, 196;
    Swi 204, 206; UK 218, 234
  parliament Au 16; Be 51; Gr 117, 118;
    No 145; Swe 195-6; Swi 206; UK 213
  provincial Au 16-17; Ge 100
  public Be 45; Ge 100; No 145; UK 210,
    234
  research Be 45; Ge 100, 102; No 145;
    Swe 194, 196
  special Gr 118; No 145
  technical Ge 100
  university Au 16-17; Ge 100; No 144-5;
    Swe 196; Swi 206-7; UK 234
  world trade Ge 100
  see also exchange (of publications); legal
    deposit; and named libraries
linguistics Be 44-5
literature Gr 112, 114; No 139-40;
  Po 167; Swe 196
literary works see books; literature
livestock Gr 114
living standards Po 165
local authorities see local government
local government Au 1, 3, 14-16; Be 24-6,
  27; Ge 56, 101-2; Gr 111; No 123,
  135, 144; Po 150, 168-9; Swe 174-5,
  185-6, 192; Swi 200, 207; UK 210,
  234, 239-40
  boroughs UK 210
  cantons Swi 200, 205, 207
  city Po 169
  communes Swi 200
  counties No 144; Swe 172, 174-5,
    185-6; UK 210
  districts Au 15; Ge 56, 101-2; Po 150;
    Swi 200; UK 210

SUBJECT INDEX

municipalities Au 3, 15–16; Be 50–1;
    Ge 56, 100; Gr 107–8; No 144; Po 150
provinces Au 1, 14–15; Be 26–7, 50;
    Ge 55, 56, 60, 64, 101–2
regions Be 24–6, 48–50; Ge 88–9;
    Po 150, 160; UK 210
Lower Austria Au 1, 16
Luxembourg Be 37
Luzern Swi 205, 207

Madeira Po 152, 168–9
Man, Isle of UK 211
manpower Gr 117; UK 224
  see also employment
maps Be 35, 48; Ge 96; No 133; Swe 187
marine *see* merchant marine
maritime affairs No 132–3; Swe 190
  see also shipping
materials testing Ge 73–4; Swe 190
mathematics, applied Ge 94; Gr 112
mayor Be 27
media Au 4
  see also broadcasting; newspapers; press;
  radio
medicine Au 8; Be 44; Ge 86–7; No 135;
    UK 224–5
merchant marine Gr 115; Po 162
meteorology Ge 79–80; Swe 193; UK 225
military affairs Ge 85
  see also armed forces; defence
mines/mining Be 35; Po 163, 164
ministers
  bills presented by Au 6; Ge 57;
    No 125–6; Po 156–7; Swe 175–82;
    Swi 201
  countersignature by Be 21
  decisions by No 126–7
  executive power of Be 21; Swe 174
  number of Au 2; Ge 66; No 131;
    UK 210
  ombudsman and No 122
  questions Be 30; Swe 179, 182
  responsibilities of Au 2, 6; Be 21;
    Swe 174; UK 210
  state enterprises and Swe 174; UK 210
  see also subjects for which responsible
ministries Au 2, 6–9; Be 21, 32–46; Ge 56,
    65–93; Gr 110–17; No 131–7; Po 152,
    157–62; Swe 174, 186–94;
    Swi 199–200, 202–5; UK 210
  see also subjects for which responsible
catalogues of publications Au 6–9;
    Ge 65–93; Gr 110–17; No 132–7,
    140–3; Po 157–62; Swe 186–94;
    Swi 202–5; UK 216–28
monarchy *see* Crown
monuments *see* ancient monuments
Mount Athos Gr 108
Mount Sinai Gr 114
municipalities Au 3, 15–16; Be 50–1;
    Ge 56, 100, 101–2; Gr 107–8; No 144;
    Po 150
  see also local government
museums Gr 112; Swe 193
music Ge 97; Gr 114; UK 218

national archives *see* archives, national
national bank Be 36–7; Gr 108, 116;
    No 125; Po 162; Swi 204; UK 217–18
national bibliography Au 13; Be 46;
    Ge 96–7; Gr 117; No 139–40; Po 168;
    Swe 193–4, 195; Swi 206; UK 218, 231
national insurance *see* social security
nationalized enterprises *see* state enterprises
nationalized industries *see* state enterprises
nature Swe 191; UK 210
  see also conservation; environment
navigation Ge 78–9; No 132; Swe 192
navy *see* armed forces
Neuchâtel Swi 205
newspapers UK 234
non-departmental public bodies
    (NDPBs) UK 210
Northern Ireland UK 210, 211, 226,
    229–30, 239
Norway No 121–48
notaries Po 163
  see also lawyers
nuclear safety Ge 92, 94
  see also radiation protection

official bulletins Po 153; Swi 202; UK 216
official gazettes Be 28–9, 30; Ge 57, 58–9,
    63, 64, 70; Gr 108; Po 154–5;
    Swi 201–2, 206
official printer *see* government printers
official publications
  bibliographies Ge 95–6; No 140
  catalogues Be 47–8; Ge 97–8; No 139;
    Swi 205; UK 239
  see also government printers, catalogues;
    ministries, catalogues
  definition Au 4; Ge 57, 94; Gr 108;
    No 123; Swe 175; Swi 200; UK 211
  guides to Be 28–46, 52–3; Ge 103–4;
    Swe 183; UK 236–8

SUBJECT INDEX

oil No 138; UK 221
 see also energy; petroleum
ombudsman Au 12; No 122, 128; Swe 173, 174, 184; UK 209, 227
orders UK 213, 229
 see also regulations; secondary legislation
ordinances Be 29; No 130; UK 230
 see also orders
overseas aid Be 33; UK 227
 see also developing countries

papers *see* parliament, documents
parishes Po 150
parliament Au 1-2; Be 20; Ge 55-6; Gr 107; No 121-2; Po 150, 152; Swe 172, 173-4, 184; Swi 199; UK 209
 bills *see* bills
 chambers Be 20, 23; Ge 55, 60; No 122; Po 150-1, 155; Swe 177; Swi 199; UK 209
 constitution Ge 55, 60; Po 150-2; Swe 174
 correspondence Au 6; Swi 201
 data base Ge 61; UK 213, 233
 debates Ge 63; Gr 109-10; No 127; Swi 201-2; UK 213, 214
 see also parliament, proceedings
 deputies *see* parliament, members
 diary Po 151, 152, 154-5, 156-7
 documents Be 29-31; Ge 61-4; Gr 109-10; No 125-30; UK 213-16, 238-9
 legislative process Au 5-6; Be 23; Swe 179-83
 libraries *see* libraries, parliament
 members Au 6; Ge 61; Po 152; Swe 174, 184; UK 209
 minutes Gr 109-10; UK 213, 215
 motions Swe 181-3
 procedure Ge 57; No 124-30; Po 155-7; Swe 175-83; UK 235
 proceedings Au 5-6; Ge 60; Gr 108, 109-10; No 124-30; Po 155-7; Swe 175-84; Swi 201-2; UK 215, 235
 questions Be 30; Swe 181-2; UK 209
 reports No 125-6; Swe 179-83; UK 209, 213, 215
 research Ge 63-64; Swe 183
 resolutions Po 153, 157; Swe 182, 185
 standing committees *see* committees, standing
parliamentary papers *see* parliament, documents

patents Au 7; Be 35; Ge 71; Swe 189-90; Swi 202
penal affairs *see* crime; prisons
penal code *see* law, code of
pensions Be 36; Swe 193
 see also social security
periodicals Au 13; Be 47, 51; Ge 96, 97-8; Gr 113-14; Swi 206; UK 219, 234
 official Au 13; Be 47; Ge 96, 97-8; Swi 206; UK 234
petroleum No 132, 135
 see also oil
philosophy Gr 112
physics UK 226
place-names Be 45; No 132
planning Be 35-6; Ge 88-9; Gr 115-16; UK 227
police Au 7, 8; Po 153, 164, 165, 166; Swe 191; Swi 199; UK 224
political education Ge 69
politics Be 32-4, 43; Ge 69; Po 151-2
pollution UK 222
population Au 8; Be 39, 41, 42; Gr 111; Po 150, 158-9, 161; Swi 202; UK 223-4, 226-7
 see also census; statistics, population
Portugal Po 149-70
postal service Au 7, 8, 9; Ge 82-3; Gr 108; No 132; Po 153; Swe 192; Swi 203
prefectures Gr 108
press Be 39; Ge 65; No 122; Swe 172, 173
 see also media; newspapers; periodicals
prices Gr 115; Po 159; Swe 190
prisons Be 33-4; Po 163; Swe 191; UK 224, 226, 228
private enterprise Ge 96; Gr 108
private organizations *see* associations; societies
proceedings *see* parliament, proceedings
proclamations *see* secondary legislation
production/productivity Gr 115
professions Au 11; Ge 77-8; No 123
project of law *see* bills
property Swe 192; UK 227
proposals, law *see* bills
provinces Au 2, 14-15; Be 26-7, 50; Ge 55, 56, 60, 64, 101-2
 see also local government
public assistance *see* social security
public corporations UK 210
public health *see* health
public-sector bodies *see* 'fringe bodies'; state enterprises

SUBJECT INDEX

public works Gr 115
publications, official *see* official
    publications
publishing *see* government printers

quality Po 163
quality of life Ge 91; Po 165
'quangos' *see* 'fringe bodies'
queen *see* Crown

radiation protection Ge 73, 94; Swe 191;
    UK 226
  see also nuclear safety
radio Ge 93
  see also broadcasting; media
railways Au 9; Ge 80–1; Swe 192; Swi 203
  see also transport
reconstruction Gr 115
regional bibliographies UK 234
regional government No 123, 143–4;
    Swi 200, 207
  see also local government
regions Be 24–6, 48–50; Ge 88–9; Po 150,
    160; UK 210
  autonomous Po 152
regulations Be 28; Ge 57; Gr 109; No 130;
    Po 153; Swe 185
  see also orders; secondary legislation
religion Gr 113–14
  see also churches
research
  agricultural Ge 74–5; No 141; UK 217
  air No 142
  applied mathematics Gr 112
  archaeology Gr 112–13
  astronomy Gr 112
  biological Ge 75, 94
  building No 141
  cancer Ge 93
  ecology Ge 75
  economic Swe 188; UK 223
  education Be 43
  fisheries Ge 75
  folklore Gr 112
  food Ge 75; UK 217
  forestry Ge 75; No 142
  general Ge 90–1; Gr 112
  health Be 41
  institutions Ge 93–4
  language Gr 112
  law Gr 112
  linguistic Be 44–5
  maritime Swe 190

  market No 140
  medical Be 44
  milk Ge 75
  ministry Au 7
  nuclear Ge 94
  philosophy Gr 112
  physico-technical metrology Ge 73
  regional Ge 89
  scientific Be 44; Ge 93–4; No 141
  social Ge 86; Gr 111; UK 223
  water No 142
revenue *see* finance
roads Ge 78; No 143; Swe 192
  see also accidents; transport
Romansch Swi 201
royalty *see* Crown

safety UK 224
  see also nuclear safety; radiation protection
Salzburg Au 1, 17
Scandinavia *see* Norway; Sweden
scholarship Gr 112
schools Au 7
  see also education
science
  agricultural Be 44; UK 217
  bacteriological Swe 193
  bibliography Be 47
  biology Ge 75, 94
  food No 135
  general Au 7; Be 36, 43–5; Ge 92;
    UK 220–1
  heavy ion Ge 94
  institutions Be 33, 44; Po 162, 164;
    UK 227
  medical Be 44; UK 210
  mineral oil Ge 93
  ministry Au 2, 7; Be 36; No 132
  nuclear Ge 94
  physical Ge 73; UK 226
  plasma physics Ge 94
  polar Ge 93
  political Be 33, 43, 44
  research Au 2, 7, 17; Be 44; Po 162, 164;
    UK 227
  social Be 31
  see also research *and* individual sciences
Scotland UK 210, 213, 220, 223–4, 227–8,
    239
secondary legislation Be 29; No 130–1;
    Po 153–4; Swe 184–5; Swi 201;
    UK 213, 229, 230
  decrees Be 29; Ge 57–60; Gr 109;

No 130; Po 153, 154; Swe 185
 orders UK 213, 229
 ordinances Be 29; No 130; UK 230
 statutory instruments UK 213, 229, 232
shipping Swe 191, 192; UK 223
 see also maritime affairs
social affairs Ge 75-8; No 135
social communication Po 164, 165
social security Be 41-2; Ge 75; Gr 117;
  No 135-6; Po 160, 164; Swe 193;
  UK 221-2, 230
 see also pensions
societies
 learned Gr 113
 scientific research Ge 93-4
 see also associations
soil UK 225
Solothurn Swi 205
standard of living *see* living standards
standards Po 160
standing committees *see* committees,
  standing
state enterprises Au 4, 11; Gr 108, 109,
  114; No 136; Po 167, 168; Swe 174;
  UK 210, 211
statistics Au 8; Be 38-41; Ge 68-9;
  No 136-7; Po 157-62; Swe 188;
  Swi 202; UK 219, 227
 agricultural Be 40; Po 159, 160;
  Swe 188; UK 228
 aviation No 137
 criminal UK 224
 demographic Be 40; Po 160
 economic Ge 68; No 136; UK 219
 education Be 40; Po 160; UK 220, 227
 energy Ge 68; Po 160
 financial Be 40; Po 160; UK 219, 222,
  228
 fisheries No 137
 foreign Ge 69
 guide to Be 38; Ge 69; Gr 111; No 136;
  Po 166; UK 219
 historical No 136
 housing Be 39, 40; Po 159; UK 222,
  227, 228, 230
 immigration UK 224
 industry Be 40; Po 159, 160
 insurance No 137
 judicial Be 41; Po 160
 mental health UK 221
 population Au 8; Be 37-9, 40; Gr 111;
  Po 158-9, 161; Swi 202; UK 223-4,
  226

 postal No 137
 prices Ge 69; Po 159
 prison No 137; UK 224
 production Be 40
 road accidents UK 222, 227
 Scottish UK 228
 social economic No 136
 social security Po 160; UK 221, 230
 sociological Be 39, 41; UK 219, 228
 telegraph No 137
 tourism Po 160
 trade Be 40; No 137; Po 159
 transport Be 40; Po 160; UK 227
 water UK 222
 whaling No 137
 yearbook Ge 68; Po 159
statutes Au 4-5; Be 28-9; Ge 57-60, 63;
  Gr 108-9; No 130; Po 152-4; Swe 179,
  185-6; Swi 201; UK 212-13
statutory instruments UK 213, 229, 232
 see also secondary legislation
stock exchange Gr 115, 116
Styria Au 1, 17
suffrage Be 21; Ge 56, 61; Swe 177
 see also elections
survey Be 34; No 133; Po 166; UK 226-7
Sweden No 121; Swe 171-97
Switzerland Swi 199-208

taxation Be 26; Po 160; Swe 188; UK 224
teaching Be 43; Gr 109
 see also education; schools; universities
technology
 associations Ge 73
 chamber of commerce Gr 115
 development board Swe 190
 general Be 37; Ge 90-1; Gr 115; Po 162,
  164
 library Ge 100
telecommunications Ge 82-3; Gr 108;
  Po 153; Swe 192
 see also radio; telegraph; telephone
telegraph Au 7; No 133
telephone Au 8; Be 39; Ge 83; No 133;
  Swi 203
 directories No 133; Swe 192
teletext Ge 83
telex Ge 83; No 133; Swe 192
theses, doctoral Be 33; Gr 112; UK 218
thought Po 167
Thurgau Swi 205
timetable No 133
tourism Po 160; UK 218

town planning Ge 88-9
trade Au 2; Be 36, 37-8; Ge 58, 73;
    Po 159; Swi 203; UK 222
  see also business; commerce; exports
trade marks Au 9; Ge 71; Swi 202
trade unions Po 160
transport Au 2, 7, 8; Ge 78; Gr 115;
    Po 160; Swe 192-3; Swi 200;
    UK 222-3, 227
  see also aviation; railways; roads; shipping
treasury UK 228
treaties Au 4; Be 5, 28, 32-3; Ge 58, 60,
    66; Gr 109, 116; No 134; Po 162;
    Swe 194; Swi 200; UK 223
tribunal Po 152; Swi 203
Tyrol Au 1, 17

United Kingdom UK 209-45
United States of America Be 51-2
universities Au 7-8; Be 43; Gr 112;
    Swe 194; UK 210
  see also named universities
Upper Austria Au 1, 17

Valais Swi 205
Vienna Au 1, 17
Vorarlberg Au 1, 17

Wales UK 210, 228
Wallonia Be 19, 25, 49
water UK 222
waterways UK 218-19
welfare Au 2, 7, 8; Swe 193
  see also social security
whaling No 137
'white papers' *see* parliament, documents
women Ge 85-7; Po 162; Swe 173, 177
work *see* employment
workers *see* labour

yearbook
  administration Be 27, 50; Ge 65
  civil service UK 211, 219
  judicial Be 27
  official Au 3, 8, 18; Swe 184
  statistical Ge 68; No 136; Po 159, 169
youth Au 2; Be 34; Ge 85-7; Po 164

AUG 3 1 1989